An Illustrated Dictionary
of the Third Reich

An Illustrated Dictionary of the Third Reich

JEAN-DENIS G.G. LEPAGE

McFarland & Company, Inc., Publishers
Jefferson, North Carolina

LIBRARY OF CONGRESS CATALOGUING-IN-PUBLICATION DATA

Lepage, Jean-Denis.
An illustrated history of the Third Reich /
Jean-Denis G.G. Lepage.
    p.   cm.
Includes bibliographical references and index.

ISBN 978-0-7864-7372-4
softcover : acid free paper ∞

1. Germany — History —1933 –1945 — Dictionaries.
2. National socialism — Dictionaries.
3. Hitler, Adolf, 1889 –1945 — Dictionaries.
4. World War, 1939 –1945 — Dictionaries.
I. Title.
DD256.47.L47 2014   943.08603 — dc23   2013044278

BRITISH LIBRARY CATALOGUING DATA ARE AVAILABLE

© 2014 Jean-Denis G.G. Lepage. All rights reserved

*No part of this book may be reproduced or transmitted in any form
or by any means, electronic or mechanical, including photocopying
or recording, or by any information storage and retrieval system,
without permission in writing from the publisher.*

On the cover: *clockwise from top center* Sperrballone — barrage balloon;
Balkenkreuz — emblem of the World War II German Armed Forces
(thick version); SS Dagger; "Gott mit Uns" Gürtelschnalle — "God
with us" belt buckle; Parabellum M08 Luger pistol; Afrikakorps Einheitsfeldmütze — standard field cap; Armbinde — armband;
The PzKpfw VI (SdKfz 181) — German World War II tank;
Panzerkampfwagen (PzKfw) — armored fighting tank;
handgranaten — hand grenades; Emblem of Thule Gesellschaft —
Thule Society; Bandenkampfabzeichen — Anti-Partisan
Guerrilla Warfare Badge; Rocket A-4/V-2 — bullet-shaped rocket;
Balkenkreuz (thin version) (illustrations by the author)

Manufactured in the United States of America

*McFarland & Company, Inc., Publishers
Box 611, Jefferson, North Carolina 28640
www.mcfarlandpub.com*

TABLE OF CONTENTS

Acknowledgments
vi

Introduction
1

The Dictionary
3

Chronology
207

Bibliography
213

Index
215

ACKNOWLEDGMENTS

The author would like to express his gratitude to Jeannette à Stuling from Rottevalle, Eltjo J. de Lang, Ben van Luik and Ben Marcarto, as well as Michèle Clermont from Groningen; and Jan à Stuling from Lelystad (the Netherlands); to Anne Chauvel and Anouk Splash from Aix-en-Provence, Simone and Bernard Lepage from Piré-sur-Seiche, Antoinette Lapaux and Nicole Genessey from Sainte-Hélène-du Lac (France); and Peter de Laet from Kapelle (Belgium) for their friendly help, advice and competent historical collaboration.

Introduction

This dictionary's purpose is to give a basic source of information on the Third Reich era by listing some German terms connected to Nazism and the Second World War. It includes ranks, badges, insignia, regalia, medals, flags and banners, weapons, uniforms, equipment, vehicles, fortifications, airplanes, battleships, main Nazi concepts and organization, slogans, sayings, code names, nicknames, slang words, some places of importance, important events and battles, treaties and alliances, industry and economics, justice, art, religion, education, political parties, newspapers, Nazi Party formations and associations, laws passed, institutions, and short biographies of the main Nazi leaders. To make the rise of Nazism comprehensible, aspects of the Weimar Republic have also been considered. As for Adolf Hitler, the Führer of the Third Reich, there is a general discussion in the entry under his name leaving readers to pursue specific interests through related entries in the book. In all there are 1,650 entries alphabetically sorted. Each entry includes the German term, its abbreviation if appropriate, its English translation, if needed a few words of explanation and—for certain important subjects—a longer article. To enhance comprehension some entries are further explained by an illustration. The aim is thus to provide a reference framework, but a vigorous selection has obviously been required to keep this book to a reasonable length. Some terms and expressions have been deliberately rejected, and those selected have sometimes been subjected to restraints. It is nevertheless hoped that all major and most important terms have been included. There is also a chronology from 1918 until 1949, and a bibliography.

This book is intended for students and any general and curious reader with an interest in the period 1919–1945. The emphasis is on an effort to achieve a more precise understanding of the events of this period.

Compiling or estimating the numbers of deaths caused during wars and other violent conflicts is always a controversial subject. Historians often put forward many different estimates of the numbers killed during World War II. The distinction between military and civilian casualties caused directly by warfare and collateral damage is not always clear. For nations that suffered huge losses, such as the Soviet Union, China, Poland, Germany and Yugoslavia, sources can give only the total estimated population loss caused by the war, and a rough estimate of the breakdown of deaths caused by military activity, crimes against humanity and war-related famine. What is certain is that World War II was the deadliest military conflict in history. More than 60 million people were killed, representing more than 2.5 percent of the world population.

It is always risky and highly sensitive to write about World War II—and especially Nazism—because of the many and passionate moral, human, racial, political and ideological issues. This is still the case in Europe today, where countless people have suffered, and where World War II has left a lot of wounds that are far from being totally healed. The author makes no attempt to apologize for Nazism, justify Nazi crimes, or encourage any form of neo–Nazism. This book is thus a historical study of what Nazism was, how it was organized, and how it functioned, without forgetting all the suffering it brought to much of humanity.

The Dictionary

AA. See Agrarpolitischer Apparat.

AA Line. The establishment of the Arkhangelsk-Astrakhan Line was the military goal of operation Barbarossa (q.v.). All territories within that line that stretched from the White Sea in northern Russia to the Caspian Sea in the south were to be Germanized according to the Generalplan Ost (q.v.). See Lebensraum and Ostwall.

AB Aktion. See Ausserordentliche Befriedungsaktion.

Abetz, Otto (1903–1958). German ambassador to the Vichy French government between 1940 and 1944. He was responsible for SD (q.v.) operations throughout France and initiated anti-Jewish drives. Abetz was sentenced to 20 years' imprisonment in July 1949 as a war criminal. He was released in 1958, and his death in that year in a motor crash was believed to be a retaliation action by former members of the French Resistance.

Abschnitt (Abschn.). Sector or regional subdivision. Also a military unit, often of regimental size, occupying a border sector.

Abteilung (Abt). Branch, section or subdivision of a main department or office. Also a military unit, generally of battalion strength.

Abwehr. Espionage, counter-espionage, disinformation, subversion and sabotage service of the German high command. The service was created in 1919 to be Germany's defense against foreign espionage. In 1935, the Abwehr was headed by captain (later admiral) Wilhelm Franz Canaris (q.v.), and became a part of the OKW — Oberkommando der Wehrmacht (q.v.) — in 1938. During the period 1935–1944, the Abwehr, a military rather than a Nazi organization, attracted non- and anti-Nazi opponents, and promoted a number of resistance activities. Besides, it was in constant rivalry with the SS security service Sicherheitsdienst des Reichsführer SS (q.v.), and as a result its functions were heavily eroded by the SS. The involvement of some of its members in a conspiracy against the Nazi regime contributed to its downfall. In February 1944, Canaris was arrested and later executed as a traitor. The Abwehr was in disgrace. The intelligence service was absorbed and put under the command of Himmler's SS, and formally dissolved.

Abwehrpolizei. Counter-espionage police, part of the Grenzpolizei (border police) controlled by the Gestapo (q.v.).

Abzeichen. Insignia, specialty badge, distinctive sign or decoration. A specialty is an activity, a trade or a job at which the person who carries it out is particularly proficient. The specialist, who attended a special course or school, was distinguished by a badge generally worn on the right forearm or on the lower right sleeve of the tunic. The specialty was indicated by an embroidered or woven yellow symbol (or a Gothic letter) on a dark green round or oval cloth background.

Abzeichentuch. Cloth badge.

Achse, Achenmächte. The Rome-Axis-Berlin — a term popularized by the Italian dictator Benito Mussolini (q.v.) to illustrate the Italian-German military collaboration. The idea of the Axis was born in autumn 1935, and was secured by treaties: the Axis pact in 1936, the anti–Kominternpakt in 1937, the Stahlpakt in May 1939 and the Dreimächtepakt in 1940. The Axis also included Japan, but Germany and Japan did not coordinate their war operations, nor share information, nor help each other in any substantial material way.

Achselband. Aiguillette or lanyard, a looped ornamental cord worn from the right shoulder by high-ranking officers. In Nazi Germany, it was awarded for skill in marksmanship and for every time it was won, a decoration was added. It was of matte silvered cord and worn from the right shoulder to the second tunic button with parade, walking-out and guard uniforms. Lanyards were awarded in eight classes. Gradually, lanyards were replaced by small metal decorations in the form of a shield. See also Abzeichen.

Achtung! Feind hört mit! "Beware! The enemy is listening!" A warning often written near telephones. Also a 1940 propaganda film directed by Arthur Maria Rabenalt, a thrilling and entertaining espionage story presenting the British as villains.

Adenauer, Konrad (1876–1967). Mayor of Cologne from 1917 to 1933. Dismissed by the Nazis, he lived in retirement during World War II, and became the first chancellor of the new German Bundesrepublik.

Adler. The eagle, symbolizing prestige and strength, referring to the German medieval Reich. To Hitler's followers, it meant the recovery of German national pride and greatness by way of Nazism. The eagle, in many styles and variations in design and coloring, was a part of the national emblem. See Hoheitszeichen.

Adlerangriffe. Eagle attack, code name for the air attack against Britain in August 1940, as a preparation for Operation Sea Lion. See Seelöwe.

Adlertag. Day of the Eagle, code name for the start of Adlerangriffe, the air offensive against Britain.

Admiral Hipper. German heavy cruiser named after Admiral Franz von Hipper. She was launched in February 1937. The *Admiral Hipper* saw a significant amount of action during the war. She was scuttled in May 1945 and scrapped after the war.

Admiral Scheer. A Deutschland-class Panzerschiff, or heavy cruiser (often termed a pocket battleship), named after Admiral Reinhard Scheer, German commander in the Battle of Jutland in 1916. She was laid down at the Reichsmarinewerft shipyard in Wilhelmshaven in June 1931, and completed by November 1934. She was sunk by bombs in April 1945.

Heavy cruiser *Admiral Scheer*.

Adolf Hitler Fund. See Adolf-Hitler-Spende der deutschen Wirtschaft.

Adolf-Hitler-Marsch. Adolf Hitler march. Beginning in 1935, Hitler Jugend (q.v.) members were obligated to perform the Adolf-Hitler-Marsch. During one week in September, all HJ units had to march in disciplined and uniformed ranks to Nuremberg to participate in the Reichsparteitag (rally of the Party).

Adolf-Hitler-Schule (AHS). Adolf Hitler school. These secondary Nazi Party schools, created in 1937 and headed by the NSDAP, were intended for Hitler Jugend (q.v.) boys between 12 and 18. AHSs were established with the concern to create a new generation of Nazi followers, and meant to turn out a technically and ideologically trained elite. The inspiration was ancient Sparta, the British public schools and the Jesuit education system, but some subjects, such as history, were falsified in a way serving Nazi aim. Similarly, biology included fake "scientific" proofs intended to develop racism. The emphasis was on forming Nazi cadres by stern teaching and physical training, and not really intellectual development. Teachers and pupils wore uniforms, and schools were militarily structured. Because of their isolated and specialized education, young people in the AHSs knew nothing about practical life. On the other hand, their arrogance and conceit about their own abilities were boundless. It is significant that most of the high NSDAP functionaries did not send their own children to such schools. It was the intention of the Nazis to have one AHS in each Gau, but in 1939 there were only ten of them. See Education in the Third Reich, Erziehung, and Nationalpolitischen Erziehungsanstalten.

Adolf-Hitler-Spende der deutschen Wirtschaft. Adolf Hitler Fund of German Economy, a donation collected and administrated by Martin Bormann, the head of the Nazi Party and Hitler's finances counselor. Established in June 1933, the Adolf Hitler fund was liberally financed by German businessmen, but also collected by more or less open extortion from Jewish businessmen. The proceeds were used for the benefit of the NSDAP in the widest sense, that is, to finance the Führer's favorite projects, support the NSDAP and participate in the nationaler Wiederaufbau (national reconstruction). At first the fund was a voluntary donation, but during the following years it became more and more a forced contribution for some concerns. As of 1945 the NSDAP had collected about 700 million Reichsmark.

Adolphe Légalité. "Adolf the Legal One." A popular nickname used to describe Hitler because of his repeatedly expressed desire to obtain political power only through legal means. Hitler had only contempt for democracy, but he was careful to maintain a public image as a strong proponent of law and order. The term was used by those Germans who believed in Hitler's sincere wish to act legally, and by those members of the early revolutionary SA elements who used it with deep contempt. The French phrase was a mocking reference to the Duke of Orleans, who called himself Philippe Egalité during the French Revolution.

Afrika Korps. See Deutsches Afrika Korps.

Aggregat 4 (A4). Original name of the V2 (q.v.) rocket.

Agrarpolitischer Apparat (AA). Agrarian Apparatus. Agricultural Affairs Bureau of the NSDAP, headed by Walther Darré. The aim of the Nazis was to make Germany self-sufficient in agricultural production. Several laws were passed, but despite some success, Nazi agriculture never achieved complete autarky.

Ahnenerbe Forschungs und Lehrgemeinschaft. Society for Research into and Teaching of Ancestral Heritage, an SS organization. Believing that Germany had been led astray for a thousand years by Judeo-Christianity, Heinrich Himmler (q.v.) wanted the restoration of the old pre–Christian Germanic culture. For this purpose, the SS organization sponsored many cultural and pseudoscientific projects, published many books and documentaries, and encouraged research on Germanic history and archaeological excavations. The Ahnenerbe Forschungs und Lehrgemeinschaft was administered by the SS, and headed by professor Walter Wüst, who specialized in Indo-Aryan language and culture at Munich University. He was made honorary SS Standartenführer (colonel), and numerous assistants and student teams with comfortable budgets, made studies of anything concerning runic symbols, Germanic customs, tales and legends, and archaeological surveys in and out of Germany. Expeditions were organized to Abyssinia and Tibet to look for supporting evidence of ancestral origins of Aryanism. There was another society with similar role, the Institut für Wehrwissenschaftliche Zweckforschung, headed by SS Standartenführer Wolfram Sievers. These research societies were, however more political than scientific, cultural and historical. They were created and controlled by the SS, and their aim was not to discover new facts, but to reinforce Himmler's racist prejudices. Hitler had little sympathy with Himmler's mythologizing of the SS. The Führer, with historical accuracy, considered the primitive civilization of ancient German forefathers inferior to the great architectural achievements and the culture of ancient Greece and Rome. Personally, Hitler would rather that part of German history be kept quiet, but as Himmler's digressions were useful to him, no attempts were undertaken to stop the reichsführer's maniacal hobby. The outbreak of World War II brought most of Ahnenerbe's activities to a halt, but it then took on new roles, including plundering of historical artifacts from occupied nations. It also organized "medical research" in concentration camps, notably the testing of chemical weapons on human subjects.

Ahnenpass. Ancestry passport. A 48-page identification book measuring 14 by 21 centimeters that was supposed to be carried by every "pure blood" German during the Nazi regime. The purpose was to demonstrate Aryan "purity" by displaying the history of the lineage up to the holder's 31st generation. As this was difficult or, in many cases, impossible to document, there was also the Ahnen-Kurzpass (short ancestry book), with only 24 pages containing family genealogy to seven generations. A lucrative business in buying and selling forged passes took place.

Aiguillette. Of French origin, the word derives from *aiguille* (needle), and refers to the pointed metal ornament at the end of a cord. Aiguillettes were ornamental tags that existed in two kinds. There were the ordinary ones worn by officers and administrative officials with parade and full dress. The other type was of silvered cord with a dull surface, which were worn by adjutants and staff officers.

Aktion Reinhard. Code name for the deportation and extermination of the Jews from the Generalgouvernement (q.v.) in the period 1942–43 to the camps of Belzec, Sobibor and Treblinka, where gas chambers were installed. See Gaskammer and Globocnik, Odilo.

Aktion T4. Code name for the extermination of mentally ill and handicapped patients by the Nazi authorities. Named after Tiergartenstrasse 4, the address of Nazi Central Office in Berlin. See Euthanasiebefehl.

Alarmeinheiten. Emergency units of the Luftwaffe (q.v.) formed on the eastern front in late 1941. Due to the shortage of regular army troops to police the occupied regions of Russia, the Luftwaffe was forced to raise its own infantry combat/police units with volunteers from airbase personnel and other rear-echelon elements to defend Luftwaffe installations (communication, dumps, airfields, etc.) against Soviet partisans. See Luftwaffe-Feld-Division.

Alarmstufe. Alarm level. See Fliegeralarm.

Alles Leben Ist Kampf. "All Life Is Struggle." See Sozialdarwisnismus (social Darwinism).

Allgemeene-SS Vlaanderen. See Burgondia.

Allgemeine SS. General SS, also named Heimat SS (Home SS) or Schwarze SS (Black SS). Originally Hitler's bodyguard, the organization grew to include other specialized branches. The General SS became a pool of SS men, a body of semipermanent, nonspecialized members structured like a military organization, including reserve and honorary members, and the broader part-time membership which turned out for parades, rallies and street actions. The structure of the Allgemeine SS was rather similar to that of the SA. The smallest unit was the Schar (squad of eight men); above this there were Zug (platoon), Sturm (company), Sturmbann (battalion) and Standarte (regiment). Above these, the Allgemeine SS included territorial units: Untergruppe, Gruppe, Abschnitt and Oberabschnitt. The Allgemeine SS territorial partition coincided with the Wehrkreise, the regular army districts. Indeed, one of the most important tasks of the Allgemeine SS was to watch over and control the Wehrmacht, the only possible force that could oppose or overthrow the Nazi regime. During the war, the number of SS-Oberabschnitte was increased following German conquests in the occupied European lands (e.g., SS-Oa Nordwest in Holland, SS-Oa Nord in Norway and SS-Oa Böhmen und Mähren in Bohemia-Moravia).

SS ranks were the same as in the SA. All ranks above SS Sturmbannführer (major) were more or less professional, and performed administrative, bureaucratic functions. Ranks below that were unpaid volunteers. Men of the Allgemeine SS had uniforms which they had to finance themselves, and which were worn on Sundays and during Nazi feasts. Except for their personally purchased side arms, they were not heavily armed, and did not live in barracks, but had their own homes and jobs. They were, however, required to undergo compulsory periods of service, notably an indoctrination evening once a week. They formed a kind of civilian political/police militia overseeing the German population which could mobilize at any moment if the Nazi regime was threatened. They also had to buy Nazi publications. They were encouraged to recruit for the active SS branches; they organized rallies and meetings, and supported and promoted all SS activities. The role of the Allgemeine SS eventually diminished as the Third Reich wore on, particularly after 1936, when Himmler became chief of all German police. The Allgemeine SS lost a great deal of its security role, which was taken over by other, more specialized SS sub-branches.

Allgemeiner Deutscher Automobil-Club (ADAC). Germany's largest automobile club, founded in May 1903, as Deutsche Motorradfahrer-Vereinigung (German Motorbiker Association), and renamed in 1911. During the Third Reich, ADAC and all other automobile clubs were subjected to Gleichschaltung (q.v.), and controlled by the Nationalsozialistisches Kraftfahrerkorps (q.v.).

Alkett. See Altmärkische Kettenfabrik GmBh.

Alpenfestung. Alpine redoubt. Rumors and "unconfirmed" Allied intelligence indicated the preparation of an impregnable German fortress in the Alpine mountains, covering almost twenty thousand square miles in upper Bavaria, western Austria and northern Italy. Its core would be the area of Obersalzberg and Berchtesgaden, where Hitler originally intended to retreat and lead a last ditch effort in the final struggle against the Allies. The fortress would be composed of concealed combat emplacements ranging from pillboxes to massive concrete artillery bunkers, camouflaged barracks and headquarters, bomb-proof factories, and caverns for food and equipment. The redoubt would be manned by a specially selected, commando-type corps of fanatical young men, mainly SS and Hitler Youth, known as Werewolves (see Werwolf). Though the Alpenfestung might have been a hoax, the threat was taken seriously by the Allies, as the possibility of its existence could not be ignored. Several strategic plans were made as a result. Hitler changed his mind in April 1945, and decided to stay in Berlin. The Alpenfestung did not exist. It was actually a huge bluff, the last great masterly lie devised by propaganda minister Joseph Paul Goebbels (q.v.).

Alte Kämpfer. "Old Fighters" or early Nazis of the Kampfzeit (q.v.), members of the SS, NSDAP, and other party-affiliated organizations having joined before the Machtergreifung on January 30, 1933. Alte Kämpfer benefited from various rights and privileges. However, Hitler was not totally loyal to the old fighters of the

Alte Kämpfer chevron.

Kampfzeit. Some of the Nazi leaders who held important positions before the seizure of power did not play any role in the Third Reich, including the brothers Otto and Gregor Strasser (q.v.), the SA leader Ernst Röhm (q.v.), and the ideologues Gottfried Feder and Alfred Rosenberg. Old Fighters wore a silver honor chevron on the upper right arm called Ehrenwinkel für Alte Kämpfer, instituted in February 1934.

Alter Art. Old-style or obsolete, according to a previously prescribed or customary manner. This term was employed for discarded vehicles, pieces of uniform and equipment, bunkers and so on.

Altmärkische Kettenfabrik GmBh (Alkett). An important company located in Berlin that produced cars and converted self-propelled guns (notably the Sturmtiger and Panzerjager).

Altreich. Old empire. German territory within the 1937 borders, and before the annexation of Austria. See Anschluß Osterreichs (an das Deutsche Reich) and Großdeutschland.

Amann, Max (1891–1957). A World War I sergeant, Amann joined the SA in 1921, and became NSDAP business manager and Hitler's literary agent. He published *Mein Kampf* (q.v.), and became a Nazi official after 1933. He was president of the Reich Association of Newspapers, president of the Reich Press Chamber, head of the Eher-Verlag (q.v.), and an honorary SS Obergruppenführer. After the war, Amann was deemed a Hauptschuldiger (prominent guilty party); he was sentenced to ten years in a labor camp in September 1948, but was released in 1953. Amann had become a very rich man in the Third Reich, but denazification and postwar trials left him penniless until his death in March 1957.

Amerika

Amerika Bomber. A spring 1942 aviation contract competition to develop a Luftwaffe transoceanic long-range strategic bomber. The only results were a few uncompleted prototype aircraft, and many advanced designs on paper.

Angeschlossene Verbände der NSDAP. Associated groups of the NSDAP. The NSDAP was formed from the union of Gliederungen der Partei (party organizations) and Angeschlossende Verbände. The Angeschlossende Verbände included:
- Dienst Frauenwerk (Service of female work)
- Deutsche Arbeit Front (DAF German Labour Front)
- Nationalsozialistische Arztebund (NSAB doctors league)
- Nationalsozialistische Juristenbund (NSJ jurist organization)
- Nationalsozialistische Volkswohlfahrte (NSV people welfare)
- Nationalsozialistische Lehrerbund (NSLB teacher league)
- Nationalsozialistische Kriegsopfer Verzorgung (NSKV, organization for veterans and war victims)
- Beamtenbund (civil servants and administrators league)

See Gliederungen der NSDAP, and Nationalsozialistiches Deutsche Arbeiter Partei.

Der Angriff. *The Assault*, Nazi polemical pamphlet and newsletter founded in Berlin by Gauleiter Joseph Goebbels in 1927. At first appearing once a week, and later twice a week, *Der Angriff* became a daily Nazi newspaper in November 1930.

Angstbrosche. Badge of Fear. Nickname jeeringly given by Nazis of the first hour to the party badge worn by new members joining after the seizure of power in January 1933.

Anschluß Osterreichs (an das Deutsche Reich). Annexation of Austria to the German Reich on March 12, 1938. The Anschluß, a burning issue in the 1920s and 1930s, was among the first major steps in Hitler's creation of an empire that would include German-speaking lands.

Antikominternpakt. Anti-Komintern Pact, a military alliance signed on November 25, 1936 between Germany and Japan for a duration of five years. The pact was intended to fight the so-called Komintern, short for Kommounisticheski Internacional (International Communist), which was established in Moscow in 1919 as a worldwide organization intended to spread communism. In 1937, Italy joined the Anti-Komintern pact, followed by Manchukuo, Hungary, Denmark, Finland, Spain, Bulgaria, Croatia, China (Nanking), Rumania and Slovakia. Germany left the Anti-Kommintern Pact in 1939, when it signed a treaty of nonaggression with the USSR (See Hitler-Stalin-Pakt). The Komintern was disbanded by the Russians in 1943, and reactivated during the Cold War as the Kominform (Information Bureau for Worker and Communist Parties) until 1956.

Anwärter. Aspirant, candidate.

Appeasement. Policy of British and French leaders in the period 1935–1938 aimed at assenting to reasonable concessions with Hitler in order to guarantee a lasting peace in Europe. See Münchener Abkommen.

Arado. Industrial airplane company. Arado designed and produced several airplanes for the Luftwaffe, notably the reconnaissance floatplanes Ar 19A-3 and Ar 196-A. The Arado company also designed the world's first operational jet bomber, the Arado Ar 234 Blitz.

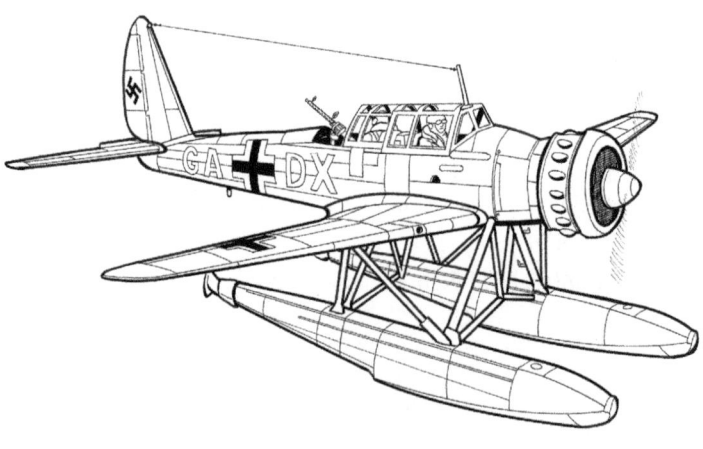

Arado Ar 196-A floatplane.

Arbeit adelt. "Labor Ennobles," the motto of the RAD. See Reichsarbeitsdienst.

RAD dagger with "Arbeit Adelt" inscription on the blade.

Arbeit macht frei. Literally "labor liberates" or "work makes free." Originally an old German peasant saying, this slogan was emblazoned on the gates of concentration and extermination camps, as part of the deception process by which it was suggested that by honest work a prisoner might be pardoned. Prisoners in Auschwitz ridiculed the cynicism and perverted humor of the slogan by saying "Arbeit macht frei durch den Schornstein ("Work brings freedom through the chimney").

Arbeitsanzug or **Drillichanzug**. Fatigue uniform issued to German recruits and to privates. This uniform, made of unbleached denim material, was white/light-gray; it consisted of a hat, a shapeless buttoned jacket with two patch pockets and a turn-down collar; the trousers, made in the same material, were simply cut with two side pockets. This uniform was easily washable and extensively used for fatigue duty, work, instruction, training maneuvers, weapon cleaning and motor vehicle maintenance.

Arbeitsbuch. Workbook, a document required by law on February 26, 1935, for all German employees. The employer would write in the book how the worker behaved. The book, which had been abolished in the 1840s, was reintroduced, and kept by the employer during the time of the work contract. Forgery, loss or falsification of the workbook was punished by fine, and even imprisonment.

Arbeitseinsatz. Work mobilization of the Third Reich. It was directed by Gauleiter and SS-Obergruppenfüher Fritz Sauckel (q.v.), given full responsibility by Hitler in March 1942, for finding workers to support Albert Speer's armaments and munitions program at all cost. The growing losses on the Russian front, increasing conscription, the heightened demands on the war economy, and the reluctance of the Nazis to employ German women forced Speer to turn to Sauckel with steadily increasing demands for more Fremdarbeiter (foreign workers). Sauckel's service turned out to be one of the greatest slave trades in history. Tirelessly and efficiently, Sauckel directed a brutal hunt for workers, and abducted approximately 5 million men and women from all over Europe during the three years he was active. Sauckel himself admitted that, of that five million, at most 200,000 had come of their own free will. See also Speer, Albert.

Arbeitserziehungslager. Educational work camp; special training and indoctrination centers for inmates released from concentration camps. After 1939, very few prisoners were released, so the "re-education scheme" was abandoned.

Arbeits-Kommando (AK). Labor detachment; secret military formations disguised as volunteer civilian laborers formed by a certain Major Buchrucker. It was funded by and attached to the Reichswehr (q.v.). Members, often men from the Freikorps (q.v.), were engaged on short-term

Arbeitsanzug.

contract, wore uniforms and were billeted in army barracks. Their number was about 20,000 in the years 1920 and 1921. The AK was disbanded in October 1924 after a failed and repressed revolt.

Arbeitslager. Work camp controlled by the SS in which all those opposed or not willingly collaborating with the Nazi regime were detained. Originally intended for German asocials and deviants, camps became also places of detention related to the concentration camps for foreign prisoners. In 1944 there were twenty Konzentrationlager (q.v.) and some 165 major work camps in Germany and in the occupied territories.

Arbeitsscheue. Literally "reluctant to work." This Nazi term designated an unemployed person deemed lazy or asocial by a law of January 1938. Work was the duty of the citizens and the glue that held German community together. Those who did not submit to this principle might be arrested and sent to a work camp. According to Nazi statistics, in December 1935 there were 2,507,000 unemployed, in January 1938 1,051,745, and in December 1938 only 450,000. See Gemeinschaftsfremde.

Architecture in the Third Reich. Architecture was one of Hitler's early passions as a young man in Vienna before World War I. Nazi architecture—like all other aspects of the ideology—reflected Hitler's personal tastes, a mixture of classical and baroque. It included monumental designs reproducing the forms of classical antiquity, neoclassicism and neobaroque, exaggerated in shapes and size. Cities such as Berlin, Nuremberg, Munich, Hamburg, and Linz were enthusiastically planned by Hitler for total transformation with colossal buildings—including monumental memorials, mighty triumphal arches adorned with Nazi symbolism, massive towers, opera houses, concert halls, and railway stations—and wide boulevards marked by large parade routes and huge bridges. The architecture also included gigantic parade grounds where large crowds could gather, participate and attend astounding spectacles: mass marches, commemorations, presentations, parades by daylight and by night with torchlight, reviews, consecrations of flags, games, meetings, exhibitions, inspections, speeches and display of force in the form of mock battles with infantry, tanks and planes.

Another aspect of Nazi architecture was cozy. Based on German tradition, country kitsch and sentimental folklore, it included thatched-roof cottages with wooden balconies and handmade oak beams, as well as whitewashed Tyrolean peasant houses. The outbreak of World War II did not at first drastically interrupt Hitler's favorite architect, Albert Speer's, construction activities, but after 1942—as the hope for a short war vanished—Hitler urged his architect to postpone the works and concentrate on weapons and ammunitions production. See Art in the Third Reich and Speer, Albert.

Arierparagraph. Aryan clause. The paragraph was a part of the anti–Jewish laws passed in June 1933, stipulating who was a Jew: "An individual of mixed Jewish blood [...] who is descended from one or two grandparents who, racially, were Jews. Full-blooded Jewish grandparents are those who belonged to the Jewish religious community." The clause banned Jews from all cultural activities, and many Jews (at least the richest) took the laws as an opportunity to leave Germany.

Arisch. Aryan. The Aryans were Indo-European people who established themselves in Iran and northern India between 2000 and 1000 B.C. The term "Aryan" was coined by the German philologist Friedrich Max Müller (1823–1900), who had warned (unsuccessfully) against extending the meaning of his neologism to race, or racism. The racist Nazi ideology borrowed a large part of the work of the French diplomat and theorist Joseph Arthur, Count of Gobineau, and also took elements from the works from various theorists and philosophers, like Fichte, Jakob Grimm, E.M. Arndt, Treitschke, Houston Stewart Chamberlain (q.v.), Paul de Lagarde, Richard Wagner (q.v.), Adolf Stöcker, Adam Muller, Rühle von Lilienstern, Hegel, Friedrich Wilhelm Nietzsche (q.v.), and Hans F.K. Günther, to mention just a few. Some of the theories of these philosophers were mixed together and additions and falsifications were made, resulting in the confused Nazi conception of human races. The Germans were the best human race; they constituted the Urvolk (people of origin); they were Ubermenschen (superhumans) belonging to the Herrenvolk (master people). The Nazis were obsessed with blood purity. The Germans were not allowed to mix with other races. Their mission was to subdue the other inferior races, to conquer and rule the world. An Aryan was someone who could prove no Jewish ancestry up to two or three generations back. The Japanese were allied to the Germans after the agreement of November 1936. Although they were of a different race — and to justify the alliance — they were considered by Hitler to possess qualities similar enough to German Nordic people to be accorded the title of "Honorary Aryans."

Arisierung. Aryanization — in fact spoliation. Jewish legal owners of businesses, shops or industry were spoliated and companies entrusted to "Aryan" Nazi followers or "pure" sympathizers. The term was also used to refer to the purging of conquered peoples by the Nazis in order to "improve" the population by removing individuals who failed to conform to their racial ideals.

Ärmelband or **Ärmelstreifen.** Lettered cloth cuff title or sleeve band, generally 15 centimeters wide. Worn on the left sleeve near the cuff, the title contained the name of the wearer's unit or a campaign he had fought, or a specialization. They came in many variations and colors: dark green, black or brown with silver, white or gold German Gothic or Sütterin lettering.

Armbinde. Armband or brassard. This piece of colored or white cloth was generally worn on the left upper arm to indicate that a soldier held a special but temporary function. The wearer could also be a German civilian or a foreign civilian officially employed in a military, auxiliary or ancillary role — a capacity not requiring the issue of a regular army uniform.

Armbinde. This armband, worn by personnel serving as auxiliary in the Deutsche Wehrmacht (German armed forces), was yellow with black Gothic lettering.

Armee. Army. See Infanterie.

Armelpatten or **Armspiegel.** Arm badge or patch, often a specialist badge. Specialists were noncommissioned officers and Unteroffizieren who were trained for a specific task. This was indicated by an embroidered yellow symbol (or a Gothic letter) on a round, dark green cloth background. The badge was generally worn on the right lower sleeve of the tunic.

Armwinkel. Arm chevron.

Art in the Third Reich. Despite his early failure to be accepted to art school in Vienna, Hitler always considered himself an artist, and his rigid taste and views formed the artistic tenets of the Third Reich. Characterized by naturalism in style and heroism and idealism in subject, the state-controlled Nazi art was militant and intended to be comprehensible to the most average person. It presented a close similarity to the Soviet propaganda art style of socialist realism. The term "heroic realism" has sometimes been used to describe both artistic styles. Nazi art (Kunst) was on the whole heavily stereotyped, cold and predictable. It was dominated by monumental power; by classical, ideal, "pure" beauty and technical perfection; by clarity, directness, accessibility, and logic; by exaltation of racial purity, blood and soil; by militarism, confidence in victory, obedience and sacrifice, martial vigor, force and bravery; and often by cheap romantic kitsch, ancestral mythology, naive idealism, sentimental simplicity, and return to rural virtues and wisdom of the past. The purpose of art was to express the Nazi view of society and glorify the regime. The subjects which National Socialist art favored and vigorously promoted showed that art was not only the direct expression of their political ideas, but also at the base of their political system in all its aspects. German artists, sculptors and other graphic designers (and musicians, film directors and writers as well) had to identify themselves with the Nazi ideology, and were required to be members of the Reichskulturkammer (q.v.), the Chamber of Culture. Created in 1933, it decided upon artistic norms and imposed political standards. There was no need for cultural experiment or expression of artists' own feelings and personal concerns in Nazi Germany. Of course, modern art movements such as expressionism, cubism, surrealism, dadaism, abstract art, and others were banned, and declared "Jewish" Entartete Kunst (q.v.) — that is, "degenerate art." Hitler's seizure of power was rapidly followed by actions intended to cleanse the culture life. Book burnings were organized, Jewish artists and musicians were dismissed from teaching positions, nonconformist artists were forbidden, and curators who had shown a partiality to modern art were replaced with Nazi Party members. See Gleichschaltung.

Artamen. See Bund der Artamenen.

Artfremd. Inappropriate. This adjective qualified anything and anyone that did not fit the Nazi ideology.

Artillerieträgerboot. Gunboat, sometimes designed to practice offensive actions.

Aryan. See Arisch.

Asoziale (Aziole). Vagabonds, tramps, beggars, jobless, nomadic Gypsies, deviating persons, modern artists, nonconformists, homosexuals and other artfremd (inappropriate) persons were considered by the Nazis as antisocial elements, dangerous for the German population and a threat to public order. They were arrested, and the SS were charged to "reeducate" them with harsh methods in work and concentration camps, where they were identified by a black triangle. See Arbeitsscheue and Gemeinschaftsfremde.

Atlantic, Battle of the. A bitter struggle fought in the North Atlantic Ocean in the period 1941–43 between Allied convoys (bringing supplies from the USA to Great Britain) and German submarines. See Kriegsmarine and Unterseeboot.

Atlantic pockets. See Festung and Atlantikwall.

Atlantikwall (AW). Atlantic Wall; fortification systems covering the west coast of Europe from northern Norway to the Franco-Spanish border intended to counter an Allied landing and the opening of a second front on the European continent. It was started in 1940; work was intensified as a result of the successful British commando raid against Saint-Nazaire in March 1942 and the repulsed Canadian landing in Dieppe on August 19, 1942. With thick concrete armed bunkers, armed emplacements and batteries covering air, sea and land, minefields, beach obstacles and antitank defenses, the Atlantic Wall was strongest around ports and in sectors deemed the most likely for Allied landing. Gradually the coasts between the main ports were filled with armed emplacements, which were deepened at the end of 1943 and early 1944 when an Allied invasion became imminent. Spurred by Field Marshal Erwin Rommel, the coastal defenses were reinforced with increased numbers of obstacles, bunkers, mines and armored forces stationed inland for counterattack. On D-Day, June 6, 1944, the Atlantic Wall was far from completion because of shortages of materials, weapons and forces, and it could not repulse the powerful Allied Operation Overlord in Normandy, France. See Festung, Stützpunkt, Stützpunktgruppe and Widerstandnest.

Atlantis. One of the German navy's deadliest sea raiders. Originally built as a freighter, the boat was converted into a militarized Hilfskreuzer (q.v.) By June 1941 she had sunk 21 ships (140,900 tons). The HSK2 *Atlantis* was sunk in November 1941 by the British cruiser HMS *Devonshire*. Another successful German commerce sea raider was HSK5 *Pinguin*.

Atombombe. Atom bomb. The fear of a German atom bomb was groundless. In spite of quantum mechanics research and experimentation carried out as early as 1932 by the German nuclear physicist Werner Heisenberg in 1938 by Lise Meitner, Otto Hahn and Fritz Strassmann (who showed that atoms of uranium could be split); and in 1940 by Professor Bothe in Heidelberg, German nuclear scientists could not match the organization and drive of the American Manhattan Project, which led to practical application in Hiroshima and Nagasaki in 1945.

Auf gut deutsch. "In plain German," a strongly nationalist, pan–German and anti–Semitic newspaper published by Dietrich Eckart (q.v.) in post–World War I Munich.

Aurora Alemà. "German Morning" in Portuguese from the German newspaper *Deutsche Morgen*. *Aurora Alemà* was a German-language Brazilian Nazi newspaper published between March 1932 and December 1941.

Ausbildungs- und Ersatzbataillon. Administrative training home depot for a German division. This was a Kazerne (barrack) in a German town where recruits were equipped and trained. During the war, men with minor wounds after their stay in the hospital were returned to the divisional Ausbildungs depot where they were trained anew to form fresh fighting units.

Auschwitz. The most infamous of all extermination camps. Situated in Poland, 160 miles southwest of Warsaw and today called Oswiecim. The place—originally a military barracks and later a factory—was opened as a prison in 1940 after the defeat of Poland. Headed by SS Hauptsturmführer Rudolf Höß, the camp greatly expanded after 1941 to carry out the "final solution of the Jewish question." A new camp was set up at nearby Birkenau and the complex became a factory producing death on industrial scale. Special installations were built, including a railway station, bathhouses—actually gas chambers where the victims were killed—and special crematoria for burning the bodies. It is estimated that about 1,500,000 persons (about 90 percent of them Jews) were murdered at Auschwitz-Birkenau. Infamous doctors such as Josef Mengele also performed a wide variety of cruel pseudoscientific experiments using inmates as guinea pigs. Auschwitz was the largest of the German camps, fulfilling the functions of work, concentration, and extermination camps. The large complex consisted of: Auschwitz I, the Stammlager, or base camp and administrative center; Auschwitz II–Birkenau, the Vernichtungslager or extermination camp, with gas chambers and crematoria; Auschwitz III–Monowitz, also known as Monowitz-Buna, an industrial center with I.G. Farben, Krupp and Siemens-Schuckert factories and processing plants using slave labor to produce synthetic oil and rubber, weapons, and many other goods; and 45 smaller satellite camps established in the vicinity termed Aussenlager (external camp), Nebenlager (extension or sub-camp), and Arbeitslager (labor camp). The largest of these were built at Trzebinia, Blechhammer and Althammer. Women's subcamps were constructed at Budy, Plawy, Zabrze, Gleiwitz (I, II, and III), Rajsko, and Lichtenwerden (Svetla). See Frankfurt Trial.

Ausführung (Ausf.). Version, model, mark, variant, batch—principally used for armored vehicles and ordnance.

Ausgehanzug. Walking-out dress, the formal military uniform, typically with order insignias and full size medals worn at ceremonies, official receptions, and other special occasions.

Ausguck. Observation post.

Auslandsdeutsche. German persons living in foreign lands. The racial doctrine of the Nazis held that such persons retained their affiliation with the homeland. There were several special agencies of the Nazi Party responsible for spreading Nazism abroad and to make contact with and supervise Germans in foreign lands. They included the Fichte World League, the German Academy, the People's League for Germanism Abroad, the League of German Business Employers, and several others. Auslandsdeutsche were rather well organized in many countries (including the United States and South Africa) and more particularly in Paraguay, Uruguay and Argentina where, after the wars, many SS, Nazi criminals and party leaders found a safe refuge.

Ausland-Sicherheitsdienst. Office of the SD dealing with intelligence in foreign countries. See also Reichssicherheitshauptamt and Sicherheitsdienst des Reichsführer SS.

Auslandsorganisation (OA). Overseas Organization, a Nazi Party department responsible for German communities overseas. In the structure of the AO, countries with important German communities were regarded as separate Gaue (political districts). Substantial funds were devoted to these organizations, which often proved an effective cover for German political interference. See Auslandsdeutsche.

Ausrüstung. Equipment and accouterments. See Sturmgepäk and Tragenriemen.

Aussenpolitisches Amt (APA). Foreign policy service of the Nazi Party, placed under command of Alfred Rosenberg (q.v.).

Ausser Dienst (a.D). On the inactive list, out of service for officers and men. After 1935, this military term was preferred to Verabschiedete (retired).

Ausserordentliche Befriedungsaktion (AB Aktion). "Extraordinary pacification action," in fact Nazi euphemistic code name for the liquidation of Polish Jews, trade unionists, intellectuals and non–Nazi leaders. The action took place during and after the Polish campaign in September 1939. It is estimated that about 3,500 persons were summarily killed from September 1939 until June 1940. The AB Aktion was entrusted to Hans Frank (q.v.) as governor-general of Poland, and to his deputy Arthur Seyss-Inquart (q.v.). See also Einsatzgruppen.

Aussichtsturm. Watchtower. Made of wood beams or metal poles or completely masoned, watchtowers punctuated barbed wire fences that enclosed airfields, economically important points, military dumps, prisoner-of-war camps and concentration camps.

Ausweiß. Identification pass or permit allowing the bearer to freely travel in Nazi occupied territories. They were very difficult to obtain for foreigners and strictly reserved to collaborators.

Auszeichnung. Decoration, distinction, medal. See Eisernes Kreuz.

Autarkie. Autarchy; national self-sufficiency, economic policy dictating that a country should produce everything it needs. It was Hitler's wish, as soon as he obtained power, that Germany should be free from — or at least should drastically reduce — imports from foreign countries in order to become immune to blockade in the future war he planned.

Autobahnen. Motorways. The Nazi Party paid great attention to modern means of transport, and Hitler was keen on cars and planes. A large scale construction program, the Autobahnprogram, was launched by the Nazis in June 1933. The Autobahnprogram served various goals. The first was the establishment of an efficient and unified network of transport routes under the control of the Reich. Secondly, the Autobahnen were political prestige objects for the Nazi regime that symbolized the rise of the Third Reich and illustrated the rebirth of Germany. Thirdly, their construction created numerous jobs, helping to resorb unemployment after the 1929 economic crisis. Fourthly, the Autobahnen served the internal political security of the Reich, enabling the rapid intervention of the SS security forces to crush any attempt to overthrow the regime. Fifthly, the new roads made military troop transport quicker and easier within the Reich. And finally, some straight sections could be used as temporary airstrips. See Organization Todt and Todt, Fritz.

Axis Sally. See Gillars, Mildred, and Zucca, Luisa Rita.

Axmann, Arthur (1913–1996). Axmann joined the Nazi Party in 1928, and became a senior official of the Hitler Jugend (q.v.) in 1932. In 1940 he succeeded Baldur von Schirach (q.v.) as leader of the Hitler Jugend. In 1941 he fought in Russia, was wounded and lost an arm. He spent the rest of World War II as head of the Hitler Jugend, overseeing the militarization and mobilization of the German youth. In 1949 he was classified as a major offender by a denazification court and sentenced to a three-year term. He was immediately released as his sentence was considered to have been served while waiting for his case to be heard. He then went on to a successful business career.

Babi Yar. A ravine near Kiev where about 30,000 Jews were murdered in September 1941. The slaughter was ordered by the German army as retaliation for an attack against the Continental Hotel, which housed a headquarters.

Bachem Natter. Viper, a small, cheap, single-seat monoplane experimental rocket-propelled fighter designed by engineer Erich Bachem in 1944. Natter had very short wings (wingspan was only 3.6 meters), and a length of 6.1 meters. It had a Walter rocket engine giving a speed of 800 kilometers per hour. Armament would have consisted of twenty-four 7.5 centimeters rockets placed in the nose. It was to be launched vertically from a guide rail and had a flight duration of about four minutes. Some 40 Natter were built but none ever achieved service status.

Bach-Zelewski, Erich von dem (1899–1972). Bach-Zelewski joined the Nazi Party in 1930, and during World War II was Höherere SS- und

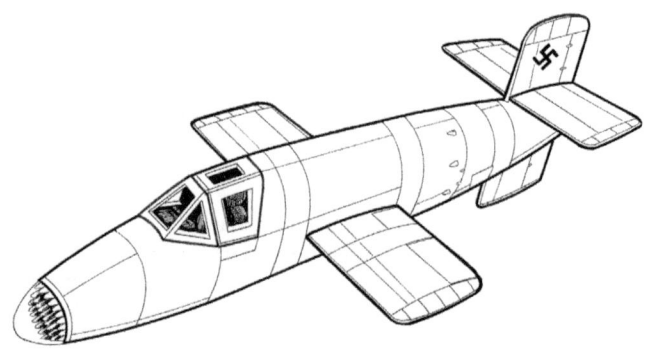

Bachem Ba 349 Natter.

Polizeiführer (q.v.) and SS General in charge of campaigns against partisans on the Russian front. Responsible for the arrest and deportation of Jews, he also suppressed the Warsaw rising of 1944. After the war, in exchange for his testimony against his former SS superiors at the Nuremberg Trials, von dem Bach-Zelewski was not accused of any war crimes, and was released from prison in 1949. In the 1950s and early 1960s he was, however, tried and sentenced to ten years house arrest for several Nazi-related murders in the early thirties. He died in a Munich prison in March 1972.

Bahnschutzpolizei. Railway protection police with auxiliary status. The Bahnschutzpolizei was put under control of the SS in 1942. Composed of Bahnhofswache (railway guards), the railway policemen were responsible for large rail centers. They checked travel papers and identity documents, they provided security and ensured the smooth flow of traffic, and they screened passengers, and hunted for deserters and soldiers absent without leave. They were lightly armed, wore a blue uniform, a gorget and an armband with the legend Bahnhofswache. See Ringkragen and Zugwache.

Bajonett. Bayonet. The German standard bayonet was the Model M84/98, produced from 1914 until 1945. The bayonet was 10 inches long with a wood or Bakelite grip. Its sharp blade was kept in a metal sheath fitting to the service belt.

Balkenkreuz. National marking, a cross of Greek type with four arms of equal length, straight and parallel sides. In the period 1938–1940 the cross was white, and later it was black with contrasting white limbs to let the cross stand out against the background color; there were two main variants, thin and thick. The Balkenkreuz was painted on planes, tanks and vehicles.

Ballastexistenzen. Burdens on the community—anyone suffering from incurable and severely crippling handicaps, injuries or mental sickness. According to Nazi eugenics those individual lives were "worthless" and were to be eliminated in the so-called Euthanasia Program. See Euthanasiebefehl.

Bamberg Conferenz. A meeting of senior Nazis held on February 14, 1926, which aimed to resolve the crisis between those Nazis who were

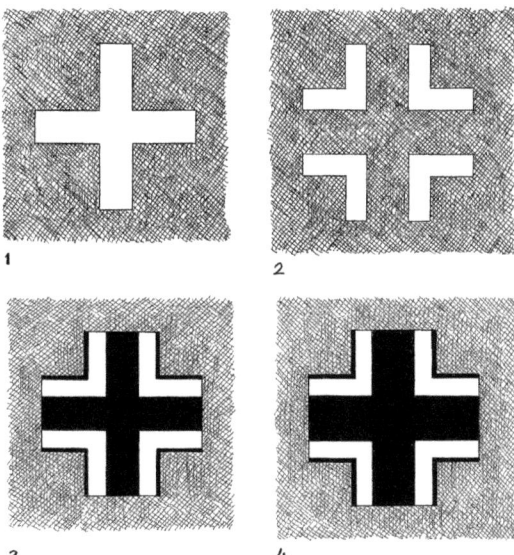

Balkenkreuz. 1. White cross (beginning of World War II). 2. White outline. 3. Thin black cross with white outline. 4. Thick black cross with white outline.

more socialist than nationalist—like Gregor Strasser (q.v.)—and the ultranationalist right wing of the party, led by Hitler. The bitter struggle between the two opposing factions went on, and was finally solved by the massacre of the Nacht der Langen Messer (q.v.) in June 1934. See Schwarze Front.

Bandenkampfabzeichen. (See illustration on page 16.) Literally "anti-gang medal"; the Anti-Partisan Guerrilla Warfare Badge established in January 1944, which rewarded military personnel that participated in antipartisan behind-the-lines battles. The badge existed in three grades: bronze, for 20 combat days; silver, for 50 combat days; and gold, for 100 combat days. Criteria were slightly different for the Luftwaffe, being based on air sorties instead of days in action.

Bandenkampfverbände. Antipartisan detachments. It was also a euphemism for extermination squads. See Einsatzgruppen.

Bandfabrik Ewald Vorsteher (BeVo). Registered trade name of a large weaving company located at Wuppertal, one of the principal makers of German World War II woven insignia. See BeVo.

Bandit. Bandit. Nazi designation of any armed civilian resistant, maquisard or partisan.

Banner

Bandenkampfabzeichen.

Banner. Banner. Each SA Standarte (regiment) had a banner copied from the ancient Roman banner. It had the form of a pole surmounted by an eagle holding a wreathed swastika, below which there was a rectangular frame displaying the letters NSDAP; from the frame was suspended a red flag with a black Hakenkreuz on a white disc. The banner had a red, white and black fringe and carried the motto "Deutschland Erwache" (Germany Awakes) on one side and on the reverse was written Nat. Soz. Deutsche Arbeiterpartei Sturmabteilung (Assault Groups of the German Workers National Socialist Party).

Barbarossa. "Red Beard"; Code name for the German attack on Russia on June 22, 1941, after the emperor Friedrich I, who was nicknamed Barbarossa (1123–1190). Hitler broke the pact of nonaggression signed with Stalin in August 1939, and as an excuse, accused the Russians of treachery. The invasion of the USSR was presented as a crusade against Bolshevism, but the real motivation was the conquest of lands providing wheat, oil, and mineral supplies, as well as the enslavement of the Russian people and the extermination of the Russian Jewish community. By his own choice Hitler opted for a fatal and disastrous two-front war.

Barbie, Klaus (1914–1991). SS-Hauptsturmführer (Captain) and Gestapo officer at Lyon (France) during World War II. He was responsible for the arrest and deportation of French Jews and Résistants, notably Jean Moulin. After the war Barbie, a skilled, experienced and anti–Communist policeman, was recruited by the U.S. Army Counter Intelligence Corps. He subsequently worked for the intelligence services of Juan Peron's Argentina, for Bolivia, and for Federal Germany. He was identified in Bolivia as early as 1971 by the Nazi hunters the Klarsfelds. It was only in January 1983 that he was arrested and extradited to France. There Klaus Barbie was the subject of a sensational and widely publicized trial held in 1987. He was sentenced to life imprisonment for crimes against humanity and died in prison in September 1991. See Klarsfeld.

Barracke or **Kazerne.** Barrack.

Bataillon. Battalion. Also called Abteilung for the artillery, and Sturmbann in the SA, SS and Waffen-SS. A Bataillon was made of several companies called Kompanie (Heer) and Stürme (SS).

Batterie. Battery, a number of artillery guns usually of the same sort and the same caliber, all of them generally firing in the same direction and against the same target.

Baustärkte StA and StB. (See illustrations on page 17.) Standardized bunker roof and wall concrete thickness. There were two main sorts, StA = 3.5 meters and StB = 2 meters (St. is short for ständig, "permanent"). See Regelbau.

Bauten des Führer. Hitler's buildings. The führer looked upon himself as a connoisseur of painting and an authority on architecture. Regarding urbanism, the Führer and his architects Troost and later Albert Speer had huge and megalomaniac plans to rebuild Berlin, Munich, Nuremberg, Linz and the main other towns of the Reich in a pompous, monumental, massive, neoclassic style which was to reflect Nazi power and would glorify the regime for a thousand years. For example, the Berlin triumphal arch would have had a volume of 83,543,640 cubic feet; the Arc de Triomphe in Paris would have fit into it fifty times. The Soldier's Hall was a cube 829 feet long, 295 feet deep and 262 feet high and the field behind this hall measured 984 by 1,476 feet. The new Berlin Town Hall was planned to have a length of 1476 feet; its central structure would have been 197 feet high. To the last days of his life, Hitler never tired of playing with models and drawings of the great German

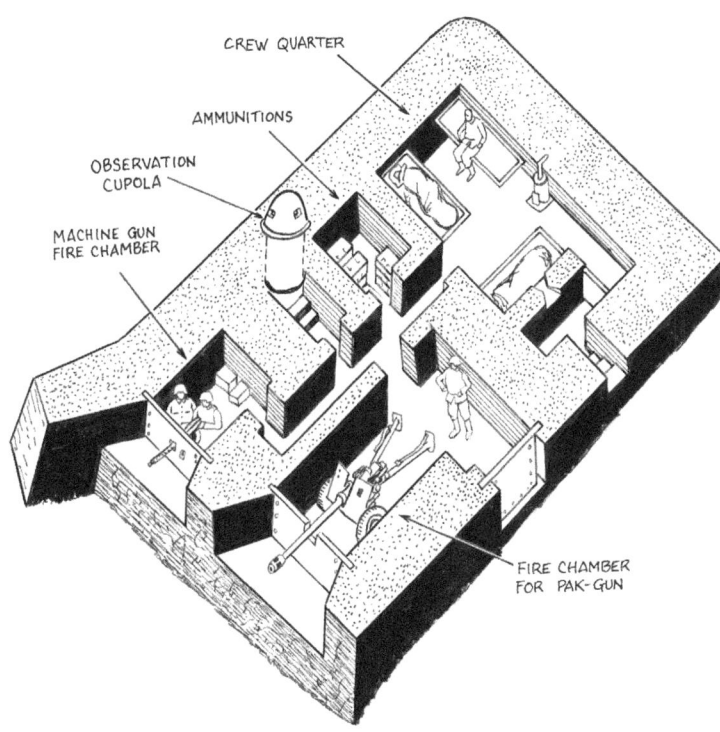

Casemate Type 116 for Pak/MG (Front view and ground plan). The bunker was in Baustärkte StB.

cities. See Architecture in the Third Reich and Speer, Albert.

Bayreuth Festival. Bayreuth, Richard Wagner's home, is located some 122 miles north of Munich. A fervent Wagnerite, Hitler made the music festival an annual National Socialist cultural event.

Beamtenbund, also called **Reichsbund Deutscher Beamter.** Civil Service League, a body of civil servants closely related with the Nazi Party and under its control. The monolithic league was intended to supersede the old professional civil servants service organizations and to implement all decrees issued by the Nazi government. See Gleichschaltung.

Beauty of Labor. See Schönheit der Arbeit.

Beck, Ludwig (1880–1944). Wehrmacht senior officer and a leading figure in the German army opposition to Hitler. General Beck was executed after the failed attempt to kill Hitler on July 20, 1944.

Beefsteak Nazi. Term of derision used to describe communists and socialists who had joined the Nazi Party after the seizure of power in January 1933. They were "brown on the outside and red on the inside."

Beer Hall Putsch. See Bürgerbräu Keller Putsch.

Befehlshaber or **Wehrmachtbefehlshaber** or **Militärbefehlshaber.** A senior commander, chief of a larger unit, commander-in-chief, or military governor. For example, the German occupying forces stationed in the Netherlands were commanded by Luftwaffe General Friedrich Christiansen, who carried the title of Wehrmachtbefehlshaber in die Niederlanden (WBN commander of armed forces in the Netherlands). From October 25, 1940, onwards, military administration in France was entrusted to general Otto von Stülpnagel, who became Militärbefehlhaber in Frankreich (MBF military governor in France). See Okkupation.

Befristete Vorbeugungshäftlinge (BV). Prisoners in limited-term preventive custody. A category of concentration camp inmates classed by the SS as criminals who had already served several sentences.

Begleit. Escort. Begleit units were security bodyguards but also fighting formations. For example, Hitler's bodyguard unit became the 1st

SS Panzerdivision Leibstandarte Adolf Hitler, and Hitler's Headquarters escort became a motorized infantry division, Führer Begleit Division. Himmler's Begleit-Bataillon was turned into the 16th Waffen-SS Panzergrenadier Division Reichsführer SS.

Beiwagen. Sidecar. The standard motorbike sidecar carried panniers, one spare wheel and often a machine gun with ammunition. The motorized soldiers were used for reconnaissance roles. They rode to battle and dismounted to fight just as in earlier centuries the dragoons using horses had done.

Bekenntniskirche. Confessional Church, formed in 1934 in response to Nazi harassment. It was a countermovement by Protestant theologians opposed to Hitler, aiming to keep the Evangelical faith in its pure form. The Bekenntniskirche declared Christianity incompatible with the Nazi doctrine of race and leadership. Many pastors of the Lutheran Church paid with their life for their opposition to Hitler. See Niemöller, Martin, and Religion in the Third Reich.

Belsen or **Bergen-Belsen.** A concentration camp situated about 10 miles northwest of Celle near Hanover in Lower Saxony. Originally a small prisoner-of-war (POW) camp (Stalag XI-C), Belsen was enlarged in 1943 and became a concentration camp where Jewish hostages were held, as well as later displaced persons and Russian POWs. Belsen was not an extermination camp, it had no gas chambers. But, as the conditions greatly deteriorated, tens of thousands of inmates died from exhaustion, disease, bad treatment and starvation. Like Auschwitz or Treblinka, the very name Bergen-Belsen became emblematic of Nazi horrors in general.

Belzec. With Sobibor and Maidanek, one of the extermination camps in the Lublin district in Poland. Belzec, situated near Lwow, was located between the large Jewish populations of southeast Poland and eastern Galicia. It was headed by SS-Brigadeführer Odilo Globocnik (q.v.), and the only business of the camp was the gassing and burning of Jews. Between 430,000 and 500,000 Jews are estimated to have been killed at Belzec, along with an unknown number of Poles and Gypsies (Roma).

Benzinekanne. A very good fuel can, nonleaking, robust, easy to carry and convenient to stack. Designed by the Germans and also known as Wehrmacht-Einheitskanister (q.v.) it was copied by all World War II combatants. The container is universally known as a jerry can, from "Jerry," a nickname given to the Germans. It had a capacity of 20 liters (5 U.S. gallons) and was made of pressed steel. Its sides were marked with cross-like indentations that strengthened it

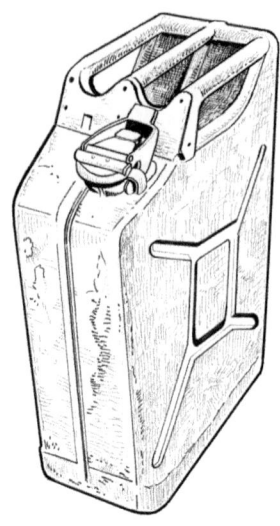

Benzinekanne (Jerry can).

while allowing the contents to expand, as did an air pocket under the handles. The jerry can has three handles, which allowed easy handling by one or two people or permitted the can to be moved bucket brigade–style. The handle design also allows for two empty cans to be carried in each hand. The containers use a cam lever release mechanism with a short spout secured with a snap closure and an air-pipe to the air pocket, which enables smooth pouring. The interior is lined with an impervious plastic, first developed for steel beer barrels, that allow the can to be used for either water or gasoline. The can is welded, and has a gasket for a leak-proof mouth.

Berchtesgaden. German town near Munich in southeast Bavaria. Here, surrounded by majestic mountains, Hitler established a large estate, the Berghof (q.v.), as his private retreat.

Berechtigt zum Tragen einer Faustfeuerwaffe. Allowed to carry a small firearm. This license was mentioned on the Ausweiß (q.v.) of noncombatant personnel such as policemen, special agents, NSDAP members, SS Ehrenführern (q.v.), civil servants, and the like.

Bergen-Belsen. See Belsen.

Berger, Gottlob (1895–1975). Head of SS Headquarters Department. Berger was responsible for, among other things, raising European Waffen-SS units. He was tried and sentenced to 25 years' imprisonment for war crimes in 1949, but was released in 1951.

Berghof. Hitler's private residence in Obersalzberg near Berchtesgaden in Bavaria. Purchased in 1936 by Martin Bormann — and paid for with funds acquired by the sale of Hitler's book *Mein Kampf* (q.v.) — the site was profoundly transformed by plans made by Hitler himself. The original small house called Haus Wachenfeld was widely extended with large rooms filled with thick carpets and tapestries, and with a huge and magnificent hall that included an enormous window giving a majestic view of the Unterberg Mountain. Apartments and studios were built to accommodate guests and visitors. The upper valley around the house was filled up with buildings, including a guest house, SS bodyguards barracks, a Nazi Party department, accommodations for employees, barns for cattle and horses, a garden for vegetables and a private guest house, the Kehlstein Haus, on the summit of a rock outcrop. The domain included roads and footpaths for communication as well as antiaircraft batteries and kilometers of high wire fences and guards to assure the Führer's peace and security. Hitler's residence was destroyed after the war to prevent its becoming a neo–Nazi place of pilgrimage. On May 13, 1946, the Allied Control Council for Germany issued a directive ordering the destruction of all military and Nazi memorials, and of all military museums "tending to revive militarism or to commemorate Nazism of such a nature as to glorify war." The directive stipulated that all such memorials dating from 1914 onwards should be destroyed, exception being made for monuments of artistic merit if they contained no offensive features glorifying militarism or National Socialism; and gravestones or their equivalent. See Kehlsteinhaus.

Bergmann. Weapons manufacturer. The company's best weapon was the 1934 submachine gun Maschinepistole MPi 34, which was based on the World War I Rheinmetall MP18. The Bergmann MPi 34 was simple, reliable and robust. It weighed 4 kilograms, and had the appearance of a short rifle. It had a one-piece wooden stock, a short steel barrel and a detachable side-loading magazine (containing 20 or 32 rounds) fitted on

Berghof.

Policeman Sicherheitsdienst with Bergmann submachine gun.

Besenstiel

the left side. Model MPi 35, an improved version, followed. Bergmann submachine guns—with a total production of about 40,000—were allocated with priority to the German police and SS forces.

Besenstiel. "Broom handle," designating the large 9-millimeter Mauser C96 pistol. It had a ten-round magazine placed in front of the trigger. The pistol could be fired with a single shot or fully automatic, it weighed 1.25 kilograms, and was kept in a large, remarkably clumsy and heavy wooden holster. It could be fitted with a detachable butt, making the weapon a small carbine. Although costly to manufacture and unsuitable for mass production, some 150,000 were manufactured before World War II, and remained in service until 1945.

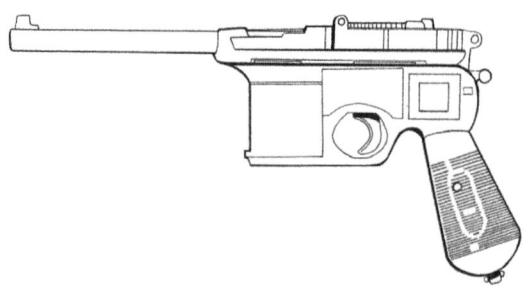

Besenstiel 9 mm Mauser C96 pistol.

Besetzte Gebiete. Territories occupied by Germany between 1939 and 1945. See Okkupation.

Besitzbürgertum. Property-owing bourgeoisie; a term applied to the bourgeoisie by the left-wing Nazis. After the elimination of the SA and the purge of June 1934, the term was no longer used. See Schwarze Front and Strasser, Gregor.

Best, Werner (1903–1989). Legal adviser to the Nazi Party and police commissioner of Hesse in 1933, Best became deputy to Reinhard Heydrich (q.v.) and legal adviser to the SS helping to build Gestapo (q.v.) and Sicherheitsdienst des Reichsführer SS (q.v.). Best was head of the SD in France from 1940 to 1942 and then German commissioner in Denmark. After the war, he was tried in Denmark and condemned to death, but the sentence was commuted to five years' imprisonment. He was released in 1951.

Bettung. Armed emplacement without a roof used to house a searchlight or an antiaircraft gun, for example.

Beutepanzer. Booty armor or captured tank. Beutepanzer included, for example, the Czech-made Skoda 38, renamed by the Germans PanzerKampfwagen 38 (t) and the Skoda 35, rebaptized PanzerKampfwagen 35 (t). After the victorious western campaign in 1940, other Beutepanzer included the French Renault R35, Renault R40, Renault AMR 33 (type VM), char FCM 36, Somua S35, Renault char B, Hotchkiss H35 and Hotchkiss H39. Many Beutepanzer chassis were converted to form self-propelled artillery hybrids.

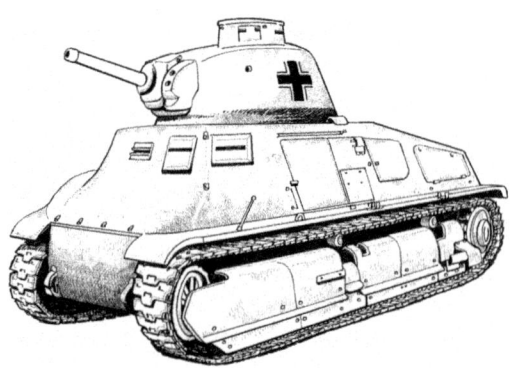

Beutepanzer, captured French Somua S 35.

BeVo. A company that manufactured uniforms, insignias and the like during the Third Reich. Although the designation "BeVo weave" is now applied to virtually all Jacquard machine-woven insignia for German uniforms from World War II, the name originally referred specifically to the firm Bandfabrik Ewald Vorsteher (q.v.) in Wuppertal-Baren. BeVo woven insignia were most often seen on German field caps and tunics.

Birds of Passage. See Wandervögel.

Birkenau. Extermination camp situated close to Auschwitz (q.v.) in Poland. It was built in 1941 with the original purpose of murdering Russian prisoners.

Bismarck. A superdreadnought, along with her sister ship *Tirpitz*, one of the most powerful warships ever built. Named after Prime Minister and Prince Otto von Bismarck (1815–1898), she displaced 42,000 tons, had a maximum speed of 30 knots, and measured 791 feet at the waterline. She mounted a main battery of eight 15-inch guns, twelve 5.9-inch guns, and sixteen 4.1-inch guns. The *Bismarck* was sunk in May 1941 by the British navy.

Black Front. See Schwarze Front and Strasser, Otto.

Black Order. See Schutz-Staffeln.

Blitz. Lightning, a term designating the sustained strategic bombing of Great Britain by the German Luftwaffe during World War II, and more particularly during the period from September 1940 to May 1941.

Blitzkrieg. "Lightning war." The tactics of Blitzkrieg were the result of Germany's appreciation of the importance of the tank in modern warfare. The essence of the tactic was that all components of the attack were geared to the speed of the basic weapon, the tank. It required a motorized infantry to keep pace with them and back them up. Blitzkrieg was a swift, sudden combined offensive beginning with reconnaissance units scouting ahead. The main attack, by combined tank and infantry forces, followed, assisted by engineers to clear artificial obstacles or prepare for the crossing of such natural obstacles as rivers, and motorized anti-tank artillery to clear away enemy armored forces while antiaircraft guns were on hand to repel enemy air attacks. Blitzkrieg aimed at a rapid disruption of enemy defenses, trying to avoid or neutralize strong points instead of assaulting them, and strokes against key targets and communication centers deep in the enemy area with the intention of stunning a surprised enemy into submission. Blitzkrieg was actuated by dynamic command and control through radio and rapidly laid line communication, simultaneously with air attacks upon enemy airfields, lines of communication and resistance centers. Sometimes, airborne troops were dropped within enemy lines to seize vital locations such as bridges, forts, ports, airfields and so on. Blitzkrieg achieved brilliant and decisive successes in the period 1939–1941 in Poland, Denmark, Norway, the Netherlands, France and the Balkans. But when the Nazis invaded the USSR in June 1941, Blitzkrieg failed because, for the first time, German logistics were unable to maintain their momentum to sufficient depth to achieve a rapid and ultimate victory.

Block. Lowest subdivision of the NSDAP, totaling about fifty households or a various number of homes with an average of 160 to 240 members. Four to eight Blocken formed a Zelle (q.v.) A Block was also a barrack or a hut in a concentration camp.

Blockführer. Guard in charge of a Block (barrack or hut) in a concentration camp. See also Kapo.

Blockleiter or **Blockwart.** Leader of a Block; block warden, the lowest rank in the NSDAP. They were above the common members, but were the immediate representative of the party to most people.

Blohm und Voss (BV). German industrial company that built ships, notably the *Bismarck* (q.v.), airplanes and flying boats. One of the most produced BV aircraft was the maritime reconnaissance flying boat BV-138. There was also the curious asymmetric BV-141, introduced in 1943.

Blohm & Voss BV 222 Viking. The large 6-engine BV 222 flying boat (so called because the body had the shape of a ship's hull) was designed in 1938 for the Lufthansa, and a few examples were militarized and used in the Luftwaffe as transport.

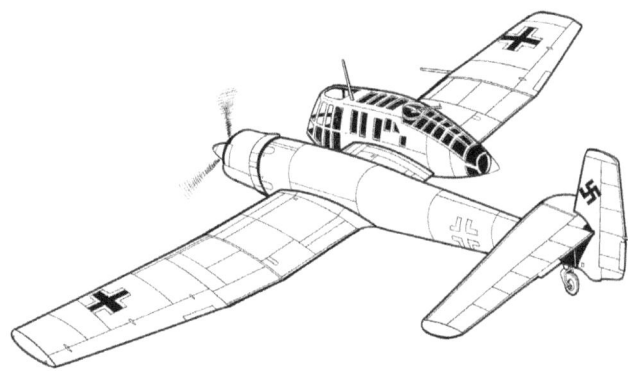

Blohm & Voss BV 141.

Blomberg, Werner von (1878–1946). General and minister of defense, Blomberg encouraged the elimination of the SA in 1934, but opposed to Hitler's plans for war. He was dismissed in 1938, allegedly because of his young wife's scandalous past. In fact, Hitler wanted more control over the German army and became himself minister of defense. Blomberg thereafter retired and was never recalled to duty. See Fritsch, Werner Freiherr von.

Blondi. Hitler's female German shepherd, to which he was much attached. Blondi was poisoned on April 30, 1945, in order to test the poison that Hitler intended to use for himself.

Blood. The symbol of blood (Blut) was widely used in Nazi ideology and propaganda. See Blut und Boden, Blutfahne, Blutorden, Blutschande.

Blood purge. See Nacht der langen Messer.

Blubo. Abbreviation of Blut und Boden (q.v.).

Blumenkriege. Flower War. Term used by Goebbels' propaganda to describe the bloodless German annexation of Austria and Czechoslovakia in 1938. These were political and diplomatic victories during which no bullets were shot but flowers were thrown to the Germans.

Blut und Boden (Blubo). "Blood and soil," a theory created by the Nazi ideologue Richard Walther Darré (q.v.). Reflecting the antiurban policy of the Nazi movement in its early days, Darré held that the roots of renewal were to be found in the native soil of Germany. For propaganda reasons, metropolises were decried and peasant virtues were extolled. Darré and Hitler cried out against what they saw as the erosion of morals in the big cities and emphasized the importance of a healthy peasantry and a country-oriented socialism as a mainstay for the state. See also Reichsnährstand.

Blut und Ehre! ("Blood and Honor!") Motto adopted by the Hitler youth. The motto was inscribed on early knife blades.

Blutfahne. Blood flag, a revered Nazi flag used at rituals. The flag was alleged to be drenched with the blood of the victims of the abortive Beer Hall Putsch in Munich in November 1923. In July 1926, the sacred Blutfahne was handed over by Hitler to the SS (q.v.) The bullet-riddled flag became a Nazi liturgy item, which was symbolically rubbed against other banners and flags in ceremonies in order to transfer the blood of the martyrs and thus prepare new units for sacrifice.

Blutorden. Blood Order Medal, instituted by Hitler in March 1934 rewarding those who had participated to the Munich Beer Hall Putsch. The order was renamed Blutenorden and awarded to Alte Kämpfer (q.v.) and to Nazi members of outstanding merit. The medal was the highest honorary decoration of the Nazi Party. Worn on the right breast, it was made of silver, attached to a red, white and black ribbon, and carried the words "Und Ihr habt doch gesiegt" (Against all odds you have been victorious).

Blutschande. Blood shame or incest. Term used by the Nazi propagandists to indicate the "violation of nature's law of racial purity" by intermarriage between "pure Aryans" and "impure non–Aryans." To protect the purity of the German blood, a special law was promulgated, the Blutschutzgesetz (Law on Protection of the Blood), which forbade sexual intercourse and marriage between "Aryans" and Jews.

Boche. French derogatory name for a German.

Böhmen und Mähren. Protectorate of Bohemia and Moravia, territories under German control after the dismemberment of Czechoslovakia in March 1939. South Slovakia and Ruthenia were annexed by Hungary. Bohemia and Moravia were autonomous Nazi-administered territories, which the German government considered part of the Greater German Reich. Böhmen und Mähren was also the name given to a Waffen-SS (q.v.) unit raised in March 1945—the XXXIst SS Freiwillige Grenadier Division Böhmen und Mähren. See Großdeutschland and Okkupation.

Bonhöffer, Dietrich (1906–1945). Evangelical Protestant theologian who maintained constant opposition to Hitler and his regime. Bonhöffer was murdered at Flossenburg KZ in April 1945. See Religion in the Third Reich.

Book burning. See Bücherverbrennung.

Bormann, Martin (1900–1945). A veteran of World War I, a member of the Rossbach Freikorps, and a Nazi of the first hour, Bormann became Gauleiter in Thuringia in 1928, party treasurer and a close associate of Hitler's entourage. Although he stayed in the background, Bormann became Rudolf Hess's chief of cabinet, and when Hess flew to Britain in 1941, Bormann was promoted to Nazi Party minister and Hitler's private secretary, who strictly controlled access to the Führer. He was made head of the Volkssturm in October 1944. Presumably Bormann died in Berlin in May 1945. He was tried in absentia at Nuremberg, found guilty and sentenced to death. See Adolf-Hitler-Spende der deutschen Wirtschaft; Berghof; Hess, Rudolf; and Volkssturm; Wirtschaft.

Bouhler, Philip (1899–1945). A Nazi of the first hour, Bouhler was business manager of the NSDAP between 1925 and 1934, head of chancery in Hitler's office, and chairman of the censorship committee. In 1939 he was responsible for the program of euthanasia. Bouhler committed suicide in 1945. See Brandt, Karl, and Euthanasiebefehl.

Boxheim papers. In November 1931 Nazi documents (named after the Boxheim estate near Worms, where groups of National Socialists had held meetings to discuss a plan for seizing power after a hypothetical communist revolution) declaring that (1) Fascist "Storm Divisions" should seize the government by a counter coup d'état; (2) Any citizen caught bearing arms or disobeying the orders of a "Storm Commander" should be shot without trial; (3) Private property should be "abolished provisionally," all bank deposits "immobilized in the banks" and interest payments stopped; (4) The fascist dictatorship should abolish wages, enroll the able-bodied citizenry (except Jews) in state labor divisions, and distribute food by a system of rationing to everyone. The documents, which contained a blueprint for a Nazi putsch and the subsequent execution of political opponents, were somehow leaked and created a scandal. Hitler (who probably knew nothing about it) was seriously embarrassed at a time when he was seeking power by legal means.

Boxing. After the Nazi seizure of power, boxing was made compulsory for students in the upper classes and was practiced in the Hitler Jugend (q.v.). Boxing was a popular sport and one of the most popular figures in German sport, was Max Schmeling (1905–2005), the only German to hold the world heavyweight championship (1936). The champion became a figurehead for Nazi propagandists who hailed his victory as a triumph of the Aryan Nordic white race. The consternation was enormous when Schmeling was defeated by Joe Louis in June 1938. See Sports in the Third Reich.

Brandenburgers. German commando force formed of trained volunteers, used to facilitate German advance or to hinder the opposing side's movements by employment of special weapons, sabotage, raids behind enemy lines, undercover agents and tricks violating the rules of war (e.g., wearing enemy uniforms). The first company, called Baulehr-Kompanie zbV 800 ("construction training for special duties") was raised in October 1939 under command of the founder Captain von Hippel. The unit grew in size and became the Baulehr-Bataillon zbV 800, subordinated to the Abwehr (q.v.) The unit expanded to a regimental force called Lehr-Regiment Brandenburg zvB 800 which included a paratroop battalion and a long-range desert patrol in North Africa. By the end of 1942, the regiment was regrouped as Sonderverband 800 (special force) then referred to as OKW Reserve Brandenburg Division, being no longer a commando unit but deployed in antipartisan operations in the eastern front. In February 1944, the unit was renamed Panzergrenadier Division Brandenburg and integrated into the army. Some soldiers volunteered for the SS Jagdverbände (q.v.) See also Skorzeny, Otto.

Brandt, Karl (1904–1948). One of Hitler's personal doctor's, Brandt was also reich commissioner for health and responsible for the Euthanisiebefehl (q.v.) in 1939. A rival to Doctor Theodor Morell (q.v.), Karl Brandt—who had approved of "medical experiments" by SS doctors in concentration camps—was tried, found guilty and hanged in 1948.

Braun, Eva (1912–1945). Hitler's secret mistress from 1932 to death. Hitler married her in April 1945 and both committed suicide.

Braun, Wernher Freiherr von (1912–1977). An engineer and rocket expert, von Braun became technical director of rocket research at Peenemünde (q.v.), where he and his team developed the model A-4 better known as V2 (q.v.). After the war von Braun lived and worked in the USA, developed intercontinental ballistic missiles, and played a central role in all phases of NASA moon flight program. See Vergeltungswaffe.

Braunes Haus. Literally, "Brown House." Situated at Briennerstrasse 45 near the Königsplatz in Munich, this palatial house called Barlow Palace was the stronghold of the Nazi Party beginning in 1931. It was purchased with funds obtained from Rhineland industrialists (particularly Kirdorf and Thyssen), and was rebuilt into a complex of offices and headquarters by Hitler's architect Paul Ludwig Troost. Imposingly furnished and decorated, it was the evidence of the NSDAP's substantial position. The Brown House was badly damaged by Allied bombardments during World War II, and the ruins were destroyed after the war to avoid its becoming a neo–Nazi pilgrimage site. See Berghof and NSDAP Headquarters.

Braunhemden. Brown Shirts, the other name for the SA. The name originates from the color of the SA uniform, which came from a surplus of German army tropical brown uniforms that were purchased for a low price in late 1925. See Sturm Abteilung der NSDAP.

Braunhemd (SA man).

Braut des Schütze. Literally, "the soldier's wife" (in other words, the soldier's best friend); a nickname designating the basic weapon of all modern soldiers: the rifle. See Gewehr.

Breker, Arno (1900–1991). German sculptor, particularly known for his neoclassic (sometimes monumentally huge) public works in Nazi Germany. Hitler regarded Breker's work as the antithesis of degenerate art. His collaboration with architect Albert Speer (q.v.) after the 1936 Olympic Games (q.v.) brought in numerous government commissions. In 1948 Breker was tried, sentenced as a "fellow traveler" of the Nazis and fined, after which he continued his artistic activity. See Art in the Third Reich.

Brigade. A military unit generally composed of two regiments.

Brigadeführer. SS senior officer. The rank was equivalent to Generalmajor in the German army, deputy Gauleiter in the Nazi Party, and major general in the British army.

Britisches Freikorps. British Free Corps, or Saint-George's Legion, a small group of 50 to 100 ill-disciplined men recruited by the Waffen-SS among British POWs. Large-scale enlistment was a total failure, and the renegade British Waffen-SS volunteers remained a symbolic unit serving only propaganda purposes.

Brotbeutel. Bread bag, a canvas haversack hung from the waist belt.

Brustschild. Gorget. A decorative half-moon-shaped piece of metal held by a chain around the neck and worn on the breast. It indicated a function like military policeman or carrier of a flag. See Ringkragen.

Buchenwald. One of the major Nazi concentration camps, located in a forest on the Etter Mountain four miles from Weimar in Thuringia. Together with Dachau and Sachsenhausen, Buchenwald was set up in 1933 to form the nucleus of the Nazi concentration camp system. Buchenwald was one of the largest concentration camps in Germany, counting some 20,000 inmates, and at times even 60,000. The prisoners were forced labor, working in an adjacent factory manufacturing weapons, ammunition and other supplies for the German army. Using two 12-hours shifts of slave laborers, the factory operated 24 hour a day. Technically Buchenwald was not an extermination camp, but conditions were so horrific that the work camp was in fact a place of extermination, with pointless humiliations, beatings, tortures, starvation, incredibly crowded living conditions, sickness, and arbitrary executions. The camp was also a site of large-scale trials for vaccines against epidemic typhus in 1942 and 1943 using inmates as test subjects. Deaths recorded in the camp averaged 6,000 per month. Buchenwald was liberated by the U.S. Army on April 10, 1945. From 1945 to 1950, the camp was used by the Soviet occupation authorities as an internment camp for Nazis, known as NKVD special camp number 2. Buchenwald KZ was demolished in 1950, and a commemorating monument was erected in 1958.

Bücherverbrennung. Auto-da-fé, or public book burning. A few months after the seizure of power, a campaign of Säuberung (purification) of libraries, bookshops and universities was launched by making lists of writers whose works the Nazis considered "immoral" or "Jewish" or not adjusted to the ideology. About 12,400 books were forbidden and collected. The interdiction was followed by public book burning in May 1933 in Berlin and in the major towns of Germany. Books by Albert Einstein, Sigmund Freud, Ricarda Huch, Thomas and Heinrich Mann, Carl Zuckmayer, Anna Seghers, Stefan Zweig and Alfred Kerr — to mention just a few — were thrown into huge bonfires. These actions were organized by the ministry of propaganda, the Nationalsozialistischen Deutschen Studentenbunde (League of German Students) and the Kampfbund für Deutsche Kultur (Combat League for the German Culture), and carried out by Nazi members as a kind of public ceremony with speeches and music. This highly symbolic and ugly action proved to be a political error as it provoked a large wave of disgust throughout the world where the press unanimously denounced the book burning as a descent into barbarism. See Gleichschaltung, Kampfbund für Deutsche Kultur and Reichskulturkammer.

Bückeberg. Mountain near Hameln (Lower Saxony), and revered Nazi meeting place beginning on October 1, 1933. The pagan feast on the Bückeberg was a part of the Blut und Boden (q.v.), a ritual intended to attract peasants from all over the Reich in order to thank the German gods for a good harvest.

Bund der Artamenen. Artaman League. Founded in the 1920s, the Bund der Artamenen was an organization of young nationalists who were devoted to the concept of soil and to the idea of German race. Members of the league wanted to work on farms in lieu of military service. The Artaman were strongly anti–Slav and urged that Polish farmers living in Germany be returned to their own country. Many Artaman journeyed to farms in East Germany to defend the fatherland against the Slavs. The movement intended to mobilize hundreds of thousands young Germans, but never succeeded in enlisting more than 2,000. It was not a success because the leaders quarreled. Also, the idealism of these young people from the cities proved insufficient to pass the severe test of daily agricultural labor. It was indeed easier to rhapsodize about blood and soil than to buckle down to a hard working day of ten hours. As the situation deteriorated in the late 1920s, some of the Artamans were drawn deeper into politics. Eventually many members of the Artaman league turned to Hitler's National Socialism. Among notable Artaman members in 1924 was Heinrich Himmler (q.v.), who later became Reichsführer SS, and Rudolph Höss, later commandant of Auschwitz (q.v.). The Artamen youth league was dismantled and incorporated into the Hitler Jugend (q.v.) as the Nazi movement gained strength. See Blut und Boden and Reichsnährstand.

Bund Deutscher Mädel in der HJ (BDM). League of German Girls, a suborganization of the Hitler Jugend (HJ) for girls aged 14 to 18. The girls were constantly reminded that their greatest task in life was service, physical fitness and particularly motherhood, as the Reich needed soldiers in the future. Their uniform

BDM girl employed as postal auxiliary.

consisted of dark blue skirts, white blouses with ties and brown jackets. The BDM was organized in units following the HJ male counterpart. See Glaube und Schönheit, Hitler Jugend and Jungmädelbund in der HJ.

Bürgerbräu Keller Attentat. Unsuccessful attempt on Hitler's life on November 8, 1939. On the celebration of the sixteenth anniversary of the failed putsch of November 1923, a bomb exploded in the historic beer hall, killing eight and injuring sixty-three Nazis. Hitler, who had cut his speech short and left about thirteen minutes earlier than planned, was unharmed. The bomb had been placed by an anti–Nazi carpenter named Georg Elser (q.v.), who had managed to stay inside the Bürgerbräukeller after closing hours each night for over a month, during which time he hollowed out the pillar behind the speaker's rostrum and placed the bomb inside it. Elser was arrested, and imprisoned for five and a half years in Dachau KZ. Although he consistently claimed to have been acting on his own, the Nazis, especially Goebbels, persisted in suspecting a British-led conspiracy, and there were rumors that the whole assassination attempt had been staged by the Nazis themselves to portray Hitler as being protected by Providence. However, no evidence involving the regime or any outside group has ever been found, and historical research made by Anton Hoch in 1969 confirmed that Elser had acted completely alone. Georg Elser was executed at Dachau by the Gestapo shortly before the end of World War II.

Bürgerbräu Keller Putsch. Unsuccessful putsch (also known as Beer Hall Putsch) led by Hitler and the Nazis to seize power in Munich in November 8, 1923. The Bürgerbräu Keller was a large beer hall where Hitler announced the breaking out of a national revolution by force. A demonstration followed the next day, and near the Feldherrn Hall a police detachment opened fire on the demonstrators. Sixteen Nazis were killed and the putsch was crushed. Hitler was later arrested and his party forbidden. On the surface, the Beer Hall putsch seemed a failure, but it allowed Hitler to achieve national fame, as the event catapulted his unimportant party into headlines throughout Germany. Hitler also learnt important lessons from this failure: He renounced violent revolution, and henceforth decided to seize power by legal means, with popular support and with the backing of wealthy industrialists.

Burgondia. Himmler envisaged the ultimate creation of a new western Germanic state to be called Burgondia, grouping the Netherlands, Belgium, Luxemburg, and northeast France. Burgondia would be policed and governed by the SS, and would act as a buffer to protect Germany proper from invasion. For this purpose, Himmler established replicas of the Allgemeine SS (q.v.) in Flanders: the Allgemeene-SS Vlaanderen was created in September 1940, and the Dutch Nederlandsche-SS was founded in November 1940. The carefully selected members of these SS organizations retained their own languages and customs, and came under the jurisdiction of their own pro–Nazi governments. Before the establishment of Burgondia (planned for implementation when the war was over and won), their primary task was to support the local police by rooting out partisans, subversives and other anti–German elements, and to promote and establish Nazi rule. In May 1942, a similar Allgemeine SS was created in Norway (Norges-SS), and in Denmark in April 1943 (Germansk Korpset, later called Schalburg Corps). The four foreign Allgemeine SS formed the Germanische SS, which totaled some 9,000 selected members.

Canada. Term used by guards in the extermination and concentration camps to describe the booty taken from prisoners. This included everything from coats, shoes, clothes and so on, to money, jewels and gold teeth, which were extracted from corpses and melted down. See Max Heiliger Deposit Account.

Canaris, Wilhelm Franz (1887–1945). Head of the Abwehr (q.v.) Canaris was arrested by the SD security service, tried on charges of treachery, found guilty and hanged at Flossenburg KZ in April 1945.

Chamberlain, Houston Stewart (1855–1927). Anglo-German prolific author and precursor of Nazi ideology. A fervent admirer of the German people, Chamberlain developed a highly romanticized concept of the Germans. The work that made him famous was *Die Grundlagen des neunzehnten Jahrhunderts* (Foundations of the Nineteenth Century) published in 1910, in which he presented the Germans as a "master race" with a mission to rule the world, and presented the Jews as a negative, disruptive and degenerating force. Chamberlain's racial theories strongly influenced Hitler and the German racist ultra-right wing.

Chamberlain, Neville (1869–1940). British prime minister from May 1937 to May 1940. His policy of Appeasement (q.v.) allowed Hitler's annexation of Austria and Czechoslovakia.

Chef der Sicherheitspolizei und des SD (CSSD). Chief of the Security Police and Security Service, title conferred on Reinhard Heydrich (q.v.) until his death in 1942, and then on his successor Ernst Kaltenbrunner (q.v.). See Sicherheitsdienst des Reichsführes SS.

Chelmno (German, Kulmhof). One of the main Nazi extermination camps, situated near the village of Zawadski, west of Warsaw and 50 kilometers north from Lodz in Poland. There were no industrial or work activities in Chelmno — the camp was strictly a killing center where people were gassed and burned. At least 152,000 people were killed in the camp, mainly Poles, Jews from the Lodz ghetto and the surrounding area, along with Gypsies (Roma) from Poland and some Hungarian Jews, Czechs, and Soviet prisoners of war. See Auschwitz and Holocaust.

Churchill, Winston (1974–1965). British prime minister from 1940 to 1945. His energy and oratory were an inspiration to Britain and her Commonwealth allies and a powerful reminder to the United States of the basic kinship of Anglo-American ideals.

Cleansed of Jews. See Judenfrei.

Colditz Castle. Fortress situated in the small town of Colditz, near Leipzig in Saxony. The castle, built in 1014, became a work camp for the Hitler Jugend (q.v.) in 1933 and a prisoner-of-war camp during World War II. The castle was a high-security Sonderlager (special camp) named Oflag IV-C. It was specially intended for captured recalcitrant Allied officers who had repeatedly tried to escape from other Oflags. These incorrigibles were held under strict surveillance.

Columbia Haus. Prison set up in 1933 by the Gestapo (q.v.) in Berlin where opponents of the newly installed Nazi regime were interrogated, beaten and tortured before being sent to a concentration camp.

Communist Party of Germany. See Kommunistische Partei Deutschlands.

Compiègne. A small town north of Paris, France, where the armistice of November 11, 1918, had been signed, putting an end to World War I. As revenge, Hitler choose the very same spot, in a little clearing in the forest of Compiegne, the very same railway coach, and the very same table to sign the armistice between defeated France and victorious Germany on June 21, 1940. Compiègne represented one of Hitler's greatest hours of triumph.

Concentration camp. See Konzentrationslager.

Condor Legion. See Kondor Legion.

Coventry. English Midlands city near Birmingham. One the numerous European cities to be destroyed by Luftwaffe (q.v.) air raids. Coventry was attacked and left in flames on November 15, 1940. There were about 1,000 dead and injured.

Credere! Obbedire! Combattere! "Believe! Obey! Fight!" Italian Fascist slogan borrowed by the SS (q.v.).

Dachau. Nazi concentration camp situated 12 miles northwest of Munich in Bavaria. Dachau was initially a makeshift holding pen that was set down amid the stone huts of a disused gunpowder factory. The camp was set up in early 1933, and soon overflowed with about 2,000 German political prisoners subjected to the ruthless rule of the SS commander, Theodor Eicke. The inmates were systematically humiliated, subjected to roll calls — standing without moving for several hours — and other brutal torments and mistreatments, underfed, beaten, worked to exhaustion in pointless hard labor — and not infrequently murdered by the camp guards. Dachau became a place of dread, a terrifying example of Nazi ruthlessness toward all opponents. It was the model for the early concentration camps that followed: Buchenwald (q.v.), near Weimar in central Germany, and Sachsenhausen (q.v.), near Berlin in the north. During World War II, Dachau was one of the largest and worst Nazi camps, and the scene of Nazi medical experiments carried out on hundreds of inmates. Dachau was also a place a detention for famous political VIPs and religious hostages such as Martin Niemöller (German anti–Nazi theologian and Lutheran pastor), Kurt von Schuschnigg (chancellor of the Austrian Republic before the Anschluß), Édouard Daladier (prime minister of France at the start of World War II), Léon Blum (three-time prime minister of France before World War II), General Franz Halder (dismissed head of the German army General Staff), Fritz Thyssen (industrialist), and Hjalmar Schacht (German economist, banker, liberal politician, and cofounder of the German Democratic Party).

DAF. See Deutsche Arbeitsfront.

DAK. See Deutsches Afrika Korps.

Daladier, Edouard (1884–1970). French premier from April 1938 to March 1940. He followed Neville Chamberlain's policy of Appeasement (q.v.) Daladier was arrested by the Vichy France (q.v.) government and deported to Dachau KZ, where he stayed till the end of World War II.

Daluege, Kurt (1897–1946). A veteran of the Freikorps (q.v.), and an early Nazi and SA-man, Daluege became Chief of the Ordnungspolizei (q.v.) After the assassination of Reinhard Heydrich (q.v.) he replaced him as protector in Czechoslovakia. Kurt Daluege was captured, tried and hanged by the Czechs in October 1946.

Darré, Richard Walther (1895–1953). Born in Argentina and educated partly in Britain, Darré was an early NSDAP member, an ideologue of Nazism, and one of Hitler's close associates. Specializing in agriculture and selective breeding, he preached the agrarian concept of Blut und Boden (q.v.), which was very much in accord with Heinrich Himmler's view. Appointed minister of food and agriculture, and in charge of the SS Race and Ressettlement Office, the corrupt Darré had the opportunity to enrich himself. In 1942 he got involved in a large-scale black-market food scandal and lost Hitler's confidence. He was suspended from duty in May 1942, finally dismissed in May 1944 and replaced by SS-Obergruppenführer Herbert Backe. In 1945 Darré was sentenced to five years' imprisonment by the Allies. See Reichsnährstand.

Death camp. Extermination camp. See Vernichtungslager.

Decree for the Struggle against the Gypsy Plague. A decree issued in December 1938 by Heinrich Himmler (q.v.), which introduced a systematic registration of Gypsies (q.v.), and which separated and segregated them from the "Aryan" population.

Degrelle, Léon (1906–1994). A Belgian-Walloon politician, founder of the ultra-right party Rex. During World War II, Degrelle favored total collaboration with Germany and joined the Waffen-SS (q.v.) Owing to his gallantry on the Russian front, he was appointed head of the SS Volunteer Sturmbrigade Wallonien. After World War II, Degrelle was condemned to death but managed to escape to Spain. He obtained Spanish citizenship and took the name José León Ramírez Reina. Until his last breath Degrelle remained a fanatical Nazi, a negationist, and a prominent figure in neo–Nazi movements.

Denazification. See Entnazifizierung.

Deutsch. German. During World War II, Jerry or Kraut (q.v.) was the nickname given to the Germans by the English-speaking Allies. In Dutch, they were called Moffen. In French slang they were commonly referred to as Boches, Doriphores, Fritz, Schleu, Frisés or Fridolins.

Deutschblütiger. According to Nazi ideology, a person with German blood. See Arisch.

Deutsche Ansiedlungsgesellschaft (DAG). German Resettlement Society, an organization devoted to encouraging the resettlement of Germans as colonists in the conquered eastern territories during World War II.

Deutsche Arbeiterpartei (DAP). German Workers' Party, a small political group formed in Munich in 1919 by a toolmaker, Anton Drexler (q.v.), and a journalist, Dietrich Eckart (q.v.). In September 1919 Hitler became a member of the DAP, and he soon became its leader. In April 1920, the name was changed to Nationalsozialistische Deutsche Arbeiterpartei (q.v.) or NSDAP.

Deutsche Arbeitsfront (DAF). German Labor Front. Soon after the NSDAP came to power, all trade unions and worker organizations were declared illegal and banned. In their place the DAF was set up in June 1933 as the sole labor organization of the German Reich. The concept of the DAF was to ensure the political stability and smooth operations of all German industry and commerce. Its function was to conciliate rather

than advance social demands. Membership in the DAF was voluntary, but any person who was a worker in any area of German industry or commerce was essentially a member by default. The DAF, headed by Robert Ley (who held the title of Führer der DAF), became a huge empire within Germany's industry and commerce. It was composed of several suborganizations including:
- Nationalsozialistische Betriebszellen-Organization (q.v.), or National Socialist Factory Organization (NSBO);
- Nationalsozialistische Handwerks-, Handels und Gewerbeorganization (q.v.), or National Socialist Handicraft, Commercial and Business Organization (NS-HagBo);
- Nationalsozialistische Gemeinschaft Kraft durch Freude (KdF) often shortened to Kraft durch Freude (q.v.)—Strength through Joy;
- Reicharbeitsdienst RAD (q.v.) National labor service. The DAF was one of the Angeschlossene Verbände der NSDAP (q.v.) of the Nazi Party, and was militarily organized.

Deutsche Ausrüstungswerke (DAW). Equipment and weapons factories established by the SS in 1939 using forced labor. See Wirtschafts- und Verwaltungshauptamt.

Deutsche Erd- und Steinwerke GmbH (DESt). German Excavation and Quarrying Co. Ltd., a company formed in 1938 by the SS with workers obtained from the SS concentration camps. See Wirtschafts- und Verwaltungshauptamt.

Deutsche Glaubensbewegung. German Faith Movement, a neopagan Nazi church whose members were sworn enemies of prior religions. The movement—an improvised offshoot of Nazism in the spiritual sphere—was designed to replace traditional Christianity. It proposed, for instance, to convert Christmas into a pagan solstice festival, to dechristenize the rituals of birth, marriage and death, and to replace the cross with the swastika.

Deutsche Kreuz (DK). German Cross, a decoration instituted on September 28, 1941 as Kriegsorden des Deutschen Kreuzes (War Order of the German Cross). It was awarded as appreciation for extraordinary individual acts of bravery, deeds of courage and leadership. The DK was awarded in two classes, gold and silver, shown by the color of the wreath around the swastika. There were two versions, cloth and metal.

Deutsche Luftsportverband (DLV). See Nationalsozialistische Fliegerkorps.

Deutsche Reichsbahn (DR). See Deutsche Reichsbahn Gesellschaft.

Deutsche Reichsbahn Gesellschaft (DRG), also **Deutsche Reichsbahn** (DR). German Railways Company. The DR was one of the most important facets of the survival, and later defeat, of Germany during World War II. The German economy during the period was centered on rail transportation. German industry, both military and civilian, could not survive without coal and the vital railways that carried it. Without rail, there was no coal, and without coal, the industrial might of Germany was doomed to failure. All other industrial necessities, as well as German passengers, goods, and freight, also required the German railways. The DR also played an important military role during the war, transporting troops and supplies from one front to another. It was also an essential part of the Final Solution (the deportation of Jews) and elimination of opponents to the regime, as it was the DR that sold a one-way ticket and transported victims to the concentration and extermination camps.

Emblem of the DRG.

Deutsche Wirtschaftsbetriebe. German Economic Enterprises, a holding company designed

Deutsche

to include all business and industry under the control of the SS. See Wirtschafts-und Verwaltungshauptamt.

Deutsche Wochenschau. Weekly newsreels organized by the ministry of propaganda. The Wochenschau lasted for about twenty or thirty minutes and it was projected before the main film in all movie theaters. Through reports, documentaries and short films, it showed political, cultural, social or sports events glorifying the Nazi regime during the period 1933–39. The Wochenschau was under severe censorship and personally viewed by Reichspropagandaminister Joseph Goebbels before being issued. During the war the emphasis was on achievements on the home front and on the Nazi battlefield victories reported by the Propagandakompanie (q.v.) and PK-Sondereinheiten der Wehrmacht (Army propaganda squads). The Wochenschau was also displayed abroad, in the occupied territories, and translated or subtitled in foreign languages. During these shows the lights in the theater stayed on to prevent manifestation of hostility against the Germans. See Propagandaministerium.

Deutsche! Wehrt euch! Kauf nicht bei Juden! "Germans! Defend Yourself! Do Not Buy at Jewish shops!" A Nazi anti–Semitic slogan encouraging boycott of Jewish businesses.

Deutscher Gruß. Nazi German salute (greeting). The salute was an adaptation of an ancient Roman salute. The saluter would be at attention, left hand on the belt buckle, right arm raised a little higher than the shoulder, and would say enthusiastically, "Heil Hitler!" with clicking heels. For the happy few who met Hitler personally, the salute was the same but one said "Heil, mein Führer!" (Hail, my leader). Also known as the Hitler Gruß, it was first used in December 1924 when Hitler was released from prison. It became common practice after 1925 during parades. After the Nazis came to power in 1933, it was compulsory at all parades, meetings, official and public events, and was strongly advised in daily life.

Deutscher Nationalpreis für Kunst und Wissenschaft. See Nobel Preis.

Deutscher Schutzen Verband (DSV). The German Rifle Association, a nonpolitical, nonmilitary organization of volunteer members who were interested in marksmanship. Created in

Germans! Defend Yourself! Do Not Buy at Jewish shops!

Deutscher or Hitler Gruß.

1861, the association had as its primary objective to promote interest among the public in competitive sport shooting. After the Nazi seizure of power in January 1933, the DSV was subjected to Gleichschaltung (q.v.) and social events had definite political overtones.

Deutscher Volkssturm. See Volkssturm.

Deutsches Afrikakorps (DAK). German expeditionary corps in northern Africa in the period 1941–43. War in North Africa began in June 1940 with Italian attacks on the British in Egypt. Because of the Italian failure, seeing the danger of losing control of the Mediterranean Sea, the Germans were obliged to intervene. In February 1941 part of the 3rd Panzerdivision was sent to Africa as the 5th Light Division. This was followed by the 15th Panzerdivision. In April 1941, the 5th and 15th formed the Deutsches Afrikakorps (DAK) proper, whose exploits under General Erwin Rommel demonstrated German expertise in mobile armored warfare. In September 1941, the DAK became Panzergruppe Afrika. In 1942, Rommel's army, including Italian troops, became Panzerarmee Afrika for the final push on Egypt, which was repulsed at El Alamein. The African campaign and the DAK episode ended in May 1943 when the Axis forces were driven from Tunisia. See Krieg ohne Hass and Rommel, Erwin.

Deutsches Frauenwerk (DFW). German Women Labor. A branch of the NS-Frauenschaft (q.v.) created during World War II that prepared women to replace men in workshops, factories, and shops. Open to all German "Aryan" women, the DFW was a noncompulsory organization.

DFW insignia. The emblem of the DFW displayed a triangle with the mention Deutsches Frauenwerk, a circular swastika, and the Algiz rune letter (symbol of life).

Deutsches Jungvolk in der HJ (DJ). Suborganization of the Hitler Jugend (q.v.) for boys age 10 to 14.

Deutsches Rotes Kreuz (DRK). German Red Cross. The International Movement of the Red Cross was founded in 1863 at the instigation of the Swiss industrialist and philanthrope Henri Dunant (1828–1910). Following the rise and triumph of Hitler's National Socialism after January 1933, the German Red Cross did not escape Gleichschaltung (q.v.) The Deutsches Rotes Kreuz was brought by force into line with other Nazi uniformed sectors and incorporated into the Nazi welfare organization NSV. Its structure was altered to fit the National Socialist control, and it became de facto a Nazi entity. Although DRK members, both male and female, were unpaid, a full-time cadre of Nazi-selected, uniformed, salaried leaders supervised them. From

Emblem of the DAK composed of a swastika on a stylized palm-tree.

1933 to 1945, Carl-Eduard, duke of Sachsen-Coburg and Gotha, was president of DRK. During World War II, the German Red Cross was the primary agency through which individual donations were funneled to the troops, and its personnel served on both the home and combat fronts. It was active in organizing first aid courses for civil defense as well as establishing shelters and emergency aid stations to nurse, feed, and house victims of bombings. The mother Red Cross organization tried to gain access to prisoner camps to carry out inspection, but the Nazi-controlled DRK refused to cooperate with the Geneva statutes, including blatant violations such as the deportation of Jews and the mass-murders conducted in the concentration and exterminations camps. After Germany's defeat in 1945, like all organizations linked to the Nazi Party, DRK was disbanded. It was reestablished in 1952 during the postwar reconstruction of both West Germany and the Eastern DDR. See Sachsen-Coburg und Gotha, Carl-Eduard von.

DRK Red Cross emblem. The emblem consisted of a black eagle with wings down, bearing a white swastika and holding in its claws a red Greek cross.

Deutschkunde. Study of German culture revisited by the Nazis. This was a required subject in all schools in the Third Reich. It stressed Teutonic greatness, the culture producing northern Herrenvolk (q.v.) as opposed to the culture-destroying Jew. It familiarized the pupils with folk culture, including music, literature, customs, heroic Nordic sagas and runes. It encouraged military discipline, respect for the Aryan heritage, love for the fatherland, and devotion and obedience to the Nazi Party. In short Deutschkunde was a preparation to war and sacrifice.

Deutschland erwache. "Germany Wakes Up," a Nazi slogan expressing the recovery of national pride, greatness and independence by means of Nazism. It was probably taken from the prose works of the composer Richard Wagner.

SA banner with Deutschland Erwache motto.

Deutschland erwache! Juda Verrecke! "Germany Awake! Perish Judah!" a variation on the slogan above, a sort of incantation shouted in unison by raiders and attackers of Jews in the early years of Hitler's regime.

Deutschland ist Hitler und Hitler ist Deutschland. "Germany Is Hitler and Hitler Is Germany," a popular Nazi slogan coined by Hitler's deputy Rudolf Hess (q.v.).

Deutschland über Alles. "Germany above All." The German national anthem since 1922, also known as "Das Lied der Deutschen" ("The Song of the Germans"). Lyrics were set by Hoffman von Fallersleben in 1841 to an early melody by Joseph Haydn composed in 1797.

Die deutsche Frau raucht nicht. "The German Woman Does Not Smoke." A slogan on signs hanging conspicuously in restaurants and public places. Smoking was considered unhealthy and bad for fertility, thus un–German, and the Nazis launched a campaign against smoking by women.

Dienstanzug. Service dress, composed of various trousers, tunics, headgear and footwear. The Dienstanzug was also used as individual combat dress, then completed by Waffen (weapons) and Ausrüstung (equipment and accoutrement). See Feldanzug and Feldausrüstung.

Dienstgrad. Rank. The right to wear a uniform and to assume rank was an essential part of the appeal of the Third Reich. To the familiar army ranks, the Nazis added party formations rankings in mostly unfamiliar terminology. The table below shows the ranks of the Heer, SS and Waffen-SS (roughly based on SA ranks) and their equivalents in the U.S. Army.

Dienstanzug.

ENLISTED RANKS
Schütze; SS-Schütze; Private or Rifleman.
Oberschütze; SS-Oberschütze; Private 1st Class.
Gefreiter; SS-Sturmmann; Acting Corporal.
Obergefreiter; SS-Rottenführer; Corporal.

NONCOMMISSIONED OFFICERS
Unteroffizier; SS-Unterscharführer; Sergeant.
Unterfeldwebel; SS-Scharführer; Staff Sergeant.
Feldwebel; SS-Oberscharführer; Technical Sergeant.
Oberfeldwebel; SS-Hauptscharführer; Master Sergeant.
Stabfeldwebel; SS-Sturmscharführer; Sergeant Major.

JUNIOR OFFICERS
Leutnant; SS-Untersturmführer; Second Lieutenant.
Oberleutnant; SS-Obersturmführer; First Lieutenant.
Hauptmann; SS-Hauptsturmführer; Captain.
Major; SS-Sturmbannführer; Major.

SENIOR OFFICERS
Oberstleutnant; SS-Obersturmbannführer; Lieutenant Colonel.
Oberst; SS-Standartenführer; Colonel.
Generalmajor; SS-Brigadeführer; Brigadier General.
Generalleutnant; SS-Gruppenführer; Major General.
General der Infanterie or General der Kavallerie or General der Panzertruppe etc; SS-Obergruppenführer; Lieutenant General.
Generaloberst; SS-Oberstgruppenführer; General of the Army.

Generalfeldmarschall; no equivalent; Field Marshal.

Dienstmantel. Service overcoat. See Mantel.

Dienstrock. Service tunic. See Dienstanzug and Feldanzug.

Dienststelle Ribbentrop. Ribbentrop's office, a duplicate organization of the German foreign office headed by the compliant Joachim von Ribbentrop. The Dienststelle was set up in 1933 by Hitler, who mistrusted the foreign office directed by Constantin Freiherr von Neurath. In February 1938, Hitler appointed Ribbentrop as foreign minister and abolished the Dienststelle.

Dienstverpflichtung. Military service. On March 16, 1935, Hitler reintroduced conscription and proclaimed his intention of building up a peacetime army, thirty-six divisions comprising 550,000 soldiers. In August 1936, the period of conscription was extended to two years.

Diet or **Landtag.** Chamber of deputies in an individual Land (state in Germany) in the days before Hitler's regime. The system of Landtag was abolished after the seizure of power by the Nazis in early 1933.

Dietrich, Joseph "Sepp" (1892–1966). A veteran of World War I and Freikorps, and a full-time SS man in 1928, Dietrich was appointed head of the select bodyguard group called Leibstandarte SS Adolf Hitler (q.v.). Dietrich's SS played a major role during the Night of the Long Knives (q.v.), and during World War II he commanded the 1st Waffen-SS Division Leibstandarte, the 1st SS Panzer Corps in Normandy and the 6th SS Panzer Armee during the Battle of the Bulge. After the war, Sepp Dietrich, one of the most decorated SS officers of the Third Reich, was sentenced to twenty-five years' imprisonment for bad treatment and killing of prisoners of war. He served less than ten, being released in 1958 for health reasons.

Disarmed Enemy Personnel (DEP). German military personnel who surrendered after May 7, 1945. A German soldier who surrendered prior to this date was a prisoner of war (POW).

Disinfektionsraum. Disinfection chamber. A deceptive name given to gas chambers in extermination camps.

Displaced Person (DP). Anyone whom the war had removed from his/her home.

Divide et impera. Latin adage meaning "divide and rule." Nazism was an incoherent and inextricable system based on this old Roman principle constructed by Hitler, who was incapable of sharing power. Many of the acts of the Nazi leaders can be seen as attempts to enhance their standing with Hitler by means of extraordinary deeds. Joseph Goebbels initiated the Kristallnacht (q.v.) on November 9, 1938. Rudolf Hess, the deputy Führer, certainly thought he was in accordance with Hitler's view when he flew to Britain in 1941. He probably hoped that bringing Hitler his long-sought-after alliance with Britain would increase his standing and influence in the Nazi leadership. Hitler's miscalculations and wrong decisions were regarded by his supporters as resulting from the Führer being "influenced by bad company"—by which they meant other party leaders with whom they were in competition—and they hoped to mitigate this tendency through their own influence.

Division der Waffen-SS. Division of the Waffen-SS (q.v.). This term designated a Waffen-SS unit composed of "impure" western, southern and eastern Europeans. The term reflected the Nazi racism even within the structure of the SS. An SS-Freiwillingendivision was composed of Volksdeutsche (q.v.), Germanic north Europeans considered as people of similar blood. An SS Division was composed of 100 percent "pure" genuine Germans.

Dolch. Dagger. Hitler, keenly interested in regalia and eager to support the world-renowned German blade makers in Solingen, encouraged

Dagger worn by the Hitler Youth leadership with inscription "Blut und Ehre!"

SS Dagger with inscription "Meine Ehre heißt Treve."

and ordered senior NSDAP functionaries and SA and SS senior officers to carry a dagger. Other Nazi organizations were quick to follow, and before long, all branches of the uniform-conscious civil servants and Wehrmacht officers had daggers of their own. The daggers were sold via the Reichszeugmeisterei (q.v.).

Dolchstoss. Stab in the back; a legendary theory largely exploited by the Nazis asserting that the German defeat of 1918 was not caused by a military action but by the subversive doings and treason of communists, socialists, pacifists and Jews. The Dolchstoß theory was believed by many (notably the army, the conservatives and nationalists), therefore it was an exploitable political issue associating the Weimar Republic—and democracy—with the humiliating defeat in 1918. As a result, the Treaty of Versailles was seen not a peace settlement but merely a humiliation and an imposed "Diktat" which had to be renounced. The truth, of course, was quite different. With the failure of the German spring offensives of 1918, the German armies were in a hopeless position, and the leading generals had ceded power to the civilian government in order to force it to bear the political burden of signing the November 1918 armistice. See Novemberverbrecher and Versailler Diktat.

Dom-Bunker. Cathedral shelter; a large concrete structure intended to shelter a submarine or a railway gun. Dom-bunkers were generally 70 to 80 meters long and 10 meters high. They were closed by heavy armored doors and constructed to resist Allied bombs. Some are preserved, notably in France at Lorient, Hydrequent and Fort Nieulay.

Dönitz, Karl (1891–1981). Founder and leader of Germany's submarine fleet, Dönitz was commander of the German navy beginning in 1943. By decree of April 1945, Hermann Göring (q.v.) and Heinrich Himmler (q.v.) having failed him, Hitler nominated Dönitz as his successor. The new Führer gathered a short-lived cabinet that surrendered to the Allies. At his Nuremberg trial, Dönitz was found guilty of planning a war of aggression and sinking neutral ships, and sentenced to ten years' imprisonment. He was released at the end of that term. See Kriegsmarine and Unterseeboot.

Dora. (1) A huge railway gun. See Eisenbahnartillerie.

(2) Code name for an ancient mine that became a large camouflaged underground factory in October 1943, located in the South Harz Kohnstein mountains close to the town of Nordhausen in Thuringia. Also called Mittelwerk, the facility consisted of two 1.6 kilometers-long tunnels connected by 43 adjacent parallel galleries (like the rungs of a ladder) with floor areas of over 95,000 square meters. Dora-Mittelwerk included numerous facilities linked by an internal electric railway. Dora-Mittelwerk was used to produce V-2 rockets, V-1 flying bombs, jet-powered airplanes, secret missiles, and other weapons. It employed forced slave labor, in atrocious conditions, and as such was also a concentration camp. Approximately 60,000 prisoners from 21 nations (mostly Russians, Poles, and French) passed through Dora, and an estimated 20,000 inmates died from exhaustion, bad treat-

Dom-Bunker.

Doriot

ment, punishment, collapse, disease and starvation.

Doriot, Jacques (1898–1945). A French communist politician turned fascist. Doriot founded the ultra-nationalist Parti Populaire Français (PPF, French Popular Party) in 1936. He and his supporters were fervent advocates of France becoming organized along the lines of Fascist Italy and Nazi Germany. After the occupation of France by the Germans, Doriot and a number of French Fascists and pro–Nazi collaborators founded in 1941 the anti-bolshevik Légion des Volontaires Français (Legion of French Volunteers, LVF). It became a French unit of the Wehrmacht, and later in 1945 a part of the French 33rd Waffen-SS Division Charlemagne. After the liberation of France in summer 1944, Jacques Doriot went into exile in Germany. He was killed in February 1945 while traveling from Mainau to Sigmaringen when his car was strafed by Allied fighters. See Fünfte Kolonne, Vichy France, and Waffen-SS.

Dornier (Do). German aircraft company founded by the engineer Claudius Dornier (1884–1969). The Dornier company was famous before the war for the construction of waterplanes. The most significant World War II Dornier airplane was the twin-engine medium bomber Dornier Do 17 produced in 1936, and its variants, and the Do 335 from 1943.

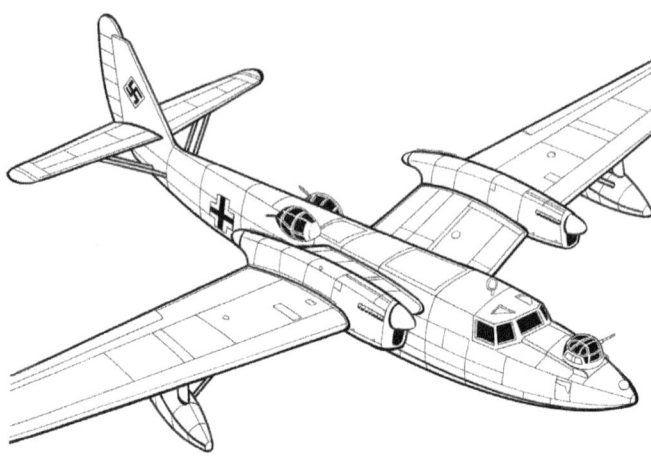

Dornier Do 26 Flugboote (flying boat).

Dragonder. Dragoon; originally (in the 17th century) a soldier moving on horseback and fighting on foot. In the modern sense, it designates a crewman on a reconnaissance vehicle, armored car or light tank.

Drahtverhau. Barbed-wire entanglement.

Drang nach Osten. "Push to the East," an expression describing the historic area of German expansion. Since the early Middle Ages, the eastern borders between the German and the Slav world had always been fluid depending upon war, colonization and evangelization. The Teutonic knights maintained the spirit of the Crusades by the Drang nach Osten, evangelizing pagan Slav populations by arms and by conquering vast territories in East Prussia and the Baltic regions.

The aggressive Drang nach Osten was revived by the Nazis as the movement of conquest for "vital space" in Eastern Europe called Lebensraum (q.v.).

Drehturm. Rotating turret. The turret was often armored, armed with guns and placed on a tank, on a warship or on top of a concrete bunker.

Drei Liter. "Three litres," a pun sounding like the greeting "Heil Hitler" (q.v.) used by rebellious young Germans as a mockery.

Dreimächtepakt. Pact of the three powers (Italy, Germany and Japan) signed on September 27, 1940. See Achse.

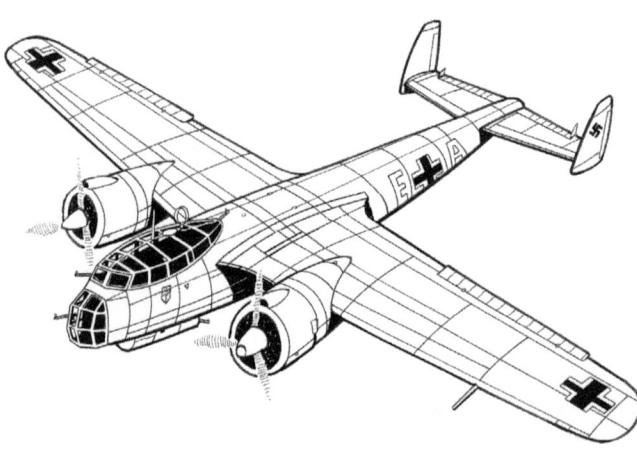

Dornier Do 17 ZO.

Drexler, Anton (1884–1942). Founder of the German Workers' Party, Drexler was one of those who drew up the Nazi 25-point program. In 1921 Hitler assumed the leadership of the NSDAP and Drexler was inexorably reduced to a background figure. He died all but forgotten in Munich in 1942. See Deutsche Arbeiterpartei.

Drillichanzug. See Arbeitsanzug.

Drittes Reich. Third Empire. Hitler's official title was chancellor of the never officially abolished Republic of Weimar and Führer, and certainly not emperor. Nazi Germany, however, was proclaimed by the propaganda das Drittes Reich (the Third Empire). The term seems to have been coined by Möller van den Bruck for his book *Das Drittes Reich*, published in 1923. It was a reference to the Erstes Reich (First Holy Roman Empire or Altes Reich, Old Empire), which lasted from A.D. 962 until 1806, and the Zweites Reich (Second Empire) ruled by the Hohenzollern from 1871 to 1918. The highly symbolic term was intended to place Hitler's dictatorship in a historical continuity. The term Third Reich is now universally used to designate the period of Nazi rule from 1933 to 1945.

Dueling. See Mensur.

Durchgangslager or **Polizeiliches Durchgangslager** (**Dulag** for short). Transit camp or prison where Jews and captured opponents of the Nazi regime were interned and regrouped before being deported by rail to concentration and extermination camps. Stays in a Dulag varied a lot, from a few hours to several weeks, perhaps months. It depended on the killing capacity of the extermination camps in Poland. There were Dulags everywhere in Nazi-occupied Europe. In France, for example, the Vichy regime established Dulags at Auvours, Baccarat, Beaune la Rolande, Chartres, Coëtquidan, Colmar, Compiègne, Doullens, Drancy, Epernay, Mailly, Pithiviers, Strasbourg, Nancy, La Chapelle-Baunay, and Châlons-sur-Marne. In the Netherlands Dulags were established at Amersfoort, Barneveld, Ommen, Oudekerk, Schoorl, Vught, and Westerbork.

Eagle's Nest. See Kehlsteinhaus.

Eckhart, Dietrich (1868–1923). A poet, a playwright, a journalist, a nationalist, an anti-Semite, and a politician; also cofounder of the NSDAP. The well-connected Eckhart was the sponsor and mentor of the young Hitler when he started his political career. He was one of the key figures in the early NSDAP, took part to the failed Beer Hall Putsch, and was briefly imprisoned with Hitler and Hess in Landsberg prison. Dietrich Eckhart, a habitual alcoholic, died shortly after his release.

Edelweiß. A rare Alpine flower, symbol of the Gebirgstruppen (mountain troops), shown on headgear and on a badge on the right upper sleeve.

Waffen-SS mountain troops' Edelweiss badge.

Edelweiß Piraten. Edelweiss Pirates, a loose group of youth culture in Nazi Germany. It emerged in western Germany out of the German youth movement of the late 1930s in response to the strict regimentation of the Hitler Youth. They were young people, mainly between the ages of 14 and 17, who had evaded the Hitler Youth by leaving school (permissible at age 14), and were also young enough to avoid military conscription, which was in effect only from age of 17. Although they rejected the Nazis' authoritarianism, the Edelweißpiraten's nonconformist behavior tended to be restricted to petty provocations. Despite this, they represented a group of youth who rebelled against the government's regimentation of leisure and were unimpressed by the propaganda touting Volksgemeinschaft ("people's community"). During the war, some Edelweißpiraten supported the Allies and assisted deserters from the German army. Some groups also collected propaganda leaflets dropped by Allied aircraft and pushed them through letterboxes. The Nazi response to the Edelweißpiraten was typically harsh. Individuals identified by the police as belonging to the various gangs were often rounded up and released with their heads shaved to shame them. In many cases, young people were sent to work camps, concentration camps or prison until they were of age to be incorporated into disciplinary units of the German army.

Education in the Third Reich. After the Nazi takeover, the German education system underwent an immediate and chilling change. During the first few months of Hitler's rule, Jewish and politically "unreliable" teachers were dismissed, while female teachers were confined to domestic tasks. Education in the Third Reich was completely revised to meet the standard of dictatorship. Hitler was contemptuous of teachers, academicians, scientists and intellectuals, whom he regarded as dangerous obstacles to the kind of compliant society he wanted to build. The Führer wanted the youth of the Nazi state to be more virile and strong than intellectually developed. Nazi education was based on these essential ideas: the sense of race; the preparation for war for the boys and motherhood for the girls. From April 1934 until the end of the war in May 1945, the school system was headed by a provincial schoolmaster and Gauleiter of the Hannover-Braunschweig district, Oberlehrer Bernhard Rust (q.v), who was promoted to the rank of Reich minister for science, education and culture. Schools and universities were re-formed and purged of Jewish and democrat teachers. Schoolteachers were encouraged to join the Nazi Party and all of them had to be members of the Nationalsozialistische Lehrerbund (q.v) or NSLB. After 1938 teachers were indoctrinated at a special compulsory one-month training course of NSLB drills and lectures where they learned what knowledge to pass on to the pupils. Sports received unprecedented attention from the elementary to the high schools. Some subjects were upgraded and converted for political and racial purposes. Pupils and students were expected to know about history revised by the Nazi system: the epics of World War I, the glory of the Munich Beer Hall Putsch of 1923, the martyrdom of the SA man Horst Wessel, and the evils of the Weimar Republic. Biology emphasized Hitler's views on race and heredity: the supposed differences between the human races, the German superman, the ignoble and hated Untermensch (Slavs and Jews). The study of Germanics stressed Teutonic greatness, the culture-producing northern race opposed to the culture-destroying Jew; emphasized were heroic Nordic sagas and runes to encourage respect for Aryan heritage and love for the fatherland. Mathematics stressed preparation for war service, with questions revolving around weaponry, artillery trajectories or bombs dropping. Religious instruction was sharply reduced and school prayer was made optional. Not content with control of the school system, the Nazis intruded even further into the lives of students, teachers and parents through the Hitler Jugend (q.v.) movement. The quality of teachers was greatly affected as the more talented were siphoned off to fill other positions or were removed. In addition, younger teachers were conscripted, and as a result the age of teachers quickly started to climb. The activities of the NSLB were suspended for the duration of the war from March 1943 onward. See Erziehung, Gleichschaltung, Nationalpolitischen Erziehungsanstalten, Nationalsozialistische Dozentenbund, and Nationalsozialistischer Deutscher Studentenbund.

Eher-Verlag. Munich publishing company taken over by the Nazis in 1922, and headed by Max Amann (q.v.) The company published Hitler's book, *Mein Kampf*, (q.v.) and became the official Nazi publishing company.

Ehestandsdarlehen. Marriage loan to help newlyweds set up housekeeping. The providing of such loans was one of a series of legislative measures that sought to encourage marriage and raise the birthrate in the Third Reich. Between 1933 and 1936, the Nazi regime financed 694,367 marriages, to which 485,285 children were born. Similar measures included prizes for large families, gifts to newborn infants, financial privileges for large families, and heavier taxes on bachelors and childless couples. See Mutterkreuz.

Ehrenliste der Ermordeten der Bewegung. List of Honor of Victims of the Movement. Nazi honor roll listing those who fought and died for the party before it came to power in January 1933.

Ehrenwinkel für Alte Kämpfer. See Alte Kämpfer.

Ehrenzeichen. Decoration, medal.

Ehrenzeichen der Deutschen Mutter. Cross of honor for the German mother. See Mutterkreuz.

Ehrewache. Guard of honor or escort. See Begleit.

Ehrhardt, Hermann (1881–1971). A Freikorps (q.v.) commander in 1919, an important supporter of the Kapp Putsch (q.v.) in 1920, a terrorist and founder of the Organization Consul (q.v.). Hitler saw him as a rival and in June 1934, Ehrhardt was on the list of people to be eliminated by the Nazis during the SA purge. Ehrhardt narrowly escaped death by fleeing to Austria. See Nacht der langen Messer.

Eiche. Oak. Code name for the daring rescue of Mussolini from captivity. In September 1943, an airborne group of commandos headed by Otto Skorzeny (q.v.) landed in the Abruzzi Apennines where Mussolini was imprisoned and rescued him from his captors.

Eichenlaubkranz. Oak leaf surround worn in combination with the Kokarde (q.v.).

Eichmann, Otto Adolf (1906–1962). One of the major organizers of the Holocaust. Because of his organizational talents and ideological reliability, Reinhard Heydrich (q.v.) charged Eichmann with the task of facilitating and managing the logistics of mass deportation of Jews to ghettos and extermination camps in German-occupied Eastern Europe. After the war, Eichmann fled to Argentina and lived and worked there under a false identity. He was captured by Mossad operatives in Argentina in May 1960 and taken to Israel to face trial in an Israeli court on 15 criminal charges, including crimes against humanity and war crimes in 1961. Eichmann was found guilty and executed by hanging in 1962.

Eicke, Theodor (1892–1943). An active member of the NSDAP beginning in 1928, Eicke was appointed head of KZ Dachau (q.v.) in June 1933, and a year later inspector of concentration camps and chief of the SS Totenkopfverbände (q.v.). In the purge of 1934, he personally shot Ernst Röhm, the SA top leader. In 1939 Eicke took command of the Waffen-SS Totenkopf Division and was killed in action on the Russian front in 1943.

Eid. Oath. Starting in August 1934, all German army officers and soldiers had to take an Eid (oath of allegiance) to Hitler: "Ich schwöre bei Gott diesen heiligen Eid daß ich dem Führer des Deutschen Reiches und Volkes Adolf Hitler, dem obersten Befehlshaber der Wehrmacht, unbedingten gehorsamheiten und als tapferer Soldat bereit sein will, jederzeit für diesen Eid mein Leben einzusetzen" ("I swear by God this sacred oath, that I will render unconditional obedience to Adolf Hitler, the Führer of the German Reich and people, Supreme Commander of the Armed Forces, and will be ready as a brave soldier to risk my life at any time for this oath"). The oath was spoken by the recruits with their right hands raised and their left hands placed on their regiment flag or on their officers' swords. The oath was taken very seriously by soldiers and officers; it was to affect profoundly all attempts to remove Hitler as the war turned unmistakably against Germany, and it kept most of the army obedient till the end of the war. An Eid was also sworn by all members of the NSDAP: "I swear loyalty to my leader Adolf Hitler. I promise to him and to the leaders he will give me, to serve always in respect and obedience." The Hitler Jugend oath said, "I swear, in the Hitler Youth, always to do my duty with love and loyalty, for the Führer and our flag." As early as November 1933, the oath sworn by the SS, later by the Waffen-SS (q.v.) and all foreign SS volunteers, was a total submission to Hitler's will: "I swear you, Adolf Hitler, as Führer and Reich chancellor, loyalty and courage. I promise you and those you appoint to command me, obedience until death, so help me God!"

Ein Volk! Ein Reich! Ein Führer! "One People! One Empire! One Leader!" Nazi slogan and battle cry popularized by the propaganda of the Third Reich.

Einheitsfeldmütze. Standard peaked field cap. Introduced in June 1943, the Einheitsfeldmütze was based closely on the style of peaked cap worn by mountain troops and Afrika Korps soldiers. Very convenient and popular, it subsequently became the most widely worn type of headgear for active service by all ranks. The Einheitsfeldmütze had a semi-stiff peak, and one type was made of canvas for warm climates. Another was made of wool for cold climates. The sides could be folded down and buttoned under the chin in cold weather.

Einsatzgruppen

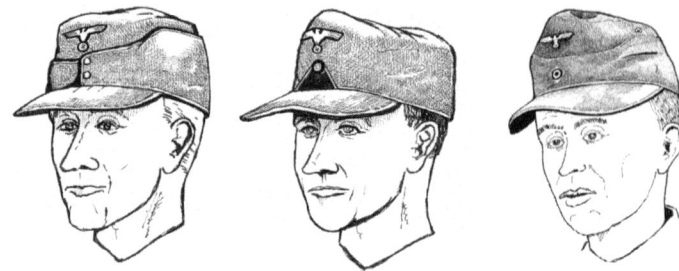

Left and middle: Einheitsfeldmütze. *Right:* Deutsches Afrika Korps Einheitsfeldmütze.

Einsatzgruppen. Intervention groups; a euphemism for murder squads. By the end of 1939, Himmler was given total control of the annexed parts of Poland and five SSEinsatzkommandos were created. Each unit, 100 or 150 men strong, was officially charged with fighting enemies behind the front line, arrestation of suspects, counterintelligence and seizure of individual civilian weapons. In reality the mission was the elimination of the Polish elite, including intellectuals, officers, politicians, trade union leaders, clergymen, civil servants and Jews. When Germany invaded the Soviet Union (June 21, 1941), the "intervention commandos" were reactivated, but on a larger scale under the name SS Einsatzgruppen (intervention or task groups). Each group counted about 600 or 900 volunteers raised among Gestapo, Kripo and SD policemen. These detachments, divided into four Sonderkommando, were officially tasked with the rearward pacification but, again, the real mission was arrest, murder and extermination of Jews and supposed or real enemies of the Reich without any juridical procedure or trial. The 3,000 policemen of the four Einsatzgruppen were responsible for the death of about 500,000 victims, mainly innocent civilians, women and children, Gypsies and Jews. Himmler rewarded the Einsatzgruppen by giving them the name Bandenkampfverbände (antipartisan detachments). They were later engaged in the Balkans, Rumania and Slovakia. By 1943 the tide turned, and when the Germans were forced to withdraw, the special Sonderkommando 1005, headed by Standartenführer Blobel, was created to erase in secret all traces of atrocities and crimes committed by the Einsatzgruppen.

Einsatzstab Rosenberg. Rosenberg Task Force, an organization headed by Alfred Rosenberg (q.v.) to confiscate art treasures in the European occupied nations.

Eintopf. One-pot meal. Propaganda campaign exhorting the German public to sobriety and moderation in food consumption.

Eisenbahn Panzerzug (Eis. Pz-Zug). Armored train. See Panzerzug.

Eisenbahnartillerie (E-Art). Artillery mounted on a railway. With the Nazi ascent to power in January 1933, and open rearmament launched in 1935, railway guns got the go-ahead. Huge long-range cannons were ordered from Krupp (Essen) and Hanomag (Hanover), reflecting Hitler's love for gigantic and prestigious weapons. See also Panzerzug.

Der Eisener. The Iron Man—the nickname of Hermann Göring (q.v.).

Eisern Faust. Mailed Fist. One of the many right-wing political groups created in 1919 that were opposed to democracy and the Weimar Republic, and which later merged with Hitler's party.

Eisernes Kreuz (EK). Iron cross decoration. In September 1939 Hitler reinstated the order of the Eisernes Kreuz (originally a Prussian decoration created in 1813) with four grades: Grand Cross (awarded only to Hermann Göring), Knight's Cross (Ritterkreuz), first class and second class. As the war progressed, higher grades of the Ritterkreuz were added. Oak leaves were introduced in June 1940, oak leaves and swords in June 1941, and oak leaves with swords and diamonds in December 1944. The iron cross was fitted to

Eisernes Kreuz 2nd Class.

a ribbon round the collar, hung on the left breast pocket or worn on the second button of the tunic (only the ribbon, the cross itself not being shown).

Elser, Georg (1903–1945). German opponent to Nazism. He was a Protestant of a simple, non-intellectual and traditional type. His opposition to Nazism was initially spurred by his concerns about working conditions, the lowering of working wages and the restrictions on civil rights and workers' freedoms. Elser, all alone, planned and carried out an assassination attempt on Adolf Hitler on November 8, 1939 in Munich. See Bürgerbräukeller Attentat.

Enabling Act. See Ermächtigungsgezetz.

Endlösung der Judenfrage. Final solution to the Jewish question; the cover name of the Nazi plan to murder all Jews in Europe. The persecution of the Jews began in 1933 with exclusion of Jews from public life, and this was followed by the infamous Nuremberg Laws in 1935. By 1941 Jews were confined in ghettos, and after the Wannsee Conference in January 1942, plans for complete elimination were made. These included establishment of concentration camps, the rounding up of Jews and transportation to the camps, where the victims were murdered in gas chambers. The project was placed under the authority of Heinrich Himmler's SS. The Endlösung was unprecedented. There has always been violence against the Jews throughout history, but nothing compares to the uniqueness of the Nazi genocide. About six million Jews were murdered during World War II in planned killing centers, a virtual industry. Even today the very word "Endlösung" is almost taboo, not easily spoken. See Auschwitz; Eichmann, Otto Adolf; Heydrich, Reinhard; Himmler, Heinrich; Konzentrationslager; Schutz-Staffeln; Sobibor; Treblinka; Vernichtungslager; Wannsee-Konferenz.

Endsieg. Final victory. This term was introduced by the German propaganda machine near the end of World War II. The Allies were winning on all fronts, but some Nazis still believed in the prospect of a German victory, which depended on a harnessing of energy and the continuation of sacrifice, as well as faith in terrifying "wonder weapons," which would theoretically restore power to the Nazis. See Totaler Krieg, Volksturm and Wunderwaffen.

Englisch. English. Designation used for all equipment, vehicles and weapons captured from the British armies and used in the German forces.

Enigma. German mechanical and electrical message encryption equipment also known as Cypher Machine E or Ultra.

Entartete Kunst. Degenerate art. This Nazi concept designated modern and abstract artwork. It was applied to the œuvres of Pablo Picasso, Otto Dix, Marc Chagall, Franz Marc, Paul Klee, Max Beckmann, Emile Nolde, Oskar Kokoschka, Paula Modersohn-Becker, George Grosz and Käthe Kollwitz, to mention only the most famous. About 5,000 oil paintings and 12,000 prints of degenerated art, also called "Jewish art," were exhibited in July 1937 in Munich to teach the Germans what this was, and to show them how "ugly, corrupted, incoherent and enfeebled" this form of art was. In May 1938 a law was passed to regulate what kind of art might be produced and exhibited in museums and galleries according to Nazi ideology. In March 1939 some 1,000 oil paintings and 3,000 prints were publicly destroyed by fire in Berlin. However the Nazis — perfectly aware of the commercial value of the entartete Kunst — sold a lot to wealthy private collectors, and during the war many chef d'œuvres were confiscated or stolen by Nazi collectors, notably Hermann Göring. See Art in the Third Reich, Meschuggismus, and Reichskulturkammer.

Entartung. The concept of Entartung ("degeneracy") became popular in Germany at the end of the 19th century when the critic and author Max Nordau (1849–1923) devised the theory presented in his 1892 book, *Entartung*. Nordau drew upon the work of the Italian criminologist Cesare Lombroso (1835–1909), whose book *The Criminal Man*, had been published in 1876. In his book Lombroso tried to prove that there were "born criminals" whose atavistic personality traits could be detected by scientifically measuring abnormal physical characteristics. Nordau developed from this premise a critique of modern art, explained as the work of those so corrupted and enfeebled by modern life that they have lost the self-control needed to produce coherent works. Explaining impressionism as the sign of a diseased visual cortex, he decried modern degeneracy while praising traditional Ger-

Entfernungmeßgerät

man culture. Despite the fact that Nordau was Jewish (so was Lombroso) and cofounder of the World Zionist Organization, his theory of artistic degeneracy was eventually seized upon by the Nazis as a rallying point for their anti–Semitic and racist demand for Aryan purity in art. See entartete Kunst, Kunst, and Reichskulturkammer.

Entfernungmeßgerät. Range finder used in artillery. Basically, the range finder was an optical instrument for calculating the distance between an observer and a distant point by triangular geometry. It consisted of a mobile tube with ends fitted with two viewers that reflected in a central eyepiece.

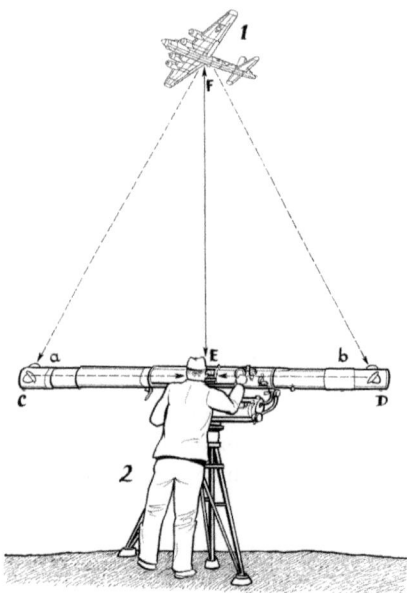

Entfernungmeßgerät (range finder). This schematic sketch shows how triangulation was used to find coordinates of the target (1), and distance from the observer (2). By measuring the angles a and b (the length of the tube CD being known obviously), it was possible according to the law of trigonometry and sines (relationship between sides and angles in any triangle) to calculate the distance EF corresponding to the height of the target.

Entnazifizierung. Denazification. A complex task undertaken by the Allies after the defeat of Germany in 1945. In October 1946 the Allied Control Council determined five categories of Nazis as follows:

(1) Major offenders, to be sentenced to death or life imprisonment

(2) Activists, militarists and profiteers, to be sentenced to a maximum of ten years of prison

(3) Lesser offenders deserving leniency, placed on probation for two or three years

(4) Followers and supporters of the regime, to be placed under police surveillance and obliged to pay a fine

(5) Exonerated individuals. The process of denazification proceeded slowly and with difficulty. Many sought to disassociate themselves from the excesses of Nazism, many minimized their role in Hitler's regime, and some of those deserving punishment were able to escape.

See Organization der ehemaligen SS-Angehöringen.

Erbhof. Hereditary estate. Special farms held by an aristocracy of farmers, a plan adopted under the Erbhofgesetz (Hereditary Farm Law) that was passed on September 1933. The law guaranteed family farm holdings of three hundred acres (1.2 kilometers) or less.

Erbkranker Nachwuchs. Program of sterilization of the mentally ill. See Euthanasiebefehl.

Erfurter Maschinefabrik Haenel und Suhl (Erma). German weapon manufacturer in Erfurt. The company's most notorious design was the formidable submachine gun Erma Maschine-

Maschinepistole MPi 38/40.

pistole MPi 38/40. The remarkable MPi 38/40 was the most common German submachine gun of the war. It was entirely made of steel and plastic (no wood at all), and weighed about 4 kilograms. It could fire about 500 rounds per minute, using 9 mm Parabellum ammunitions fitted with a 32 rounds detachable magazine used as forward handgrip.

"Erika" (Auf der Heide blüht ein kleines Blümelein). A popular German military marching song. The song was composed by Herms Niel in the 1930s specifically for the SS, but it soon came into usage by the Wehrmacht in general, especially the Heer and, to a lesser extent, the Kriegsmarine. Like "Heidi Heido Heida" (q.v.), the lyrics were not bellicose at all but rather poetic, as they compared a nice blonde girl to a flower blooming on the moor.

Erkennungsmarke (EK). Standard identification disc or dogtag. The Erkennungsmarke was first issued in August 1939 to all members of the Wehrmacht (q.v.) It was composed of a thin metal oval disk made of aluminum, zinc, steel or tin, and was worn around the neck on a chain or string. Upon enrollment into the armed services the tag was stamped with the issuing unit's name, the soldier's ID number and his blood type. In the event the soldier was killed in action, perforations in the center of the disk allowed it to be easily broken in two parts. The laced half stayed with the body, and the other half was taken to graves registration. See also Soldbuch.

Erler, Fritz (1868–1940). German painter, graphic designer and scenic designer, best remembered for several propaganda posters he produced during World War I and the Third Reich.

Erma. See Erfurter Maschinefabrik Haenel & Suhl.

Ermächtigungsgezetz. Enabling Act, passed under duress by the Reichstag on March 23, 1933. The legally obtained act gave Hitler absolute power. Hitler's dictatorial power was to last for four years unless renewed by the Reichstag, which occurred twice. The formal name of the Enabling Act was Gesetz zur Behebung der Not von Volk und Reich (Law to Remedy the Distress of People and Reich).

Ersatz. Reserve, replacement or substitute product. The term could refer to replacement troops or any substance used in place of another, for instance ersatz coffee or ersatz rubber.

Ersatzheer. Replacement army. The training cadres and recruitment apparatus for the German military inside Germany itself.

Erziehung. Education. The Nazis saw education as the most important means for instilling a new collective mentality, a new Volksgemeinschaft (national community), and the infusion of the Nazi Weltanschauung (world view) to the German youth. On April 30, 1934, Bernhard Rust (q.v.) was appointed Reich Minister of Science, Education and National Culture. It was the task of the Nazi Party to control schools and universities, to reshape history, to forge scientific proofs, and to clearly define who the enemies were in order to educate the Volksgenossen (national comrades), young and old, to view war as normal, and to secure their loyalty to the Heimat (fatherland) and their willingness to fight for Germany's honor. As Hitler envisaged it, education was a preparation for war. It was not to be confined to stuffy classrooms, but to be furthered by a spartan political and martial training in the youth groups, and to reach its climax, not so much in the universities and engineering colleges—which were attended by only a small minority—but at the age of eighteen, first in compulsory labor service, and then in military service as conscripts in the armed forces. See Education in the Third Reich, Hitler Jugend, Nationalsozialistische Lehrerbund, and Reichsarbeitsdienst.

"Es war ein Edelweiss." "There Was an Edelweiss," a popular marching song composed by Herms Niel in 1941 for the Heer (German army ground force).

Essai sur l'Inégalité des Races Humaines. Essay on Unequality of Human Races, a book published in 1853 by the French diplomat and theorist Joseph Arthur, count of Gobineau (q.v.).

Euthanasiebefehl. Nazi euthanasia program. The secret operation was code-named Aktion T4 (q.v.) after the headquarters situated at Tiergartenstraße 4 in Berlin. The program was the mass killing of those declared biologically "unworthy of life." Measures were taken to eliminate undesirable elements of the population, notably the mentally handicapped, the incurably sick, and physically disabled babies, children and adults who were starved to death or killed by poisonous injection (some 70,000 by August 1941). The murder program was organized by Philipp Bouhler, chief of the party's leadership, and by Dr. Karl Brandt, Hitler's Begleitartz (personal surgeon). The program started in September 1939, and, due to protest from families and German churches, was officially stopped in August 1941. In fact, it continued unofficially under cover in concentration camps until the end of the Nazi regime in 1945.

Expert. Ace; a military aviator credited with shooting down many enemy aircraft during aerial combat. The most successful Luftwaffe top aces flew on the eastern front, among them Erich Hartmann (with 352 credited kills), Erich Gerhard Barkhorn (301), Günther Rall (275), Otto Kittel (267), Walther Nowotny (258), Wilhelm Batz (242), Theo Weissenberger (238), and Erich Rudorffer (222).

F. See Flammpanzer, Feldmäßig, and Französisch.

"Die Fahne hoch." "Up with the Banner." Official NSDAP anthem beginning in 1930, officially called the "Horst Wessel Lied" (q.v.).

Fahneneid. Flag Oath. Oath to the Führer taken by the armed forces of the Third Reich from August 1934. Sworn upon the national colors, it bound soldiers and officers not merely during their period of service but for the term of their natural lives. It originated from the medieval feudal oath, which the knightly nobility swore to their liege lord. The sacred Fahneneid proved for many an insuperable obstacle to their participation in any conspiracy against Hitler. See Eid.

Fahnenflucht or **uberlaufen.** Literally, "abandonment of the flag" or "running away," figuratively, desertion. Desertion was regarded in Nazi Germany as an offense against the Führer, the Volksgemeinschaft (national community) and the Wehrkraftzersetzung (a brutal law against subversion of the war effort). In April 1940, Hitler issued guidelines, which prescribed death as being the normal punishment. Estimations show that, during World War II, about 35,000 soldiers of the German force were accused of desertion, resulting in about 22,750 death sentences, of which at least 15,000 (may be more) have been carried out. This amazingly high figure can be largely explained by the extreme measures imposed by the SS on German commanders and troops during the last year of the war. Indeed, any soldier not wounded who was picked up outside his unit area was to be tried and shot.

Fahnenjunker. Cadet on active service.

Fähnrich. A non-commissioned officer rank, equivalent to Feldwebel (q.v.) but with additional responsibilities. If successful, a Fähnrich might be promoted to Oberfähnrich (equivalent to Hauptfeldwebel, or sergeant first class), before being made an officer.

Fahrer. Driver of a horse-drawn vehicle.

Fallschirmjäger (Fsch-Jg). Paratrooper. The Fallschirmtruppen (FsT, Parachute troops) were created by General Kurt Student and were a branch of the Luftwaffe. They were successfully involved in 1940 in Blitzkrieg (q.v.) tactics. However, after the mitigated success of the attack on Crete in May 1941, when they suffered heavy ca-

Fallschirmjäger.

a rate of fire of 750 rounds per minute. Ammunitions were contained in a 20-round detachable magazine feeding from the left side.

Fangrost. (See illustration below.) Additional layer of concrete intended to protect the roof of submarine bunkers. It was composed of two rows of concrete beams (each 2 meters high and 1.5 meters wide). The Fangrost framework was intended to explode bombs before they actually hit the roof.

Feder, Gottfried (1883–1941). An early member of the DAP, and cofounder of the NSDAP, who helped draw up the Nazi 25-point program. Feder represented a strand in early Nazi thinking not unlike the populist, rural-based, anticapitalist, socialist radicalism of the Strasser (q.v.) brothers. Feder took part to the failed 1923 Beer Hall Putsch, but ultranationalist Nazis regarded the views he held as incompatible with Hitler's views. After Hitler's seizure of power in January 1933, Feder fell out of favor and was given only a junior post. Dispirited, he resigned and worked as a teacher in the University of Munich until his death in obscurity in 1941.

Feiertagen. "Holy days" of the Nazi calendar. Party meetings, mass rallies, torchlight marches, theatrical celebrations, and ceremonies a with festive air, flags and anthems were intended to sanctify the regime, to inculcate a note of reverence for the Nazi Party, and also to serve as sub-

Fallschirmjäger with parachute.

sualties, the parachute troops were no longer used as assault forces attacking from the sky but as elite infantry.

Fallschirmjäger Gewehr FG 42. Self-loading assault rifle for paratrooper model 1942. The Fallschirmjäger Gewehr FG 42, issued in 1942, was designed and produced for the Luftwaffe. It was intended to give paratroopers the extra firepower that they needed when operating in small detached groups. The FG 42 was actually the first of what are now called assault rifles. The remarkable and advanced weapon weighted 4.5 kilograms, shot 7.92-millimeter rifle cartridges, and was capable of single-shot or full automatic operation with

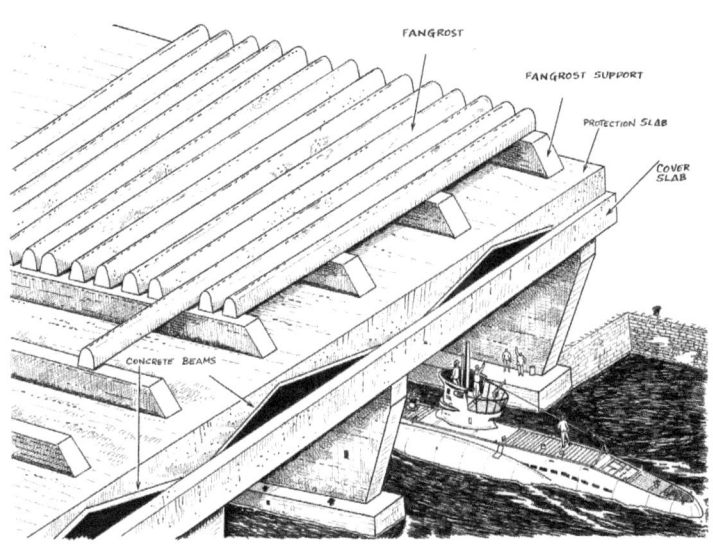

Fangrost at U-Boot bunker, La Pallice, France.

Feindhörer

stitutes for traditional religious high holy days. January 30 was the day of the Machtergreifung (Seizure of Power), when Hitler had assumed the chancellorship in 1933. February 24 was the day of the foundation of the NSDAP in 1920. March 16 was the National Day of Mourning, or Heroes' Remembrance Day, for the victims of World War I and Nazi martyrs. April 20 was Hitler's birthday (b. 1889), an important day in the ritual of Führer worship with extensive ceremonies, torchlight parades, choruses and mass initiation rites. May 1 was National Labor Day, appropriated from the socialists, with maypole dances, bonfires and parades. The second Sunday in May was Mothering Day, during which prolific mothers were rewarded at public ceremonies. The summer solstice (when the sun reaches its highest point relative to the celestial equator on the celestial sphere) was dedicated to NSDAP martyrs and war heroes, with evening bonfires, parades and official speeches. In September, the Parteitagen (Party Rally) was held in Nuremberg during three days with parades, marching, a consecration of party colors and—as climax—a speech by the Führer. In autumn, the Harvest Thanksgiving Day was a tribute paid to the German farmers. November 9 was the anniversary of the abortive 1923 Beer Hall Putsch in Munich; survivors of the putsch reenacted their solemn march through the streets of Munich. The winter solstice was a celebration designed to replace the Christian festivals; it did not, however, supplant the traditional Christmas and New Year. Christian festivals like Easter, Pentecost, Ascension Day and Christmas continued but, of course, were not Nazi Party events.

Feindhörer. Literally "listeners to enemy radio." Listening to enemy broadcasts—notably the BBC—was considered by the Nazis as a major offense. Feindhörer were regarded as Volksschädling (q.v.), or enemies of the people. "Good Germans" were encouraged to denounce them to the authorities.

Feindmächte. Enemy powers. This term was made up by the Ministry of Propaganda in January 1940. The words Alliierte (Allies) or Entente (Alliance) were officially forbidden in the press because they recalled the Allied victory in November 1918. Other terms allowed were Franzosen (French), Engländer (British) or westliche Demokraten (western democrats).

Feldanzug. Field service dress, the typical German Feldgrau (q.v.) uniform composed basically of steel helmet M35, shirt, tunic, trousers and marching boots. See Dienstanzug.

Feldausrüstung. Field equipment composed of gas mask container and accouterments including waistbelt, shoulderbelts, suspenders and straps supporting ammunition pouches, pistol holster, drinking bottle, bread bag, entrenching tool, bayonet, and Tarnkappe (q.v.). See Sturmgepäk and Tornister.

Feldausrüstung.

Feldgendarmerie des Heeres. Military police (MP) of the ground force. The MP was intended to maintain order and security among the fighting units. Military policemen were also responsible for control duties in ports and airfields, administrative control of aliens, patrol duties, collecting and evacuating prisoners of war, rounding up of deserters and also to regulating movement and organizing road traffic. The military field policemen wore the regular army uniform with, on the upper left arm, a national emblem (in orange color) composed of eagle and swastika set against an oval wreath of oak leaves; on the cuff of the left sleeve they had a brown cuff title inscribed with the word "Feldgendarmerie" in silver Gothic lettering. They often

Feldjägerkorps

bodied a shrine to the sixteen fallen Nazis who were killed during the failed putsch. In September 1936, SA ceremonial units called Wachstandarte (guard regiment) were regrouped to form a regiment named Standarte Feldherrnhalle. In January 1937 the regiment Feldherrnhalle was placed under command of Göring and became a Luftwaffe paratrooper fighting unit and later an infantry Luftwaffe division. See Bürgerbräu Keller Putsch.

Feldjägerkorps (FJK). A kind of military police of the Sturm Abteilung (q.v.) created in October 1933. The FJK was disbanded in April 1935 and incorporated into the regular Prussian Schutzpolizei (q.v.).

Feldgendarme.

wore the standard Schutzmantel (q.v.). On duty their most notable feature was the Ringkragen (q.v.). See Gendarmerie and Kettenhund.

Feldgrau. Field gray. Term used to describe the color of the ordinary German soldier's tunic and, by extension, the soldiers themselves. Feldgrau was actually grayish-green but there were some variations in its actual shade depending on age and amount of cleaning of the uniform. It could be anything from slate gray to a distinct light green.

Feldherrnhalle. Hall of Heroes; name of the building in Munich in front of which the bloody confrontation between the Nazis and the Bavarian police took place on November 9, 1923. After the Nazis came to power the Feldherrnhalle em-

SA Obertruppführer Feldjägerkorps 1933.

Feldmaßig

Feldmaßig (F. or f.) Field fortification. Feldmäßiger Ausbau was made of earth reinforced with sandbags, planks and beams and was used to make temporary defenses such as trenches, machine gun nests or simple artillery emplacements considered "schußsicher," which means protecting only against small projectiles and shell splinters.

Feldmütze. Peakless field service cap. Worn by all ranks from private to general, the very popular service forage cap or garrison cap was made of gray material, designed so that it could also be worn under the steel helmet. Feldmütze existed in various styles and qualities. Some were designed to allow the sides to be pulled down and buttoned around the wearer's ears. Sewn on the front of the cap was the national eagle/swastika insignia as on the tunic, and the Reichskokarde (see kokarde) without oak leaves for low ranks, beneath an inverted chevron of Waffenfarbe arm of service piping. The national tricolor kokarde was surrounded by a wreath of oak leaves for senior officers.

Feldmütze (peakless field service cap) Left: Model 1938. Right: Model 1942.

Feldwebel (Fw). German noncommissioned officer rank roughly equivalent to company sergeant major (British army) or technical sergeant (U.S. Army).

Feldzug. Military campaign.

Feldzugschild. Campaign medal awarded for "just being there." The campaign medals were often circular, oval or shield-shaped; they were awarded without reference to a soldier's performance but merely in recognition of the fact that a man had been involved in a specific campaign. For example, the Demjanskschild (Demjanskcampaign medal) was instituted in 1942 in commemoration of the defensive battle in the pocket of Demjansk (north of Moscow) in early 1942. The campaign rewards also took the form of Armelstreifen (cufftitles). Consisting of a cloth band worn on the right under sleeve, they illustrated great combat such as Spain (1936), Africa (1941), Crete (1942), Metz (1944), Kurland (1945) and others.

Feme. From Vehme, meaning "punishment" in ancient Germanic. These were medieval secret courts that rendered death penalty sentences on perceived enemies by public opinion rather than formal legal proceeding at a time when lawlessness among the feudal barons had rendered the imperial court impotent. In the early 1920s, the term was revived to designate political assassinations and acts of violence perpetuated by the ultraright, notably the Organization Consul (q.v.).

Ferdinand. See Jagdtiger (P) SdKfz 184 Elefant.

Fernschreiber. Teleprinter; a communication device composed of a typewriter keyboard and a printer linked to a telegraph system using multichannel-carrier frequency. The keystrokes generated electrical impulses, which were translated into the printed word at the receiving end. Developed in the 1920s, teleprinter circuits were extensively used throughout World War II.

Festung (F). (See illustration on page 49.) Generic term for fortress. As the Allied menace became more and more urgent, Hitler decided by directive number 51 in November 1943 to complete the Atlantic Wall; in January 1944, he ordered creation of the so-called Festungen (fortresses). This measure affected Saint-Malo, the British Channel Islands, Le Verdon and all Verteidigungsbereiche (q.v.). Festungen had priority in men, arms and defense. Their commanders had to personally swear to the Führer to resist till the last cartridge. Some fortresses were fitted with a Kernwerk (q.v.). The territory around the fortress was called Festungsbereich (FB). The program was still not completed in June 1944, but Festungen formed powerful hedgehogs. They were the most formidable strong points in the Atlantikwall (q.v.) These "Atlantic pockets" remained desperately held by their defenders till the end of the war.

Submarine pen Keroman III at Festung Lorient, France.

Festungspioniere (Fest. Pi). Fortification engineering corps.

Feuerschutzpolizei. Fire-brigade police.

Feuertaufe. Baptism of fire, when a soldier is in real combat for the first time.

Feuerwehr. Fire brigade.

Fieseler (Fi). The Gerhart Fieseler aircraft building company. It produced in large number the light reconnaissance highwing airplane Fieseler Fi 156 Storch. The company also produced the flying bomb V1 (q.v.), officially named Fieseler Fi 103.

Film Industry in the Third Reich. Like all other aspects of cultural life in the Third Reich, the film industry was "cleansed" and coordinated by Gleichschaltung (q.v.) The Reich Film Law was enacted in February 1934, establishing a censorship committee. Under this law, a Reichsfilmdramaturg (Reich Film Supervisor) was designated to examine scripts and given full authority to accept or reject those scripts. After a screenplay passed the Reichsfilmdramaturg, the completed film was shown to the censorship committee, consisting of permanent members and four judges nomi-

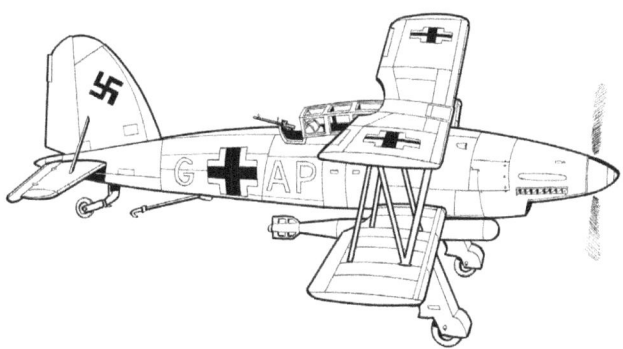

Fieseler Fi 167 (Naval torpedo bomber). The Fi 167 was intended to be the standard topedo carrier to arm the German aircraft carrier *Graf Zeppelin*. As the ship was never completed, the few planes built were never used.

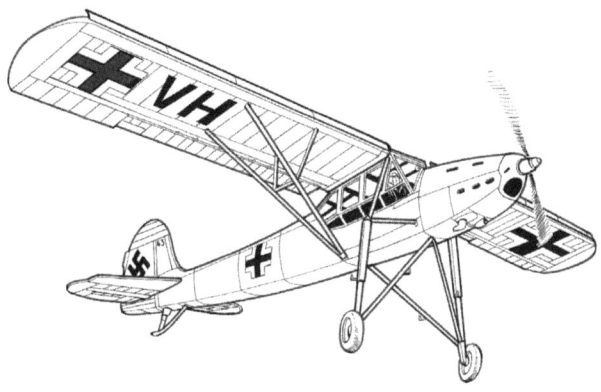

Fieseler Fi 156 Storch.

nated by the propaganda minister. This body was empowered to withhold permits for films if they did not hew to Nazi lines. Foreign films were also included under this law. Dr. Joseph Paul Goebbels (q.v.), Reichminister für Volksaufklärung und Propaganda (Minister for Public Enlightenment and Propaganda) was fully aware of and very interested in the potential of film as a propagandistic tool, and he took an active role in the development of Nazi movies. From 1933 to 1945, the Nazi film industry produced some 1,363 feature films. A string of nationalistic films and documentaries were produced. However, these films were so boring and political that the public stayed away. So Goebbels quickly realized that propaganda would have to be delivered in the form of entertainment, notably by pseudo-historical films. Another important facet of wartime Nazi cinema was illusion and escapism with light comedy and romantic stories for pure entertainment, in order to sustain morale and keep good spirits. See *Hans Westmar* and Riefenstahl, Leni.

Final Solution. See Endlösung der Judenfrage.

Flak. Antiaircraft artillery. See Flugzeugabwehrkanone.

"Flak nach vorn!" "Flak Forwards!" Marching song of the German World War II antiaircraft artillery. Lyrics and music were by Unteroffizier Nils Cederborg.

Flakboote. A ship armed with antiaircraft guns, intended to protect harbors, shipyards and submarine bases, and the like.

Flakhelfer. Often underage auxiliaries from the Hitler Youth used to load and operate flak batteries and man searchlight batteries.

Flakhelferrin. Woman serving as auxiliary in antiaircraft service.

Flak-Kampfabzeichen. Flak medal representing an 8.8 centimeters gun turned to the sky, hemmed with oak leaves and crowned with the Luftwaffe (q.v.) emblem. The medal, issued in January 1941, was awarded to gunners who shot down five enemy aircraft.

Flakpanzer. Antiaircraft gun mounted on an armored vehicle, intended to protect transport, tanks and troop columns against aircraft attacks. These weapons, provided with armor-piercing ammunition in addition to high-explosive rounds, could also be used against ground targets. Many types were used on halftrack and full-track vehicles. See Möbelwagen.

Flakpanzer IV Kugelblitz.

Flakturm. Antiaircraft tower. A large concrete building fitted with a terrace armed with flak guns. A flak tower was mostly a little higher than the average urban buildings around it so that guns and searchlights could have a wide arc of fire, and they were often camouflaged as normal civilian buildings. Towers were connected to radar stations and Luftwaffe command posts, which coordinated and conducted antiaircraft fire. The different floors were arranged as ammunition stores, shelters for rescue teams, doctors and medical personnel, police squads, firemen, and bomb clearance squads. There was often also room for civilians from the neighborhood. See Luftschutzraum.

Flammenwerfer. Flamethrower. Carried by a single operator, the flamethrower was composed of a canister filled with a fluid fuel (such as thickened gasoline) with a tank of pressurized nitrogen to propel the liquid, which was ignited as it left the launcher. The weapon had a limited range (about 30 to 40 meters), which made the operator quite vulnerable, but it had a terrifying effect on enemy morale as well as a formidable physical effect. The most common type of German portable flamethrower — reliable and easy to operate — was the Flammenwerfer Model 40, which was slung in a web harness. The impressive device, generally issued to assault engineers, weighed about 23 kilograms and had a range of about 30 meters. Larger flamethrowers, also part of armored vehicles' armament, were called Flammpanzerwagen, (F) for short.

Flammpanzer (F). A tank armed with a flamethrower.

Flaschenbiergustav. Beer-Bottle Gustav, a term of derision used by the early Nazis to describe one of their worst enemies: Gustav Stresemann (1878–1929). Stresemann was a staunch supporter of democracy, a liberal politician and statesman who served as chancellor and foreign minister during the Weimar Republic. He also achieved reconciliation with France, and for this, was co-laureate of the Nobel Peace Price in 1926 (together with the French statesman Aristide Briand).

Flecktarn. Spotted camouflage. A disruptive pattern designed for use in temperate woodland terrain. It commonly consisted of dark green, light green, black, red-brown and green-brown. The use of spots created a dithering effect, which eliminated hard boundaries between the different colors. See Tarnung.

Fliegeralarm or **Luftalarm.** Air raid alarm. There were three levels of alarm. Voralarm (three long tones by public sirens) warned the population to prepare for an attack. Vollalarm (one long screaming tone) indicated the imminence of an attack. Entwarnung (all clear) marked the end of the attack. The sounding of the alarm was the responsibility of the Luftschutz Warndienst, (q.v.) or LSW, Air Raid Warning Service. When the frequency of Allied raids increased, refinements and a more elaborate system were introduced, giving 12-minute and 6-minute warnings. Information on the movements of Allied bombers was improved by 1942 (notably by the development of radar) and progress of attack formations and raids was broadcasted.

Fliegerfaust. Literally "airplane fist," a one-man portable antiaircraft weapon, composed of a bundle of nine 2-centimeter caliber barrels set together into a portable device about 1.70 meters long with a weight of 6.5 kilograms. It had a fore handgrip, a pistol-like electrical firing grip, and a simple optical sight for aiming. For firing, the weapon was shouldered like a bazooka. At the beginning of 1945, some 10,000 of them were ordered, but only a few prototypes were ever built, none of which ever reached combat troops on the field. See also Panzerfaust.

Flossenbürg. Concentration camp in the Oberpfalz region of Bavaria, near the Czech border. Flossenbürg KZ was established in May 1938, originally intended for German criminals, "asocial" persons, and Jews. During World War II the camp grew to include political prisoners and foreign prisoners of war, particularly Russians. The site was chosen for its granite hills, and prisoners were put to exhausting work in a large quarry. Flossenbürg was liberated by the U.S. Army in April 1945. By that time, some 30,000 inmates had died in Flossenbürg and its subcamps from slave labor, starvation and maltreatment.

Flottenkriegsabzeichen. High sea fleet badge created by the well-known artist Adolf Bock, approved and adopted in April 1941 by then–Grand Admiral Raeder, Commander in Chief of the German Navy. Although the decoration

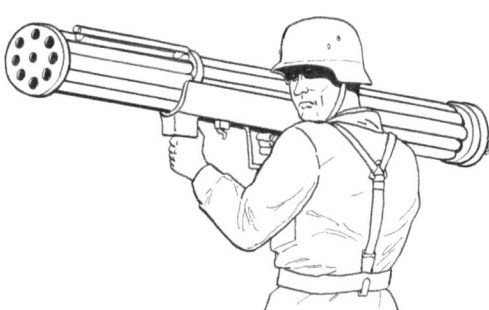

Fliegerfaust.

Flottenkriegsabzeichen.

Flugzeugabwehrkanone

was instituted in 1941, awards could be rendered in retrospect of service from the beginning of World War II. Required qualifications included active duty of 12 weeks at sea, wounds or being sunk in action.

Flugzeugabwehrkanone or **Fliegerabwehrkanone** (Flak). Antiaircraft artillery. The flak artillery was a branch of the Luftwaffe (q.v.), but other arms of the Wehrmacht (Heer and Marine) and the Waffen-SS developed their own flak. The flak was divided into two categories. (1) Light flak was directed against low-flying planes and thus shot directly on sight. Troops were armed with machine guns and rapid-firing light guns with calibers of 2 centimeters or 3.7 centimeters and the formidable 2-centimeter Flak-Vierling. (2) Heavy flak was fired at high-flying level planes. It comprised long-range pieces such as the famous 8.8-centimeter or the 10.5-centimeter flak guns.

Flugzeugtrager. Aircraft carrier. The only World War II German aircraft carrier was the *Graf Zeppelin*, which was never completed as priority was given to the construction of submarines.

Focke-Wulf (Fw). German airplane company created in 1923 by Heinrich Focke and Georg Wulf. Its most produced plane was the modern and advanced fighter Focke-Wulf Fw 190, introduced in 1942. Another remarkable plane was the four-motored long range Focke-Wulf Fw 200 Kondor, which was designed right before the war as a civilian airliner and which was converted to anti-shipping bomber and sea reconnaissance aircraft. The company also designed the light-bomber/ground-attacker/reconnaissance Focke-Wulf Fw 189 Uhu with double fuselage.

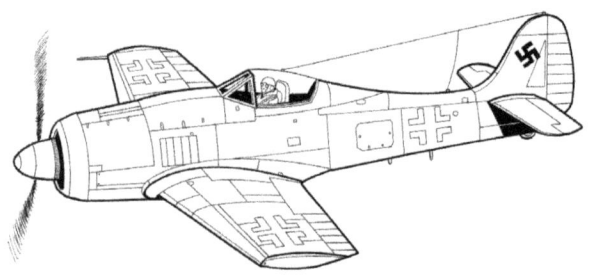

Focke-Wulf 190.

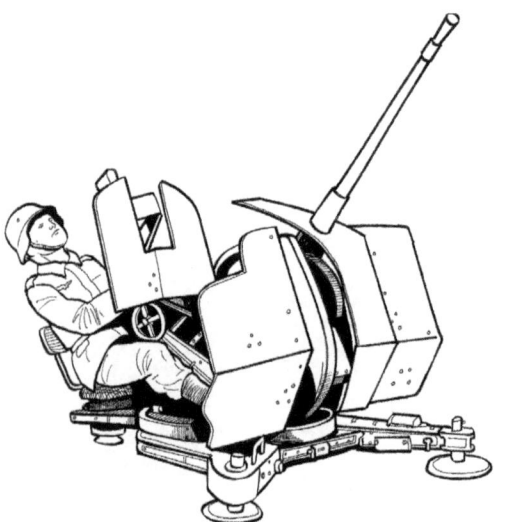

Flugzeugabwehrkanone: Light 2 cm flak 38.

Fördernde Mitglied der SS (FM-SS). Patrons of the SS who made regular contributions to SS funds. Fördernde Mitgliedern were usually Germans of lesser wealth who might benefit from some of the SS order's prestige and privileges by paying a modest sum. Introduced in 1934, this convenient system collected an average of 581,000 reichsmarks per year.

Four Years' Plan. See Vierjahresplan.

Fraktur. A fashion of Gothic black letter popularly associated with Nazi Germany. Fraktur came into use when Emperor Maximilian I (1493–1519) established a new typeface created specifically for the purpose of printing books. In the 19th century, the use of Fraktur increased, leading to the Antiqua-

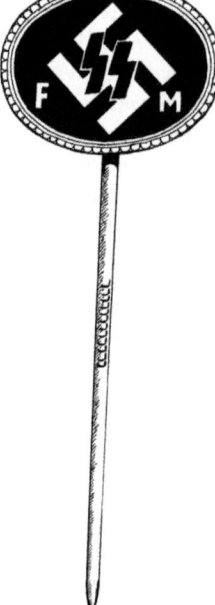

Lapel badge FM-SS.

Fraktur dispute, which lasted until the Nazis abandoned Fraktur in 1941 (on grounds of it being Jewish). Since it was so common, all kinds of Gothic black letter tend to be called Fraktur.

Franco, Francisco (1892–1975). Spanish general, leader of the Nationalist military rebellion in the Spanish Civil War, and dictator of Spain from October 1936 until his death in November 1975. Although Hitler and Mussolini had given him significant help to defeat the Republicans in the Civil War, Franco refused to engage Spain on the Axis side during World War II. See Hendaye and Kondor Legion.

Frank, Anne (1929–1945). A young Jewish girl who had to go into hiding during the occupation of the Netherlands. The Frank family was originally from Frankfurt. They had immigrated to the Netherlands in March 1933 to escape Nazi persecutions. After Holland was occupied by the Germans in 1940, anti–Jewish measures were taken and the family went into hiding in 1942 in a building at Prinsengracht 263 in Amsterdam. After two years in hiding, the Franks were betrayed by an unknown informer, arrested by the police and deported. Anne Frank died in early 1945 at the camp of Bergen-Belsen. While in hiding she had written a diary in Dutch in which, with intelligence, warm spirit and sensitivity, she described the vicissitudes of people living together under dangerous circumstances, facing hunger, boredom, the ever-present threat of being discovered, and all the cruelties and kindnesses of human behavior. The diary was retrieved after the war by a close friend named Miep Gies, who gave it to Anne's father, Otto Frank, the only known survivor of the family. The diary was published and received widespread critical and popular attention. It has now been published in more than 60 different languages. The secret annex in the office building on the Prinsengracht where the family was hidden is now a museum open to the public.

Frank, Hans (1900–1946). A veteran of World War I and Freikorps (q.v.), an early Nazi Party member and Alt Kampfer (q.v.), Frank became legal adviser to the NSDAP, and ran the internal disciplinary court Untersuchungs-und Schlichtungs-Ausschuß (q.v.). In late 1939 he was made governor-general of Poland. There he established a regime of terror, directed the enslavement of the Polish people and organized the extermination of the Jewish community. One of the major Nazi war criminals, he was condemned to death at the Nuremberg Trials and hanged. See Generalgouvernement.

Frankfurt Trial. A trial held at Frankfurt am Main of the SS officers who worked at Auschwitz (q.v.), hence also known as the Auschwitz Trial. It took place from December 1963 to August 1965.

Französisch (f). French. Designation used for all equipment, airplanes, tanks and weapons captured from the French armies after the defeat and occupation in 1940.

Frauenlager. Women's camp, the official designation for a concentration camp whose inmates were exclusively female. See Ravensbrück.

Free corps. See Freikorps.

Freemasonry. See Freimaurerei.

Freiburg Kreis. Freiburg Circle, a liberal resistance movement opposed to Hitler, composed of intellectuals and led by the historian Gerhard Ritter at the University of Freiburg.

Freie Indien. Free Indians, a curious Waffen-SS Legion of about 2,000 volunteers originating from India. These men were enlisted in the British army, captured by the Germans in North Africa and recruited in the prisoner-of-war camps by Subhas Chandras Bose, leader of the independence movement. The Indian volunteers, wearing their turbans with German uniforms with swastika, never saw action and merely played a propaganda role.

Freiherr (Frhr). Free lord or baron, a low-ranking old military title of nobility especially in Austria and Bavaria. The title was normally written between Christian and family names, for example General der Panzertruppen Leo Dietrich Franz Freiherr Geyr von Scheppenburg (1886–1974).

Freikorps. Free corps. Right-wing paramilitary units recruited at the end of 1918 among "reliable" ex-officers and soldiers from the demobilized German imperial army. The Freikorps were illegally organized by captain Kurt von Schleicher (q.v.). They were given covert support by the army as a means of evading the demilitarization imposed by the Treaty of Versailles. They were charged with maintaining order, notably

Freimaurer

the repression of the political left-wing conspirators and revolutionaries. Freikorps units fought — with Allied approval — against the Bolsheviks in Lithuania and Latvia in 1919. They were also intended to protect the newly instituted Weimar Republic from being invaded from the East, notably in Silesia, which was disputed by Germany and Poland in 1920. At first, the Weimar Republic supported the formation of the freebooter Freikorps, but the rough behavior of some units eventually made them obnoxious to the traditional military command and an embarrassment to the civilian authorities. In early 1921, all citizens' militias were forbidden and disbanded, and many troopers of the Freikorps went to Munich where they joined nationalist parties — notably Hitler's movement. See Schutz-Staffeln, Spartakusbund, and Sturm Abteilungen der NSDAP.

Freikorps trooper 1919.

Freimaurer. Freemason.

Freimaurerei. Freemasonry. The Nazis claimed that Freemasons were members of the "Jewish conspiracy" whose aims were control of the world and destruction of the Aryans. They also considered that Freemasonry was one of the causes of Germany's World War I defeat. In August 1935, Freemasonry was outlawed, assets were confiscated, and Masons declared the "most implacable and dangerous enemies of the German race." They were persecuted, arrested and imprisoned in concentration camps where they were harshly treated as political opponents, conspirators and traitors. During World War II Freemasons in Nazi-occupied countries were also persecuted.

Freisler, Roland (1893–1945). A prominent and ardent Nazi lawyer and judge, Freisler was appointed state secretary of the Reich Ministry of Justice and president of the Volksgerichtshof (People's Court), which handled political actions against the regime. Freisler contributed to the Nazification of the German Laws and presided over the (mock) trials of the Scholls (see Weisse Rose) and the July 20, 1944 conspirators. Freisler was killed in February 1945 in Berlin during an Allied air raid. See Zwanzig Juli 1944.

Freundeskreis Reichsführer-SS. Reichsführer Himmler's friends circle. This special association made contacts between the SS and German industrialists, bankers and high-ranking civil servants. It collected substantial sums of money and obtained economic facilities and financial help, notably by negotiating cheap loans. The funds were used to finance the Nazi election campaign in 1932–33 and during the war to equip Himmler's Waffen-SS (q.v.) In return industrialists and businessmen were made SS Ehrenführer (q.v.) and had various benefits. These included priority status for the allocation of cheap slave laborers from the SS concentration camps. See Wirtschafts- und Verwaltungshauptamt.

Freya. German radar. Early warning Freya radar (called Funkmeßgerät 80 or FuMG 80) ranged from 150 to 200 kilometers. It was composed of a complete 360-degree rotating cabin resting on a concrete base. The cabin contained all instruments, equipment and the operators. On top of the cabin there was a framework holding reflectors and two 6.20-meter-high aerials. Freya was often placed in an open concrete pit.

Frick, Wilhelm (1877–1946). An early adherent of National Socialism, Frick participated in the failed Beer Hall Putsch in November 1923, for which he was jailed for several months. In 1924, he was elected as one of the first Nazi deputies to the Reichstag. Six years later he became minister of the interior in Thuringia. During his tenure he purged the police force of Weimar sympathizers and promoted Nazi candidates for office over all others. After the Nazi seizure of power, Frick was appointed Reich Minister of the Interior, a position he held until August

1943. His training as a jurist was put to use in the drafting of legislation that removed Jews from public life, abolished political parties, and sent dissidents to concentration camps. After helping Hitler to consolidate power, Frick steadily lost influence. In 1943, he was appointed Reichsprotektor of Bohemia and Moravia. After the war, Frick, one of the major Nazi war criminals, was tried before the International Military Tribunal at Nuremberg and hanged in October 1946.

Fritsch, Werner Freiherr von (1880–1939). Army commander-in-chief under the minister of defense General Werner von Blomberg (q.v.) from 1934 to 1938. As a general staff officer of the old school he was hostile to the Nazis. Fritsch was framed on charges of homosexuality, and although found not guilty and later reinstated, his career had been ruined. In September 1939 he was killed in action in Poland.

Fritz Thyssen Foundation. See Thyssen, Fritz.

Fritz Todt Ring. An honorary ring, an award to the memory of Fritz Todt (q.v.) The ring and its impressive silver box were designed by H.J. Wilms, the celebrated jeweler who also made Hermann Göring's sumptuous marshal batons. The ring was awarded to only three persons. Albert Speer (q.v.); Dr. Julius Dorpmüller (minister of transport and director-general of the State Railway Company); and Dr. Wilhelm Ohnesorge (minister of post). See Nationalsozialistischer Bund Deutscher Technik.

Fritz-X. Luftwaffe's radio-controlled glide bomb.

Frontbann. After the abortive Munich Beer Hall Putsch in November 1923, Hitler was tried and imprisoned, the NSDAP forbidden and the SA disbanded. The SA troops were then temporary turned into clandestine units called Frontbann. When Hitler was released from prison in December 1924, the Frontbann were abolished and the SA and Nazi Party reactivated. See Sturm Abteilung der NSDAP.

Frontgemeinschaft. Front-line comradeship or community, or group of front-line combat soldiers and veterans.

Frontkämpfer. Front-line soldier.

Führer. Leader or guide; title assumed by Hitler to signify his role as supreme head of Germany. This was in imitation of the Italian fascist leader Benito Mussolini (q.v.) who called himself Il Duce, the Guide.

Führer und Reichkanzler. Leader and chancellor of the Reich. Adolf Hitler's official title.

Führer worship. The Führer principle had as a result a personality cult and worship of the leader. Hitler was presented by Goebbels' propaganda as a larger-than-life military strategist, an idol endowed with superhuman qualities. At the same time Hitler was also presented as a simple man coming from the people, a World War II front-line veteran, as a teetotaler, vegetarian, nonsmoker, an asexual bachelor totally devoted to his holy mission, a chosen savior who exemplified his followers' yearning for greatness and perfection. Some Nazi leaders, notably Rudolf Hess (q.v.), spoke of their master in biblical terms and words of praise approaching hysteria.

Führerhauptquartier (FHQu). Hitler's operational headquarters during World War II. There were underground concrete bunkers and command systems in Berlin, Rodert, Bruly, Obersalzberg, Munich, Salzburg, Bad Nauheim, in Silesia and Thuringia, and at Rastenburg in East Prussia, the scene of the plot of July 1944. These complexes were guarded, fenced, and included accommodations for escort troops and staff, and were linked by a communication system. Nearby there was often access to the railway, and possibly an airfield. See Zwanzig Juli 1944.

Führerlexikon. Nazi Who's Who, published in 1934. The directory gave a brief account of NSDAP leaders, Alte Kampfer (q.v.), party martyrs, pro–Nazi politicians, industrial managers, civil servants, lawyers and technologists. There were some deliberate omissions, though, notably the names of Joachim von Ribbentrop, who at the time was in disgrace as parvenu, and Ernst Röhm, the SA leader who had been murdered because he was an obstacle to Hitler's power. No women and no military figures were mentioned.

Führerprinzip. Leader principle. Italian Fascism and German Nazism held for basic truth that parliamentary procedures by elected deputies would not work to produce comprehensive planning. As early as July 1922, negotiation, election, compromise and democracy were denounced by Hitler as nonsense. Instead, all power had to be concentrated into the hands of one leader or guide, whose will represented the nation, whose vision, ideas and plan were truth, and whose command and decision were law. The absolute leader concept outlined the authoritarian character of the Nazi regime. The Third Reich was a dictatorship based on discipline and blind obedience to the Führer, who had absolute power and responsibility. This principle of leadership was also applied to all the Nazi organizations. At all levels, Germany was ruled by a multitude of appointed senior and junior führers. The Nazi hierarchy (described by the term Führer-Korps, Leader Corps) was based on respect for the strong man, obedience to a local, regional or provincial potentate who considered himself above the other people. One of the results of the Führerprinzip was corruption and an intense rivalry at all levels for promotion into this Nazi "aristocracy."

Führersbunker. Hitler's bunker, a subterranean concrete headquarters situated some 8.2 meters (50 feet) beneath the garden of the Reich Chancellery in Berlin. It was reached by descending a stairway from the butler's pantry. The bunker had two levels. The upper level included kitchen, servants' quarters, additional guest rooms and others. The lower level included seventeen small cramped and uncomfortable rooms, bathrooms, an emergency telephone center, a drawing room, guardrooms, an anteroom and cloakroom. Hitler had a suite of three rooms and a map/conference room. Two rooms were reserved for Eva Braun (q.v.) who was Hitler's girlfriend, one room for Joseph Goebbels (minister of propaganda), and one for Dr. Ludwig Stumpfegger. From the cloakroom, there was an emergency exit leading up into the Chancellery garden. It was in this bunker that Hitler committed suicide on April 30, 1945.

Führerstaat. Leader state, a descriptive and popular term for Hitler's regime in which the will of the leader was the highest law of the land.

Führertreu. Loyal to the leader, a term applied to those who remained utterly faithful to the Führer under all circumstances.

Führerweisung. Leader's directive. Hitler was convinced that he had messianic skills as a warlord. He alone might lay down the strategy, and his will was to be obeyed through a series of Führerweisungen (directives), which were issued and transmitted through the Oberkommando der Wehrmacht. Generals and field marshals were discouraged from strategy and confined to operational and tactical levels.

Führungshauptamt-SS. Operational headquarters of the SS, main office of the Schutz-Staffeln (q.v.) responsible for the training of its members.

Fünfte Kolonne. Fifth Column. Traitors within a country willing to help foreign enemies. The term was first used by a nationalist general during the Spanish Civil War who claimed he had four columns of troops converging on Madrid and a fifth column of waiting supporters ready inside the city. Nazi Germany had indeed active fifth columnists in Austria and in the Sudetenland before World War II. During the war, men such as Léon Degrelle (q.v.) in Belgium, William Joyce (q.v.) in Britain, Vidkun Quisling in Norway, Anton Mussert in the Netherlands, Jacques Doriot (q.v.) and Marcel Déat in France for example, were zealous pro–Nazi collaborators. See Quisling.

Funk, Walther (1890–1960). A financial journalist and a valuable link with industry, Funk became a prominent Nazi official, and served as minister for economic affairs from 1937 to 1945. Standing with other Nazi leaders at the Nuremberg Trials, he was accused of conspiracy to commit crimes against peace; planning, initiating and waging wars of aggression; war crimes and crimes; against humanity. Funk was sentenced to life imprisonment and released in May 1957 for medical reasons.

Funkmeßgerät (FuMG). Detection device; radar. Radar is a detection method based on broadcast of strong and short radio impulses. Waves are reflected if they meet a solid flying object; measuring time from the departure of the impulse until the return of the echo allows for calculating the distance between the radar station and the target. German radar devices, used by both the navy and the air force, included early warning devices such as Mammut (q.v.), Wassermann (q.v.) and Freya (q.v.), and short-range equipment such as Würzburg (q.v.) and Würzburg-Riese (q.v.).

Fusilier. Infantry rifleman, a historic term often used to refer to light infantry, originally named after the fusil that such troops once were armed with. During the last stage of World War II, the term was given to boost morale of infantry units with a reduced number of battalions (generally 6 instead of 9).

Fw. See Focke Wulf.

Galen, Clemens August Graf von (1878–1946). Galen, the aristocrat cardinal archbishop of Münster, had conventional views and at first welcomed aspects of Hitler's nationalism. He was, however, opposed to Nazi violation of human rights and Nazi racial doctrines, and made effective public protests against euthanasia. The Nazis were furious, but preferred to wait to arrest him until the end of World War II to avoid undermining German morale in the heavily Catholic area of Münster. Galen was beatified on October 9, 2005, by Pope Benedict XVI. See Euthaniebefehl and Religion in the Third Reich.

Gamasche. Gaiters made of canvas worn more and more frequently by German troops in place of boots when leather became scarce after 1943.

Gamasche (gaiters).

Gaskammer. Gas chamber. A gas chamber is an apparatus for killing humans (or animals) with gas, consisting of a sealed area into which a poisonous or asphyxiant gas is introduced. The most commonly used poisonous agent used by the Nazis was hydrogen cyanide, but carbon dioxide and carbon monoxide were also used. Gas chambers were used as a method of execution for condemned prisoners in the United States beginning in the 1920s. During the Holocaust, large-scale gas chambers designed for mass killing were used by the Nazis as part of their genocide program.

The Auschwitz gas chambers had a capacity of 2,000 persons at one time, and at the height of its activity the camp could provide for the gassing and incineration of 12,000 people a day. Gas chambers in extermination camps were disguised as shower or disinfection rooms. See Gaswagen and Vernichtungslager.

Gasmaske. Gas mask carried in a cylindrical container.

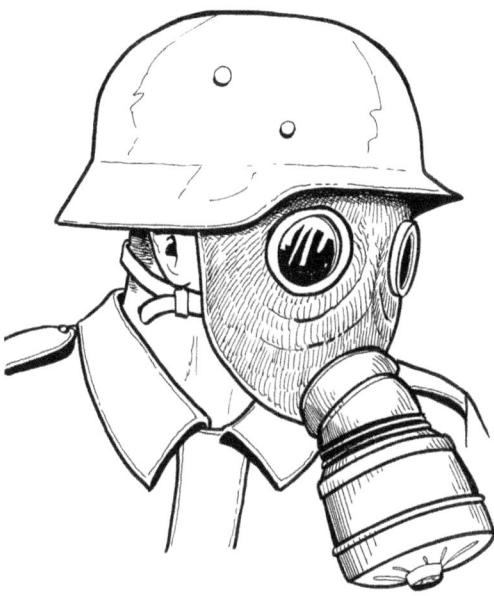

Gasmaske model M38.

Gaswagen. Gas truck, also known as Sonderwagen (special truck). Gaswagen, used for mass murder, were converted so that when the engine was started the exhaust gas was led inside the airtight body of the vehicle, causing death to the occupants. The trucks, varying in size, could each take from fifteen to twenty-five persons, who were told when climbing into them that they were to be transported elsewhere. Once the doors were closed, the inside of the truck, tightly sealed, became a gas chamber on wheels. In late 1942, the Nazis operated these for several months in Russia, Poland and Czechoslovakia, but the gas trucks failed to dispose of sufficient numbers. The Nazis did not want only hundreds or thousands people killed; their ambition was the extermination of millions. The Gaswagen scheme was quickly abandoned, and soon the Nazis embarked upon a comprehensive "Final Solution" of their Jewish population on a larger scale in extermination camps equipped with gas chambers and crematoria. See Endlösung der Judenfrage and Vernichtungslager.

Gau. Region (plural Gaue), main territorial division of the NSDAP. Nazi Germany was divided into 42 Gaue. The 43rd was the Auslands Organization (party agency for the supervision of Germans living abroad). The Gau corresponded roughly to the electoral district and to the civil defense region. Each Gau was headed by a Gauleiter (q.v.) and was divided into Bezirken, and Kreisen (q.v.), which were in turn divided into Ortsgruppen (q.v.), themselves subdivided into Zellen (q.v.).

Gauleiter. Head of a Gau, a regional leader appointed by Hitler. The Gauleiter (sometimes called Gauführer) was the highest-ranking Nazi official responsible for civil, economic and political affairs, civil defense and organization of labor, as well as in some cases taking on police duties. Below the Gauleiter were the Kreisleiter (q.v.). All of the 43 Gauleiters (and also the Kreisleiter) were required to swear unconditional and personal allegiance to Hitler.

Geballte Ladung. Concentrated charge, a stick grenade with six additional grenade heads, handles removed, lashed around it.

Gebirgstruppen. Mountain troops. Gebirgsjäger or Gebirgstruppen included Bergführer (mountain guides), Ski-jäger (skiers) and Alpinisten (mountaineers) specially trained to wage combat in mountainous areas. The Gebirg corps formed an elite troop whose esprit de corps and pride were enhanced by a distinctive emblem, the Edelweiß flower. Their Waffenfarbe (official color) was light green. Special uniforms and equipment were issued to meet the extreme conditions in which they operated, such as a special cap, windproof anoraks (Windblusen), skis, ice axes and snowshoes. To facilitate their vertiginous scrambling they were issued standard MGs (machine guns), MPs (sub-machine guns), short rifles such as the 7.92-millimeter Gewehr 33/40, and special pieces of artillery capable of being dismantled, carried piecemeal on mules and then readily reassembled for firing.

Gefolgschaft. (1) Disciplined Nazi partisan, faithful follower. (2) A group of four Scharen (platoons) of the Hitler Jugend (q.v.), roughly a company of 160 boys commanded by a Gefolgschaftführer.

Gefreiter. Lance corporal heading a Gruppe (squad of ten soldiers) in German infantry. This was also Hitler's rank in the army during World War I. Hitler was sometimes—not openly, though—referred to as the Gefreiter by his generals and marshals as a mark of contempt.

Gefrierfleischorden. "Order of Frozen Meat." See Ostmedaille.

Geheime Feldpolizei (GFP). Secret field police under army control. Created by OKW in July 1939 and recruited among professional policemen, the GPF was tasked with counterespionage, countersabotage, and detection of treasonable activity. The GPF's reach was also extended to all matters concerning the security of the Wehrmacht, including personal escort of military VIPs, interrogation of captured enemy prisoners, and the repression of illegal activities of the German army soldiers such as spying or dealing on the black market. GFP commandos were also used when the German troops retreated to capture deserters and to establish roadblocks and barrages in order to rearm disorganized wandering units and stragglers who were sent back to the front. In 1942, the GFP's duties were taken over by the Sicherheitsdienst des Reichsführer SS (q.v.).

GFP policeman in 1940.

Geheime Staatspolizei or **Gestapo.** State secret police. Originating from the small political department of the Prussian State Police in Berlin, the Gestapo was established in April 1933 by Hermann Göring (q.v.) who removed anti–Nazi police officials and replaced them with Nazi

Party members. The small service was reorganized and became in April 1934 one of the most dreadful and efficient SS secret police departments later to be placed under command of the SS-Reichssicherheitshauptamt (q.v.), RSHA or Reich Security Main Office. Himmler had studied the organization of the Russian Secret Police, the dreaded Cheka, and he boasted that his Gestapo could do better. Indeed the Gestapo in Germany (before and during World War II) kept a watchful eye over the people. It was a small secret police service designed to track down and eliminate all dissidents, complainers and opponents. It was largely composed of career policemen and had 32,000 full-time employees in 1944. With the aid of denunciation, intimidation, preventive custody in concentration camps and even summary execution, the Gestapo was a very effective police force in Germany and the symbol of the Nazi regime of terror. During the war in all occupied lands in Europe, the Gestapo was charged with infiltration, arrestation and interrogation (using torture) of all opponents and resistance members. It also employed foreign volunteers and even criminals as spies, informers, infiltrants, extortionists, torturers and killers in an auxiliary police force. The Gestapo was also responsible for the arrests and mass deportation of Jews to extermination camps. Gestapo policemen were officially registered as members of the Sicherheitsdienst des Reichsführer SS (q.v.), but they did not wear the SS uniform. The wore civilian clothes often a long black leather overcoat and a hat.

Geheimer Kabinettsrat. Secret Cabinet Council, a special cabinet set up by Hitler in February 1938 to guide him in the conduct of foreign affairs. The cabinet never functioned and never met as Hitler refused to share his power.

Geheimes Staatspolizeiamt or **Gestapa.** Secret State Police Office. In April 1933, Hermann Göring, initially acting as Prussian minister of the interior and then as Prussian minister president, established the Secret State Police Office (Geheimes Staatspolizeiamt, or Gestapa). As the initials GPA would be too similar to the Soviet GPU, the service was renamed Geheime Staatspolizei (q.v.).

Gemeinnutz geht vor Eigennutz. "Common Good Goes before Private Interest." A popular Nazi slogan popularized by Rudolf Jung in his book *Der Nationale Sozialismus*, published in 1922. This became Hitler's basic stance on the subordination of the economy to the national interest.

Gemeinschaftsfremde. Community aliens, a flexible term used by the Nazis to include all those who failed to live by the social norms of the national community, including habitual criminals, the "work-shy," tramps and beggars, alcoholics, prostitutes, homosexuals and juvenile delinquents. The Nazis explained the deviance from their norms in terms of biologically determined degeneracy. They saw these problems as a racial matter rather than a social welfare issue. In September 1933 the police initiated a major roundup of beggars and tramps. Some 300,000 homeless and jobless persons were registered, but the regime lacked the means to provide shelter and work. As the German economy had advantages in having a mobile and cheap labor force, the Nazis made a distinction between "orderly" and "disorderly" persons of no fixed abode. Those who were healthy, willing to work and with no previous convictions were given a Wanderkarte (permit to travel and work). Disorderly people, on the other hand, were arrested and placed in work camps and concentration camps. Another large roundup of tramps and "community aliens" took place right before the Olympic Games (q.v.) held in Berlin in 1936 in order to give a "clean" image of Germany. See Asoziale.

Gendarmerie. The term indicates policemen, but it is derived from the French *gens* (men or people) and *arme* (weapon), or "armed men." The Gendarmerie in Germany was the rural uniformed police, including motorized units for traffic control. It was a part of the Ordnungspolizei (q.v.).

Generalfeldmarschall (Gen. Feldm.). Field marshal, the highest and most prestigious rank in the German army. Field marshals were appointed (and dismissed) by Hitler himself as he was head of the German armed forces.

Generalgouvernement (GG). General Government, official name for the eastern part of Nazi-occupied Poland after the German victory of 1939, the western part being named Wartheland. Of all conquered European nations, Poland was treated most savagely by the Germans. Nowhere had Nazi terror reached such monstrous proportions, such a height of ferocity unknown in other countries (possibly excepting the Soviet Union). Millions of people were displaced, enslaved, deliberately starved and killed, including the Jewish community. The Polish intelligentsia was eliminated, the territory was carved out, towns destroyed, wealth confiscated, and industry dismantled. The General Government was ruled by Hans Frank (q.v.).

Generalplan Ost. Master Scheme East, a Nazi plan for the colonization of Eastern Europe. The plan, prepared in the years 1939–1942, was part of the Nazi Lebensraum (q.v.) policy and a fulfillment of the Drang nach Osten (q.v.) The plan effectively called for the extermination, expulsion, Germanization or enslavement of most or all eastern and western Slavs, and Jews living behind the front lines in Europe. The body responsible for the drafting of this plan was the Reich Main Security Office (RSHA). Nearly all the wartime documentation on Generalplan Ost was deliberately destroyed shortly before Germany's defeat in May 1945. See AA Line; Himmler, Heinrich; and Reichssicherheitshauptamt.

Generalquartiermeister (GenQu). Principal staff officer responsible for supplies for the whole German army.

Generalstab des Heeres (GenStdH). General Staff of the Army, highest administrative staff of the army.

Genesende. Convalescent. Because of a shortage of combatants by the end of the war, some combat units were filled with sick and recovering soldiers. The 70th Infanteriedivision, for example, was composed of infantry regiments 1018, 1019 and 1020, and artillery regiment 170. Most recruits were stomach patients, so the unit was nicknamed Weißbrotdivision (white bread division) illustrating the special diet its soldiers were on. The 70th Infanteriedivision was totally destroyed in November 1944 on the island Walcheren in the Netherlands.

Genfer Konvention. Geneva Convention. The term refers to various international conventions signed in Geneva (Switzerland) in 1864, 1906 and 1929. The convention (through the channel of the Red Cross) dealt — and still deals — with care for the wounded and sick in the field, the armed forces at sea, the respect of prisoners of war and the protection of civilians in time of war. The convention had not been signed by the USSR, and this was taken as an excuse by the Nazis to behave with inhuman savagery. In the shadow of the excesses of World War II, the only partially effective convention was reestablished in 1949 with rules that threatened penalties through international laws.

Genocide. Genocide, from the Greek *genos* (race, kind, people) and *-cide* (killing). The term was coined after 1945 to describe the use of a deliberate, systematic policy intended to eliminate an entire racial, political or cultural group of a nation or a people. Genocide was a part of Hitler's racial program.

George-Kreis. George Circle, an exclusive group of nationalist and anti–Semitic intellectuals gathered around the poet Stefan Anton George (1868–1933) at the beginning of the 20th century. After World War I, in Munich, the young Hitler was much impressed by the virulent nationalist and anti–Semitic tone of the speakers of the circle.

German States. See Länder.

German-American Bund or **Amerikadeutscher Bund.** Probably the largest of the numerous pro–Nazi organizations that emerged in the United States in the 1930s. Headed by Fritz Kuhn, the bund (taking advantage of the First Amendment to the U.S. Constitution) organized training camps for its members as well as meetings, public parades and events in order to promote a favorable view of Nazi Germany. It had contact with the NSDAP but received no financial or verbal support from Germany. Officially Hitler (who was concerned with American public opinion) disavowed the existence and the activities of the bund. The organization made little headway in the U.S. and vanished during World War II.

Germanische-SS. Germanic SS. See Burgondia.

Gesamt-SS. Total SS, a term used to describe all the SS branches. See Allgemeine SS Schutz-Staffeln, and Waffen-SS.

Geschwader. Operational squadron in the Luftwaffe. A Geschwader, commanded by a Kommodore, counted between 80 and 120 aircraft; each Geschwader was composed of three or four Gruppen and each Gruppe included three or four Staffeln. A varying number of Geschwader formed a Fliergerkorps (flying corps). Geschwader were of different types: bomber, dive-bomber, single-engine fighter, twin-engine fighter, night-fighter, ground attacker and transport.

Gesellschaft zur Förderung gewerblicher Unternehmungen (GEFU). Company for the Promotion of Industrial Enterprises; actually the cover name of a secret organization intended to develop and coordinate military collaboration between Soviet Russia and the German Reichswehr (q.v.) in the 1920s. Headed by General von Borries, with offices in Berlin and Moscow, GEFU was disbanded when Hitler decided to break up military cooperation with the Red Army by autumn 1933.

Gesellschaftsanzug. Evening dress (or mess uniform) for military personnel.

Gesetz zur Erhebung der Not von Volk und Reich. Literally "Law to remove the Distress of People and State," better known as Enabling Act. This single law, passed on March 24, 1933, provided the constitutional foundation of Hitler's dictatorship.

Gestapa. See Geheimes Staatspolizeiamt.

Gestapo. State secret police. See Geheime Staatspolizei.

Gesundes Volksempfinden. Healthy folk sentiment or sound national feeling. This notion of "natural law" held that there was no authority and ultimate source of law other than the conscience of the German nation, and since Adolf Hitler was seen as the keeper of the nation's conscience, his word was law. See Feme and Justice in the Third Reich.

Gesellschaftsanzug.

Getarnte Drillichanzug. Camouflage service dress introduced in 1944 for the Waffen-SS. The suit consisted of a tunic and trousers similar in cut and style to the standard army uniform but it was made in cheap camouflage drill material; with it was worn the peaked camouflage cap in matching patterns and the regular steel helmet with camouflage cover.

Getarnte Drillichanzug M44.

Gewehr. Rifle. In 1939 all rifles issued to the German forces were virtually the same as those their forebears had used during World War I. The only changes were minor adaptations intended to make mass production easier. Indeed, on the whole, the German manually-operated rifles of World War II were largely confined to the Mauser originating from the 1890s and in service since 1904. The basic standard German infantry rifle was the traditional Mauser Karabiner Modell 1898k (Kar 98 K) which used a bolt

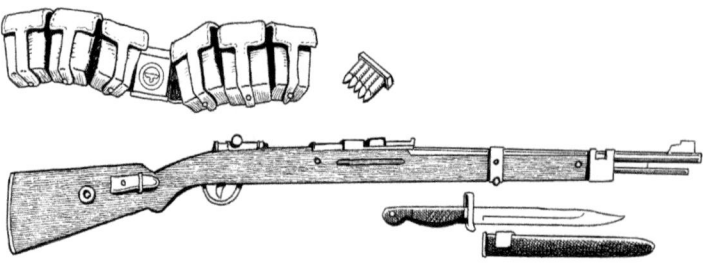

7.92 mm Mauser Gewehr 24 with accessories.

action that facilitated rapid loading and ejection of the spent cartridge, and could fire about ten shots per minute.

Ghetto. A neighborhood in a city predominantly occupied by a group relegated there especially because of social, racial, economic, or legal stigma. Many medieval European and Middle Eastern cities had a Jewish quarter and some still do. Jewish ghettos existed because Jews were viewed as aliens due to being a cultural minority and due to their non–Christian beliefs in a Christian society. During World War II, the Nazis established Jewish ghettos notably in occupied east Europe in order to segregate, confine and concentrate Jews before shipping them to concentration and extermination camps. Living conditions in these ghettos (e.g., Warsaw) were so appalling that they were de facto extermination camps. In early 1943, Himmler ordered the liquidation of the ghettos, which were transformed into concentration camps. See Endlösung der Jugenfrage and Warschauer Getto.

Gillars, Mildred née Sisk (1900–1988). American student who went to Europe and Germany in the 1920s. Gillars found a job in German radio and during World War II she broadcast Nazi propaganda, for which she was nicknamed Axis Sally, Berlin Bessie, Berlin Babe, or the Bitch of Berlin. After the war she was arrested, tried, and sentenced to twelve years' imprisonment. She was paroled in 1961. Another "Axis Sally" was Luisa Rita Zucca (q.v.).

Glaube und Schönheit. Faith and Beauty, a female youth organization created in 1937 in which girls from the ages of seventeen to twenty-one received advanced training in fashion design, domestic science and preparation for marriage. Glaube und Schönheit was also intended to develop the spiritual and physical graces. Some pretty girls were to become prize exhibits for the National Socialist conception of ideal womanhood. The organization was a part of the female Hitler Jugend (q.v.) See also Bund Deutscher Mädel in der HJ and Jungmädel Bund in der HJ.

Gleichschaltung. Literally unification, regimentation, coordination, and conformity. It was a series of laws aiming to restructure of German society and government into streamlined, centralized hierarchies of power, with the intention of gaining total control and coordination of all aspects of society. This process was begun after the seizure of power in January 1933. All political parties were forbidden, institutions and government were Nazified, trade unions were abolished, industry, trade and agriculture were focused on war preparation, the country was purged of "undesirable" elements and organized hierarchically according to the racial and leadership principle, youth was indoctrinated, people were forced to conform, and opponents were arrested and placed in the newly created concentration camps. The Nazis demanded total involvement by creating numerous organizations, fronts, corporations, agencies and associations run or directly affiliated with the Gliederungen der NSDAP (q.v.) and the Angeschlossene Verbände der NSDAP (q.v.). The process of Gleichschaltung concentrated the effective political power in the hands of Hitler to a degree unknown in Germany since the days of Frederick the Great, king of Prussia (1712–1786). Gleichschaltung was a devastating assault on the political, social and cultural institutions of the old Germany. It was a massive restriction of the rights of the individual. From the stream of legislation new power groups developed, notably the NSDAP, the Deutsche Arbeitsfront (q.v.) and the Schutz-Staffeln (q.v.) It would take time before the German churches, army and industry were fully subjected to Hitler's will, but Gleichschaltung provided the legislative weapons necessary for the complete takeover of Germany by the Nazi clique.

Gleiwitz. A small town in Upper Silesia at the border between Germany and Poland, today called Gliwice. In the night of August 31, 1939, the Germans staged an incident in the form of an alleged provocation attack (code name Fall Himmler) on a radio station by "Polish" troops (actually camp prisoners dressed in Polish uniform who were shot). The entire operation was intended to give the appearance of Polish aggression against Germany, and used as an excuse to justify the invasion of Poland.

Gliederungen der NSDAP. Nazi Party organizations. The NSDAP was formed of the reunion of Gliederungen der Partei and Angeschlossene Verbände der NSDAP (q.v.) (associated groupments), which enabled the Nazis to control all police and administrative functions, and cultural and social life. The Gliederungen included the following: Sturm Abteilung der NSDAP (SA, assault battalions); Schutz-Staffeln der NSDAP (SS, defense detachments); Nationalsozialistische Kraftfahrer Korps (NSKK, transport corps); Hitler Jugend (HJ, Nazi youth movement); Nationalsozialistischer Deutscher Studentenbund (NSDStB, Nazi student league); Nationalsozialistischer Deutscher Dozentenbund (NSD-DB, Nazi professorial league); and Nationalsozialistische-Frauenschaft (NSF, Nazi women's organization). Although on the surface Nazism appeared to be a rigidly structured, monolithic entity, it was very difficult to bring to light the jumble of authorities and functions which grew, overlapped and changed among the Gliederungen der NSDAP and Angeschlossene Verbände through the impact of the war, and the dynamism of the Nazi movement. From Hitler, there was a deliberate contra- and juxtaposition of state and party institutions with overlapping functions. Nazi rule is often described as "organized chaos." See Nationalsozialistische Deutsche Arbeiter Partei.

Globocnik, Odilo (1904–1945). An Austrian Nazi, Globocnik became Gauleiter of Vienna in May 1938 after the Anschluß Osterreichs (q.v.). He lost this position at the end of January 1939 due to financial irregularities and mismanagement of Nazi Party funds. Pardoned by Heinrich Himmler, he was appointed SS- und Polizeiführer (q.v.) to the Lublin district in Poland in November 1939, and tasked to carry out Himmler's orders regarding Aktion Reinhard (q.v.), which resulted with the death of 1.7–1.8 million Jews, and a booty of about 178 million Reichsmark stolen from the victims. Later in the war, Globocnik was responsible for the final liquidations of the Warsaw Ghetto and the Bialystok Ghetto. Globocnik also directed the resettling—ethnic cleansing—of a large number of Poles, particularly around Zamosc. Appointed by Himmler as head of the SS company OSTI (Ostindustrie GmbH), he was in charge of 45,000 Jewish workers in forced labor camps, among them Trawniki and Poniatowa. Globocnik also organized a part of the network of concentration/work camps in the Lublin (q.v.) district, including the extermination camp Maidanek. Following the completion of Aktion Reinhard and the cessation of the Generalplan Ost (q.v.), Globocnik was ordered to Trieste (Italy) as Höhere SS- und Polizeiführer (q.v) Adriatisches Küstenland, along with the majority of the Aktion Reinhard personnel. There he led Aktion R, the persecution of partisans and Jews in Istria. Globocnik was arrested by British troops in Austria in May 1945. He committed suicide by poisoning himself while in custody.

Glücks, Richard (1889–?). Inspector of concentration camps and successor to Theodor Eicke (q.v.). Glücks vanished without a trace after World War II.

Gneisenau. (See illustration on page 64.) Battleship/battlecruiser named after Admiral August von Gneisenau. She was completed in May 1938, launched in December 1936, and heavily damaged in an air raid in February 1942. She was then decommissioned, scuttled as a blockship in March 1945, and scrapped after the war.

Goebbels, Joseph Paul (1897–1945). Rejected for military service in World War I for a deformed right foot, Goebbels earned a Ph.D. from Heidelberg University in 1921. A failed writer of novels and plays, he worked as a journalist and later as a bank clerk and caller on the stock exchange. Goebbels came into contact with the Nazi Party in 1923, became a member in 1924, and was appointed Gauleiter (q.v.) of Berlin. In this position he put his propaganda skills to full use, fighting the local socialist and communist parties with the help of Nazi papers and the paramilitary SA. By 1928, he had risen in the party ranks to become one of its most prominent members. In 1933 Goebbels was appointed propaganda minister, and one of his first acts was the

Gneisenau.

burning of books deemed unsuitable by the Nazis. He exerted totalitarian control over the media, arts and information in Germany. From the beginning of his tenure, Goebbels organized attacks on German Jews, commencing with the one-day boycott of Jewish businessmen, doctors, and lawyers on April 1, 1933. His attacks on the Jewish population culminated in the Kristallnacht (q.v.) of 1938. Further, he produced a series of anti–Semitic films (most notably *Jud Suss*), and used modern propaganda techniques to psychologically prepare the German people for a war of aggression. During World War II, Goebbels increased his power and influence through shifting alliances with other top Nazi leaders. By late 1943, the tide of the war was turning against the Axis powers, but this only spurred him to intensify the propaganda by urging the Germans to accept the idea of Totaler Krieg (q.v.)—total war—and mobilization. The faithful Goebbels remained with Hitler in Berlin until the end. He and his wife, Magda, killed their six young children and then both committed suicide.

Gobineau, Joseph Arthur, Count of (1816–1882). French diplomat and writer of "Essay on the Inequality of Human Races," which asserted the superiority of the white race over others and labeled the Aryans or Germanic peoples as the summit of civilization. Drawing upon distorted views of anthropology, linguistics and history Gobineau claimed that white societies flourished as long as they remained free of black and yellow strains and that dilution would lead to corruption and decadence. Gobineau's book provided the classic synthesis of ideas that largely determined the nature of modern racist thought. His theory of racial determinism in the essay influenced the racist beliefs of such figures as Houston Stewart Chamberlain (q.v.) and Adolf Hitler. See Arisch and Ubermensch.

Goldenes Partiabzeichen. Party Golden Badge of Honor, a special decoration given by Hitler as a reward to persons who had performed outstanding services for the Nazi Party.

Goldfasan. Golden cock-pheasant. Nickname of ridicule, mockery applied to the Höheren

Politischen Leiter der NSDAP (Nazi Party functionaries having important official function). Many of those administrators were corrupt and the common people regarded them as ostentatious and filled with a ridiculous sense of self-importance. The derogatory term derived from the gold braided insignia, and golden brown collar patches worn on the gaudy uniform. See also Führerprinzip and Gauleiter.

Goliath. Experimental weapon. The SdKfz 303 Goliath was a small tracked robot vehicle equipped with a petrol or an electrical engine and carrying an 80 kilogram charge of explosive; it was remote controlled and driven to a speed of 10 to 20 kilometers per hour in direction of the enemy where it was detonated. Some of those vehicles were used during the battle of Kharkov in 1943 and during the Allied landing in Anzio (Italy). But, vulnerable even to small arms fire and often breaking down, Goliath proved a failure.

Goose step. See Stechschritt.

Göring, Hermann (1893–1946). Göring was a World War I hero who won fame as a pilot in the notorious crack Richthofen squadron. An early Nazi, he was seriously wounded during the abortive Beer Hall Putsch, and for some years lived in exile in Italy and Sweden. Back in Germany, he resumed Nazi activism. He became a politician and Hitler's closest colleague. He was responsible for organizing and training of pilots and the supply for the secret air force and became air minister and commander-in-chief of the Luftwaffe in 1935. As Hitler's right-hand man, he ably and ruthlessly eliminated political opposition and directed the Four Years Plan. As a military commander, Göring made several major mistakes, such as allowing the British forces to withdraw at Dunkirk in 1940, losing the Battle of Britain, and ordering the wasteful assault on Crete in 1941. He was also responsible for the failure to supply Stalingrad by air, and for being unable to prevent the Allies bombing Germany on large scale after 1943. In the last years of World War II, Göring retired to a life of luxury and drug use at his estate, Karinhall (q.v.). On the whole, Reichsmarschall Göring by his incompetence very much contributed to Germany's defeat. Hermann Göring was condemned to death for war crimes at the Nuremberg trials and committed suicide in his cell in 1946.

Göring-Werke. See Reichswerke Hermann Göring.

Gott mit Uns. "God with Us," an old German slogan reused by the Nazis. It was notably inscribed on army service belt buckles.

"Gott mit Uns" belt buckle.

Götterdämmerung. Twilight of the Gods, term used to describe the last days of Hitler in Berlin in late April 1945. The term (occasionally used in English to refer to a disastrous conclusion of events) comes from the fourth and final cycle of Hitler's favorite opera, *Der Ring des Nibelungen*, composed by Richard Wagner between 1853 and 1874.

Goulashkanone. Goulash gun; affectionate nickname given by German troops in both world wars to their army mobile field kitchens because the chimney of the stove resembled an ordnance piece when disassembled, lowered and limbered for towing.

Graf Spee. German pocket battleship named after Graf Maximillian von Spee (1861–1914), a German World War I naval hero. Launched in 1934, the *Graf Spee* was a fast, light, heavily armored warship. She had six 11-inch guns, eight 6-inch guns and eight 19.7-inch torpedo tubes. The captain of the *Graf Spee*, Hans Langsdorff, scuttled her in December 1939 near Montevideo, Uruguay, where the ship was blockaded by the British navy.

Granatwerfer (GrW). Grenade launcher or mortar (also called Mörser). A mortar is a specific kind of gun whose projectile is shot with a high-curved trajectory, between 45 degrees and 75 degrees. This is called plunging fire, permitting projectiles to hit concealed objectives or targets protected behind fortifications or hidden in a trench. The main German mortars were the Granatwerfer 8-centimeter GrW 34, which had a maximum range of 1.8 kilometers, and the heavy Granatwerfer 42, ranging up to 6 kilometers.

10-centimeter Granatwerfer 35 Mortar.

Greater Germany. See Großdeutschland.

Grenadier. Originally a soldier armed with hand grenades, then an elite soldier generally a member of a special guard corps. The term was adopted during World War II from mid–war onward as a morale-building honorific often indicative of German low-grade units. Other resurrected terms given to infantrymen were Fusilier (rifleman) and Musketier (musketeer).

Grenadierdivision. After October 1942, all German infantry divisions were renamed Grenadierdivisions in the hope of increasing morale by establishing a link with their elite counterpart of the past.

Grenzpolizei (Grepo). Frontier control police, administrated by the Sicherheitsdienst des Reichsführer SS (q.v.).

Grenzwacht. Frontier guard, border patrol.

Gröfaz. Mocking acronym for Größter Feldherr aller Zeiten (greatest general of all time), a title initially publicized by Nazi propaganda to refer to Adolf Hitler during the early years of World War II.

Großdeutscher Bund. Greater German League. A nationalist youth organization headed by Admiral Adolf von Trotha (1868–1940). The league was incorporated by force into the Hitler Jugend (q.v.) after the Nazi seizure of power.

Großdeutschland or **Großdeutsches Reich.** Greater Germany, including the Volksdeutsche (q.v.), people of German "race" and language who had been kept out of the German community after 1918. Großdeutschland—a tenet of pangermanismus (q.v.) or pan–Germanism—was intended to unite all German-speaking people in Europe in one political state. The idea originated in the early 19th century, and was presented by Ernst Moritz Arnd and others. In theory Greater Germany included: Austria; Luxemburg; Sudetenland, Bohemia and Moravia in Czechoslovakia; Memel, Upper Silesia and Posnania in Poland; Schleswig-Holstein in Denmark; Eupen-Malmédy in Belgium; and Alsace-Lorraine in France. As for the German-speaking part of Switzerland, its neutrality was respected by the Nazis for financial and diplomatic reasons. The Germans of south Tyrol, too, were left alone because of the alliance with Mussolini's Fascist Italy. There were also supporters of the Kleindeutsche Lösung ("Lesser German solution"), which sought only to unify the northern German states (not including Austria) under the leadership of the Kingdom of Prussia. The term was also given to a World War II armored Heer elite unit: Panzer-Grenadier-Division Großdeutschland.

Großraumwirtschaft. Contintental economic zone similar to Lebensraum (q.v.).

Groß-Rosen. Nazi concentration camp located near Stiegau in Lower Silesia, Poland. The camp was established in mid–1940 as a subcamp to Sachsenhausen. It became an independent concentration/work camp in May 1941, intended to exploit a large stone quarry owned by the SS-Deutsche Erd-und Steinwerke GmbH. The camp soon grew in size, and inmates included mostly Jews from all over Europe, but also political prisoners, Russian POWs, and Nacht und Nebel Erlaß (q.v.) prisoners from Poland, Hungary, Belgium, France, the Netherlands, Greece, Yugoslavia, Slovakia, and Italy. They were put to work in such appalling conditions and treated so badly that life expectancy was less than two months. At its peak activity in 1944, the Groß-Rosen complex had up to sixty subcamps located in eastern Germany and occupied Poland. A total of 125,000 inmates of various nationalities passed through the complex during its existence, of whom an estimated 40,000 died on site and in evacuation transports. The camp was liberated by the Russian army on February 14, 1945.

Gruppe. Generic term for group.

(1) The Gruppe was the smallest unit in the German infantry, composed of eight or ten soldiers under command of a Gefreiter (corporal).

(2) In the SA and SS, the Gruppe was a unit as large as a division, composed of several brigades under command of a Gruppenführer (major general in the SA or lieutenant general in the SS).

(3) In the Luftwaffe a Gruppe numbered about forty airplanes. It was a subdivision of a Geschwader (q.v.).

Gruppenführer (Gruf.) Rank of major general in the SA. Rank of lieutenant general in the SS and Waffen-SS, commanding a division.

Gruppenführer Winter. General Winter, the ironic nickname given to the extremely cold winter of 1941–1942, which was a terrible ordeal for the ill-prepared German troops engaged in the Russian campaign.

Guderian, Heinz (1888–1954). German general, a specialist in the innovative use of armor and Blitzkrieg (q.v.) tactics. Guderian never seriously questioned the objectives of Nazi policy. Like many other German senior officers, he was a gifted but blinkered soldier.

Guernica y Luno. A small town situated east of Bilbao (Baskenland) in Spain. On April 26, 1937,

Infanterie Gruppe.

the town was bombed by the air unit of the German Kondor Legion (q.v.) The great painter Pablo Picasso (1881–1973) made an allegorical painting in commemoration of this tragic and phenomenally cruel event. Picasso's *Guernica*—a remarkable monochromic painting in white, gray and black—is exhibited in the Prado Museum in Madrid, Spain.

Gummimantel. Rubberized waterproof overcoat, often worn by motorcyclists and military police. See Mantel.

Gummimantel.

Günther, Hans F.K. (1891–1968). German social anthropologist who developed racist theories similar to those of Joseph Gobineau (q.v.) and Houston Stewart Chamberlain (q.v.). Günther's views became Nazi doctrine and he was regarded as the official spokesman for Hitler's racial ideology.

Gypsies or **Roma.** An ethnic group that originated from India (their language, Romany, is directly descended from Sanskrit). For unknown reasons, they took to a wandering lifestyle in the late Middle Ages. Eventually they reached Europe and became part of the ethnic mix of many countries. Because they were nomadic strangers to many of the people among whom they moved, strong prejudices grew, and indeed continue to this day. Although they were indisputably "Aryan" according to the Nazi racial typology, they were classed Fremdrasse (race alien), and divided into several tribes: Sinti (German), Rom (Hungarian), Gelderati, Lowari, Lalleli (Bohemia-Moravia), and Balkan Gypsies. Before the war they were discriminated against and pursued relentlessly, and from 1942 onward physical elimination started, first by Einsatzgruppen (q.v.) and later in elaborate extermination camps. Total losses are hard to ascertain, but perhaps some 200,000 Gypsies were deported and murdered by the Nazis.

Haarschnitt. Hair cut. German men's hair fashion in the 1930s and 1940s as well as Wehrmacht regulations stipulated a very distinctive soldier's look. Hair was shaved from the neck and tapered up to the top above the ears all the way around. The hair could be long on top, neatly combed and slicked (with pomade or Vaseline) straight back from the forehead. If parted, the part was high on the head.

Habicht Turm. Experimental artillery, a rotating concrete turret designed by General-Major Franz Rollomann Habicht, belonging to the navy engineering corps. Habicht and his team, working in the navy engineer experimental center in Gennevilliers near Paris, France, designed scale models for 38- and 40.6-centimeter guns and one prototype for a 15-centimeter gun. Marshal Rommel visited the center on Saturday, April 1, 1944, and showed enthusiasm for the project. However, Habicht's design was not accepted by the German high command, and only one rotating concrete turret was ever built. Today it is preserved at navy battery MKB Waldam, northeast of Calais, France.

Hakenkreuz. (See illustrations on page 69.) Hooked cross or swastika. The Hakenkreuz is the symbol most readily associated with the Nazis, but they did not invent it. The swastika is an adapted Greek cross with four arms of equal length extended at right angles. The Nazi swastika was often represented standing on one point to give the dynamic impression of an advancing movement. The swastika and the traditional German eagle were combined with a wreath of oak leaves and acorns to form the most distinctive Nazi insignia: the Hoheitszeichen (q.v.). The swastika and national emblem appeared inevitably everywhere in the Third Reich in many shapes and forms, on buildings, uniforms, badges, medals, flags, administrative applications and seals, official mail and printing works, and so on.

Handgranate

Various forms of Hakenkreuzen.

Hakenkreuzbinde. Armband made of red cloth with a black swastika in a white disc. It was worn on the upper left arm by party members, members of Nazi organizations, SA and SS.

Hakenkreuzfahne. Nazi flag consisting of a red background with a black swastika in a white disc.

Halbjude. Half Jew. In Nazi parlance, people with two grandparents of Jewish origin. Also defined as Mischling (q.v.) of the first degree. People with one Jewish grandparent were defined as Vierteljude (quarter–Jew) or Mischling of the second degree.

Halbketten-Zugkraftfahrzeuge. Halftrack. See Panzerspähwagen and Schützenpanzerwagen.

Medium 5-t Büssing-NAG SdKfz 6 halftrack.

Hall of Heroes. See Feldherrn Halle.

Handgranate. Grenade, a small antipersonnel bomb filled with high explosive, mostly thrown by hand for close-quarter warfare. Designed in 1915 and used until 1945, the German Stielhandgranate (stick grenade or "potato masher") was one of the most characteristic weapons associated with World War II German soldiers. The Stielhandgranate weighed about 0.59 kilograms, and it operated with a friction igniter inside the handle. The other type of grenade used by the Germans was the M 1939 Eiergranate (egg grenade), which weighed 0.34 kilograms and had an exploding blast of about 13 meters.

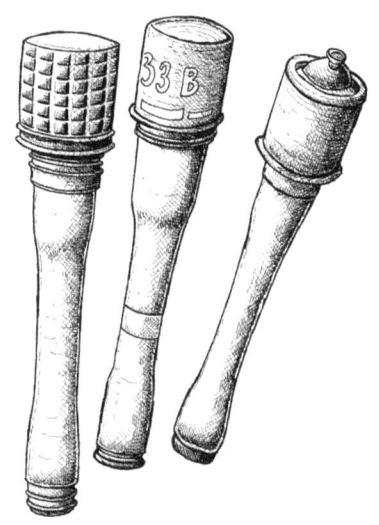

Stielhandgranate.

Igniting the German Stielhandgranate PH 39.

Hanfstängl, Erna (1885–1981). Elder sister of Ernst "Putzi" Hanfstängl (q.v.). Erna was also an acquaintance of Adolf Hitler, and the emerging leader of the NSDAP was romantically involved with this beautiful, charming, cultured and intelligent woman. In the period 1922–1923, there were rumors that the two were lovers and on the point of being engaged. Erna was also a friend of Unity Mitford (q.v.) and lived with her for a while.

Hanfstängl, Ernst (1887–1975). A Harvard-educated and rich German-American businessman who was an intimate of Adolf Hitler in the 1920s and early 1930s. Nicknamed Putzi, Hanfstängl loaned Hitler money for the purchase of the newspaper *Völkischer Beobachter* (q.v.), played piano for him, helped polish his image, and introduced him to Munich high society. Fluent in English, with many connections to higher society in both England and the United States, Putzi became head of the Foreign Press Bureau in Berlin. As the Nazi movement grew in popularity and Hitler in power, Putzi's value lessened. In 1937 he fell out of favor, escaped to England where he was imprisoned for a while and then went to live in the United States. He later worked as adviser to the Harvard Psychological Clinic on senior Nazi personalities, including Hitler. After World War II he returned to Germany and wrote several books about his experiences.

Hannoversche Maschinenbau AG (Hanomag). A company producing military vehicles, notably the SdKfz 251 medium-armored halftrack.

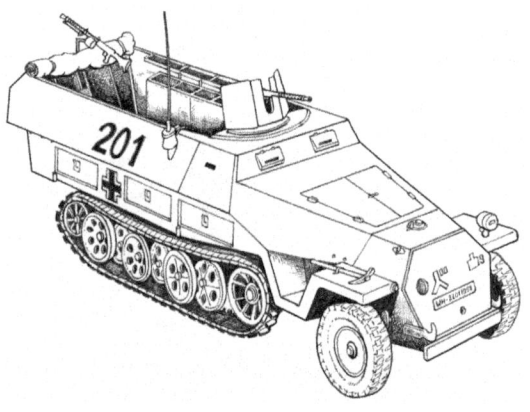

Hanomag SdKfz 251 armored medium halftrack.

Hans Westmar. A Nazi propaganda film retelling of the Horst Wessel legend, made in 1933. *Hans Westmar* (originally titled *Horst Wessel*) was an idealized film biography of the small-time pimp in which all unsavory details of his life were suppressed. As Wessel's actual life and "martyrdom" in a street brawl were laughable, the film was retitled *Hans Westmar* and was recut after a private showing to boost its propaganda value. It had Paul Wegener playing the communist leader, and Emil Lohkamp playing Wessel/Westmar, trying to recruit the East Berlin masses to National Socialism before being shot by the communists. The film imitated Soviet techniques of documentary realism, particularly in the final funeral sequence. It ended with a vision of the Nazis seizing power, the usual hagiography in front of swastika flags and marching masses with martial music thundering. For the same purpose, glorifying the SA, several films were produced in 1933, such as SA-Mann Brand. See "Horst Wessel Lied."

Harzburger Front. An ultra-right-wing political alliance in Weimar Germany formed in October 1931 as an attempt to present a unified opposition to the government of Chancellor Heinrich Brüning. It was a coalition of the national conservative German National People's Party (DNVP) under millionaire press baron Alfred Hugenberg with Adolf Hitler's NSDAP Nazi Party, the leadership of the Stahlhelm paramilitary veterans' association, the Agricultural League and the Pan-German League. As there was strong rivalry between the chief actors, the front was very short-lived.

Hauptamt Persönliche Stab des Reichsführer-SS (Pers. Stab RfSS). Himmler's personal headquarters. This was the top of the labyrinthine SS pyramid headed by Himmler's assistant Karl Wolf and many other secretaries, such as Rudolf Brandt. It was the centre of the Reichsführer's empire where all intelligence, data and information were gathered, where all significant decisions were made, and from where all orders were issued. It was a huge and very important organization as it had direct and absolute command over all SS suborganizations, notably the Allgemeine SS (q.v.), the Totenkopf Wachverbände (q.v.), the SS-VT/Waffen-SS (q.v.) and all the other SS Hauptämter. The Pers. Stab RfSS covered the wide field of activities of Himmler's organization, having power and control over armed forces, intelligence, economics, genocide and so on. The Pers. Stab RfSS also included many permanent, semipermanent or temporary subdepartments directly connected with Himmler's personal interests. See Himmler, Heinrich; and Wewelsburg.

Hauptamt SS. Central office of the SS, responsible for welfare, education, recruitment and training of the SS.

Hauptamt SS-Gericht. SS justice department. This department was concerned with what the SS considered crimes committed by its members and all auxiliary/police personnel in Germany and later in occupied Europe. In October 1939, the SS introduced its own penal code as a form of military justice. The SS-Gericht was headed by Paul Scharfe and after 1942 by Franz Breithaupt. However, Hitler and Himmler had the right to pardon or to overturn any decision made by the martial courts. There were three main sorts of tribunals; the first was the Oberstes SS- und Polizeigericht, established in Munich, which handled serious crimes like corruption, treason, sabotage or attempts against the regime allegedly committed by the rank of Brigadeführer (major general) and higher; the second were SS-und Polizeigerichte, which were established in each SS Abschnitt; the third were field martial courts at division level for minor offenses. At the end of 1943 there were 31 permanent courts and 20 in the field, with a total of 204 judges; between 1939 and 1944, these courts condemned about 1,000 SS men.

Hauptamt Volksdeutsche Mittelstelle (VoMi). Main office for Germanic people. Originally an NSDAP organization, it came under SS's jurisdiction under Werner Lorenz' command. The VoMi—completing the Rasse- und Siedlungshauptamt (RuSHA) (q.v.)—was charged to make contact with and take care of the "racial" Germans living abroad. The VoMi played an important role in infiltrating racial German communities in Austria and Czechoslovakia in the late 1930s, paving the way for the Nazi occupation of these lands. After 1941, the VoMi took a part of the RuSHA's tasks in organizing the settling of German populations in the conquered eastern territories. For this task there was also another organization, the Stabshauptamt of the Reichskommissar für die Festung deutschen Volkstums (StabHa RKFdV, the Reich commission for the consolidation of Germanism) headed by Himmler himself. Entanglement and rivalry between RuSHA, VoMi and StabHa RKFdV were very complex but they allowed Himmler to get the SS involved in Central and Eastern Europe. This led to criminal practices and ethnic atrocities such as confiscation of large agricultural lands and liquidation of entire communities. See Volksbund für das Deutschtum im Ausland.

Hauptkampflinie (HKL). Main resistance line. The line could be composed of mobile troops deployed on the front. It might also be constituted of field or permanent fortifications.

Heer (H). German ground forces. The Heer was sometimes wrongly called Wehrmacht, this term including all three German armed forces: Heer, Kriegsmarine (navy) and Luftwaffe (air force). The ground force was directed by the OKH, Oberkommando des Heeres (q.v.).

Heeresgeistliche. Army chaplain. Chaplains of the Catholic and Protestant Lutheran churches were present in the German army. Clergymen were not supposed to be armed. They were issued the normal army officer's uniform but they were recognizable by their Waffenfarbe (q.v.) which was violet, with a small Christian metal cross placed at the front of the cap between the eagle/swastika and the Reichkokarde (q.v.), a golden crucifix hanging on a chain around the neck, scapulars and rosaries, gray doeskin gloves, gilded and silver-white buttons as well as the collar patches displaying ranks: fieldbishop, senior army chaplain and army chaplain. The role of the army chaplain (Heerespfarrer), or Padre (Feldgeistliche) was similar to the duties they performed in civilian life, such as conducting services of mass, communion, marriage, funerals, and so on.

Heeresgruppe. Army group. Commanded by a Generalfeldmarschall, this was an organizational formation made up of a number of armies. It was the largest German military group during World War II. Usually it consisted of hundreds of units and hundreds of thousands of men, operating widely dispersed at the front. In the period 1939–1940 the German Heer (ground army) was composed of three army groups: Heeresgruppe A, commanded by von Rundstedt, Heeresgruppe B, commanded by Bock, and Heeresgruppe C, commanded by Leeb. Another example would be Heeresgruppe Africa, which controlled all units fighting in North Afrika at the time of its formation. All Heeresgruppen were placed under command of the Oberkommando des Heeres (q.v.)—OKH, or army high command directed by General Brauchitsch and Chief of Staff Halder. The OKH was a part of the Oberkommando der Wehrmacht (q.v.)—Wehrmacht high command, directed by Hitler and chief of staff Keitel. See Infanterie.

Heeresküstenartillerie (HKA). Army coastal artillery. The HKA, hastily created in the summer of 1940, was on the whole ill-prepared, lacking instruments and qualified personnel, and missing guns and bunkers specially adapted to this function. Furthermore, the Heeresküstenartillerie was considered by the navy more as a rival than as a partner. The HKA was organized on the navy model and divided in army coastal batteries (Heeresküstenbatterien or HKB). The general structure of an HKB was rather similar to a MKB (navy battery). It included a fire leading post called Befehlstand (command station) giving orders and firing instructions to four, six or even ten guns placed in bunkers or open emplacements; various shelters, ammunitions stores and service facilities were installed behind the firing line. See Atlantikwall.

Heeresküstenbatterie (HKB). Army coastal battery. See Atlantikwall and Heeresküstenartillerie.

Heeresstreifendienst. Army patrol service, tasked with traffic control duties and maintaining order and discipline in garrison areas. The Luftwaffe and the Kriegsmarine had their own street patrol services but all were combined in 1943 to form the Wehrmachtstreifendienst (armed forces patrol service).

"Heidi Heido Heida" ("Ein Heller und ein Batzen"). A popular World War II German military march song. The lyrics were written in the 1830s by Albert Graf von Schlippenbach, but the composer remains unknown. The lyrics are not bellicose at all but rather funny, about drinking and girls.

Heil Hitler! "Hail Hitler!" or "Long live Hitler!"—part of the Nazi salute. See Deutscher Gruß.

Heil Hitler! Juda Verrecke! "Hail Hitler! Death to the Jews!"—another favorite Nazi slogan.

Heimat. Fatherland, homeland.

Heimatabend. Patriotic evening. This term was applied to evening meetings and gatherings attended by Nazi members, including boys and girls of the Hitler Jugend (q.v.).

Heimatflak. Home air defense artillery. The Heimatflak was manned by boys and young men of the Hitler Jugend (q.v.) and German workers. Antiaircraft guns, searchlights and fire control devices were set up in case of Allied bombardments. Heimatflak units generally received poor training and thus were of questionable use.

Heimatroman. Patriotic novel, a literary form that focused on national mystique and regional and traditional Germanness. This was of course favored and encouraged by the Nazis. See Literature in the Third Reich.

Heimatschuß. Homeland shot; in military slang a wound not severe enough to be permanently disabling, but of sufficient severity to require evacuation from the battlefront. The German soldier's equivalent of the American G.I.'s "million-dollar wound" or the British soldier's "blighty wound."

Heimtücke Gesetz. Treason Law, a special regulation starting in December 1934 designed to punish wartime offenders and political dissenters.

Heimwehr Dantzig. Defense force of Danzig. This force was raised in August 1939 with the SS Totenkopf (q.v.) battalion Götz and local volunteers in order to suppress the Polish forces in the town of Danzig. On September 1, 1939, the SS Heimwehr Dantzig attacked the Polish garrison with the help of the German navy. After the victory, SS Heimwehr Dantzig became a Kampfgruppe (q.v.) headed by Gauleiter Forster. It was used to pacify by force and retaliation in the city of Danzig. Later in World War II, the unit was incorporated into the Waffen-SS 3rd Panzerdivision Totenkopf.

Heinkel (He). Professor Dr. Ernst Heinkel (1888–1958) was the designer of significant airplanes in World War I, including the Albatross types. In 1922 Ernst Heinkel created an industrial company building civilian aircraft at Warnemünde and established another plant in Sweden. After the Nazi seizure of power in early 1933, the Heinkel Company produced the Heinkel He 51 biplane fighter and the highly successful medium twin-engine monoplane bomber Heinkel He111 (5,656 built). There were also jet-engine planes produced by the advanced Heinkel. As early as August 1939 the company designed the world's first jet aircraft, the Heinkel He 178. The experimental Heinkel He 162 Salamander was a cheap combat jet-engine fighter introduced late in the war. The Heinkel He 280 was the first efficient twin jet engine combat plane, but the Luftwaffe preferred the Messerschmitt Me 262.

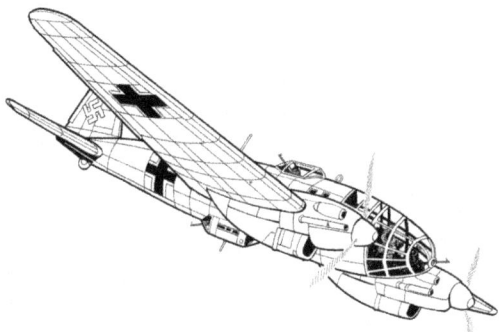

Heinkel He 111.

Heldengedenktag. Heroes Memory Day, March 16, instituted in 1934 to commemorate fallen soldiers of World War I, but also Nazi "heroes and martyrs" fallen in action before the seizure of power. See Feiertagen.

Helferin. Uniformed female auxiliary. During the war, many male Army personnel were drafted for service at the front. Women replaced them in subaltern posts such as teleprinter operator, telephone or wireless operator and other administrative areas. In 1944 there were about 100,000 women serving as auxiliaries to the Luftwaffe (q.v.) in air warning, telephone and teletype departments.

Helferin.

Helfershelfer. Literally "helper's helper." Secondary auxiliary members of the Sicherheitsdienst des Reichsführer SS (q.v.), usually informants who acted from highly questionable and selfish motives.

Helicopter. See Hubschrauber.

Hemmbalk. Strand beam, a beach obstacle mainly used in the Atlantikwall (q.v.) consisting of a tree trunk about 8 meters long or a concrete beam resting on supports. The beam made a 30- to 40-degree angle with the ground. Hemmbalken were placed in alternating rows on the beach with the intention of stranding landing crafts. Its destructive potential was increased by placing sharp blades (Stahlmesser), which would rip boat hulls like can openers. Hemmbalken could also be fitted with antitank mines.

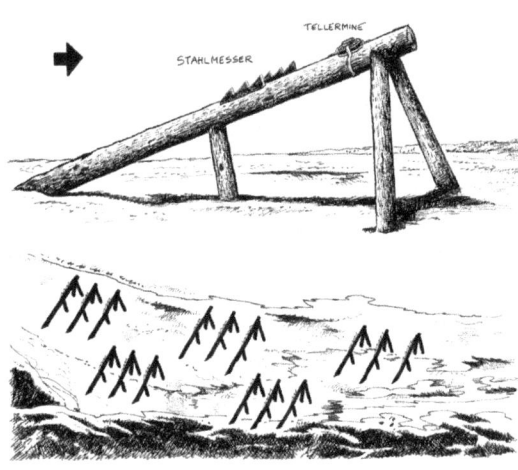

Hemmbalk.

Hemmkurven. Strand bars. A German antitank obstacle designed in 1937 to oppose 36-ton tanks. Hemmkurven were formed of four or five bent steel bars grouped as a unit; each bar was about 2.30 meters high, resting on a strong metal framework and placed at 1.40 meters distance from its neighbor. Obsolete in 1944, Hemmkurven were then used as beach obstacles to strand landing craft in the Atlantikwall (q.v.).

Hendaye. A city in southwest France close to the Spanish border. There, on October 23, 1940, a meeting took place between Hitler and the Spanish dictator Francisco Franco (q.v.). The German dictator tried to convince his Spanish counterpart to join the war on his side, but Franco's demands were unacceptable to Hitler. Actually neither side trusted the other and the meeting ended without any agreement. Spain, which had been bled white by three years of civil war followed by a harsh repression of the defeated Republicans, remained neutral and did not get involved in World War II.

Henschel (Hs). German industrial company. Henschel built airplanes such as the biplane fighter Henschel Hs 123. Other Henschel wartime airplanes include the Recce Hs 126 and the twin-engine Henschel Hs 129 armed with a powerful antitank gun and used as tank killer on the Russian front. The Henschel Company also designed and built locomotives, tanks (notably the Tiger and the Panther), trucks and cars and the Henschel Hs 293 guided antiship missile.

Henschel Hs 126.

Herr. In past and modern German military protocol, "Herr" (meaning lord, mister or sir) is said before rank when addressing a person of higher rank. For example, a lieutenant (Leutnant) would address his captain as "Herr Hauptmann" (Sir Captain).

Herrenvolk. "Master people," according to Nazi ideology. A term expressing the Germanic "Aryan racial superiority." A Herrenmensch (master man) was a member of the Herrenvolk. This term was opposed to Untermensch, "subhuman." See Arisch.

Hess, Rudolf (1894–1987). Hess served in the same regiment as Hitler and later as a junior officer in the German air force during World War I. After that he was a volunteer in the Ritter von Epp Freikorps (q.v.). Rudolf Hess joined the Nazi Party and, having a penchant for occultism, became a member of the Thule Society. He marched with Hitler in the Beer Hall Putsch. Imprisoned with his leader, he took Hitler's dictation of *Mein Kampf* (q.v.) and played a leading part in the reorganization of the NSDAP. After the seizure of power in January 1933, Hess, burning with a religious fervor for Hitler, became Stellvertreter (Deputy Leader). By 1939, however, his great days were over, and Hess felt himself cut off from his idol. Probably to recover favor, the unbalanced Hess flew to Britain on May 10, 1941, in order to persuade the British to make peace with Nazi Germany and align with Hitler against the Soviet Union. Hess's diplomatic coup failed, and instead he was taken straight into custody and remained in a British prison until the end of World War II. At Nuremberg, Rudolf Hess was tried for war crimes and sentenced to life imprisonment. See Bormann, Martin.

Heu Aktion. Hay Action, an order issued in June 1941 by Alfred Rosenberg for the rounding up in Poland of 40,000 to 50,000 young people for shipment to Germany as forced labor.

Heute Deutschland! Morgen die Welt! "Today Germany, Tomorrow the World!" A popular Nazi slogan illustrating the thirst for power and the drive for world domination.

Heydrich, Reinhard (1904–1942). Reinhard Tristan Eugen Heydrich was a member of a Freikorps in 1919 and 1920. He enlisted in the German navy in 1922. He was promoted to the rank of leutnant in 1926 but was expelled in 1931 for dishonorable conduct towards a young woman. In that year he became a member of the NSDAP, became a close associate of Himmler, and was promoted to head of the SS Sicherheitsdienst (SD). In 1936, Heydrich was chief of the Sicherheitspolizei (q.v.) and Sicherheitsdienst (q.v.), and head of the Reichssicherheitshauptamt (q.v.) in 1939. In this function, Heydrich was one of those who organized the machinery of the Holocaust (q.v.). In September 1941 he was promoted to Reichsprotektor in Bohemia-Moravia. On July 4, 1942, he was assassinated by the Czech resistance. In retaliation, the Germans destroyed the village of Lidice and murdered the whole male population. See also, Himmler Heinrich, and Kaltenbrunner, Ernst.

Hierl, Konstantin (1875–1955). A veteran of World War I, a Nazi activist starting in 1927, and a high-ranking member of the NSDAP in charge of what was known as Organization Department II, Hierl was appointed Reichsarbeitsführer (Reich Labor Leader) in 1933, heading the Reichsarbeitsdienst (q.v.) until the very end of World War II. Hierl was also appointed Reichsleiter in 1936 and a Reichsminister in 1943. Hierl survived World War II, was tried as a major offender by the Nuremberg tribunal in 1946, and spent five years in prison. He was released soon after, and died in 1955.

Hilfsgemeinschaft auf Gegenseittigkeit (HiaG). Mutual Aid Association. A welfare organization for veterans of the Waffen-SS in need. Created after the end of World War II, the association aimed at helping veterans who had fallen on hard times or who found it difficult to find work. It also tried lobbying the German federal government for financial, personal and political rehabilitation. The successive chairmen were former SS Obergruppenführer (General) Paul Hausser and former SS Brigadeführer (Major General) Kurt "Panzer" Meyer. The HiaG's headquarters was set up in Lüdenscheid in the province of Westphalia. In 1993, the HIAG evolved into an organization called "Kriegsgräberstiftung-Wenn alle Brüder schweigen" ("Foundation for War Graves—When All Brothers Are silent"), whose objective is to raise money for the maintenance of veterans' cemeteries.

Hilfskasse. Relief Fund, a special account used to help members of the Nazi Party who had been injured and disabled in street fighting against the communists. The Hilfskasse was set up in 1930, and was administered by Martin Bormann (q.v.).

Hilfskreuzer. Auxiliary cruiser or sea raider. The German navy requisitioned several civilian merchant ships and converted them into armed corsairs with hidden guns and concealed torpedo-launching tubes. Displaying various flags, their mission was to avoid Allied warships and instead approach unsuspecting Allied merchant ships and either capture or sink them. See *Atlantis*.

Hilfspolizei (HiPo). Auxiliary police, groups of SA deputized into the regular police force in the period February–August 1933. The HiPo had been formed by Hermann Göring (then occupying the function of Minister of interior in Prussia) in late February 1933. The result was a rampage of law and order directed against political enemies of the Nazi movement, an official sanctioned continuation of previously illegal methods. The extra-legal SA was involved in outbreaks of violence, and to resist a gang of SA men was to confront the power of the official state. The SA Hilfspolizei organized vast raids, searched houses, arrested and kidnapped people, confiscated goods, held interrogations and imprisoned suspects. Once the Nazi dictatorship was established, the usefulness of the SA Hilfspolizei was limited to Germany's new leadership. In August 1933 the SA were no longer part of the auxiliary police organized by Göring, and a year later the SA leadership was murdered by the Nazis themselves. See Sturm Abteilung der NSDAP.

Hilfswerk Mutter und Kind. Mother and Child Welfare Association, a special social office set up for the benefit of "Aryan" mothers and children. The office was administered by the Nationalsozialistische Volkswohlfahrte (q.v.), the Nazi People's Welfare Organization.

Hilfswillige (HiWi). Non-German voluntary worker, especially Russians and Ukrainians who joined the German army during the last years of World War II. In return for a precarious preferential treatment, HiWis fulfilled menial duties, manned antiaircraft guns, helped build and manned fortifications, and performed all sorts of noncombatant duties. They did not necessarily have any commitment to the Nazi ideology, but only wished to survive by escaping from the inhumane conditions suffered in the camps by Russian prisoners. Of 5,754,000 Russians captured by the Germans, 3,700,000 died. About one million prisoners chose to take some form of service as HiWis (Hilfswillingen, pl.).

Himmler, Heinrich (1900–1945). Too young to take part in World War I, Himmler obtained a diploma in agriculture from Munich Technical High School, where he studied from 1918 to 1922. After working briefly as a salesman for a firm of fertilizer manufacturers, the young Himmler joined the paramilitary, nationalist Freikorps (q.v.), and participated in the Munich Beer Hall Putsch of November 1923 as standard-bearer at the side of Ernst Röhm (q.v.). In January 1929, he was appointed head of Hitler's personal bodyguard, the Schutz-Staffeln (q.v.), at that time a small body of less than 300 men, which was subsequently to become under his leadership an all-embracing empire within the Nazi state. A very able organizer and administrator, meticulous, calculating and ambitious, Himmler was also a curious mixture of bizarre, romantic fantasy and cold, unscrupulous efficiency. His astonishing capacity for work and irrepressible power-lust showed itself in his rapid promotion and his perfecting of the methods of organized state terrorism against Jews, political opponents and others counter to the Nazi regime. The diabolically skillful organizer of rationalized modern extermination methods, and the supreme technician of totalitarian police power who saw himself as a reincarnation of the pre–Christian Duke of Saxony, Henry the Fowler (861–936), Himmler fell out of favor in the last month of World War II, and committed suicide. See Himmler-Kersten Pakt.

Himmler-Kersten Pakt. A late agreement signed by Chief of the SS Heinrich Himmler in March 1945 when the Third Reich was collapsing. Himmler, the very man who directed the Holocaust, foolishly hoped to play a political role in postwar Germany. Felix Kersten, Himmler's personal doctor and masseur, arranged a meeting with Norbert Masur, a member of the Swedish branch of the World Jewish Congress. "In the name of Humanity," the Reichsführer SS agreed to spare the lives of the remaining 60,000 Jews left in Nazi concentration camps days before their liberation by the Allies. On behalf of Himmler, Felix Kersten also made contact with the Swedish diplomat Count Folke Bernadotte in order to start peace negotiations with the Allies. When Hitler heard of the agreement and attempt of negotiation, he was furious and stripped Himmler of all his ranks and functions.

Hindenburg, Paul Ludwig von Beneckendorff und (1847–1934). German field marshal during World War I and second president of the Weimar Republic from 1925 to 1934. His presidency was wracked by political instability, economic depression, and the rise to power of Adolf Hitler, whom he appointed chancellor in 1933.

Hindenburg line. See Siegfried lines.

HiPo. See Hilfspolizei.

Hitler, Adolf (1889–1945). Führer und Reichskanzler (leader and chancellor) of Germany from 1933 to his death in 1945. He was leader of the National Socialist German Workers Party (better known as the Nazi Party). Hitler rose from the lowest of origins to lead one of the most powerful nations in Europe with devastating early success but ultimate failure. He legally seized power in January 1933 and began an expansion of Germany through the annexation of Austria and invasion of Czechoslovakia. Germany's invasion of Poland provoked World War II. At the height of the Third Reich, the armies of Nazi Germany and its allies controlled the larger part of Europe. Hitler's ambitions went further, embracing notions of a thousand-year Reich, some form of world order under his command and war and racial determinism in pursuit of which he and the Nazis were responsible for the death over 11 million people, including 6 million Jews, in a genocide now known as the Holocaust (q.v.). The planned "thousand-year Reich" ended shortly after his death by suicide, in the Führerbunker (q.v.) in Berlin during the final days of World War II.

Hitler, Alois. born Alois Schicklgruber (1837–1903). Austrian civil servant and Adolf Hitler's father. See Pölzl, Klara, and Schicklgruber, Maria Anna.

Hitler Gruß. Hitler salute. See Deutscher Gruß.

Hitler Jugend (HJ). (See illustrations on pages 77 and 78.) Hitler Youth. The Jugendbewegung (youth movement) was created in March 1922 with the purpose of organizing young Germans within the Nazi Party (NSDAP). The movement, regrouping less than 2,000 members, officially became a Nazi Party organization (see Gliederungen der NSDAP) called Hitler Jugend, or HJ, in May 1925. In October 1931, the young and dynamic Baldur von Schirach became its leader. HJ boys were paramilitarily organized, and deeply and fanatically indoctrinated in Nazi racist ideology. The HJ was a kind of juvenile brotherhood with sectarian rules, customs and rituals. The boys had insignia, flags, banners, badges and an emblem stating "Blood and Honour." Girls were not forgotten; they could join the Hitler Youth in two suborganizations: the Jungmädelbund, or league of young girls (ages 10 to 14), then the Bund Deutscher Mädschen (BDM), or German girls league (ages 15 to 18). Girls from 18 to 21 became part of the Glaube und Schönheit (q.v.) association. Units and ranks of HJ were copied from the army and the other Gliederungen der NSDAP. From ages 10 to 14, boys were called Pimpfen (meaning "little boys"), and belonged to the Deutsches Jungvolk (DJ, or German young people). From 14 to 18 years old, members were Hitlerjung (Hitler's boys), and belonged to the Hitlerjugend proper. As young as 10 years old, all boys and girls had to swear an oath of loyalty and obedience. HJ members wore a uniform composed of a light brown shirt, a black scarf, an armband with swastika, black shorts, a waist belt, a shoulder belt and a dagger, white stockings and heavy marching shoes. The HJ was by no means an innocent youth movement. At twelve, boys trained in the use of rifles and machine guns, and at fourteen they attended military training camps for one month. Teenagers ages 16 to 18 had to serve in the Reichsarbeitsdienst (q.v., the German labor service). Discipline, hierarchy, and physical training were strictly observed and conducted by Hitler Jugend staff. At the end of 1933 the HJ counted two million members, and in 1935, four million. In 1936, BDM and HJ membership became compulsory for all youth between 6 and 18 years old. The HJ was a mainstay of the Nazi regime, and its influence became pervasive in Germany. It was a propaganda machine in the schools. When World War II started in 1939, eight million HJ boys and girls were available to replace the mobilized soldiers as auxiliaries in various branches of production, agriculture, transport and administration. Education, indoctrination, esprit de corps, ranks and training foredoomed the HJ to get more and more involved in military activities. When the Allied bombardments began to strike Germany, HJ boys were issued uniforms and equipment to serve in the Feuerwehren (fire brigades), Feuerschutzpolizei and Luftschutzpolizei (emergency and rescue squads as well as police units); they were allowed to enlist in the transport corps, Nationalsozialistische Kraftfahrer Korps (q.v.). As the war progressed, the youthful loyalty of its members was ruthlessly exploited. By mid–1943, a new Luftwaffe flak artillery branch was created, called Heimatflak (homeland antiaircraft artillery); the Hitler Jugend was encouraged to serve in it as Luftwaffe-Helfern (air force auxiliaries). The Hitler Jugend's members were also recruited in the Streifendienst, a patrol/police auxiliary service officered by the SS, and principally intended to capture shot-down Allied airmen. The final step towards complete militarization was reached in 1943. The HJ leader Arthur Axmann (who replaced Baldur von Schirach in 1940) encouraged HJ members to join a special Waffen-SS unit composed of HJ boys born in 1926. The 12th SS Panzerdivision Hitler Jugend was created in June 1943. During the last months of the war, the Hitler Jugend became an important part of the Volkssturm (q.v.), and during the Battle of Berlin many teenagers fought in the front line; few survived. A number of HJ were also enlisted into the werewolf scheme (see Werwolf).

Hitler Jugend member with flag.

Hitler

Hitler Youth knife with inscription "Blut und Ehre!" ("Blood and Honor!") on the blade.

Hitler Jugend Feuerwehrscharen. Young volunteers of the Hitler Youth who formed firefighting companies. They were trained, equipped, and placed at the disposal of the local fire and police officers.

Die Hitler Jugend. Idee und Gestalt. *The Hitler Youth. Idea and Form.* A book written by Baldur von Schirach (q.v.) and published in Berlin in 1934. The book was not a success and was described in 1941 by Schirach's press agent Günther Kaufmann as being entirely "outdated in all sections."

Hitlerism. Another term for Nazism.

Hitlerproleten. Hitler's proletariat. The term used by Berlin working-class Nazis to designate themselves in order to distinguish themselves from the rest of the (communist and socialist) proletariat.

Hitler's bunker. Hitler's headquarters under the Reich Chancellery in Berlin. See Führersbunker.

Hitler's citizenship. By birth Adolf Hitler was Austrian. However, he dodged the military draft in Austria, and thus lost his nationality, which made him stateless for some years. At the outbreak of World War I, he was accepted in the German army, apparently with no check on his nationality. After the abortive Beer Hall Putsch, the German authorities jailed Hitler and tried to deport him "home" to Austria. The Austrian government refused to accept the stateless troublemaker, pointing out that he had served in the German army, which effectively negated his Austrian citizenship. In February 1932 the stateless champion of German nationalism was finally made honorary Councillor to the State of Brunswick legation in Berlin, thus automatically acquiring German citizenship only months before becoming chancellor.

Hitler-Stalin-Pakt. Nazi-Soviet pact signed in Moscow on August 23, 1939, by Joachim von Ribbentrop and Vyacheslav Molotov, both ministers of foreign affairs. The pact stipulated friendship, nonaggression and economic cooperation. There was also a secret protocol in which they agreed to invade and divide the doomed Poland. The pact came as a bombshell to the French and British Allies who had been making tentative moves towards Stalin. Yet everyone — Germans, Russians and all other political observers — knew it was an unnatural alliance, for Hitler had been battling communism for two decades, and Stalin had denounced the Nazis as fascist beasts. In the very short term, both dictators saw benefits in the pact. This allowed Hitler to have a free hand to launch his campaign in the West against France and England without the fear of a two-front war. It allowed Stalin to gain time for the reorganization of his forces, and gave him a wide zone of influence in Eastern Europe.

Hitler's testament. Before committing suicide on April 30, 1945, Hitler dictated his political testament. In the first part, he defended his work and career and placed the blame for World War II on international Jewry. In the second part, he expelled from the NSDAP the men whom he regarded as traitors to his cause, notably Hermann Göring (q.v.) and Heinrich Himmler (q.v.).

Hitlers Zweites Buch. See *Mein Kampf*.

HiWi. See Hilfswillinge.

HJ. See Hitler Jugend.

Hochleitstand. (See illustrations on page 79.) A nonstandardized concrete fire control tower. These huge works — particularly imposing on the British Channel Islands — represented naval architecture designs put in place to allow calculators and observers a large, panoramic view over the horizon. See Atlantikwall and Leitstand.

Höckerhindernisse. "Dragon's teeth," a permanent antitank obstacle. The Höckerhindernisse was formed of several tiers of concrete blocks whose distance and height were calculated so as

Höhere SS- und Polizeiführer

Hochleitstand Begot at Plouharnel, France.

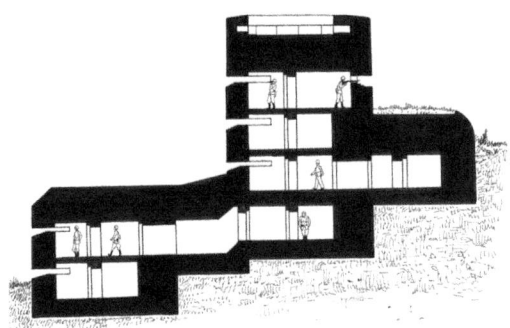

Cross-section of Hochleitstand Gull Bay at Guernsey (British Channel Islands).

Höckerhindernisse model 1942.

wreath containing the NSDAP's swastika. It was worn as a cloth badge over the right breast pocket by all ranks of the German army, and on the upper right arm by the SS. In a smaller metal version it decorated all army cloth headgear. It was used by the army starting with the seizure of power in 1933. The Hoheitszeichen also existed in the form of a seal stamped on all army, police, party and civil administrative official cards, IDs, papers and applications.

Hoheitszeichen.

to make crossing impossible for any tanks. Höckerhindernisse were effective but very expensive and time-consuming to build.

Hoffmann, Heinrich (1885–1957). Official photographer to Hitler and the Nazis. Eva Braun (q.v.) was introduced to Hitler by Hoffmann while she was employed as a shop assistant. Owing to his Nazi connection, Hoffmann's business became highly profitable. After the war, in 1947 he was tried for profiteering and heavily fined.

Hoheitszeichen. Official national army emblem. The Hoheitszeichen was a badge combining the traditional German imperial eagle with outstretched wings clutching in its claws an oak

Höhere SS- und Polizeiführer (HSSuPF). Senior SS and police leader. Because of the complexity of the Schutz-Staffeln (q.v.) corps, there was a real danger that some branches and their local suborganizations could split off or become independent; for example the Waffen-SS could be split from the SS and be integrated into the regular German army. To prevent centrifugal movements and separatist tendencies within the SS, Heinrich Himmler (q.v.) created in November 1937 the function of Höhere SS- und Polizeiführer. These senior officers were selected inspectors who represented personally the Reichsführer at regional Oberabschnitt level. The HSSuPf enjoyed vague, illegal, and effective prerogatives allowing them to coordinate and maintain the cohesion of the SS and control local NSDAP workers, policemen, Allgemeine SS members, and to watch over the regular Army Wehrkreise. However, the task of the HSSuPf was not always easy, and it gave rise to numerous complaints, quarrels and conflicts as the local Allgemeine SS Oberabschnitt leaders, NSDAP functionaries and local Ordnung Polizei officers did not want to have their power diminished or checked by an outsider. In many cases only the Höhere SS- und Polizeiführer who combined this function and that of the SS Oberabschnittführer could actually impose his authority. After the outbreak of World War II, the Höhere SS- und Polizeiführer network was extended to the occupied territories where the populations were much more unreliable and hostile than in Germany. HSSuPf were then no longer political inspectors but dreaded Befehlshaber — police and military commanders with reinforced power, who conducted and coordinated the intelligence, repression and retaliation actions of the local police and security services (SD, Gestapo, Orpo), but also organized the liquidation of entire populations in Poland and Russia by murder squads (Einsatzkommando) and in extermination camps. They might also conduct military and "peacekeeping" operations involving Waffen-SS and Wehrmacht units against revolts in ghettoes or resistance movements. In late 1944 and 1945, Himmler promoted many HSSuPF to the ranks of Gruppenführer or Obergruppenführer (generals) in the Waffen-SS. This was apparently to give them a status of combatant and thus place them under protection of the Hague Convention rules of warfare.

Holidays in the Third Reich. See Feiertagen and Parteitagen.

Holocaust. Holocaust (from the Greek *holókaustos*). *Hólos* means "whole" and *kaustós*, "burnt." The term designates the genocide (q.v.) of approximately six million European Jews during World War II, a program of systematic state-sponsored murder by Nazi Germany throughout Nazi-occupied territory. Also known as Shoah ("catastrophe") in Hebrew.

Homosexuality in the Third Reich. Homosexuality had been outlawed in Germany under the Penal Code of 1871, but in the liberal climate of Weimar Germany, and especially of Berlin with its café life, bars, cabarets and nightclubs, the law was relaxed and there had been proposals for repeal. After the seizure of power by the Nazis in January 1933, homosexuality was strongly repressed. According to obsessive Nazi concerns about high birthrates, homosexuals merited no mercy. It was more arithmetic than morality; in terms of population policy, homosexuals were zeroes who harmed the community by failing in their duty to produce children. Persecution of male homosexuals varied in intensity throughout the period of the Third Reich. While many members of the performing arts and political leaders (notably the SA leadership) enjoyed an unofficial immunity, police supervision, castration, imprisonment in concentration camps, and the death penalty were included in the range of punishments applied to others. Lesbianism, too, was forbidden, but persecution was generally on a much smaller scale. It presented no practical reproductive problems because even a married lesbian could and must bear children at the behest of her spouse.

Horchgerät. Sound locator. The Horchgerät — rather in the manner of a cupped ear or an ear trumpet — was a mobile, orientable acoustic double sound amplifier horn (much more accurate and sensitive than the human ear), some with microphones incorporated to detect sound made by aircraft propellers. They made it possible to warn of the approach of planes, for searchlights to find and illuminate targets, and for antiaircraft artillery to fire. Developed by the British and the Germans as early as 1915, this detection method was discontinued for air defense when, by 1942, radar made it obsolete.

Horchgerät (sound locator).

"**Horst Wessel Lied.**" A song written by a young Nazi student, a member of the SA who made a living from prostitution. Horst Wessel (1907–1930) was a small-time pimp who was killed in February 1930 in the early Kampfzeit, not for political reasons but during a fight in the criminal world. The Nazi Party made a martyr and a hero of him by proclaiming that he had been murdered by communists. Wessel's real murderer, named Ali Höhler, was later killed by SA men. Horst Wessel's song, also called "Die Fahne Hoch" (q.v.), became the official NSDAP anthem. Horst Wessel was the inspiration for heroic propaganda movies such as *SA-Mann Brand*, and *Hans Westmar* (q.v.) made in 1933. In 1944 the hero's name was even given to a Waffen-SS unit, the 18th Freiwillige Panzergrenadier Division Horst Wessel.

Hose. Trousers. The German soldiers usually wore dark gray Hose with a belt or suspenders. The trousers had two side pockets; they were straight legged and cut in such a way as to be fairly high waisted. Some NCOs, officers and generals wore riding breeches and high leather riding boots with adjustable straps at the top, sometimes with spurs attached. Generals' trousers were decorated with a double red band running down the outside seam of the leg.

Höss, Rudolf (1900–1947). A veteran of World War I and the postwar Freikorps (q.v.) and an early Nazi, Höss joined the SS and worked at Dachau (q.v.) in 1934 and Sachsenhausen in 1938. From 1940 to 1943 he was in command of Auschwitz (q.v.) and was noted for his brutal efficiency. So successful was Höss that he was appointed deputy inspector general of the SS-WVHA, controlling concentration camps and SS businesses. At his trial, Höss explained that the extermination of millions of people was only carrying out orders. Höss was hanged in Auschwitz in 1947. See Wirtschafts-und Verwaltungshauptamt (WVHA).

Hossbach Niederschrift. Memorandum or recorded by Colonel Friedrich Hossbach, Hitler's military adjutant from 1934 to 1938. The Hossbach Memorandum, sometimes known as the Hossbach Protocol, was the record of a secret conference held on November 5, 1937, during which Hitler informed his closest advisers that he planned war. He outlined the steps he intended to take in achieving his goals, notably autarky. He also defined Lebensraum (q.v.), war of conquest, and enslavement of the conquered. The Hossbach Memorandum was introduced in evidence before the International Military Tribunal at Nuremberg in November 1945.

Hubschrauber. Helicopter. The first helicopter, the autogyro, was designed by Juan de la Cierva in 1923. In 1936 the first practical vertical takeoff piston-engine Focke Wulf 61 flew at a speed of 76 miles per hour to an altitude of 11,000 feet. Other types designed by the Germans were the Flettner Kolobri ("hummingbird") and the heavier Drache ("kite"). In spite of this development, the military use of helicopters in World War II was extremely limited. It was not until 1946 that the American Bell 47 really met military requirements.

Hubschrauber: the Flettner Fl 282 Kolibri.

Hundertschaft. Action squad of one hundred SS men of the Totenkopfverbände (SS-TV, q.v.), part of the SS Hauptamt headed by Obergruppenführer August Heißmeyer. Formed in 1936, they were employed as guards in the concentration camps. They were originally organized in Hundertschaften (groups of 100 men) but their growth necessitated the constitution of military regiments with structure and ranks similar to that of the Allgemeine SS (q.v.).

"I decide who is or is not a Jew." See "Wer Juden ist, bestimme ich."

IG Farben AG. Short for Interessen Gemeinschaft Farbenindustrie Aktiengesellschaft (Community of Interests of Dye Industries, Incorporated). This was the largest and most powerful German industrial cartel. The name was deceptive, for dyestuffs were only a small part of IG Farben, which in fact had a monopoly over chemical production and trade. The cartel, formed in 1925, was a merger of several companies: BASF, Bayer, Hoechst including Cassella and Chemische Fabrik Kalle, Agfa, Chemische Fabrik Griesheim-Elektron, and Chemische Fabrik-Weiler Ter Meer. It had some 900 factories and controlled about 500 other concerns that produced ammunition, explosives, tires, synthetic coal, synthetic oil, synthetic rubber and many other products that were vital to keep the Nazi war machine rolling. During the war, IG Farben AG employed many slave laborers from the concentration camps in inhuman conditions. The cartel also held the patent for the pesticide Zyklon-B (q.v.), used in Holocaust gas chambers. After the war the directors of IG Farben AG who were involved in Hitler's regime were brought to trial, fined and imprisoned. The cartel was split up into its original constituent companies.

Illustrierter Beobachter. *Illustrated Observer*, a monthly and later (in 1943) biweekly magazine used by the Nazi Party as an illustrated complement to the daily *Völkisher Beobachter* (q.v.). Published by the Eher-Verlag (q.v.), the first edition was issued in November 1926. The *Illustrierter Beobachter* was a popular combination of polemical text and eye-catching photographs designed to appeal to a large public. The last edition appeared in April 1945.

Industrieklub. Industry Club, a wealthy and influential organization of industrial magnates in Düsseldorf who chose to support Hitler after January 1932 as the champion against communism and trade unions. The important financial contribution of the Industry Club paved the way for Hitler's rise to power.

Infanterie (I). Infantry. The German ground army (Heer) was divided into the following units (starting with the smallest): Gruppe (squad); Trupp (troop); Zug (platoon); Kompanie (company); Abteilung (battalion); Regiment (regiment); Brigade (brigade); Infanteriedivision (ID, infantry division); Armee-Korps (army corps); Armee (army); Armeegruppe or Heeresgruppe (army group). The German infantry was placed under command of the OKH (Army High Command) directed by general Brauchitsch and chief of Staff Halder. The OKH was a part of the OKW (Wehrmacht high command) directed by Hitler and Chief of Staff Wilhelm Keitel (q.v.). By 1939 the Wehrmacht had 4.5 million soldiers, including those in training. Fresh divisions were formed for the invasion of the USSR in June 1941, but as the war progressed and as casualties grew, the German army was increasingly obliged to reduce exemptions from conscription to seek out men for combat service and to cast its recruiting net wider. By 1943 Hitler became a prisoner of his own conquests, for he no longer had the military strength to hold them. The Wehrmacht forces were scattered and unable to stem the Allies on all fronts. The disasters at Stalingrad and in northern Africa cost Hitler close to 600,000 soldiers. German morale had plummeted and even the Führer was forced to change his attitude. To replace the genuine Germans, enlistment was gradually imposed on Volksdeutsche (q.v.). Germanic volunteers from northern Europe (Flanders, the Netherlands, Denmark, Norway), considered as people of "similar" blood, were welcomed in army regiments and Waffen-SS formations. The army was also strengthened by allied units composed of pro–Nazi volunteers (Romanian, Hungarian, Italian, Slovak, French, and Spanish). By the end of the war, the foreign contingents represented 10 percent of the army's strength, but they proved unreliable and of limited military use. In 1944 German military manpower continued to shrink, and attempts by Hitler to build up a strategic reserve failed as the new divisions were swallowed up by the eastern front. The great gamble at Kursk in the summer of 1943 cost the Germans dearly and proved their last large-scale offensive on that front. The German military authorities had to manipulate the numerical strength of the divisions, which existed at least on paper. Thus, as World War II drew to a close, infantry divisions were on the whole far smaller than their former establishment. In September 1944, Volksgrenadier Divisions (q.v.) were formed. By the end of the war, it was the entire male population, which was raised to take arms in the so-called Volkssturm (q.v.).

Infanterie Greift an. *Infantry Attacks.* A classic book on innovative infantry tactics written by General Erwin Rommel (q.v.) and published in 1937.

Infanterie Sturmabzeichen. Infantry Assault Badge, instituted in December 1939 by Generaloberst Walther von Brauchitsch for award to all ranks of nonmotorized infantry and mountain infantry units who participated in three different assaults on three different days.

Infanteriedivision (ID). Infantry division. See Infanterie.

Infanteriegeschütz (IG). Infantry gun.

Infanteriehaubitz (IH). Infantry howitzer.

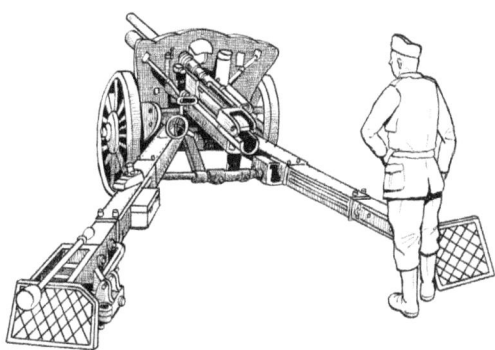

Infanteriehaubitz (howitzer) 10.5-centimeter leFh 18.

Institut für Wehrwissenschaftliche Zweckforschung. See Ahnenerbe Forschungs und Lehrgemeinschaft.

International Military Tribunal (IMT). See Nürnberger Prozeß.

Israel und Sara. By decree of August 1938, all Jewish men and women in Germany and Austria had to add to their names on their official papers the mention of Israel (for the men) and Sara (women). This way, policemen and civil servants could see that the holder was a Jew—a second-class citizen after the promulgation of the racial Nuremberg Laws. See Judenstern and Judenverfolgung.

Iwan. German slang for a Soviet soldier.

Jagdbomber or **Jabo.** Fighter-bomber, light bomber, or ground-attacker aircraft or fighter on strafing mission.

Jagdgeschwader. A Luftwaffe fighter airplane group composed of three Gruppen. See Gruppe.

Jadgkommando. Jagd means hunting, so a jagdkommando was a pursuit or raiding detachment that specialized in hunting partisans and armed resistance groups.

Jagdpanther. The Jagdpanther V (SdKfz 173), produced in February 1944, was a self-propelled gun. It was a converted Panther (q.v.) tank chassis armed with an 8.8 centimeter Pak 43/3 L/71 enclosed in a massive sloping armored superstructure. About 350 were produced and, although it demanded a lot of maintenance, the Jagdpanther V was often considered as the best tank destroyer of World War II.

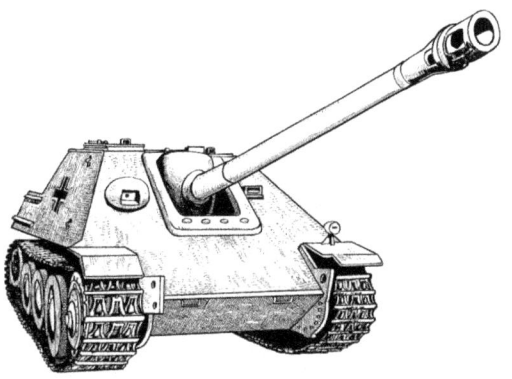

Jagdpanther V SdKfz 173.

Jagdpanzer. Tank hunter, a new type of Panzerjäger (q.v.)—tank destroyer—brought into service in late 1943. The Jagdpanzer was designed to improve the Sturmgeschütz (q.v.) concept.

Jagdtiger (P) SdKfz 184 Elefant. (See illustration on page 84.) The most formidable self-propelled antitank gun used by the Germans. Originally named Ferdinand after its designer, professor Ferdinand Porsche, it was a heavy, solidly armored, hard-hitting powerful tank-hunter built in February 1944 on the chassis of the Porsche Königstiger (Royal Tiger). It weighed 68 tons, had a speed of only 21 kilometers per hour (12.5 miles per hour), a range of 153 kilometers (95 miles), a crew of six, and was armed with one 8.8-centimeter Pak 43/2 L/71 gun and one 7.92 millimeter MG. Only 48 of these fortresses on tracks were manufactured, and they were issued too late to the troops on the field to play a significant role.

Jagdverbände. Hunting detachments formed in October 1944 from the old SS-Jägerbataillone and units of the army's Brandenburgers (q.v.).

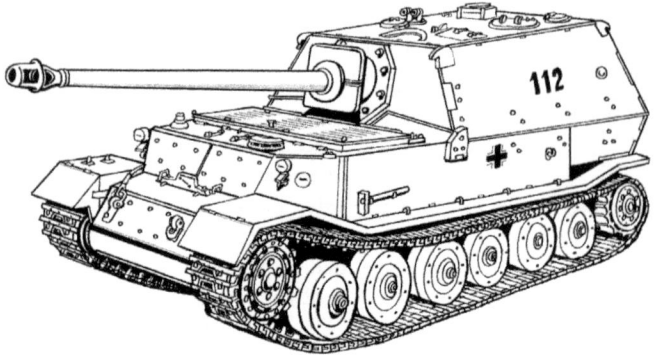

Jagdtiger (P) SdKfz 184 Elefant.

The new formation took over all functions of sabotage and secret operations in occupied territories. These units often included highly trained men of the Fallschirmjäger (paratrooper) formations. The most notorious of these small units was the special Jagdverband Friedenthal led by the famous SS Obersturmbannführer Otto Skorzeny (q.v.).

Jäger. Literally hunter or forester. The term has three meanings.

(1) In the German armed forces, a mobile infantry private, or a rifleman in a mountain or paratrooper unit.

(2) A self-propelled antitank gun mounted on a tank chassis. See Jagdpanther V and Jagdpanzer.

(3) In the Luftwaffe a Jäger was a fighter airplane used for reconnaissance, ground attack, low-level bombing, bomber interception and combat against enemy fighters. See Focke-Wulf and Messerschmitt.

Jedem das Seine. German translation of *Suum cuique*, the Latin expression meaning "to each his own" or "to each what he deserves" made famous by the Roman orator, politician and author Cicero. The phrase was placed over the gate of Buchenwald (q.v.) concentration camp. See Arbeit macht frei.

Jehovah's Witnesses. As pacifists who refuse to do military service or to salute national flags, and as nontrinitarian believers in the imminent return of a Messiah, who considered secular society to be morally corrupt and under the influence of Satan, members of this religious group were victims of ruthless repression in Nazi Germany between 1933 and 1945. Unlike Jews and Gypsies (Romani) who were persecuted on the basis of their ethnicity, Jehovah's Witnesses had the opportunity to escape persecution and personal harm by renouncing their religious beliefs. The Nazi government, although linking Jehovah's Witnesses to "international Jewry," gave them the option of release by signing a document indicating renouncement of their faith, submission to state authority, and support of the German military. Few renounced their faith. Jehovah's Witness prisoners were identified by a purple triangular badge in Nazi concentration camps. See Religion in the Third Reich.

Jerry can. See Benzinekanne.

Jew. See Jude.

Jodl, Alfred (1890–1946). Hitler's chief of Wehrmacht operations from 1939. Jodl was a professional soldier and an outstanding staff officer, but his sense of obedience to orders blinded him to their evil. He was tried among the major Nazi war criminals at Nuremberg, found guilty and hanged.

Joyce, William (1906–1946). Nicknamed Lord Haw-Haw, Joyce was an Irish-American fascist politician and Nazi propaganda broadcaster to the United Kingdom during World War II. Although he claimed German citizenship, he was hanged for treason by the British as a result of his wartime pro–Nazi activities.

Juda Verrecke! "Death to Judaism!" A favorite Nazi anti–Semitic slogan.

Judas-Jude. Judas-Jew, a Nazi insulting term indicating the supposed direct connection between Jews and traitors.

Jude. Jew. The Ahnenpass (q.v.) and Nuremberg Laws classified people as Jews if they descended from three or four Jewish grandparents. A person with one or two Jewish grandparents was a Mischling (q.v.), a "crossbreed" of "mixed blood." One could not become a non–Jew in the eyes of the Nazis by becoming non–practicing, marrying outside the religion, or converting to Christianity. Only people with at least two grandparents of "German blood" could be German citizens. A "half–Jew" not practicing Judaism could not be considered a Jew under the Nazi dictate. See also Ahnenpass, Arisch, Arierparagraph, Endlösung der Judenfrage, and Nürnberger Gesetze.

Juden unerwünscht. Literally, "Jews undesirable," meaning forbidden for Jews. This inscription was placed at the entrance of public parks, movie theaters, public swimming pools, shops and many other public places, which were officially forbidden to the Jews according to the 1935 Nuremberg laws. Like the yellow Judenstern (q.v.), this inscription was another means of public humiliation and discrimination intended to create a massive and continuous anti–Jewish hysteria.

Juden-Christen. Jew-Christian, historically a term used for Jews who converted to Christianity but kept their Jewish cultural heritage and traditions.

Judenfrei. Free of Jews, in the sense of cleansed free. Nazi term to describe cities or areas where total Jewish deportation had taken place.

Judenrat. Jewish council established by the Nazis in ghettoes to have them carry out necessary duties.

Judenreservat. Jews' Reservation. See Ghetto.

Judenstern. Jewish star, also known as star of David or yellow star badge. In Nazi Germany, the Judenstern was a yellow cloth badge in the form of a star of David (with six points), black outline and the word Jude (Jew) in the middle. The badge had to be purchased, and had to be worn visible on the left side of the chest, tightly sewn onto the garment. The badge, one of the numerous humiliations inflicted on the Jewish people, was a further step in the racial repression of the Jews. Its aim was to discriminate, segregate and identify the Jews. It was also intended to facilitate the rounding up of wearers for arrest. Mass deportation of German Jews to the killing centers in the east started in December 1941. In Germany the wearing of the badge was compulsory for Jews older than 6 years of age starting in September 1941 and later for all Jews in the occupied European countries (in France since June 7, 1942). See Pour le Sémit.

Judenverfolgung. Persecution of the Jews. The Nazis considered the Jews their foremost enemies and persecuted them from 1933 onwards. Analysis of Jewishness never went beyond superficial clichés, pseudo-scientific statements, and was more often expressed in the violent images of Julius Streicher's newspaper *Der Stürmer* (q.v.). Persecution of the Jews started in earnest after August 20, 1935, when the Nazi government decided on a firm policy against them. Two main measures were announced at the annual party rally in Nuremberg, becoming known as the Nuremberg Laws. The first law, the Law for the Protection of German Blood and German Honor, prohibited marriages and extramarital intercourse between "Jews" and "Germans," and also forbade the employment of German females under forty-five in Jewish households. The second law, the Reich Citizenship Law, stripped Jews of their German citizenship and introduced a new distinction between "Reich citizens" and "nationals." All this led to the final step, which was the systematic annihilation of the Jews in extermination camps. See Endlösung der Jugenfrage.

Jüdische Grundspekulationsgesellschaften. "Jewish property speculation companies," a Nazi slang term for Jewish businesses.

Jüdischer Wohnbezirk. Jewish district. See Ghetto.

July 1944 Bomb Plot. Unsuccessful attempt to kill Hitler on July 20, 1944. See Stauffenberg, Graf Claus Schenk von; and Zwanzig Juli 1944.

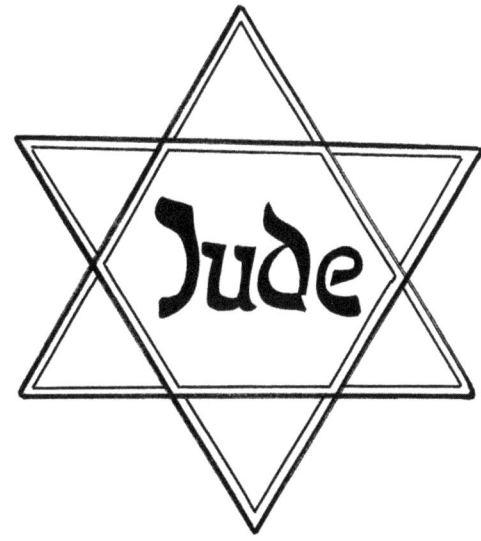

Judenstern.

Jungmädelbund

Jungmädelbund in der HJ (JM). Suborganization of the Hitler Jugend (q.v.) for girls age 10 to 14. See Bund Deutscher Mädel in der HJ.

Jungmädel.

Jungstahlhelm. Young Steel Helmet, the youth organization of the Stahlhelm (q.v.). The Stahlhelm was formed in December 1918 with nationalist ex-servicemen. In July 1933, the Jungstahlhelm was incorporated into the Hitler Jugend (q.v.).

Jungvolk. Suborganization of the Hitler Jugend (q.v.) for boys aged 10 to 14. See Deutsches Jungvolk in der HJ.

Junkers (Ju). An aircraft company. Dr. Hugo Junkers (1859–1935) was a technically educated innovator who began an engine factory in Dessau in 1895. The aging Hugo Junkers was a socialist and a pacifist, and when the Nazis seized power in 1933 he was placed under house arrest and his company was nationalized. He died in 1935. During World War II the Junkers Company produced some famous planes, notably the transport trimotor Junkers Ju 52, the dive-bomber Ju 87, and the twin-engine medium bomber Junkers Ju 88. The Junkers company was also involved in developing the first jet engines.

Justice in the Third Reich. Hitler held all lawyers in deep contempt, and the Third Reich was in fact lawless. It was a police state characterized by Schutzhaft (q.v.)—arbitrary arrest and imprisonment without trial of political and ideological opponents not in ordinary prisons but in concentration camps ruled by the SS. The Third Reich has been called a dual state, since the normal judicial system coexisted with the arbitrary power of Hitler and the SS police. But the law was extravagant, purblind, a pomposity remote from the true interest of the litigants and the community at large. It was the exercise of objective-seeming power in support of purely arbitrary and subjective decisions. Its true criminal character was in no way hidden but emphasized by the mock formality of its own wordings. Indeed, like most areas of public life after the Nazi seizure of power in 1933, the German system of justice underwent Gleichschaltung (q.v.). All professional associations involved with the administration of justice were merged into the National Socialist League of German Jurists. In April 1933, Hitler passed one of the earliest anti–Semitic laws, purging Jewish and also socialist judges, lawyers, and other court officers from their professions. Further, the Academy of German Law and Nazi legal theorists, such as Carl Schmitt, advocated the Nazification of German law, cleansing it of "Jewish influence." Judges were enjoined to let "gesundes Volksempfinden (healthy folk sentiment) guide

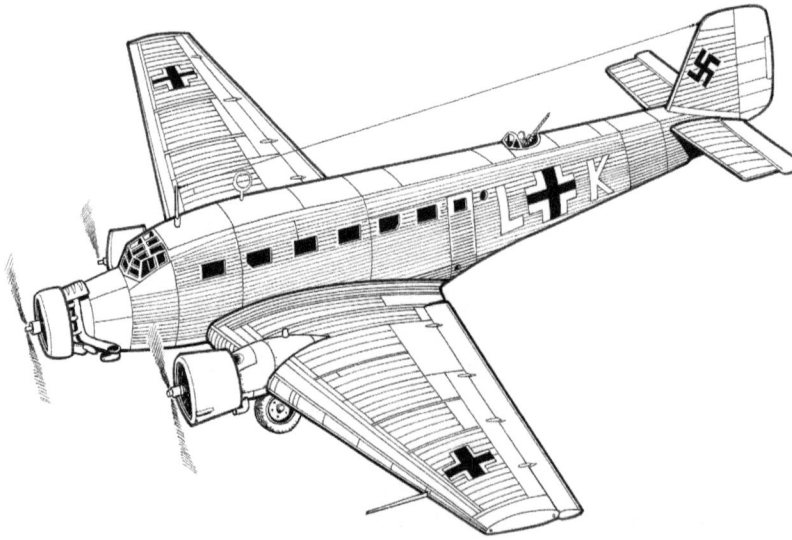

Junkers Ju 52.

them in their decisions. Hitler was determined to increase the political reliability of the courts, and in 1934 he ordered the creation of the so-called People's Court (Volksgerichtshof) to try treason and other important and sensitive "political cases." Under Roland Freisler (q.v.) the People's Court became a mockery, merely a part of the Nazi system of terror, condemning to death thousands of people. The trial and sentencing of those accused of complicity in the July 1944 Bomb Plot (q.v.) was especially unfair. After the war, prominent Nazi jurists were tried in the Jurists' Trial of the subsequent Nuremberg trials on charges of "judicial murder" and other atrocities. See Gesetz zur Erhebung der Not von Volk und Reich and Nationalsozialitische Reichswahrerbund.

Kahr, Gustav von (1862–1934). The leader of the right-wing nationalist Bavarian People Party, Kahr was prime minister of Bavaria from 1920 to 1921. In 1923 he was appointed state commissioner with full emergency powers to suppress all Communist revolution by force. He withdrew his support of Hitler in the Beer Hall Putsch, and was mistrusted and even hated by the Nazis. In the purge of June 1934, the then seventy-one-year-old Kahr was murdered, hacked to pieces and thrown into a swamp near Dachau.

Kaltenbrunner, Ernst (1903–1946). Ernst Kaltenbrunner was originally an Austrian lawyer. In mid-1934 he took part in the assassination of Chancellor Dollfuss that was intended to overthrow the Austrian government. For this Kaltenbrunner was sentenced to jail. By the time of the Anschluß Osterreich (q.v.) in March 1938, he was state secretary for security and head of the Austrian SS. After the death of Reinhard Heydrich (q.v.), Kaltenbrunner replaced him as the head of the Reichssicherheitshauptamt (q.v.) in January 1943. When Hitler ordered the dissolution of the Abwehr (q.v.) in 1944, Kaltenbrunner took over the intelligence service. Found guilty of crimes against humanity at the Nuremberg trial, he was executed by hanging in October 1946.

Kamerad. Comrade. The customary form of address within the Nazi Party.

Kameradschaft. Literally comradeship. A group of ten to fifteen boys, the smallest unit of the Hitler Jugend (q.v.). A Kameradschaft was commanded by junior leaders called Kameradschaftführer and Oberkameradschaftführer. Three or four Kameradschaften formed a Schar (a squad of 50–60 Hitler Jugend).

Kampf dem Verderb. "Combat against spoilage." A Nazi educational slogan issued by the Nationalsozialistische Volkswohlfahrt (q.v.) in 1936 encouraging people to conserve food and to avoid spoilage and waste.

Kampfbund. League of Combat. An umbrella organization for various small groups of Bavarian extremist paramilitary formations and rightist activists in Munich in the early 1920s, including Hitler's SA (Sturm Abteilung [Assault Detachment]). Hitler became the head of the league and used the men for his failed Beer Hall Putsch (q.v.) of 1923. The Kampfbunde was later absorbed by Hitler's Nazi Party.

Kampfbund für Deutsche Kultur (KfdK). League of Combat for the German Culture. An organization created by the Nazi "philosopher" Alfred Rosenberg in 1929. The aims of the league were to promote the Nazi beliefs on the nature of culture and to combat perceived Jewish influence in the German cultural life. The KfdK was one of the most active Nazi organizations in the early Kampfzeit (q.v.). It published inflammatory brochures and reviews of Jewish and modernist musicians, and pursued practices of disrupting concerts and performances by intimidating audiences and threatening "undesirable" performers. See Art in the Third Reich, and Music in the Third Reich.

Badge worn by members of the Kampfbund für Deutsche Kultur (KfdK).

Kampfgruppe. Combat group often comprising various military formations according to the requirements of a battle. Kampfgruppen were generally titled after their commander's name. They were essentially ad hoc organizations of different units organized temporarily for a specific operational task.

Kampfstand. Armed bunker, a concrete construction sheltering machine guns, field guns, antitank guns or coast-defense guns. The weapon was placed in a Kampfraum (combat chamber).

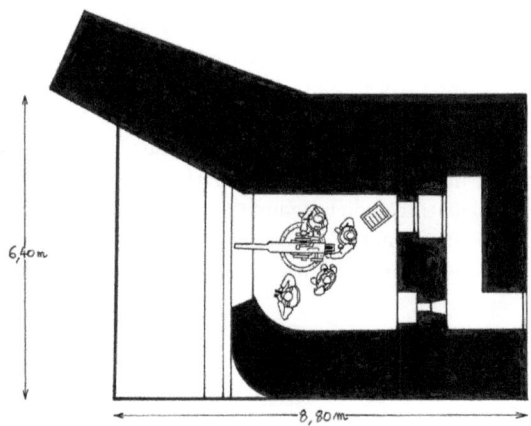

Kampfstand type 667. Top: Front view. Bottom: Plan.

Cross-section Casemate type 667.

Kampfwagenkanone (KwK). Gun specially designed to be mounted on a tank, often semiautomatic in operation and fired electrically.

Kampfwagensperren. Antitank obstacles. See Hemmkurven, Höckerhindernisse, Mine, Panzergraben, Panzermauer, Rollbock, Tschechenigel.

Kampfzeit. The period of struggle (1920–1933) before the Nazis took over power in Germany. After 1933, the Kampfzeit was used in schools as a compulsory history subject and students were expected to know all about the early age of Nazi martyrs and heroes. Playwrights and novelists were encouraged to produce epics on the period. See Alte Kämpfer.

Kanalinseln. British Channel Islands off the Cotentin Peninsula, Normandy, France—the only part of British territory to suffer German occupation during World War II. For propaganda and symbolic purpose, the islands of Jersey and Guernesey were heavily fortified by the Organisation Todt (q.v.) The garrison (entrenched in impressive concrete fortifications) was totally ignored by the Allies and surrendered without fighting in May 1945.

Kapo. A foreman or trustee in a concentration or extermination camp, usually a promoted and slightly privileged common criminal. Kapos were charged with supervising a group of political or racial prisoners. They had to oversee the work of inmates, but were also responsible for the results.

Kapp Putsch. A right-wing coup d'état attempted in March 1920 against the Weimar Republic. The conspiracy was led by the journalist Wolfgang Kapp (1868–1922), and General Walther von Lüttwitz (1859–1942) who, with the support of 6,000 soldiers of a Freikorps (q.v.) headed by Hauptmann Hermann Ehrhardt (q.v.), occupied Berlin and proclaimed a new government with Kapp as chancellor. The legal German government was obliged to flee to Dresden and then to Stuttgart. A general strike was thereupon called by the trade unions and after four days the ill-prepared coup failed. Kapp fled to Sweden and men of the Erhrardt Brigade fled to Munich where they mixed with other nationalist activists, notably with Hitler's NSDAP.

Karinhall. Hermann Göring's sumptuous private estate situated in the Schorfheide near Berlin. It was named after his first wife, the Swede Karin von Kantzow, who died in October 1931. The luxurious estate was the place where the Reichsmarschall lived in idleness and comfort, where he played with his model trains, received his guests, and displayed his huge collection of looted art. After the war — like many other official Nazi buildings — Karinhall was totally destroyed to avoid it becoming a neo–Nazi place of pilgrimage. See Berghof.

Karl. Charles, name given to a series of six enormous self-propelled mortars (Mörser). The Karl series showed German technical achievement but there was little else to praise. The amount of action the enormous guns saw and the effect they had on the battlefield, and on the outcome of the war, did not match the effort, money and time that went into their design and manufacture. See also Dora.

Kasemat. (1) Casemat, concrete pillbox, armed bunker. (2) Armored substructure fitted on a tank chassis to form a self-propelled gun.

Kasemat-Kanone (KK). Gun mounted on a special carriage or a fixed mount for exclusive use in a concrete casemat.

Katyn. A small town near Smolensk in Russia. When the Russians invaded Poland in 1939, they captured about 240,000 soldiers and officers. When the Germans invaded Russia in June 1941, Katyn fell into their hands and they found mass graves in the forest near the town with the remains of some 22,000 Polish soldiers who obviously had been executed by the Russians. The Nazis exploited the massacre by making the news known to the world. The affair had international repercussions and caused diplomatic embarrassment and serious tension as both Poles and Russians were in the Allies' camp. The Polish government in exile in London appealed for an international tribunal, but Stalin denied any responsibility and accused the Germans of lying.

A Red Cross International Committee made an investigation, but the Russian war crimes of Katyn were not mentioned at the Nuremberg trials despite its concern with the treatment of prisoners of war. Not until November 2010 did Russia approve a declaration blaming Stalin and other Soviet officials for having personally ordered the Katyn massacre.

Kavallerie. Cavalry. Although ineffective in modern mechanized war, the military horse did not disappear completely. In World War II its use was limited to those parts of the world where topography and climate were such that mechanized transport was impossible, such as in Russia or in mountainous sites. As for motorized vehicles, the Heer was a massive army of drafted soldiers, a body so large that German industry could not fully equip. Furthermore, in spite of captured and controlled oil fields and synthetic fuel production, the fuel supply was to remain a constant and critical problem for Germany throughout the war. Motor vehicles were allocated to elite units like the armored divisions and Waffen-SS. As for the average infantry division, particularly after 1943, the number of motor vehicles was decreased, heavy equipment and artillery were horse-drawn and infantrymen just had to walk. In 1940 and all through the war, the mobility of over 80 percent of the German army depended on horses. The cavalry's color was golden yellow, and that of veterinary officers was crimson.

Kazerniert. Literally, barracked — that is, permanently living in barracks. This adjective was obviously applied to regular troops but also to permanent Nazi paramilitary units. For example, the full-time SA Stabswachten (staff guards), SA Wehrmannschaften (armed militia), SS-Totenkopfverbände (death's head camp guards units) and SS-Verfügungstruppen (task troops at Nazi Party's disposal later to be known as Waffen-SS) were kazerniert. Nonpermanent members such as the Allgemeine SS were part-timers with their own homes and jobs in civilian life.

KdF. See Kraft durch Freude.

Kehlsteinhaus. Eagle's Nest. Hitler's sumptuous mountaintop teahouse built on a peak of the Hoher Göll (altitude 1834 meters) known as the Kehlstein. It was built as an extension of the Obersalzberg complex in the mountains above

Berchtesgaden. The Kehlsteinhaus, commissioned by Martin Bormann (q.v.), was completed in April 1938, and was a gift for Hitler's 50th birthday. The luxurious chalet-style house (as well as an access road, a tunnel and a richly decorated elevator bored through the rocks) cost a fortune. Hitler, however, visited the property only ten times and each visit was under 30 minutes. Today the building is owned by a charitable trust and serves as a restaurant. See Berghof.

Keitel, Wilhelm (1882–1946). As chief of staff of the OKW—Oberkommando der Wehrmacht (q.v.)—Keitel attended all significant conferences on the conduct of the war and signed operational and political orders. A loyal toady for Hitler, he was sentenced to death and hanged at Nuremberg in 1946. See Laikaitel and Nacht und- Nebel Erlaß.

Keppler Kreis. A group of wealthy and influential conservative capitalists led by the industrialist Wilhelm Keppler (1882–1960), who financially helped Hitler in 1931. Like many other rich businessmen who contributed to Nazi coffers, they believed Hitler could be tamed. They expected to manipulate him for their own purposes (to combat communism and trade unions), but to their dismay they learned too late that he was skillfully using them.

Kernwerk (K). Redoubt, citadel, keep. A Kernwerk was a fortified zone inside a fortress. It had the same function as the keep in a medieval castle: It formed the last entrenchment, the ultimate place of resistance where combat still could be continued even when the rest of the stronghold was taken. See Festung.

Kersten, Felix (1898–1960). A masseur who treated Heinrich Himmler (q.v.) for stomach pains. His postwar memoirs were a major source of information on Himmler and his plans. See Himmler-Kersten Pakt.

Kesselschlacht. From Kessel (cauldron or kettle) and Schlacht (battle), thus encirclement battle or pocket. The encirclement battle was part of Blitzkrieg (q.v.), but after 1942, the Germans experienced enveloping offensives and many German troops were caught up in a Kesselschlacht.

Kette. Literally, chain. A track fitted to tanks and halftracks. Also a combat formation of three aircraft in the German air force.

Kettenhund. Chained dog, slang for a German army military policeman, derived from the metal gorget worn on a chain around the neck. See Feldgendarmerie and Ringkragen.

Kettenkrad. Caterpillar bike. The NSU Kettenkrad HK 100 was a motorcycle fitted with a small halftrack chassis and an Opel car engine giving a maximum speed of 70 kilometers per hour on good road. The halftrack bike was originally designed to tow airborne light artillery (2.8-centimeter or 3.7-centimeter guns); its weight (1,560 kilograms) and its dimensions were calculated in order to fit in a transport plane, Junkers Ju 52. The Kettenkrad was also successfully employed by the German ground army on the muddy Russian front to haul light guns or ammunition/supply trailers, as well as to tow bogged or wrecked small vehicles.

NSU Kettenkrad HK 100.

KG 200. A special Luftwaffe unit that used secret weapons for extraordinary missions. This unit was formed in February 1944 and included four groups. Group I/KG 200 received its orders from the SS Sicherheitsdienst des Reichsführer SS (q.v.). It employed various airplanes, notably a few captured USAAF bombers for special espionage or reconnaissance missions. Group II/KG 200 operated a secret weapon called Mistel (q.v.). Group III/Kg 200 was composed of specially adapted Focke-Wulf 190 fighters, which never saw action. Group IV/KG 200 was a technical unit charged with maintenance and training of groups I, II and III. Group IV/KG 200 also included about 80 men called Totaleinsatz (total effort) who had volunteered for suicide missions. One of these missions (Operation Zeppelin) was an attempt to assassinate Stalin. Another experiment of Group IV was the project codenamed Reichenberg or V4 (q.v.).

Kinder, Kirche, Küche. "Children, Church, Kitchen." A Nazi slogan indicating that the German woman's place was at home. The "Three Ks" were part of the indoctrination of young girls and was intended to be the rule governing their lives. The woman's status in the Third Reich was regarded as auxiliary, ranking below the male.

Kinderlandsverschickung (KLV). Evacuation of children to the countryside. In September 1940, the Nazi regime decided to evacuate children from cities at risk of bombing. Initially the evacuation was to apply only to children of school age from Berlin and Hamburg who lived in suburbs and parts of the cities that did not have sufficient air raid shelters. The project soon became more and more extensive. In April 1942, there were already 850,000 evacuated boys and girls. These children were regrouped in camps, homes and Kindertagesstätte (nursery schools) and placed under the tutelage of the Hitler Jugend and the Nazi Party. Separating children from their parents was also intended to standardize education for further indoctrination in Nazi values and mobilization for war.

Kindersegen. Blessed with children, an emotional term constantly used by the Nazis leaders to increase the birthrate. Hitler called for an ever-greater population, and his regime adopted eugenic measures such as marriage loans, child subsidies, and family allowance as well as a strong propaganda campaign and the creation of honorific rewards for prolific mothers. See Ehestandsdarlehen and Mutterkreuz.

Kirchenkampf. Battle of the church. Campaign directed by Martin Bormann against the German churches. The relationship between Christian religions and Nazism is still a complex, controversial and much debated issue. Hitler regarded the issue of religion as important but boring. Some aspects of Nazism had a quasi-religious aspect, such as the cult around Hitler, with huge congregations, banners, sacred flags and flames, processions, a style of popular and radical preachings, prayers-and-responses, memorials and funeral marches. In confidential circles it was clear that Nazism was incompatible with Christianity and that in the end the power of the churches must absolutely and finally be broken. However, Hitler had to be patient and in the meantime, he considered that the German Christian churches were strong and conservative elements absolutely necessary for the people. Hitler had no problem at all with the total eradication of Judaism but not the Christian churches in Germany. The Nazis' policy towards Christian religions was complex and shifting, resulting in a kind of status quo, that allowed freedom of religion as long as the churches, both Catholic and Lutheran, did not interfere in political matters, but many opposing and anti–Nazi priests and pastors were harassed or dismissed. Some were arrested and murdered in camps and prisons. See Reichskonkordat and Religion in the Third Reich.

KL. See Konzentrationslager.

Klarsfeld. Serge (born in September 1935, Bucharest, Romania) and Beate (born in February 1939, Berlin, Germany) Klarsfeld are a French Jewish couple known for engaging in Holocaust documentation and Nazi-hunting activism. They were involved in catching Klaus Barbie (q.v.), René Bousquet, Jean Leguay, Maurice Papon, and Paul Touvier to seek prosecution for their World War II crimes. In 1984, they were awarded the Legion of Honor by President François Mitterrand. Their son, Arno Klarsfeld (b. 1965), is a human rights attorney.

Kleiderkarte. Textile card. At the beginning of World War II, in November 1939, food and textiles were rationed for German civilians, and a system was established consisting of a card valid for one year with 100 dated, numbered and detachable Punkten (coupons). Similar cards were used for winter clothes, workwear, blankets, sheets, shoes, tobacco and other goods. For food there was the Lebensmittel-Karte (food card) that rationed each family's food supply. Starting in March 1943, the Sonderbezugsscheine für Fliegergeschädigte (special bureau for air victims) offered help to (exclusively German) people who had lost all or a part of their belongings because of Allied bombardments. From 1940 onwards the Jews were excluded from the distribution and assistance systems, and had to fend for themselves to get textiles, daily needs and food.

Kleinstand. Small pillbox, a maximally simplified small bunker with only one function, part of the Atlantikwall (q.v.) starting in early 1944 because of delay in the initial 1943 program. Kleinstände (series 700) were less thick than all previous bunkers, which made them cheap and quick to build but of course less effective.

Klepper. A large, long, thick, rubberized raincoat designed for motorcyclists. See Schutzmantel.

KLV. See Kinderlandsverschickung.

Knickebein. "Crooked leg" or "bent leg." A German navigational system using radio beams to guide bombers to their target.

Knochensack. Bonesack. Nickname for German paratrooper combat smock. See Fallschirmjäger, Luftwaffe, and Tarnung.

Kokarde. Cockade or rosette. The Reichskokarde was worn on headgear. It was circular and made up of the three German national colors: red center, white or silver in the middle and black outer. On officers' caps the rosette was often surrounded by a wreath of oak leaves and acorns.

Kokarde.

Kolonne. Column. A transportation unit varying in size (platoon or company), but consisting of a set number of horse-drawn or motor vehicles capable of transporting a fixed tonnage.

Kommandantur (Kmdr). Military administration bureau in the occupied European lands. See Okkupation.

Kommando. Command or commando unit; in general a group with a special assignment, also a special task detachment.

Kommandostab Reichsführer SS. Himmler's command staff. This staff was a part of the Hauptamt Persönliche Stab des Reichsführer-SS (Pers. Stab RfSS, Himmler's personal headquarters), created in April 1941 and headed by SS Brigadeführer Kurt Knoblauch. The command staff was charged with Himmler's personal security in Berlin and when the Reichsführer was traveling. It included an escort and bodyguard battalion. This Begleit-Bataillon Reichsführer SS, totaling about 3,000 armed guards, was drafted in late 1943 to form the 16th Waffen-SS Panzergrenadierdivision Reichsführer SS. See Begleit and Hauptamt Persönliche Stab des Reichsführer-SS.

Kommissar Erlaß. The infamous Commissar Decree, issued by Hitler on June 6, 1941, ordering the execution without trial of all captured Soviet political commissars (supervisory political officers responsible for the ideological education and loyalty of the military to the Stalin government).

Kommunistische Partei Deutschlands (KPD). Communist Party of Germany, the main opponent of the Nazis in the 1920s and early 1930s. The communists named themselves as antifascist, and the Nazis often referred to them as Bolsheviks after the radical doctrine of Lenin. After World War I, the KDP was a large, disciplined, and well-organized party that enjoyed considerable favor among the lower working classes. They had Moscow's support, and their propaganda—based on the teachings of Marx and Lenin—was powerful and convincing. But to many Germans it seemed to aim at bloody revolution, the renunciation of private property, and the elimination of the middle classes and intelligentsia. Many Germans lived in fear of a Bolshevik takeover. The KPD had strong-arm squads, the Rotfront Kämpferbund (q.v.), or Red Front Fighters' Association, whose men were trained on Russian political lines and partly financed by Moscow. See Spartakusbund.

Kompanie. Company in the German army. A Kompanie was composed of three or four Züge (squads). It included from 90 to 160 soldiers and was commanded by an Oberleutnant (lieutenant) or a Hauptmann (captain). Three or four companies constituted a Bataillon, or Abteilung (battalion), placed under a major's command. In the Waffen-SS, the company was called Sturm.

Kondor Legion. The Condor Legion, formed in November 1936, was a German combat formation engaged in the Spanish Civil War (1936–1939) in support of Franco's Fascist Nationalist forces. The unit included transport airplanes Ju 52 (also used as bombers), fighters, seaplanes, communications, ground-support units and flak artillery. There were also two tank companies under command of Oberst Ritter von Thoma. German warships, including the battleship *Deutschland* and submarines U-33 and U-34, operated off the Spanish coast and assisted in interdicting supplies and shore bombardments. The legion's total strength was about 20,000 men. The Kondor Legion was first led by air force Generalmajor Hugo Speerle until November 1937, then by Generalleutnant Helmut Volkmann and finally by Generalmajor Wolfram Freiherr von Richthofen (a cousin of Baron von Richthofen, the World War I ace known as "Red Baron"). Unlike Mussolini, Hitler was not concerned with bringing about a victory for Franco. On the contrary, it suited him that the Spanish Civil War should continue indefinitely, as he and Göring found it marvelously convenient to test their new weapons at other people's expense. Civil War in Spain indeed gave the Germans valuable experience in tank and air warfare. See Franco, Francisco; and Hendaye.

Konkordat (Kirchenvertrag). Concordat. An agreement or treaty, especially one between the Vatican and a secular government relating to matters of mutual interest. See Religion in the Third Reich, Pius XI and Reichskonkordat.

Konzentrationslager (KZ). Concentration camp. The correct abbreviation would have been KL, but KZ was chosen for the tougher sound (ka-tzett). Basically a concentration camp is defined as "a guarded compound for the detention or imprisonment of individuals, aliens, members of ethnic minorities, political opponents, who are arbitrarily detained and confined, typically under harsh conditions." The term grew in prominence during the Second Boer War (1899–1902) in South Africa, when concentration camps were operated by the British. During the 20th century, the arbitrary internment of civilians by the state reached a climax with Nazi concentration camps between 1933 and 1945. The first Nazi concentration camp was Dachau (established in March 1933), and soon the number greatly expanded. Concentration camps were intended to detain political prisoners, opponents of the Nazi regime, and other "undesirables." The number of camps quadrupled all over occupied Europe between 1939 and 1942, when about 1,200 camps, subcamps and work camps were run by the SS in countries occupied by Nazi Germany. Labor camps were concentration camps where interned inmates had to do hard physical labor under inhumane conditions and cruel treatment. Some of these camps were subcamps of larger camps, or "operational camps," established for a temporary need. Millions of slave laborers, Jews, political prisoners, criminals, homosexuals, Gypsies, the mentally ill, people with disabilities, Jehovah's Witnesses, clergymen, Freemasons, "deviant" artists and intellectuals, members of the Resistance movements, and others from across Europe were incarcerated, most often without any judicial process. Camps were also sites for secret "medical experiments." Eugenics experiments, freezing of prisoners to determine how downed pilots were affected by exposure, and experimental and lethal medicines were all tried at various camps. The KZ were run by the SS through the Concentration Camps Inspectorate headed by Theodor Eicke (q.v.), and later by Department D of the SS Office of Economics and Administration under Oswald Pohl. Although many of the prisoners died in the concentration camps through deliberate maltreatment, disease, starvation, and overwork, or were executed as unfit for labor, and although all concentration camps had some of the elements of an extermination camp, a distinction is drawn between concentration camps and extermination camps. The latter were established by the Nazis for the systematic, industrial-scale mass murder of the Jewish and Gypsy populations. The most important KZs were Vught in the Netherlands; Natzweiler in French Alsace; Neuengamme, Bergen-Belsen, Ravensbrück, Sachsenhausen, Buchenwald, Flossenburg, and Dachau in Germany; Mauthausen in Austria; Groß-Rosen in Poland; and Theresienstadt in Czechoslovakia. The main extermination camps were all located in Poland and included Strutthof, Chelmno, Treblinka, Sobibor, Maidanek, Belzec and

Auschwitz-Birkenau. See Vernichtungslager and Wirtschafts-Verwaltungshauptamt.

Koppel. Service belt.

Koppelschloß. Belt buckle, often decorated and bearing a motto. See Gott mit Uns.

Körper-Schürze. Body apron issued to German soldiers. The apron was made from a large piece of cotton. It had a V-shaped collarless neck opening and tapes that could be tied under the arms. The item was large enough so equipment could loosely fit under it. The cloth was reversible; on one side it had camouflage patterns for use in spring and summer and on the other side plain white for winter use in snow.

Körper-Schürze (camouflage body apron).

Krad or **Kraftrad.** See Motorrad.

Kraft durch Freude (KdF). Officially named NS-Gemeinschaft Kraft durch Freude (National Socialist Organisation Strength through Joy), KdF was a sub-organization of the Deutsche Arbeitsfront (q.v.), or DAF, created in November 1933. All members of the DAF were also members of KdF. The KdF organization was the velvet glove of the Nazi regime. It was essentially designed for the purpose of providing organized leisure for the German working class, including trips, cruises, concerts, plays, operas, and many other forms of Nazi-approved cultural activities and outings. It was through KdF that the NSDAP hoped to bring to the common man the pleasures once reserved only for the rich. By opening the door for the working class to easy, entertaining activities and attractive, affordable cultural events, it was believed that the labor force could be lulled into being more flexible, obedient and productive. Another aspect of the KdF organization was the provision for workers to have a right to vacation and paid holidays, a concept totally unique to the period in nearly all nations of the world. Another attractive aspect of the KdF was the attempt to make the automobile a reality for as many Germans as possible. To this end, the world famous Volkswagen (q.v.) was created. KdF was a Nazi organization, and of course all activities and events were strictly reserved for "true German Aryans." When World War II began in 1939, there was no longer time for fun, and KdF activities were drastically reduced.

Kraftfahrer. Driver of a motorized vehicle in a mechanized unit.

Kraftfahrerbewährungsabzeichen. Driver Award, a medal instituted in October 1942 to reward drivers who had distinguished themselves in operations between 90 and 185 days.

Kraftfahrzeug (Kfz). Motor vehicle. A Sonderkraftfahrzeuge (q.v.), or SdKfz, was a vehicle specially designed for military purposes.

Kragenpatten or **Kragenspiegel.** Collar patch. The collar of the service tunic and other parts of the uniform were used to display rank and branch of service. The collar patches were a feature of all German uniforms, and assumed particular importance during the period of the Third Reich. Each patch was faced in very dark bottle-green material upon which a standardized patch was worn on each side; this consisted of a Doppellitze (double bar) woven in silver-gray thread and with a central strip in each bar in the Waffenfarbe color. Collar patches were also used to display rank on the uniforms of the Nazi Party and its many affiliated organizations.

Krätzchen. Scratcher, a short-lived Imperial-style "pork-pie" field hat worn by the SS in the late 1920s. The Krätzchen had a rough texture (hence its name), and it was black, peakless and roundish in form. Its front was decorated with a massive eagle and swastika.

SS Krätzchen 1925.

Krauss-Maffei. The J.A. Krauss-Maffei AG from Munich-Allach, established in 1931, was a German company that specialized in producing locomotives. During World War II the company produced various trucks and halftracks.

Kraut. Literally "cabbage" or "weed," a slang term for Germans used by Allied soldiers.

Kreisen. Districts (literally circles).

Kreisleiter. Official of the Nazi Party, leader of a Kreis. See also Gau.

Krieg. War. The martial tradition in Prussia dated from Frederick the Great (1712–1786). The empire founded with the unification of Germany in 1871 had a profoundly military ethos, and militarism reached new heights with the Nazis. In Hitler's mind history was an interracial struggle and war, the "father of all things." It was seen as inevitable, determining the life of individuals and nations. War made sure that races were graded on a scale of merit, and struggle for survival was permanent. War was seen as an inspirational experience and as the highest expression of the life force of a nation. It was not a morale issue but the physical and legitimate means for the survival of the superior Germans. For the Nazis there was no distinction between the home front and the combat zone. The full force of Germany had to engage and strike all enemies within and without the Reich with no legal restraints. The Nazi ideology, no less than Nazi economics, was one of preparation for war. Both depended for their continued success upon the maintenance of a national spirit and a national effort, which in the end had to find expression in aggressive action. War, the belief in violence and the right of the stronger were not corruptions of Nazism, they were its essence.

Krieg ohne Hass. "War without hate," a reference to the fighting in North Africa. It is generally admitted that both sides behaved with (relative) humanity. The Deutsches Afrika Korps (q.v.) were never accused of any war crimes.

Kriegsfischkutter (KFK). A confiscated civilian fishing boat transformed into a small patrol or gun warship.

Kriegsgefangener (KG). Prisoner of war (POW). "KG" was often written or painted in large white letters on the back of POW tunics and coats for immediate recognition, thus making escape impossible.

Kriegsgericht. Martial court.

Kriegshilfsdienst. War Help Service. A compulsory extension of six months of the Reichsarbeitsdienst (q.v.), or RAD (Reich Labor Service), to be served by women between ages 17 and 45, in munitions factories, communication centers and hospitals, and in general duties for the German armed forces. This measure was taken in the summer 1941. Later in the war, the RAD/Kriegshilfsdienst included another branch, the Luftwaffeneinsatz (q.v.).

Kriegsmarine (KM). German navy. The Kriegsmarine (called Reichsmarine until 1935) was headed by Admiral Erich Raeder from 1928 until 1943 and by Admiral Karl Dönitz from 1943 to 1945. The navy's supreme headquarters was the Oberkommando der Marine (OKM), which was established in Berlin and divided into geographical fleet commands (Marinegruppekommando). After the June 1940 German victory in West Europe, the Germans occupied all North Sea, Channel and Atlantic Ocean shores. Having control of numerous important harbors, they engaged in a sea war against Britain and, at the end of 1941, against the United States. The so-called Battle of the Atlantic was a bitter fight to control communication between Britain and the United States. On the German side, air force and surface warships did not play a decisive role. The *Bismarck* was sunk in 1941, the *Gneisenau* was disarmed, the *Tirpitz* was blocked in Norway and the *Scharnhorst* was destroyed in December 1943. The main German weapon was thus the submarines (U-Boote). The German U-Boote arm grew from 57 boats at the beginning of the war to a peak strength of 445 in early 1944. Commanded by OKM and Admiral Dönitz, the U-Boote arm became an operational branch run by Admiral Eberhart Godt who in March 1943 was promoted to Befehlhaber für Unterseeboote (submarine commander). The U-boote fleets were organized in operational U-Flotille (flotillas), each based on a port and usually numbering up to 20 submarines, of which at least half were at sea. They would attack in "wolfpacks" at night (Rudeltaktik). The actions of the German U-Boote were made more effective by Allied lack of experience and shortages of destroyers, escort ships and planes. At the beginning of 1942, two million tons of merchant ships were sunk, and the Battle of the Atlantic reached its climax at the end of the same year when Allied losses reached more than 600,000 tons per month. Progressively the Allies learned how to strike German submarines. Merchant ships crossed the ocean in convoys escorted by planes and destroyers equipped with sophisticated and reliable detection means (ASDIC, sonar) as well as powerful antisubmarine weapons (depth charges). American shipyards were mobilized and rapidly produced numerous standardized cargo boats known as Liberty Ships. In spite of German technological innovations such as Schnorchel (allowing complete and durable submersion), better weapons (acoustical torpedoes) and new submarine types XXI and XXIII with increased performance, the Allies achieved victory by the end of 1943. If German U-Boote remained a threat, they could no longer prevent the Allies from crossing the ocean. Northern Africa and Britain then became military platforms where weapons, material, vehicles, equipment and men were regrouped to undertake landings and liberation of occupied Europe. Between 1941 and 1945, 268 million tons of equipment and 4 million soldiers crossed the Atlantic Ocean while 17 million tons of war material were shipped to the USSR. From 1939 to 1945, the Germans sank 14 million tons of ships. They lost 782 U-Boote and about 20,000 submariners were killed.

Kriegsschuldlüge. "War guilt lie." Term often used by the Nazis in denouncing Article 231 of the Treaty of Versailles, the provision that placed full responsibility on Germany for causing World War I (1914–1918). See Versailler Diktat and Versailler Vertag.

Kriegswinterhilfswerk (KWW). Wartime winter help collection scheme. See Winterhilfswerk.

Kriminalpolizei (Kripo). Criminal police. After 1939 the Kripo became a branch of the SS. It was the Amt V (department 5) of the Reichssicherheitshauptamt (q.v.), or RSHA, Central Security Reich Main Office. The Kripo, the normal criminal investigation police, totaling some 12,000 persons in 1944, was headed by Arthur Nebe. It dealt with common thieves and other lawbreakers, but the Kripo also applied racial criteria, viewing criminal behavior as biologically inherited. Accordingly, justification was provided for the protection of society from alleged potential criminals through the use of Schutzhaft (q.v.).

Kripo. See Kriminalpolizei.

Kristallnacht or **Reichskristallnacht.** "Crystal Night" or "Night of Broken Glass." Initiated and coordinated by Propaganda Minister Joseph Goebbels on the night of November 9, 1938, Kristallnacht was a large scale anti–Semitic pogrom throughout Germany and Austria. Goebbels used as an excuse for the pogrom the assassination in Paris of the German diplomat Ernst von Rath by a Jew named Herschel Grynspan. The broken glass littering the streets gave name to the attacks. It was a new step in the escalation of hatred, and a premeditate act of violent terror against the German Jewish community. During that night, with an unpreceded savagery, Nazi members sacked Jewish shops, looted Jewish homes, and set hundreds of synagogues on fire. The police and the fire brigades were ordered not to intervene. Some ninety Jews were murdered and 20,000 were carted off to concentration camps. The ugly riots — which continued in several cities until November 13, 1938 — were viewed in Germany with both enthusiasm and silent indignation. Abroad, Kristallnacht presented the free world with the evident savagery of the Nazi regime. Of course, the rioters were never prosecuted.

Kroll Opera House. Location of the Reichstag (q.v.) after the original building was destroyed by fire in February 1933. See Reichstagsbrand.

Krupp. The Krupp Company was founded in Essen in 1801 by Friedrich Krupp, who had developed modern methods of making high-quality steel. His son Alfred expanded the foundries to produce rails and wheels for railways. In 1851 the company began to produce weapons, notably the first breech-loading gun. Krupp's main activity was from then onwards the production of artillery, warships and other weapon systems. It came to be known as "the Arsenal of the Reich" until 1945.

Kübelwagen. (See illustration on page 97.) Literally "bucket car." The term was applied to all light carrier personnel cars, but more particularly to the open-topped military version of the 1936 Volkswagen (q.v.) "Beetle," a sort of a small personnel car.

Kulmhof. See Chelmno.

Kultur. Culture in a broad sense, also taking into consideration the entire way of life of a people. Nazi Kultur was closely associated with its Weltanschauung (q.v.).

Kübelwagen Kfz 1 Volkswagen 82.

Kunst. Art. See Art in the Third Reich.

Küstenvorfeldsperre (K-Sperre or KS). Beach obstacle in the Atlantikwall (q.v.).

Kyffhaüserbund. Kyffhäuser League, World War I veterans association. The name comes from a commemorative monument called Kyffhäusen Denkmal located on the summit of the Kyffhäuser Mountain near Bad Frankenhausen in the state of Thuringia in central Germany. The Kyffhaüserbund was an umbrella organization for war veterans' and reservists' associations in Germany. After the Nazi seizure of power in 1933, the league was subjected to Gleichschaltung (q.v.), and members over forty-five years of age were attached to SA Reserve No. 2. The name was changed to NS-Reichskriegerbund Kyffhäuser e.V. (National Socialist Reich Warriors Association Kyffhäuser). The Kyffhäuser Association was swiftly and unceremoniously disbanded during World War II in March 1943, by Adolf Hitler himself. Apparently the reason was the German defeat in the Battle of Stalingrad. The association's assets in the whole Reich were transferred to the NSDAP. After Nazi Germany's defeat in 1945, the league was disbanded and de-Nazified. It was reestablished in 1952 in the German Federal Republic. See Stahlhelm.

Kyffhaüserbund badge.

KZ or **Kazetlager.** Common abbreviation for concentration camp. See Konzentrationslager.

Labor Front. See Deutsche Arbeitsfront (DAF).

Labor Service. See Reichsarbeitsdienst (RAD).

Lagarde, Paul de (1827–1891). German orientalist, philologist, and political forerunner of National Socialism. Criticizing materialism, calling for moral cleansing and the end of the "spiritual and economic power of the Jews" in Germany, Lagarde was held in high esteem by Alfred Rosenberg (q.v.). His severe strictures against the Jews helped pave the way for Nazi policy of genocide.

Laikaitel. Sarcastic term used by fellow officers to describe the subservient General Wilhelm Keitel (q.v.). It was a play on words using the German term Lakai (lackey or flunky) and Keitel.

Kyffhaüser monument.

Länder. German states. Before Hitler unified Germany with Gleichschaltung (q.v.), the country was a federation of states including the large and dominating Prussia and Bavaria, and smaller states including Saxony, Württemberg, Baden, Thuringia, Hesse, Mecklenburg-Schwerin, Mecklenburg-Strelitz, Oldenburg, Brunswick, Anhalt, Lippe, Waldeck and Schaumburg-Lippe. In addition there were three independent cities originating from the Hansa (medieval trade league): Lübeck, Bremen and Hamburg.

Landsberg Prison. A penal facility located in the town of Landsberg am Lech in the southwest of the German state of Bavaria, about 65 kilometers (40 miles) west of Munich. Hitler was imprisoned there following the failed Beer Hall Putsch (q.v.) He was very well treated. He wore his own clothes, had his own rooms, was provided with a special diet, and was allowed free association with the forty other Nazis detained with him. He had many visitors and enough free moments to dictate his book *Mein Kampf* (q.v.) to his faithful fellow prisoner Rudolf Hess (q.v.). After 1945, the prison was used by the Allies during the occupation of Germany for holding Nazi war criminals.

Landsdienst. Agricultural service. The Nazis had a strong desire for urban youth to commune with rural folk. In addition to their regular activities, Hitler Jugend (q.v.) members were required to help with the harvest each year in the summer. Combining the ideologically desirable and the economically useful, the agricultural service was intended to harden the HJ and to ease the rural labor shortage. Some students who had completed their elementary education spent a nine-month stretch in the Landsdienst in camps, working in the morning and receiving lessons in Nazi ideology in the afternoon. The youngsters at these camps were allowed no vacations, no leave, no parental visits and no religious services. The subjection to authoritarian rule and the exploitation of cheap labor were justified by the National Socialist leadership with the claim that everyone's welfare was at stake, and concern with the individual's needs was regarded as synonymous with irresponsibility.

Landsturm. (1) Historically, infantry units of nonprofessional soldiers levied by decree by Prussian King Frederick William III in 1813 to harass Napoleon's rear areas during the War of Liberation; (2) a kind of militia or secondary military reserve for men over 45.

Landwacht. Auxiliary rural police established in 1942 to help the regular police. The Landwacht was composed of old Germans, mostly World War I veterans.

Landwehr. A term referring to several organized militias created in the 19th and early 20th centuries. See Landsturm and Volkssturm.

Langbehn, Julius (1851–1907). A German writer and intellectual who lauded the Aryan Germanic people as a master race destined to dominate the world. His hazy theories, quite similar to those of Paul de Lagarde (q.v.), Joseph Arthur, Count of Gobineau (q.v.) and Houston Stewart Chamberlain (q.v.), were later appropriated and exploited by the Nazis.

Langemarck. A World War I battle in Belgium, also a name given to the 27th SS Freiwillige Grenadier Division. This unit, composed of Belgian Flemish volunteers, was raised in autumn 1944.

Lanyard. Originally a woolen cord worn in a variety of ways. See Achselband.

Laufgrabe or **Schützgrabe.** (See illustration on page 99.) Trench. Trenches were communication and combat emplacements. They could be simple excavations hastily dug under enemy fire or semipermanent positions reinforced by planks, corrugated plates or wooden beams; they could also be permanent and made of concrete. Their profile often widened upwards so that soldiers could pass with equip-

Lanyard worn by a SS Standartenführer in evening dress.

Laufgrabe (cross-section).

ment, arms and ammunition. Trenches were sometimes camouflaged and were always given a zigzag layout to reduce enfilading fire. Combat trenches were fitted with a banket (firing step), a narrow platform allowing soldiers armed with rifles to shoot above the parapet (breastwork). The glacis, a gentle slope extending to the no-man's-land on the enemy side, was covered with obstacles, mines and barbed wire. Where dead angles (blind spots) could occur, machine gun and mortar nests were placed.

Lebensborn eingetragener Verein (e.V.) or **Lebensborn** for short. Fountain of Life Society, name given to a Nazi human breeding scheme intended to expand the "Aryan race." Organized by the SS, the Lebensborn society was created in December 1935. It was intended to give aid to unmarried women who bore children by "Aryan" fathers, and to take care of wives and girlfriends of police and SS members. Special maternity homes were established in order to encourage a higher birthrate even for unmarried women. Most girls using the homes belonged to the Bund Deutscher Mädel (BDM, League of German Girls) the female section of the Hitler Jugend (q.v.). Girls were taught that their duty was to make children for the Third Reich. They were encouraged to get pregnant by SS men who, married or not, were relieved of any responsibility for the children. Estimates showed about 12,000 babies born under these conditions. Some were raised by their own mothers but most were adopted by selected "racially sound" foster parents. Children born with a physical or mental handicap were killed in a euthanasia program. The Lebensborn program also included the importation—kidnapping—of Aryan-looking children from occupied countries. They were placed by the society with "reliable," suitable German families and sent to special schools. The number of kidnapped children is difficult to know, but estimates show probably some 340,000, stolen from Russia, Poland, Yugoslavia and other occupied lands.

Lebensraum. "Vital space" or "living space," a concept used by the Nazis for expansionism, especially eastwards. Hitler never really rejected colonies abroad, but he asserted that security and vital space for Germany were to be conquered in Eastern Europe (mainly in the rich plains of Poland, Ukraine and Russia), if need be by force. Conceived by Hitler and his secretary Rudolf Hess during their stay in prison in 1924 and clearly exposed as early as 1925 in *Mein Kampf*, Lebensraum was not seen by Hitler in terms of restoring the pre–1914 borders. Lebensraum formed one of the main bases for the Nazi program of security and expansion which was the resumption of the ancient struggle against the Slavs carried out by the Teutonic knights in the Middle Ages. Lebensraum offered the opportunity to build the Nazi order, the empire of the Herrenvolk based upon the slave labor of the inferior races. Hitler's program was no detailed blueprint but an amalgam of various elements. The logical consequence of this policy was obviously war with Poland and Russia, and territorial reshaping of Germany and east Europe. Lebensraum indeed included conquest, expulsion, enslavement, extermination and annihilation of the resident population justified by the principle that "might is right." Hitler's determination to wage war and apply the criminal Lebensraum policy were proved by the so-called Hossbach Niederschrift (q.v.). See Drang nach Osten.

Ledermantel. Leather greatcoat. See Mantel.

Legion. A German military unit without fixed size (from battalion to brigade); term used by both the German army and Waffen-SS. Often, but not always, composed of foreigners in German service, such as Croat Army Legion, Spanish Legion Azul, French anti–Bolshevik Legion, Georgian Legion, Azerbaijan Legion, and so on. See Kondor Legion.

Lehr. Demonstration or model. The term was usually part of the name of an elite formation whose members were mobilized from instructional troops, such as Panzer-Lehr-Division.

Leibstandarte SS Adolf Hitler (LSSAH). SS ceremonial armed honor unit, Hitler's personal bodyguard, raised in March 1933. Organized, formed and headed by Joseph "Sepp" Dietrich (q.v.), the unit became later the first Waffen-SS division, called 1st Panzerdivision Leibstandarte SS Adolf Hitler.

Leichenkommando. Corpse commando. In Nazi concentration camps, inmates designated to collect every morning the bodies of those who had died during the night.

Leicht (le). Light; of artillery, projectile, vehicles and tanks, and formations and units.

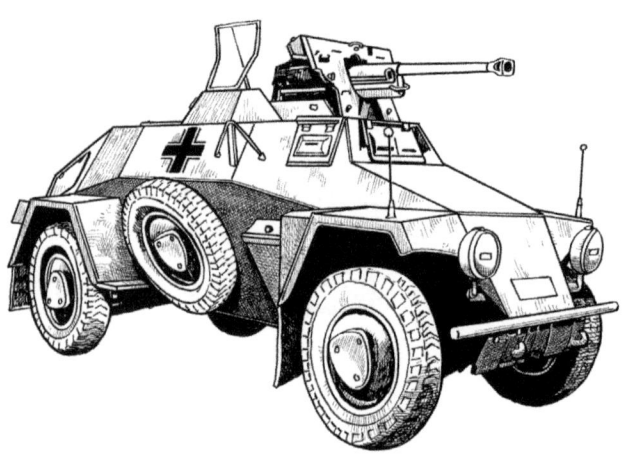

Leichter Panzerspähwagen SdKfz 221 armed with a 2.8-centimeter gun.

Leistung. Performance, proficiency, good result. Often rewarded in the form of a medal.

Leistungsabzeichen or **Heeres Leistungsabzeichen.** Army arms badge. Special proficiency arms badges represented a qualification going further than a trade or a specialty. Heeres Leistungsabzeichen were regarded with more esteem and distinguished the wearer as possessing special skills and training related to the type of military unit in which he served. This applied, for example, to elite formations such as mountain troops (whose Leistungsabzeichen was an Edelweiß flower), armored troops (death's head), paratroopers (diving eagle), Afrikakorps (swastika on a palm tree) or Waffen-SS (double lightning SS rune). See also Abzeichen.

Leitstand or **Feuerleitstand.** Fire control station for artillery, often a standardized bunker. As the central organ of an artillery coastal or flak battery, the Leitstand was placed in the middle of the battery or slightly ahead of it in order to have maximal view. Fire control stations were composed of several working and computing rooms. The upper terrace, often covered by a thick concrete plate, was equipped with a range finder to calculate distance between battery guns and targets. Leitstände (pl.) crews were highly trained specialists who determined firing angles and calculated distances, taking into account many factors. Officers indicated which ammunition to use and gave orders to fire; after firing, results were observed and corrections were made.

Leuchtgranate (Lg). Flare shell.

Leuchtpistole. Flare pistol used for signal on the field.

Ley, Robert (1890–1945). An airman in World War I, an ardent Nazi starting in 1924, and a close henchman to Hitler, Robert Ley was appointed head of the Deutsche Arbeitsfront (q.v.) in May 1933. Despite his wide range of power, his relative importance within the party leadership greatly declined when World War II started. Ley was only a marginal figure in the Nazi hierarchy, but he was a highly dangerous criminal. An enriched plebeian and radical Nazi, a violent and bitter anti–Semite, a notorious and incorrigible drunk with an ostentatious lifestyle, Robert Ley exemplified the coarse, corrupt and criminal face of Hitler's regime. He committed

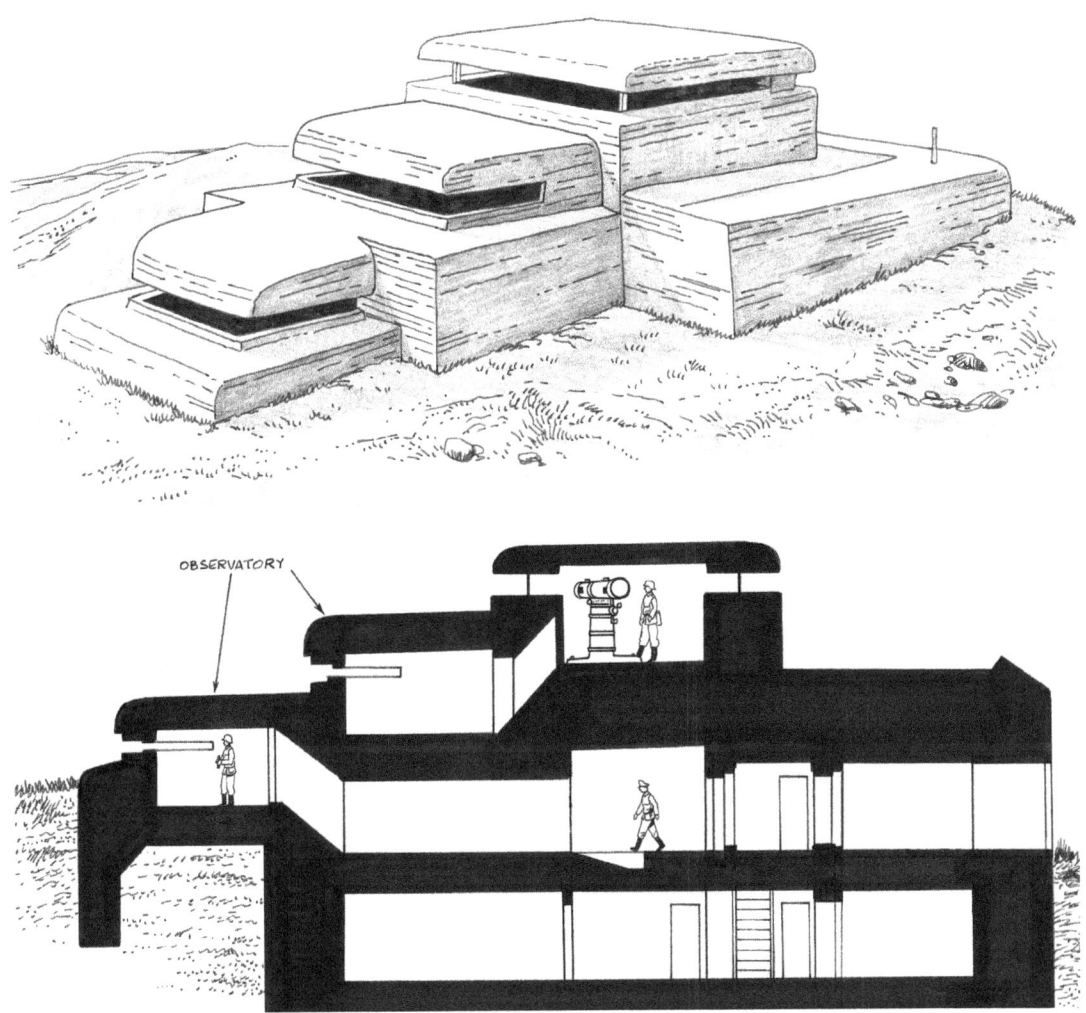

Leitstand type S414. Top: Exterior. Bottom: Cross-section.

suicide in his cell in 1945, right before judgment by the Nuremberg Trial.

Lichterfelde Barracks. Headquarters and barracks of the Leibstandarte SS Adolf Hitler (q.v.) Located near Berlin, the barracks became notorious as place where opponents of the regime were shot by SS firing squads.

"Lili Marleen." A famous German song sung in 1939 by the Swedish-German singer Lale Anderson. The lyrics (originally a poem titled "Das Lied eines jungen Soldaten auf der Wacht") were written in 1915 by a German soldier called Hans Leip. The music was composed by Norbert Schultze in 1937. The song transcended the hatreds of war and was popular among both Allied and German troops, particularly in North Africa—so popular indeed that the BBC decided to make a cover version (with English text by Tommy Connor) sung by Anne Shelton.

Lindemann. Coastal battery situated near Sangatte in northern France. The battery regrouped three imposing artillery bunkers (Turm Anton, Turm Bruno and Turm Cäsar) in 3.5-meter "StA" thickness, each one sheltering a 40.6-centimeter gun originating from the discarded warship *Bismarck* and firing 594-kilogram shells. The Lindemann battery was part of an ensemble of artillery positions that included the batteries Todt, Friedrich-August, and Großer Kürstfurst, ranging up to 54 kilometers, further than Dover. These heavy batteries were built after the fall of France in June 1940 and made part of the preamble of Operation Sea Lion, the projected invasion of Britain. They planned to block the Strait of Dover to any non–Axis shipping and intended to shell Dover and the southern part of Kent. See Atlantikwall.

Liska, Hans (1907–1984). One of the best known, most talented and most prolific World War II illustrators, who served with the German armed forces during the war. In 1942 and 1943 German publishing house Carl Werner in Reichenbach, sponsored by Junkers Flugzeug und Motorenwerke AG, published two albums with Hans Liska's sketches and color illustrations. Liska's art lived up to the expectations of his peers, and he used propaganda clichés that were highly recognizable in his paintings and drawings. However, at the same time he was also able to create something more valuable than NSDAP-commissioned propaganda. Liska convincingly demonstrated that he had a great talent, with a dynamic hand and an eye for the real war drama, with all its pain, suffering, desperation, hard work, and endurance.

Literature in the Third Reich. German literature was greatly affected by the Nazis, as Hitler placed writers first on his list of detested intellectuals. Hitler did not read with the open mind of the intellectual but for confirmation of what he already believed, and for lending legitimacy to his prejudices. Following the process of Gleichschaltung (q.v.) some 2,500 authors went into exile either voluntarily or under duress. Nazi literature, like all other aspects of cultural and artistic expression, was reduced to a level of predictable and boring mediocrity. The best-selling book of the Nazi period was Hitler's *Mein Kampf* (q.v.), which sold more than 6 million copies. See Bücherverbrennung and Heimatroman.

Litzen. Collar braid. See Kragenpatten.

Locarno Treaties. When World War I ended, the Treaty of Versailles was signed in Paris in 1919. In this treaty, the Germans lost land and all their colonies, and were also required to make reparations of material goods and cash payments. Germany was not happy with this, and the Locarno Treaties signed in October 1925 included a number of agreements meant to improve this tense postwar situation by reaching compromises in order to help prevent future wars.

Lord Haw Haw. See Joyce, William.

LSSHA. See Leibstandarte SS Adolf Hitler.

Lubbe, Marius van der (1909–1934). A Dutch bricklayer found in the Reichstag building at the moment of the Reichstag fire in February 1933. Van der Lubbe was tried, sentenced to death and executed. It is still debated, however, whether van der Lubbe was the arsonist or whether the fire was deliberately set by the Nazis themselves. See Reichstagsbrand.

Lublin. Concentration and forced labor camp, but a de facto extermination camp. Also known as Majdanek or Maidenek, this camp, located near the city of Lublin in Poland, was in operation from October 1941 to July 1944. The estimated number of victims murdered there is about 79,000, of whom 59,000 were Polish Jews.

Ludendorff, Erich (1865–1937). A talented military strategist, Ludendorff had early successes in World War I that were obscured by Germany's defeat and his pro–Nazi political activities in the postwar period. Ludendorff participated in the unsuccessful Beer Hall Putsch in Munich in 1923, and in 1925 he ran for president against Paul von Hindenburg (q.v.), now a bitter enemy. From 1924 to 1928 he was a Nazi member of the Reichstag. After falling out with the Nazis he retired, and he died in December 1937. See Dolchstoss.

Luftballon. Balloon. Though vulnerable to fighter attack, unmanned balloons were extensively used during World War II to protect vital ground targets and naval convoys against low-flying aircraft.

Luftflotte. Air fleet, composed of Fliegerkorps (air corps) and Geschwadern (squadrons). See Geschwader, Luftwaffe, Oberkommando der Luftwaffe, and Staffel.

Luftgau. Air region. See Luftwaffe.

Lufthansa. German civilian air transportation company created in 1926. After the seizure of power by the Nazis, the company grew, as the regime was eager to expand its prestige all over the world. During World War II Lufthansa was militarized. It was liquidated in 1945. The company was recreated in 1953.

Luftlandesperre (LL-Sperre). Obstacles against paratroopers and gliders. See Rommelspargel.

Luftschutz. Civilian air raid protection service. Aerial defense was viewed as a component of the country's military defense. Led by the Luftwaffe, various antiaircraft units were created, such as the Ziviler Luftschutz (civil air defense) or the Heimatflak (home antiaircraft artillery). This artillery was to be the decisive element of the Reich active defense, mobilizing more than 300,000 men to operate some 7,813 antiaircraft guns. However, as the demand for soldiers fit for front-line duty increased during the war, so, too, did the Luftwaffe conscription of schoolboys in the Hitler Jugend (q.v.) aged between 16 and 18 to man the antiaircraft guns.

Luftschutz Warndienst (LSW). Air Raid Warning Service; a civilian service composed of volunteers (including many women) who were responsible for the timely warning of incoming enemy air raids and attacks on German cities, towns and installations. It functioned at all times, day and night, by taking reports from its members, from the Flugmeldedienst (Warning Service) and from the various related police organizations, after which they processed the information so as to set in motion the sounding of air raid sirens prior to an attack. The LSW was incorporated into the Luftwaffe in 1942. See Fliegeralarm.

Luftschutzpolizei. Air Defense Police, a highly mobile rescue organization for immediate help to trapped and injured air raid victims. It was created in May 1942 and placed under the command of Reichsführer SS Himmler in his capacity as chief of the German police. Members were exempt from military conscription. See Sicherheits und Hilfdienst.

Luftschutzraum. (See illustration on page 104.) Shelter for civilian population. Luftschützräume (pl.) were always placed in the middle of a city. They were huge, rectangular concrete buildings with 2- to 3-meter-thick roof and walls, camouflaged as a normal urban buildings. Some of them were round towers; others were shell-shaped (anthill) in hopes of deflecting bombs. Luftschützräume consisted of a vast reception hall, staircases and lifts leading to many rooms; they usually included an infirmary, water supply and lavatories. When Allied air raids started, these shelters were not numerous, but with the intensification of Allied bombardment, their number was considerably increased. Arrangement and disposition were standardized, allowing protection of 500, 1,000, 2,000 or 4,000 people. Some shelters could even hold up to 12,000 or 18,000 persons. See Reichsluftschutzbund.

Luftschutzwart. Worthy of being defended from air attack, such as a town, an industrial center, a shipyard, and the like.

Luftverteidigungszone West (LVZ-W). Zone of air defense west. This zone was formed shortly before the war, in 1938, as a part of the Westwall (q.v.). The LVZ-W was a massive deployment of light and heavy antiaircraft guns in a belt 30 kilometers deep stretching from the Black Forest to the Saar and later extended, first to Aachen, then to the Heligoland Bight and finally to Schleswig-Holstein.

Luftschutzraum at Aachen.

Luftwaffe (L, Lw). German air force. The Luftwaffe, unlike the other two branches of the Wehrmacht (Heer and Kriegsmarine), was wholly created by the Nazis, since the World War I air force had been part of the army and any other air force had been forbidden by the Treaty of Versailles. Headed and created in 1935 by Reichsmarschall Hermann Göring (q.v.), the Luftwaffe was consequently looked on much more favorably by the Nazi hierarchy than were the Heer and Kriegsmarine. Hitler saw the air force as an important tool for achieving his territorial conquest and the Luftwaffe expanded greatly in the late 1930s. The main characteristic of the Luftwaffe was tactical, concentrating air power in support of ground operations in so-called Blitzkrieg (q.v.). Although a few strategic long-range bombing airplanes were developed, they never went into full production and this lack proved a significant weakness. The Luftwaffe also suffered from serious organizational weakness at the top. Göring was both Luftwaffe commander-in-chief and Reich aviation minister, having control over all air matters through the Reichsluftfahrtministerium (Reich Aviation Ministry). Personal enmity between various services did not help, and the situation was made worse by Göring's incompetence and laziness, as the Reichsmarschall often accepted over-optimistic reports rather than realistic ones. Because of Göring's standing within the Nazi hierarchy, Hitler allowed him to run the air force with little interference for much of the war. By mid–1944 Göring had lost all interest in his air force and Hitler increasingly concerned himself with Luftwaffe affairs, making the situation even worse. The Oberkommando der Luftwaffe (OKL, air force high command) was placed under command of the Oberkommando der Wehrmacht (OKW, high command of all three German armed forces). The Luftwaffe was divided into Luftflotten (air fleets), Fliegerkorps (flying corps) and Fliegerdivisionen (flying divisions), Geschwadern (groups), Gruppen (wings) and Staffeln (squadrons). Although the production of planes peaked in 1944, the Luftwaffe eventually lost the war in the air not so much through inferior aircraft but through lack of fuel and shortage of experienced instructors and airmen. The Luftwaffe also possessed a number of ground troops, as Göring was a private empire builder. He helped the creation of the German paratrooper force and developed Luftwaffe infantry divisions. The Reichsmarschall also had his own armored division, the

The Luftwaffe Hoheitsabzeichen represented a diving eagle holding a swastika in one of its claws.

elite Hermann Göring Panzerdivision (q.v.) See Fallschirmjäger and Luftwaffe-Feld-Division.

Luftwaffe-Feld-Division (LFD or Lw-Feld-Div). Air force infantry division. During 1942, Alarmeinheiten (q.v.) of the German air force became regiments and infantry divisions, not only for defensive purpose, but also because of a dire need for front-line combatants deployed as regular infantry troops. They fell under the tactical command of the Heer while in operation in the field, but remained under Luftwaffe control for personnel and administrative purposes. Twenty-one LFD divisions were created during World War II, but because they were poorly equipped, under regular strength, and badly led, their combat performances were on the whole rather mitigated.

Luftwaffeneinsatz. A branch of the RAD/Kriegshilfdienst (q.v.) comprising militarized women employed in air communication (e.g., operation of radar, searchlights and fighter direction stations), and air raid services. In all, the compulsory call-up of women in the Luftwaffeneinsatz brought in between 300,000 and 350,000. See Reichsarbeitsdienst.

Luger. A pistol. The well-known and quasi-legendary P08 9mm Parabellum pistol was commonly called the Luger after its designer, the Austrian Georg Luger (1848–1922). Designed in 1908, the long-lived Luger was a 9-millimeter caliber semiautomatic with an eight-round magazine contained in the grip. It weighed 0.87 kilograms. It existed in several versions, and was the common sidearm used by all German forces during both world wars.

Lüger, Karl (1844–1910). The mayor of Vienna between 1897 and 1910, when Hitler lived there

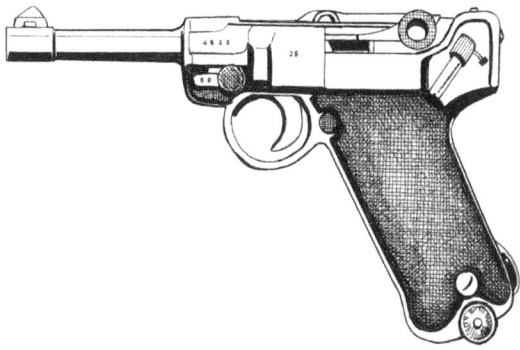

Parabellum M08 Luger pistol.

as a youth. In *Mein Kampf* (q.v.) Hitler called him "the last great German to be born in Austria."

Lutze, Victor (1890–1943). An SA senior officer who secretly helped the Nazis for the preparation of the Nacht der Langen Messer (q.v.). After the assassination of Ernst Röhm (q.v.), as a reward, Lutze was appointed leader of the SA. But it was now an SA in decline, with limited power and no longer in a position to challenge either the German army or Hitler's leadership. See Sturm Abteilung der NSDAP.

M19. 5-centimeter automatic mortar. The M19 grenade launcher was especially designed to equip bunkers and was generally placed in a Turm (armored cupola). Designed and produced by Rheinmetall-Borsig AG Company of Düsseldorf, the mortar had a range of 50 to 600 meters with a rate of 20 shells a minute when manually loaded and a formidable 100 grenades a minute in automatic mode.

Machtübermahme or **Machtergreifung.** Seizure of power by Hitler and the Nazis on January 30, 1933.

Madagaskarplan. Operation Madagascar, a pre–World War II scheme in which all German Jews would be deported to the island of Madagascar in the Indian Ocean. The plan would have been very difficult to implement, and one may wonder whether it ever was a serious proposal. By 1941 it was no more than a smokescreen for the true nature of the Endlösung der Judenfrage (q.v.).

MaFla. See Marineflakabteilung.

Maidanek. See Lublin.

Mammut. Mammoth. German radar. The Funkmeßgerät FUMG 51 Mammut, designed and produced by the Telefunken Company, was an early-warning instrument with a range of 200 to 300 kilometers. Its aerial, weighing some 150 tons, was a large, flat vertical frame 15 meters high and 30 meters wide. It could not rotate, and searching was accomplished by means of electronic compensators giving a directional angle of 120 degrees forwards and 120 degrees backwards. The huge aerial was fixed on strong concrete poles resting on the roof of specially designed bunkers: Luftwaffe types L485–1 and L485–2, and navy bunker type V143.

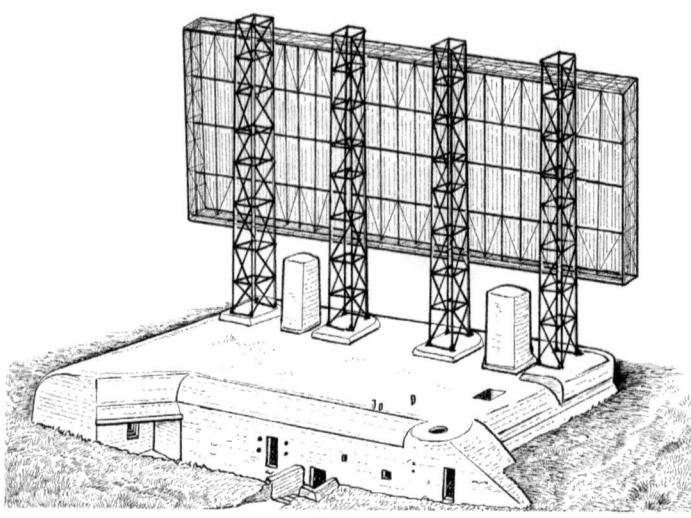

Mammut radar on bunker L 485 (1).

Männerbund. Bond of men; a distinctly masculinist mystique that became an essential part of Nazi ideology.

Mannschaft. Crew, team, group or — in the German infantry — a squad of ten men.

Mannschaftraum. Troop chamber in a bunker generally for the accommodation of a Gruppe of eight to ten soldiers.

Mantel. Greatcoat. The Mantel was a standard pattern throughout the German army and NSDAP formations. Issued in a large variety of qualities and colors, the Mantel was a long double-breasted garment reaching to the wearer's calf. It had two rows of six gray metal buttons (gilded for officers), deep turn-back cuffs and two side slash pockets. After 1943, for reasons of economy, the Mantel for privates was made from inferior quality material. There was a rubberized version designed as a raincoat known as Klepper.

Mantel worn by **NSDAP Bereichsleiter.**

Marburg Rede. A public speech given in June 1934 at Marburg University by Reich Deputy Chancellor Franz von Papen (q.v.), criticizing Nazi methods, condemning the brutal implementation of Gleichschaltung (q.v.) and calling for a return to democracy and freedom. The speech was written by Edgar Jung and Erich Klausener. Both were murdered within a week during the Nacht der Langen Messer (q.v.).

Marine (M). German navy. See Kriegsmarine.

Marineflakabteilung (MaFla, MFLA). Navy flak (antiaircraft artillery). The MaFla mission was to protect the airspace above harbors, navy installations and U-Boote bases. Navy flak batteries (called Marineflakbatterieen, or MFLB) were placed on ships or permanently installed as ground units. An MFLB was quite similar to a standard Luftwaffe Flak battery. Guns, searchlights, measuring instruments, range finders and radar were the same, but each arm designed its own installations and bunkers. A permanent navy heavy-flak battery was generally composed of a fire control station, various flak gun emplacements, ammunitions store, radar, shelters for searchlights and a power plant. The battery was arranged as a Stützpunkt (q.v.) and fenced with barbed wires and mines.

Marineflakbatterie. Navy flak battery. See Marineflakabteilung.

Marineküstenartillerie (MKA). Navy coastal artillery. The Marineküstenartillerie's principal purpose was to defend the main German-held harbors. The MKA was divided into three categories: light artillery with caliber up to 10.5 centimeters; medium artillery, from 10.5 up to 22 centimeters caliber; heavy artillery, with caliber greater than 22 centimeters. All MKA categories were organized in navy batteries (Marineküstenbatterien, or MKB, also called Seezielbatterieen). A navy coastal heavy battery included a fire leading post called Feuerleitstand (fire control station); four (sometimes six) guns sheltered in bunkers disposed in line facing the sea; ammunitions stores; and personnel shelters as well as various service and logistic buildings. The battery was arranged as a Stützpunkt (q.v.).

Marineküstenbatterie (MKB). Navy coastal battery. See Marineküstenartillerie.

Marinesignalstelle (MSS). Navy signal post.

Marsch auf die Feldherrnhalle. Nazi demonstration held in Munich on November 8, 1923, that was repressed by the police. See Bürgerbräu Keller Putsch.

Märzgefallene or **Märzveilchen.** See Septemberling.

Maschinegewehr (MG). Machine gun. During World War II, the Germans did not produce separate heavy and light MGs but used the dual-purpose air-cooled Maschinengewehr MG 34 and Maschinengewehr MG 42. Both MG 34 and MG 42 were general-purpose weapons combining the characteristics of a light machine gun—limited weight, manageability—and the formidable fire rate of a heavy machine gun. The MG 34 weighed 12 kilograms and shot about 800 rounds per minute. Production of the MG 34 continued until 1945, concurrent with the later heavier MG 42. The remarkable Maschinengewehr MG 42 weighted 11 kilograms and could fire up to 1,500 rounds per minute. Both used the standard German 7.92-millimeter cartridge fed either by a 250-cartridge belt or by a cylindrical magazine (Gurttrommel) containing 50 projectiles. Both could be adapted to various mountings, such as a portable infantry bipod, or be fitted on a vehicle (tank) or in a bunker with a special fortress mounting.

Maschinegewehr Werkzeug Tasche Modell 35. The MG gunner leather tool pouch M35 was carried on the waist belt, generally on the right side. Its dimensions were 19.5 centimeters by 15.5 centimeters by 6 centimeters. It contained the following standard item: an oil can; a belt tag for repair purposes; a complete MG spare bolt; a ruptured cartridge remover; a wrench MG13; a screwdriver/case extractor; a spanner wrench for the cradle spring assembly; an antiaircraft ring sight; spare muzzle covers; and a hot-barrel hand protector.

Maschinenfabrik Augsburg-Nürnberg (M.A.N.). Augsburg-Nuremberg Machine Factory, a German company engineering and manufacturing tanks and other vehicles during World War II.

Maschinepistole (MPi). Submachine gun. German World War II submachine guns were generally simple and cheap to produce. They worked on the blowback principle. They were lightweight and always intended for close combat ranging up to about 100 meters and not for precision sniping. The most produced MPis were the MPi 38 and the MPi 40, which could fire about 500 rounds per minute, using 9-millimeter ammunition, fitted with a 32-round magazine, weighing about 4 kilograms with foldable butt. The MPi 38 and the MPi 40 were sometimes called Schmeißer after the German weapon designer Hugo Schmeißer (wrongly, though, because Schmeißer had little to do with the design of the weapon). Other German submachine guns were the older MPi 35 Bergmann 9 millimeter (mainly issued to SS before the war), the Erma MPi 9 millimeter, the MPi 3008 (a copy of the British Sten gun) and the improved assault rifle Sturmgewehr MPi 44, intro-

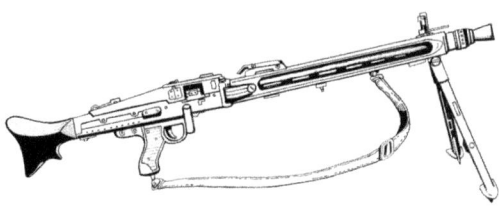

Maschinegewehr MG 42.

Machinepistole MPi 40.

duced at the end of the war. See Erfurter Maschinefabrik Haenel und Suhl.

Master race. See Herrenvolk.

Maurice, Emil (1897–1972). A watch- and clockmaker by profession, Maurice joined the Nazi Party in 1919, and soon became head of Hitler's bodyguard unit at public meetings, and his personal chauffeur. He took part in the Munich Putsch in 1923 and was imprisoned with Hitler in Lansberg prison. Maurice was friendly with Geli Raubal (q.v.), and there were rumors that he had an affair with her. Maurice was with Hitler during the Night of the Long Knives (q.v.) and was responsible for the execution of SA leader Edmund Heines and his boyfriend. He was also responsible for the killing of Father Bernhard Stempfle, who had been talking too much about Hitler's rela-tionship with Geli Raubal. In 1937 Maurice kept his distance from the Nazis and returned to his former endeavor by becoming head of the Landeshandwerksmeister, a society of professional handicraft workers in Munich. From 1940 to 1942, he served in the Luftwaffe. After the war in 1948, Maurice was sentenced to four years' imprisonment for his early involvement in pre–World War II Nazi crimes.

Maus. Mouse. Name given to the PzKpfw VIII SdKfz 205 superheavy assault tank. The Maus—designed by the engineer Ferdinand Porsche (q.v.) as early as 1942—appeared in late 1944. It cost the Germans much time and money, and only two test prototypes were produced. These never saw action but were captured by advancing Soviet troops. The Maus, described by Porsche himself as a mobile fortress, was armed with a heavy 12.8-centimeter gun with a coaxially mounted 7.5-centimeter gun. Its weight (about 180 metric tons) and length (11 meters) made it slow and hard to handle. The vehicle's huge proportions reflected Hitler's megalomaniac enthusiasm for large tanks.

Mauser. The common name of the German arms manufacturer Mauser-Werke Oberndorf Waffensysteme GmbH, formed in the 1870s. See Gewehr and Sturmgewehr.

Mauthausen-Gusen. A concentration/work camp located near Linz in Upper Austria. Established after the Anschluß Osterreichs(q.v.) in 1939, and initially a single camp intended to be the toughest camp for the "incorrigible political enemies of the Reich," Mauthausen greatly expanded over time. During World War II, the Mauthausen-Gusen camp, headed by SS Sturm-

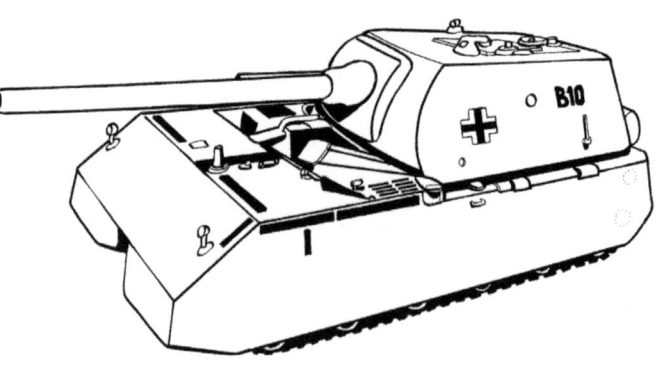

Maus Super heavy tank PzKpfw VIII.

bannführer Franz Ziereis, became one of the largest forced labor complexes in German occupied Europe. Apart from the four main sub-camps at Mauthausen and nearby Gusen, more than 50 subcamps, located throughout Austria and southern Germany, used the inmates as slave labor. Several subordinate camps of the KZ Mauthausen complex included stone quarries, ammunitions factories, mines, arms factories and Messerschmitt 262 fighter-plane assembly plants. Officially Mauthausen was not an extermination camp, but in practice prisoners were exterminated through hard labor, starvation and horrific living conditions. The death toll remains unknown. The official Totenbuch (q.v.) indicates 36,318 executions, but other sources indicate between 123,000 and 320,000 victims. Franz Ziereis was shot by American soldiers when trying to escape in May 1945, and his dead body was later hung on the fence of the camp by former prisoners.

Maybach (M). A German automotive and engineering company created in 1909. Wilhelm Maybach was the inventor of numerous engines and his inventions became landmarks in the history of automotive engineering. During World War II the company produced engines for armored vehicles and tanks.

Max Heiliger Deposit Account. Cover name for an SS bank deposit consisting, among other things, of the macabre booty stolen from the victims of extermination camps. The whereabouts of Nazi treasures that disappeared in 1945 have been the subject of numerous books, speculations and conspiracy theories. In April 1945, as the Russians closed in on Berlin, Ernst Kaltenbrunner (q.v.) ordered a raid on the Reichsbank and cleared out the last of the valuables, worth some $10 million, which he regarded as belonging to the SS. Before this, Oswald Pohl (q.v.)— who wisely had taken care to make himself a director of a Swiss bank—had moved SS gold, jewelry, and foreign currency (valued then at over $300 million) to mines in Thuringia in February 1945. Within a month part of this consignment was captured by American troops. It is clear, however, that the Americans did not recover all the Nazi treasure, and most probably this money was used to finance SS escape routes and later set up SS survivors in civilian business. See Canada and Wirtschafts-und Verwaltungshauptamt.

Mefo Bills. See Metallurgische Forschung GmbH.

Mein Kampf. (*My Combat* or *My Struggle*). Although extremely averse to writing anything down and preferring the power of speech, Hitler wrote a book in 1924 during his stay in prison, in which he attempted to set out his political ideas. The first volume, four hundred pages long and costing the high price of twelve marks, was published in summer 1925. By the end of the year the book had sold 9,473 copies. Sales went down from 6,913 in 1926 to 3,015 in 1928, and shot up to 50,000 in 1930 and 1931. From 1925 until 1933 the royalties from *Mein Kampf* and the high fees received for newspaper articles published in the Nazi press were Hitler's principal source of personal income. After 1933, *Mein Kampf* made Hitler a wealthy man. By 1940 six million copies were sold. In 1928 Hitler had written another book, on foreign policy, but this manuscript, known as "Hitlers Zweites Buch" (Hitler's second book), remained unpublished until 1961. "Turgid," "monotonous" and "repetitive" are the familiar terms that commentators have used to convey something of the flavor of Hitler's prose. See Amann, Max; Hess, Rudolf; and Tischgespräche im Führerhauptquartier.

Meine Ehre heißt Treue. "My Honor Is Loyalty," the SS's motto.

SS motto "Meine Ehre heißt Treue" on belt buckle.

Memel. A city and Baltic seaport with its territory in East Prussia, belonging to Germany since the time of the Teutonic knights, now known as Klaipeda, part of Lithuania. Memelland, the area separated from Germany by the Treaty of Versailles, had a substantial German-speaking community. After the bloodless and successful seizure of the Sudetenland in 1938, Hitler demanded the return of Memel. Lithuania con-

Mengele

ceded and the region became a part of Germany again. See Großdeutschland and Volksdeutsche.

Mengele, Joseph (1911–1979?). The notorious Auschwitz doctor, known as the "Angel of Death," in charge of pointless medico-racial experiments in the period 1943–1945. No information of medical value is known to have emerged from the tortures inflicted on those Mengele called his "patients" (twins, dwarfs, hunchbacks and persons with physical abnormalities). After the war the "Angel of Death" escaped to South America and became one of the most hunted Nazi war criminals. Mengele was never found and is believed to have died in 1979.

Mensur. Duel. Dueling was forbidden during the Weimar Republic, but it was legalized by the Nazis as a means of instilling students with discipline, courage, and indifference to pain. In November 1935 Heinrich Himmler (q.v.) stipulated that every SS man had the legal right and duty to defend his honor by force of arms under certain precisely recorded conditions.

Meschuggismus. Cult of insanity (from the Yiddish *meschugge*, meaning crazy). Term used by the Nazis to denounce modern "degenerate" art like expressionism, surrealism, impressionism and dada. See Entartete Kunst and Kunst.

Messerschmitt (Me). Engineer Willy Emil Messerschmitt (1898–1978) became head of the company Bayerische Flugzeugwerke (Bf) in 1927. The most significant plane designed in 1935 and produced by Willy Messerschmitt's company was the all-metal, one-seat, single-spar wing fighter Messerschmitt Bf 109, which proved one of the most outstanding fighters of World War II. Another Messerschmitt/Bayerische Flugzeugwerke production was the less successful twin-engine, two-seat, escort fighter/light bomber Messerschmitt Me/Bf 110. Worthy of mention is the gigantic Messerschmitt Me 323 transport airplane with six engines (adapted from the Me 321 glider). Messerschmitt was also a pioneer in the domain of jet aircraft, such as the experimental rocket-propelled fighter Messerschmitt Me 163 Komet, and the first operational twin jet-propelled combat airplane, the Messerschmitt Me 262. The revolutionary Me 262 was a break-through in aeronautics and the inspiration to many postwar jet fighters.

Metallurgische Forschung GmbH (Mefo). Metallurgical Research, Inc. Cover name for special banknotes invented by Dr. Hjalmar Schacht (q.v.). Mefos were issued by the Reichsbank and guaranteed by the Nazi regime as a means of maintaining secrecy in rearmament. Used to pay arms manufacturers, Mefo bills were accepted by all German banks, but their mention was strictly forbidden. About 12 billion marks in Mefo bills was issued between 1935 and 1939.

Milch, Erhard (1882–1972). During World War I, Milch served in the German army as an ar-

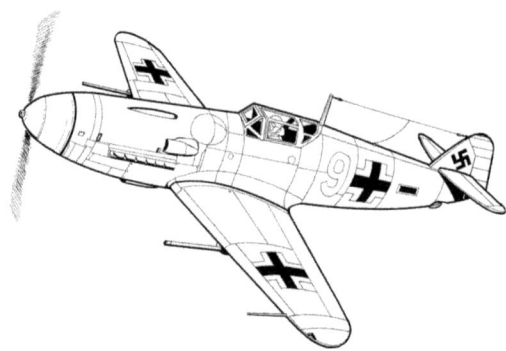

Messerschmitt Bf 109 F.

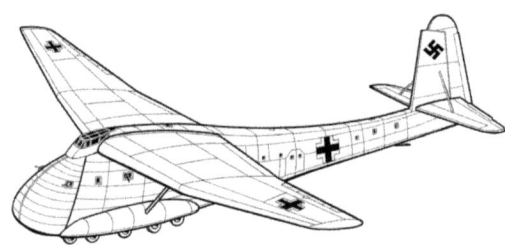

Cargo glider Messerschmitt Me 321 Gigant.

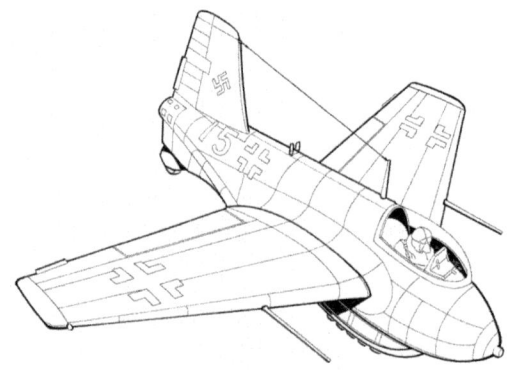

Messerschmitt Me 163.

tillery officer and then as a pilot flying observation planes, and later commanded a squadron. In the 1920s he worked in various civilian air companies and became managing director of Deutsche Lufthansa (q.v.) in 1926. In the 1930s Milch entered government service as the state secretary of the newly formed Reichsluftfahrtministerium and was instrumental in establishing the Luftwaffe (q.v.) During World War II, he commanded Luftflotte V during the Norwegian campaign, and as general air inspector and field marshal was placed in charge of the production of military aircraft in Germany. Milch was tried at Nuremberg, and sentenced to life imprisonment for war crimes and crimes against humanity. In 1951, his sentence was commuted to 15 years, and he was released in June 1954.

Mimoyecques. See V3.

Mine. Explosive devices concealed under the ground or at sea. A mine is composed of a main charge in a container, a detonator that sets off the main charge, and a firing mechanism, which sets off the detonator. There existed three main sorts of mines. Antipersonnel mines exploded when walked on or when a wire was disengaged; antitank mines were high explosives used to destroy tanks and vehicles; sea mines were spread in large numbers at sea to create a strategic blocade.

Minensucher. See Räumboot.

Minenwerfer. Literally "mine thrower." A mortar, a short-barreled, smoothbore high-angled weapon for dropping projectiles on top of and behind enemy defense. See Granatwerfer and Mörser.

Mirus. The battery Mirus established in Guernsey (British Channel Isles) was one of the most powerful artillery positions of the Atlantikwall (q.v.) It comprised four 30.5-centimeter guns originating from a Russian warship. The guns, housed in special huge concrete bunkers, could fire to a range of 50 kilometers.

Mischling. People of mixed race according to Nazi racial criteria.

Mistel. Mistletoe. The name for a program that included various types of planes, most commonly

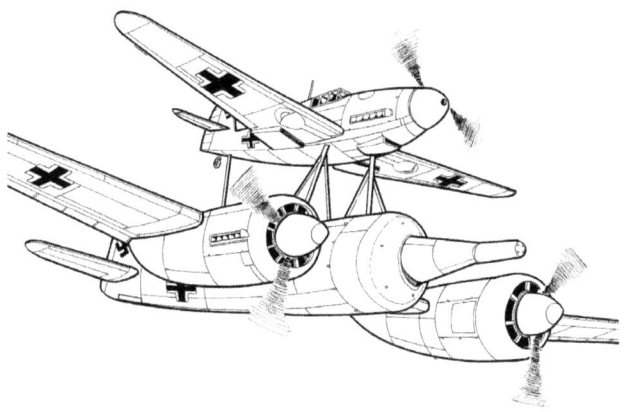

Mistel 1 (Me 109 with rebuilt Ju 88).

rebuilt Junkers Ju 88s, having their forward fuselage filled with explosives, which were guided by an attached fighter (Messerschmitt Bf 109 or Focke Wulf 190). These were developed for long-range attack with maximum destructive power, using the bomber's engine to reach the target. Once above the objective, the bomber was released and either radio-controlled or left to dive onto the target on autopilot while the fighter's pilot had sufficient fuel to return to his base. Mistel was employed in March 1945 to destroy bridges across the river Oder but it never made any significant tactical impact on the war. See also KG200.

Mit brennender Sorge. *With Deep Anxiety*, an encyclical addressed to German bishops (written in German and not in the usual Latin), issued in March 1937 by Pope Pius XI (q.v.) to warn against Nazism and to express the Vatican's dissatisfaction with the Nazi application of the terms of the Concordat of 1933. See Pius XII and Reichskonkordat.

Mitford, Unity (1914–1948). British aristocrat (daughter of the 2nd Baron Redesdale) who became one of Adolf Hitler's friends. Mitford's parents held right-wing political views and supported the British Union of Fascists, and in 1936 their daughter Diana Mitford married its leader, Oswald Mosley (q.v.) Unity, already filled with racist views, was dazzled by the Nazis. She went to Germany and within months she was part of Hitler's inner circle and thought to be his mistress. Hitler told newspapers in Germany that Unity was "a perfect specimen of Aryan womanhood." On the outbreak of World War II

Unity — torn between love for her homeland and dedication to Hitler — tried to commit suicide. She survived and returned to England suffering from gunshot wounds. She died from her brain injury in 1948.

Mitglied der NSDAP or **Parteigenosse** (Pg). Member of the Nazi Party. For admission as Mitglied, three main conditions were demanded: to be a Reichsdeutsche (German national); to be eighteen years old; and to be of non–Jewish and non–Slav descent since 1800. If many Parteigenossen were convinced National Socialists, a majority joined for opportunistic and personal motives, to make a career, to profit from various advantages, from greed, or to become a local Führer, what the Germans call "mitlaufen" (freely translated as "following" or "just walking along" with the Nazis).

Mittel (M. or m. in short). Medium, notably for artillery, planes, tanks and other vehicles.

Mittelstand. The German middle- and lower-middle class, socially composed of shopkeepers, petty white collar workers, clerks, factory foremen, schoolteachers, low-level managers, and small businessmen, was the main target population for the NSDAP. In the late 1920s and early 1930s, a large part of the embittered Mittelstand, squeezed by inflation, economic crisis, uncertainty and unemployment, was prepared to believe that the Jews were responsible for their misery and that the Nazi Party was the only political formation that would improve their situation.

Mittelwerk. See Dora.

Mjölnir. In ancient Germanic mythology, Mjölnir was the name of Thor's hammer. It was also the pseudonym of artist Hans Schweitzer (1901–1980). Hans Schweitzer signed his posters Mjölnir for dramatic effect rather than to hide his real identity. One of Hitler's favorite artists, Mjölnir produced many propaganda posters for the Nazi Party. In 1937, he was appointed reich commissioner for artistic design and chairman of the Reich Committee of Press Illustrators. After the war, Schweitzer was fined 500 deutsche marks, and was boycotted as "Goebbels' illustrator," but nonetheless found work designing posters for the West German federal press and information office and as an illustrator in the German right-wing press.

Möbelwagen. Literally, "removal van"; nickname given to the Panzerflak IV F. The Möbelwagen, put into production in late 1943, was composed of the chassis of a Panzerkampfwagen PzKfw IV upon which a four-barreled 2-centimeter gun (Vierling 38 with a devastating rate of fire of 800 rounds per minute) was centrally mounted. There were also other versions armed with one 3.7-centimeter flak 43, and others armed with one 8.8-centimeter antiaircraft gun.

Möbelwagen.

Moffen. Dutch insulting slang word for Germans.

Morell, Theodor (1890–1948). Hitler's personal physician. Morell was presented to Hitler by his photographer Heinrich Hoffmann (q.v.), and for nine years the Führer submitted to his treatment, which greatly contributed to wreck his health. Morell was a quack who prescribed fancy nostrums, fake medicines, narcotics, addictive remedies and artificial stimulants, a therapy which in the end ruined the patient's health by slow poisoning. Though rejected by Hitler in 1944, Morell came back into grace and exercised total control over Hitler in the last six months of his life. The greedy Morell became an immensely rich man. He built factories, manufactured his own patent remedies, and secured a monopoly for his own brands. The purchase of Morell's lice powder was made compulsory throughout the German army. Morell died at Tegernsee in 1948.

Morgenthau Plan. A scheme devised by U.S. President Roosevelt's Secretary of the Treasury, Henry P. Morgenthau, to reduce Germany after its defeat to an agricultural economy. The announcement of the plan at the Quebec Conference in September 1944 was a serious mistake on the part of the Allies, enabling Goebbels to present the plan as the alternative to fighting to the last man. Besides, Morgenthau was a Jew, another reason to continue the fight. See Totaler Krieg.

Mörser. Mortar. See Granatwerfer and Karl.

Mosley, Oswald (1896–1980). A British aristocrat (6th Baronet of Ancoats) and politician, known principally as the founder of the British Union of Fascists (BUF) in 1932. The BUF was dissolved in 1940 and Mosley was interned. After the war he formed the Union Movement, calling for a single national party in Europe.

Motor SA. Motorized units of the SA. See Nationalsozialistisches Kraftfahrkorps and Sturm Abteilung der NSDAP.

Motorisiert (Mot.). Motorized, mobile; an artillery or infantry unit that was equipped with significant wheeled transport. Often used as an adjective and thus not capitalized.

Motorrad or **Kraftrad** (Krad). Motorcycle. Bikes were used in the German army as early as the 1930s. The Germans mainly used Zündapp, NSU and BMW motorbikes with sidecars, equipped with powerful 750-cubic centimeter engines that drove both the rear wheel of the bike and the sidecar wheel to greatly improve performance. Whole battalions were issued motorcycles with sidecars mainly for reconnaissance or communications purposes. A biker was called a Motorradfahrer or Kradfahrer. See Spähtruppen.

Müller, Heinrich (1896–?). A Bavarian SS expert on politics and police, Müller was appointed by Reinhard Heydrich (q.v.) head of the infamous Gestapo (q.v.). Heinrich Müller together with Otto Adolf Eichmann (q.v.) carried the final solution into action. The criminal Müller vanished in Berlin by the end of World War II, most presumably having planned his escape long in advance.

Müller, Ludwig (1883–1946). Outspokenly nationalist, anti–Semite and pro–Nazi, Ludwig Müller was elected Reich Bishop of the Protestant Church in 1933. The opposition to this pro–Nazi Protestant group was the Confessional Church. See, Bekenntniskirche, Martin Niemöller, and Religion in the Third Reich.

Münchener Abkommen. Munich Agreement, signed September 29–30, 1938, between Germany, Italy, France and Britain, ceding the German-speaking Sudetenland of Czechoslovakia to Nazi Germany. The region was handed over without any consultation with the inhabitants. The Munich Agreement was a result of the Franco-British policy of "appeasement," a policy of negotiations and compromises to prevent Hitler from taking international law into his own hands.

Münchener Beobachter. *Munich Observer.* A völkisch newspaper edited by Rudolf von Sebottendorf (q.v.). In the course of 1920 it became the official Nazi organ, renamed the *Völkischer Beobachter* (q.v.).

Munich agreement. See Münchener Abkommen.

Munich Beer Hall Putsch. See Bürgerbräu Keller Putsch.

Munich Putsch. See Bürgerbräu Keller Putsch.

Music in the Third Reich. Hitler's regime highly favored music, which alluded to a mythic, heroic German past, and embraced classical "German" composers such as Bach, Beethoven, Wagner, and Richard Strauss. Important music festivals (Wagner at Bayreuth, Mozart at Salzburg) were sponsored and used as Nazi propaganda tools. The Nazis made concentrated efforts to shun modern music, which was considered degenerate and Jewish in nature. Avantgarde and atonal music was forbidden, and composers like Schoenberg, Mahler, Mendelssohn and many others were banned because they were Jewish. After January 1933, a stream of musical emigrants—composers, conductors and performers—began to leave Germany for a friendlier environment. Mass culture was less stringently regulated than high culture, possibly because the authorities feared the consequences of too heavy-handed interference in popular entertainment. Thus, until the outbreak of World War II, leading English and American jazz bands continued to perform in major German cities. After 1939, dance bands officially played "swing" rather than the banned "Negro jazz." The Nazis emphasized military marches and songs. They also strongly encouraged the revival, practice and performance of German traditional songs and folk music. Dance music was governed by a policy that tried to take into account both the seriousness of the war and the widespread desire for frivolous diversion. See Kunst, Reichskulturkammer, Swing Jugend and Wunschkonzert.

Musikerschutze. Private musician.

Musquetier (or Musketier). Musketeer, infantryman or rifleman. This term was exclusively applied to privates of the Panzerkorps Großdeutschland as a morale booster.

Mussert, Anton (1894–1946). A Dutch engineer, founder of the Nationaal-Socialistisch Beweging (NSB, National Socialist Movement), in imitation of Hitler's party. During World War II, Mussert and the NSB worked closely with the German occupiers. Arrested in 1945, Mussert was tried and hanged in May 1946. See Fünfte Kolonne.

Mussolini, Benito (1883–1945). Italian dictator and founder of Italian Fascism. Mussolini's seizure of power through the Marcia su Roma (March on Rome) in October 1922 impressed Hitler and was the inspiration for his 1923 Beer Hall Putsch. The Germano-Italian collaboration was marked by the formation of the Rome-Berlin Axis in 1936 and the signing of the Anti-Comintern pact in 1937. During World War II, both countries were allied, but soon the humiliating defeats suffered by Mussolini made Italy little more than a cumbersome client to Germany. Nevertheless, Hitler never stopped admiring Il Duce, and when Mussolini was destitute, he ordered his rescue, and had him brought to northern Italy to head a new Italian state, a puppet of Germany. Benito Mussolini and his mistress Clara Petacci were captured and shot by Italian anti–Fascist partisans in April 1945, and their bodies were taken to Milan and strung up by the heels, a fate Hitler did not want to suffer (he instead decided to commit suicide). See Achse and Skorzeny, Otto.

Mutterkreuz. Mother cross. Motherhood was the highest aim for German girls and women. Families were encouraged to have at least four children. A special medal was created in December 1938 for this purpose. The Mutter Kreuz, or Ehrenzeichen der Deutschen Mutter (cross of honor for the German mother), was bestowed on mothers of large families in three classes: bronze for four or five children; silver for six or seven children; and gold for eight or more children.

My Struggle. See *Mein Kampf.*

Der Mythus des 20. Jahrhunderts. The *Myth of the Twentieth Century,* a book written by the Nazi "philosopher" Alfred Rosenberg (q.v.). Published in 1931, and with 713,000 copies sold, *der Mythus* was regarded as the second standard text for Nazi ideology, the other being Hitler's *Mein Kampf* (q.v.) Rosenberg's 700-page book developed the main Nazi ideas, such as Lebensraum (q.v.); defense of the white Aryan race; the eternal struggle for survival; rejection of churches; mythisizing of the northern Germanic blood; hatred against the Jews, who were held responsible for all the decaying international movements and aiming at the destruction of the Aryan; hatred against Roman Catholicism, Freemasonry, and Marxism. Worthy of mention is that Hitler and other Nazi leaders mocked Rosenberg's idealistic mysticism. Albert Speer reported that Hitler once said that *der Mythus* was "stuff nobody can understand" written by "a narrow-minded Baltic German who thinks in horribly complicated terms."

Mutterkreuz.

Nachrichten (N, Nachr.). Signal, news, transmission, communication.

Nachrichtendienst. Intelligence service.

Nachschub. Supply.

Nacht der langen Messer. The Night of Long Knives, also called Blood Purge or Röhm Purge. A campaign of assassination unleashed by Hitler on the weekend of June 29 and 30, 1934, against the growing power of the Sturm Abteilung der NSDAP (q.v.) and the deviant SA chief Ernst

Röhm (q.v.). The massacre was directed against the so-called socialist left wing of the party, which was a challenge and a potential threat to Hitler's power. The elimination of the SA leadership was also an excuse for the murder of several internal opponents annoying to the Nazi regime. Officially the Nazis spoke of 77 casualties, but it is more probable that the purge cost the lives of some 1,000 SA leaders and opponents not connected with the SA. The bloody purge was later presented to the German people and to the international public opinion as an act of high justice perpetrated by Hitler in a moment of intense emergency.

Nacht und Nebel Erlaß. Decree of Night and Fog, December 1941. Ordered by Hitler and issued by the OKW and General Wilhelm Keitel (q.v.), the decree stipulated that any person found guilty or suspected of anti–German activity would be deported to a concentration camp. Tried in Sondergerichte (special courts of justice), or often without trial at all, real or supposed enemies of the Reich were disposed of without leaving any traces. The aim of the decree was deliberately to initiate a new dimension of intimidation, repression and fear. German authorities applied the decree principally in German-occupied Western Europe: Belgium, France, Luxembourg, Norway, Denmark, and the Netherlands. German occupation authorities and their collaborators arrested approximately 7,000 individuals under the provisions of the Night and Fog decree, nearly 5,000 of them in France. The code name stemmed from Germany's most acclaimed poet and playwright, Johann Wolfgang von Göthe (1749–1832), who used the phrase to describe clandestine illegal actions often concealed by fog and the darkness of night.

Napola. See Nationalpolitischen Erziehungsanstalten.

Nationalpolitischen Erziehungsanstalten (NPEA or Napola). National political education institutes. Created in April 1933 under the direction of August Heißmeyer, these schools were established for the purpose of training a Nazi elite for high posts in the government of the Third Reich. Though part of the Ministry of Education, Napolas were under the SS's tutelage, and candidates were nominated by high SS functionaries responsible only to Himmler and Hitler. Most candidates came from the rural and labor elements of the population. The teaching was greatly influenced by the Nazi ideology, with a strong emphasis on racism and anti–Semitism, soldierly spirit, physical courage and training, sense of duty and simplicity, and forming of a Nazi personality rather than intellectual development. There were three Napolas in 1933 and twenty-three by 1938, including four in Austria and one in the annexed Sudeten area of Czechoslovakia. This number grew to about forty during World War II. See Adolf-Hitler-Schule, Hitler Jugend, and Ordensburgen.

Nationalsozialistische (NS, Natsoz, or Nazi). National Socialist, pertaining to the official German Nazi Party (NSDAP) unit or organization, and not to the German government.

Nationalsozialistische Betriebszellen-Organisation (NSBO). National Socialist Factory Cell Organisation. The NSBO was created in 1928 by Nazi-led workers as an alternative to democratic and Christian labor and trade unions. By means of aggressive propaganda and violence, the NSBO participated in the Kampfzeit (q.v.). After the seizure of power in January 1933, all non–Nazi trade unions were outlawed by decree in May 1933. The NSBO then became the only official workers' organization in Germany. This moment of triumph, however, was short lived, for the Nazi leadership had decided that there would be no role whatsoever for trade unions in the new Reich. Instead the German Labor Front (DAF) was established a few days later. More organized and better represented at national level,

Emblem of the NSBO, here shown as metal badge worn on headgear by members. The same emblem was also displayed as a small metal lapel badge, and as a black cloth rhombus worn on the upper left sleeve of the uniform.

the DAF finally absorbed the NSBO in 1935. See Deutsche Arbeitsfront (DAF) and Robert Ley.

Nationalsozialistische Deutsche Arbeiterpartei (NSDAP). German Worker National Socialist Party. Hitler's party originated from the anticapitalist, anti–Semitic, and nationalist extreme right-wing Deutche Arbeiterpartei (DAP, German Workers Party) founded in Munich in 1919 by the locksmith Anton Drexler (q.v.). Right after World War I, Adolf Hitler was commissioned by the army to obtain intelligence about right-wing parties in Bavaria. In this role he infiltrated the DAP, and decided to enter politics. He joined the party in September 1919, soon became its head, and renamed it Nationalsozialistische Deutsche Arbeiterpartei (NSDAP). In February 1920, the nascent NSDAP outlined its political platform in twenty-five points. Drawn up by Drexler, Gottfried Feder (q.v.) and Hitler, the Nazi 25-point program remained the official Party guideline until the end of the Nazi movement in May 1945. In essence, the Nazi ideology stood in sharp contrast to modern Western democratic values such as liberty, equality, tolerance, state sovereignty and justice. The Nazi platform was simple, even simplistic, and often contradictory. It was designed to appeal to everyone with a grievance of some kind. Rather than an intellectually constructed doctrine, it was a flexible movement aiming at aggressive action. The 25 demands in the NSDAP program were as follows:

(1) The union of all Germans in a Groß Deutschland (Greater Germany) based on the right of self-determination;

(2) The revocation of the Versailles Treaty of 1919;

(3) Land and territories to feed the German people and settle its surplus population (Lebensraum or "living space");

(4) The restriction of state citizenship to those of German blood, with no Jew to be a German;

(5) Non-Germans in Germany to be only guests and subject to appropriate laws;

(6) Official posts to be filled only according to character and qualification;

(7) The livelihood of citizens to be the state's first duty;

(8) Non-German immigration to be stopped;

(9) Equal rights and duties for all citizens;

(10) Each citizen must work for the general public good;

(11) All income not earned by work to be confiscated by the state;

(12) All World War I profits to be confiscated;

(13) All large business trusts to be nationalized;

(14) Profit-sharing in all large industries;

(15) Adequate provision for old age;

(16) Small businessmen and traders to be strengthened and large department stores to be handed to them;

(17) Reform of land ownership and end to land speculation;

(18) Ruthless prosecution of serious criminals and death penalty for profiteers;

(19) Materialist Roman law to be replaced by German law;

(20) A thorough reconstruction of the national education system;

(21) The state to assist motherhood and youth;

(22) Abolition of the paid professional army and the formation of a national draftees army;

(23) Newspapers to be owned by Germans, and non–Germans banned from working on them;

(24) Religious freedom, except for religions which endanger the German race;

(25) A strong central government for the execution of effective legislation.

The Nazi Party had some 27,000 dues-paying members in 1925, 49,000 in 1926, 108,000 in 1928, and 178,000 by the end of 1929. The NSDAP had 210,000 members in March 1930, and 850,000 in January 1933. By September 1939 this had increased to more than 4 million with 150,000 officials. By January 1943, the NSDAP numbered 6.5 million, and 8.5 million in 1945.

NSDAP Gemeinschaftsleiter.

The hierarchy of the NSDAP included the following:
- Der Führer. Adolf Hitler, undisputed party leader;
- Stellvertreter des Führers. Deputies (first Rudolf Hess, later Martin Bormann).
- Reichsleiter der NSDAP. Senior officers with specific areas of responsibility. Propaganda (Goebbels); foreign policy (Rosenberg); law (Frank); finance (Schwartz); court (Buch);
- Landesinspekteur (Regional Inspector). Originally nine, each responsible for four Gaue (regions). (This level gradually became insignificant.).
- Gauleiter. Leader of a Gau;
- Kreisleiter. Leader of a "circuit" or district;
- Ortsgruppenleiter. Local group leader, responsible for a group of villages or a town;
- Zellenleiter. Cell leader, responsible for a village or a neighborhood in a town;
- Blockwart. Warden responsible for several households;
- Parteigenosse (PG). Member of the NSDAP.

The NSDAP was composed of various sectors, including the Gliederungen der Partei (q.v.) and the Angeschlossene Verbände (q.v.).

Nationalsozialistische Deutscher Arztebund (NSDAB). National Socialist German Physicians' League, founded in August 1929. Headed by Dr. Leonardo Conti, it included all physicians, surgeons, dentists, veterinary surgeons and pharmaceutical chemists. The league was charged with coordinating all measures of health and the political training of its members. It was composed of two main sections, the Reichszahnärztekammer (Dentists' Chamber) and the Reichsärztekammer (Doctors' Chamber).

Nationalsozialistische Deutsche Oberschule Starnbergersee. National Socialist German High School Starnbergersee. This was a Sturm Abteilung der NSDAP (q.v.) (SA) school for boys situated at Feldafing on the Starnbergersee south of Munich. This school, opened in April 1934, was intended to train future SA leaders. The selected pupils were known as SA Jungmannen (Young Men). Graduates could enter the SA corps with the rank of Truppführer (Staff Sergeant). The newly created Starnbergersee school survived the elimination of the SA in June 1934 but in February 1936, control passed from the SA to Nazi Party hands, although the headmaster remained an SA officer—Obergruppenführer (Lieutenant-General) Julius Görlitz. In 1941 all connection with the SA was severed. Pupils were enrolled in the Hitler Jugend, and the staff in the NSDAP.

Nationalsozialistische Dozentenbund (NSDB, National Socialist lecturers league), a professional association of university lecturers designed to keep them in line with the Nazi ideology. The universities were purged of Jewish, liberal, and social-democrat personnel. They were harassed, dismissed, forced into exile and retirement or even imprisoned. They were replaced with inexperienced and unqualified but reliable Nazi professors. This was a terrible loss for Germany, which had held a position of world leadership in science, but the purge was a gain for the free world, where many educators fled. See also Education in the Third Reich.

Nationalsozialistische Fliegerkorps (NSFK). Nazi Flyers Corps. According to the stipulations of the Treaty of Versailles in 1919, Germany had no right to possess an air force, but in the 1920s a highly centralized civil aviation appeared in the framework of the commercial airline company Lufthansa. At the same time flying, gliding and ballooning were popular sports developed and performed in private clubs and in the *Deutsche Luftsportverband* (DLV German Air Sports League). The DLV was created by the Nazis in 1932 to channel and develop air-mindedness in Germany. The DLV continued to exist after the Luftwaffe (q.v.) was founded in 1935 but to a much smaller degree. In 1937 the DLV was dissolved and replaced with a new organization named the *Nationalsozialistische Fliegerkorps* (NSFK, Nazi Flyers Corps). The NSFK was a State-registered association subordinate to the *Reichsluftfahrtministerium*—RLM Reich Minister for Air Travel (q.v.) The NSFK was mainly a voluntary organization with a small core of paid personnel. Like the DLV before it, the NSFK's main purpose was to promote interest and development of air sport, notably gliding and ballooning, to channel energy, to exploit youth enthusiasm in aeronautic with a view of training future combat pilots and technical support personnel. Right before and during the Second World War one important task of the Flying

Nationalsozialistische

Emblem of the NSFK.

Corps was training the *Hitler Jugend* (q.v.), and to provide voluntary recruits for the Luftwaffe. As World War II proceeded members of the NSFK were gradually involved in combat roles, notably performing air defense duties in flak (antiaircraft artillery) service.

Nationalsozialistische Frauenschaft (NSF). National Socialist Womanhood. Women formed a distinct social group forced into compliance with Hitler's regime. The Nazi Party was ideologically antifeminist, and women's position in society was inferior. Women had little official influence. They were expelled from work, and the removal of women from many sectors of employment caused resentment. However, Nazism had a certain appeal resulting from family allowances and benefits reinforced by improved provision for maternity. Furthermore, the creation of new roles within party and public organizations—such as the Nationalsozialistische Frauenschaft (NSF women's organization)—made possible the active involvement of many women. The NSF was a Gliederung (limb) of the NSDAP. It was created in October 1931 and led by Elsbeth Zander. The NSF was reorganized after the Nazi seizure of power in 1933 under the leadership of Gertrud Bäumer and then under Gertrud Scholtz-Klink (q.v.) who was promoted to Führerin of the NSF and other women's organizations. The duty of the NSF members was to rear their children as patriots, and to see that all commands of the Nazi Party were unconditionally carried out in daily life.

Emblem of the NSF.

Nationalsozialistische Führungsoffizier (NSFO). National Socialist Leadership Officer. These were political officers commissioned by the NSDAP and the SS who were attached to regular German units after the failed coup against Hitler in summer 1944. They were tasked with providing for the indoctrination of troops in Nazi values, and were given a free hand to boost morale and repress defeatism by all means.

Nationalsozialistische Gemeinschaft Kraft durch Freude. See Kraft durch Freude.

Nationalsozialitische Handwerks-, Handels- und Gewerbe Organisation (NS-Hago). National Socialist Handicraft, Commercial and Business Organisation. A Nazi-controlled organization created in August 1933 for the industrial middle class, intended to promote the interests of small tradesmen and self-employed craftsmen. In October 1934, NS-Hago became a part of the Deutsche Arbeitsfront (q.v.). In practice, NS-Hago proved to be more of a liability than an asset. Hitler was obliged to order its members to stop attacking Jewish-owned businesses, which were, in a time of economic depression, providing much-needed employment for German workers. Never officially dissolved, the NS-Hago was allowed to fade into obscurity, as Robert Ley (q.v.) created his own shopkeepers and artisans organization called the Reichsstand des deutschen Handwerks (RDHdw or National Corporation of German Handicraft).

Emblem of NS-Hago.

Nationalsozialistische Kriegsopferversorgung (NSKOV). The National Socialist War Victim's Care. As the name implies, this was a Nazi social welfare organization for wounded and disabled veterans and victims of the World War I, and widows and orphans. The NSKOV was established in 1933 and was one of the Angeschlossene Verbände der NSDAP (q.v.). After the war, like all organizations affiliated with the Nazi Party, the NSKOV was disbanded.

Badge of the NSLB.

NSKOV emblem.

NSLB emblem.

Nationalsozialistische Lehrerbund (NSLB) National Socialist teacher league. The NSLB was established in April 1929 by Hans Schemm and had its seat in the House of German Education at Bayreuth (Bavaria). After the Nazi takeover of power in 1933 the Nazi Party validated the NSLB as the sole organization of teachers in the German Reich. In July 1935 the NSLB was merged with the existing organization of lecturers to form the Nationalsozialistischer Dozentenbund (q.v.) (NSDDozB)—National Socialist German University Lecturers League. The league subjected all teachers to strict Nazi Party control. It had responsibility for the integration of political and ideological training, and the planning of general school curriculum. Membership in the NSDDozB was originally not mandatory, however it was tactically advantageous, if not unavoidable, as the district leaders had a decisive role in the acceptance of an Habilitationsschrift (highest academic qualification), which was a prerequisite to attaining the rank of Privatdozent (private lecturer) necessary to becoming a tenured university lecturer. Membership became compulsory in May 1941. By August 1942, the league had 360,000 members. See Education in the Third Reich.

Nationalsozialistische Monatshefte. *National Socialist Monthly*, a magazine edited by Alfred Rosenberg (q.v.) and devoted to propagating Nazi ideology.

Nationalsozialistische Reichsbund für Leibesübungen. See Reichssportbund.

Nationalsozialistische

Emblem of the NSAO.

Nationalsozialistische-Reichskriegerbund Kyffhäuser e.V. See Kyffhäuserbund.

Nationalsozialistische Reichsverband der Deutschen Arbeitsopfe (NSAO). National Socialist Association for Work Victims, a group that took care of the welfare of German workers who became victims of industrial injury or accident.

Nationalsozialitische Reichswahrerbund (NSRB). National Socialist Jurists' League. Founded in October 1928 by Hans Frank (q.v.), the league was composed of representatives of the legal professions and teachers of jurisprudence. Its headquarters were originally at Munich in the Haus des deutschen Rechts (House of German Law). It later came under the jurisdiction of the Ministry of Justice in Berlin. With a membership of 90,000 in 1938, the Jurists' League was divided into eight Reichsgruppen (groups), including judges and public prosecutors; attorneys; notaries; administrative personnel; teachers at universities; administrative jurists; industrial lawyers; and young jurists. The NSRB was suspended in March 1943 for the duration of the war.

Nationalsozialistische Volkswohlfahrte (NSV). Nazi People's Welfare Organisation. The NSV was devoted to the welfare of party members and their families, especially mothers and juveniles. The NSV was founded in September 1931 by a Nazi municipal councilor, Erich Hilgenfeldt, in the Wilmersdorf district in Berlin. Originally its function was modest. The NSV was designed as an emergency aid group providing relief for party members during the depression of 1929–1932. Soon its activities encompassed the whole town of Berlin with the support of Joseph Goebbels and the patronage of Hitler. After the seizure of power in January 1933, the NSV grew in influence and stature as Erich Hilgenfeldt received Hitler's mandate for all matters of charity and the people's welfare at national level. Hilgenfeldt soon usurped the place of both private and public welfare agencies, effectively subordinating organizations like the German Red Cross. It became the second largest party organization, with some sixteen million members in 1942. The NSV was structured after the organization of the Nazi Party and was divided into Block, Kreis and Gau. The NSV had several subagencies, including the WHW (Winter Relief), the Tuberculosis Relief, the Dental Relief, the Mother and Child Relief, among others. The Nazi welfare organization constituted a large empire within Germany, disposing of millions of Reichmark raised by millions of "voluntary" dues-paying members, state funds, collections and donations. During World War II, the NSV's task was to feed and house German civilians who were injured or who had lost everything because of Allied mass air raids. Apparently an innocuous organization, the NSV—as much as the other branches of the Nazi Party—had an inhuman vocation: the implementation of Hitler's racial policy. In fact the NSV was not solely or primarily a welfare and charitable organization. It was designed to strengthen the collective biologically and politically, not to feed the hungry, give drink to the thirsty or clothe the naked. Instead of pursuing social policies and assisting needy individuals, it participated in political indoctrination, the "purification" and strengthening of the body of the nation in accordance with strict racial lines. From the start Jews, Gypsies, the "asocial," the "hereditary ill" and other "enemies of the regime" were excluded and disqualified from the benefit of the organization. Racial objectives were also pursued by the NSV's Mother and Child Relief. Only the "biologically valuable parts of the German nation" received support. Women who were allegedly "hereditarily ill and inferior" and those who had "asocial disposition" were disbarred from postnatal care. From 1935, the NSV became involved in the field of adoption with racial-political objectives, and by 1937 a new subagency was created, the NSV Reich Adoption Service, providing only "healthy and racially pure" children. During World War II, the NSV's attempts to appropriate the field of adoption led to conflicts with the Lebensborn agency (q.v.) Both NSV and Lebensborn eingetragener Verein were involved in kidnapping "Aryan" children in occupied Europe. Orphans of "German blood" were taken from homes or from their foster parents, or were simply abducted from kindergarten, schools, or off the streets. They were placed in NSV homes, given new names and educated in military and racial fashion.

Nationalsozialistischer Bund Deutscher Technik (NSBDT). National Socialist League for German Technology. The NSBDT was first headed by Gottfried Feder (q.v.), then by Dr. Fritz Todt (q.v.), and then by Albert Speer (q.v.). The league was intended to foster a greater public awareness of technology and raise productivity through technical expertise. It comprised Germany's elite engineers. The NSBDT had 43,000 members, covering all aspects of technology. Members of the NSBDT were simultaneously members of the Deutsche Arbeitsfront (q.v.). The league had a training center at Plassenburg in Bavaria and its own periodical called *BDT Zeitschrift*. The NSBDT sponsored a ring to honor the memory of Fritz Todt. See Fritz Todt Ring.

Nationalsozialistischer Deutscher Studentenbund (NSDStB). National Socialist Student League. The NSDStB was devoted to the furtherance of the Nazi way of life among students, indoctrination with National Socialist philosophy, physical training and military drill. Its curriculum emphasized the basic elements of Nazi ideology: racism, nationalism, Germanics, duty, loyalty to the Führer, soldierly spirit, obedience and discipline. Between summer 1928 and October 1931, the NSDStB was directed by Baldur von Schirach (q.v.), who later was the head of the Hitler Jugend (q.v.). The NSDStB was notable for strong social revolutionary traits and the use of violence, such as the burning of books in April and May 1933 (see Bücherverbrennung). The educational "reforms" instituted by the Nazi regime had catastrophic results. The traditional German humanism was replaced with politico-racial institutions dedicated to militarism, racial hatred and aggressive expansionism. Education, from the elementary schools to the universities, became merely an appendage of the Propaganda Ministry, intellectual standards declined precipitously and a whole generation was the victim of odious indoctrination. See also Education in the Third Reich.

Nationalsozialistischer Volksbund (NSVB). National Socialist People's League. Before Hitler secured absolute control over the Nazi Party machine in 1927, the National Socialist movement was multiform and made up of several streams. The NSVB was one of the small splinter Nazi groups opposed to Hitler in 1925. The NSVB was later dismantled. See Strasser, Gregor, and Strasser, Otto.

Nationalsozialistisches Kraftfahkorps (NSKK). National Socialist Driver Corps. The NSKK originated from the Nationalsozialistischen Automobil Korps, or NSAK (national socialist automobile corps), which was founded in 1930. It included wealthy car owners who sympathized with the Nazis and put themselves at the party's disposal in their free time. It comprised a group of mechanics, drivers and vehicles to transport Nazi Party formations and leaders. The Sturmabteilung der NSDAP (SA) had its own transport service, Motor Sturm Abteilung (MSA). Both MSA and NSAK played a significant role during the Kampfzeit (q.v.). After the elimination of the SA in June 1934, the MSA was disbanded and its members were transferred to the NSAK, which from then on was reorganized and called Nationalsozialistischen Kraftfahkorps, or NSKK (national socialist motorized corps). Until the end of the Nazi regime, the NSKK was an important official Gliederung der NSDAP (q.v.), placed directly under Hitler's authority. The NSKK (counting 500,000 members in 1938) was headed by Major Hühnlein until his death in 1942, then by NSKK-Korpsführer Erwin Krauss until 1945. The Corps was militarily organized, and divided into units in five geographic Obergruppen (North, East, South, West and Middle regions). These were divided into Motorgruppen, Motorstaffeln, Motorstürme, Scharen, and Rotten. Members of the NSKK were given Nazi hierarchy ranks, which were similar to those of the SA, the SS and the Waffen-SS. Members were recruited from the Nazi party, the Hitler Youth and men discharged from military service for medical reasons. The NSKK had not only a logistical role—driving and maintaining vehicles—they were also technological specialists in military matters. They had close contacts with the army, notably with the armored forces headed by Heinz Guderian. They gave mechanical advice and driving lessons to Wehrmacht candidate truck and tank drivers in Fahrschulen (driving schools). The technical efficiency of the motor corps was a major benefit for the formation of tank crews and the development of the Blitzkrieg (lightning war), which gave Germany tremendous victories in the period 1939–1941. Closely connected to the Nazi Party, NSKK members were often politically active. They participated in party rallies and ceremonies, gave Nazi ideology lectures, and organized visits to factories and manufactures for propaganda aims. In addition, the politically involved NSKK allowed Hitler to have a grip on the Wehrmacht, as all transport and army logistics were controlled by the Nazi organization, thus placing the regular national armed forces in a totally dependent position. After 1940 the NSKK also recruited French, Belgian, Dutch and other volunteers from occupied nations. In 1942, all transport units were renamed "Transportkorps Speer" after the minister of war production and ammunition Albert Speer (q.v.). By the end of the war, due to manpower shortage, NSKK members, both German and foreign, were armed to form new fighting units. Other NSKK men were incorporated into the Waffen-SS (q.v.) and the Volkssturm (q.v.).

Nazi. Acronym formed of the first syllable of *NA*tional and the second syllable of So*ZI*alistische. Convenient acronyms were very popular in the Third Reich, such as Blubo, Ostuf, Flak, VoMi, Jafu, PaK, Gestapo, Schupo, Hiwi, Schuma, Napola, Kripo, Stuka, MaFla, Stubaf, and the like.

Nazi art. See Kunst.

Nazi holy places. For many fanatic followers, Nazism was a spiritual path akin to a religion. The movement naturally had some sites of pilgrimage that one might call holy sites. These included the following: Berchtesgaden, Hitler's home on the Berghof (q.v.); Braunau am Inn, his birthplace; Feldherrnhalle (q.v.), site of the failed 1923 Munich Putsch; Leonding, where the parents of Adolf Hitler were buried; Linz, where Hitler went to school; Landsberg am Lech, where Hitler was imprisoned; Nürnberg (q.v.), a highly symbolic Nazi city, notably for enormous rallies; Wewelsburg (q.v.) Castle, one of the SS's headquarters.

Nebeltruppen. "Fog troops." Smoke was used in warfare as a hindrance to the enemy's accurate firing and concealing tactical movement. Chemical substances

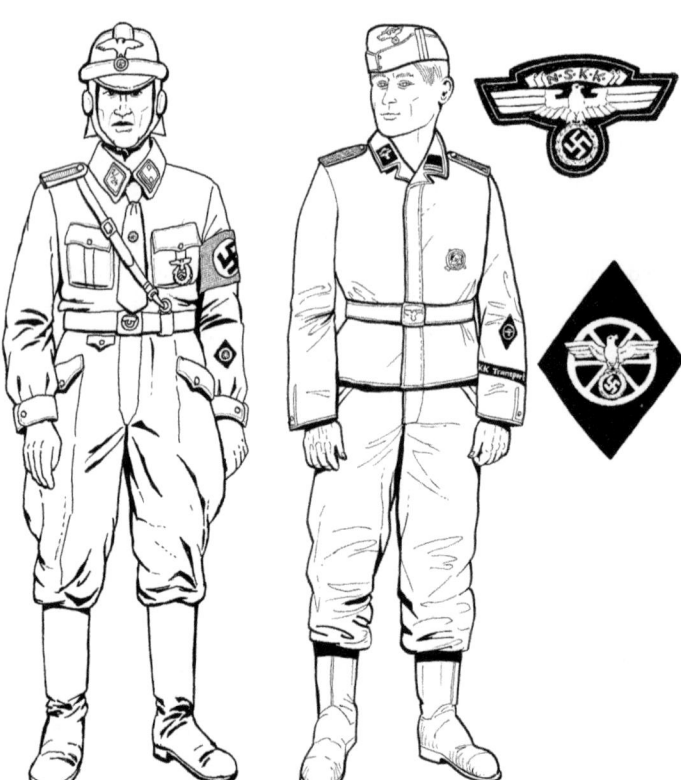

Left: **NSKK man wearing crash helmet.** *Right:* **NSKK Obersturmmann.** *Inset, top right:* **Emblem of NSKK.** *Inset, bottom right:* **Driver's badge.**

were used which, when ignited or exposed to the atmosphere, produced the "fog of war," or artificial screening smoke. Contained in small canisters, grenades or shells that burst on impact, smoke was always subject to the vagaries of wind and weather and therefore could be a friend or a foe on the battlefield. See Nebelwerfer and Wurfkörper.

Nebelwerfer. Literally, "fog-thrower." The Nebelwerfer 5 cm rocket launcher (nicknamed Moaning Minnie by the Allies) was the most widely used of the family of artillery launchers developed by the Germans. The Nebelwerfer was a heavy (35 kilograms) self-propelled projectile containing explosive or smoke. It was electrically launched to a range of about 7 kilometer by means of a short barrel; six or ten barrels were fixed together on a two-wheeled carriage or on a mobile halftrack.

Negationismus. Negationism or historical revisionism. The illegitimate distortion of the historical record such that certain events appear in a more or less favorable light or are simply denied. Since World War II the term is often associated with skepticism regarding the existence of gas chambers and extermination camps, as well as a denial, or minimalization of the Holocaust.

Neo-Nazism. A general term for the related fascist, nationalist, white supremacist, anti–Semitic beliefs and political tendencies of the numerous groups that emerged after World War II seeking to restore the Nazi order or to establish a new order based on doctrines similar to those underlying Nazi Germany.

Nero Befehl. Nero Order, a nihilistic directive issued by Hitler in March 1945 aiming at a total scorched earth policy. This suicidal strategy included the large-scale and deliberate destruction of towns, communications and factories, dams and bridges, mines, railways and rolling stock, and any other economic, industrial and public facilities as an attempt to let the whole German people perish with himself. Owing to the efforts of Albert Speer (q.v.) who tried to nullify as much as possible the order by preserving what was still standing, and surrendering intact industrial sites to the Allies, the Nero Befehl was fortunately only partly carried out.

Neue Front. New Front. A cigarette brand promoted and sold in the 1930s by Nazi merchants and others sympathetic to the NSDAP.

Neue Westwall. The New West Wall, first name of Atlantikwall (q.v.).

Neuengamme. Concentration camp located southeast of Hamburg in northern Germany. Established in 1938 originally as a subcamp of Sachsenhausen (q.v.) concentration camp, it was begun by the SS-owned Deutsche Erd-und Steinwerke (German Earth and Stone Works Corporation), and intended to be a brickworks using cheap labor from concentration camp prisoners. In all, the SS incarcerated approximately 104,000–106,000 people in Neuengamme from December 1938 until May 1945; approximately 13,500 of the prisoners were women. The largest groups by nationality were Soviets (34,350); Poles (16,900), French (11,500), Germans (9,200), Dutch (6,950), Danes (4,800), and Belgians (4,800).

Neuer Art (nA or neu). Literally, "new type." This term was employed for new, revised or improved vehicles, pieces of uniform and equipment, bunkers and so on, that replaced or improved on older designs.

Neurath, Constantin Freiherr von (1873–1956). Aristocratic diplomat and ambassador in Copenhagen, Rome and London, foreign minister in 1932, and protector of Bohemia-Moravia from 1939 to 1941. In 1941 he was replaced with Reinhard Heydrich (q.v.). At Nuremberg Von Neurath was sentenced to 15 years' imprisonment, but he was released in 1954 on health grounds.

Newspapers. See Presse.

Niemöller, Martin (1892–1984). A committed churchman, pacifist, nationalist and anticommunist, Pastor Niemöller at first supported the Nazi regime. However, soon deeply disillusioned by the Nazi Gleichschaltung (q.v.), he was one of the few Germans willing to speak out against Hitler. He formed the Confessional Church and protested against the Nazis' actions against the Jews. For this he was arrested in 1937 and detained at KZ Dachau until the end of World War II. See Bekenntniskirche and Religion in the Third Reich.

Nietzsche, Friedrich Wilhelm (1844–1900). German philosopher of the late 19th century who challenged the foundations of Christianity and traditional morality. He was interested in the enhancement of individual and cultural health, and believed in life, creativity, power, and the realities of the world we live in, rather than those situated in a world beyond. Central to his philosophy is the idea of "life-affirmation," which involves an honest questioning of all doctrines that drain life's expansive energies, however socially prevalent those views might be. Aspects of Nietzsche's theories were espoused by Nazism and Italian Fascism. It was possible for Nazi interpreters to assemble and twist, quite selectively, various passages from Nietzsche's writings whose juxtaposition appeared to justify war, aggression and domination for the sake of nationalistic and racial self-glorification.

Night of the Long Knives. Campaign of assassination unleashed by Hitler on June 30, 1934, to decapitate the SA leadership. See Nacht der langen Messer; Röhm, Ernst; and Sturm Abteilung der NSDAP.

Nobel Preis. Nobel Prize. During Hitler's regime, Germans were forbidden to accept the Swedish Nobel Prizes, which were regarded as a manifestation of "international Jewry." Instead the Führer, to emphasize German cultural freedom, had instituted in 1937 the Deutscher Nationalpreis für Kunst und Wissenschaft (German National Prize for Art and Science) which were generally announced and given to the winners by Joseph Goebbels. Hitler would congratulate the winners. The reward consisted of a sum of 100,000 Reichsmarks and a decoration on a star of platinum and gold featuring a profile of Athena, the Greek goddess of wisdom. The recipients of Nationalpreis between 1937 and 1939 were aircraft designers Ernst Heinkel and Willy Messerschmitt (shared award), engineer and vehicle manufacturer Ferdinand Porsche, engineer Fritz Todt, architect Paul Troost (posthumously), Reich leader Alfred Rosenberg, explorer Wilhelm Fichner, and surgeons August Bier and Ferdinand Sauerbruch (shared award).

Nordhausen. See Dora.

Novemberverbrecher. November criminals. In Hitler's view, the men who had agreed to the November 11, 1918 Armistice. Implicit was the idea that traitors and war profiteers (Jews, Democrats and socialists) were responsible for the "stab in the back" which brought Germany to defeat. See Dolchstoss and Versailler Diktat.

NS. Short for Nationalsozialistisch (National Socialist).

NS-Briefe. NS-Letters, a fortnightly national socialist newsletter created by Gregor Strasser (q.v.).

NSDAP. The Nazi Party. See Nationalsozialistische Deutsche Arbeiter Partei.

NSDAP Headquarters. Located in Munich, this was in the Sterneckerbräu beer hall in 1920; then at Corneliusstrasse 12 in 1922 and 1923; for six months in 1925 it was in the Eher Verlag, Thierstrasse 15 (later the party publishing house); Schellingstrasse 50 in the period 1925–31; and finally from 1931 to 1945 in the Barlow Palace, Briennenstrasse 45, rebuilt by architect Paul L. Troost as Braunes Haus (q.v.).

NSDAP 25-Point Program. See Nationalsozialistische Deutsche Arbeiterpartei.

NSKF. See Nationalsozialistische Fliegerkorps.

NSKK. See Nationalsozialistisches Kraftfahrkorps.

NSKK Katastrophendienst. Nazi Drivers' Corps Emergency Service. These were units of the Nationalsozialistisches Kraftfahrkorps (q.v.)—NSKK, National Socialist Drivers's Corps created in 1943 in order to support the various existing rescue teams on the home front. They performed various roles, including transport, evacuation, and ambulance driving, but also had police, protection, heavy rescue, firefighting, and debris-clearance duties.

NSV. See Nationalsozialistische Volkswohlfahrte.

Nuremberg rallies. See Feiertagen and Parteitage.

Nuremberg trials. See Nürnberger Prozeß.

Nürnberg. Nuremberg. A city in the administrative region of Middle Franconia, in the German state of Bavaria. Because of the city's relevance to the Holy Roman Empire and its position in the center of Germany, the Nazis chose the city to be the site of huge annual party conventions. At the 1935 rally, anti–Semitic measures were passed and announced there, known as Nuremberg Laws, which revoked German citizenship for all Jews. The city was also the home of the Nazi propagandist Julius Streicher (q.v.), the publisher of *Der Stürmer* (q.v.) During World War II, Nuremberg was an important industrial site for military production, including aircraft, submarine parts, and tank engines. For this reason, the city was severely damaged by Allied strategic bombing from 1943 to 1945. Despite the intense degree of destruction, the highly symbolic city was chosen by the Allies to house in 1945 and 1946 the International Military Tribunal (IMT), which became known as the Nuremberg Trials. See Feiertagen, Nürnberger Gesetze, Nürnberger Prozeß, and Parteitagen.

Nürnberger Gesetze. Nuremberg laws. A series of laws against Jews promulgated in 1935. The Law for the Protection of German Blood and Honor forbade intermarrying between Reichsbürger (citizens of "pure German blood") and Staatsanhörigen ("unpure subjects of the state"). Other laws excluded Jews from official professions and positions, and later from economic and social life, obliged them to wear a star of David, and forced them to live where ordered. A later decree, anticipating the final solution, made Jews outlaws in Nazi Germany. See Endlösung der Judenfrage and Judenstern.

Nürnberger Prozeß. Nuremberg trials. The International Military Tribunal, known as the Nuremberg trials, were held from November 20, 1945, to October 1, 1946. They brought the main Nazi leaders before international justice for three main charges: crimes against peace; war crimes; and crimes against humanity. If Hitler, Himmler, Goebbels, Bormann and Ley were dead and thus not judged, Göring, von Ribbentrop, Keitel, Kaltenbrunner, Rosenberg, Franck, Seyss-Inquart, Frick, Streicher, Sauckel and Jodl were sentenced to death and hanged. Heß, Funk and Raeder were sentenced to life imprisonment. Speer and von Schirach were sentenced to twenty years, von Neurath to fifteen years and Dönitz to ten. Fritsche, Schacht and von Papen were acquitted. The various Nazi organizations, such as the SS and Waffen-SS, were deemed criminal and forbidden. A second set of trials of lesser war criminals was conducted under Control Council Law No. 10 at the U.S. Nuremberg Military Tribunals (NMT); among them were the Doctors' Trial and the Judges' Trial.

Oath. See Eid.

Oberbefehlshaber (Ob). Commander in chief, top commander of units in the German Wehrmacht (q.v.). See Befehlshaber.

Oberführer (Oberf). Brigadier general in the SS (q.v.).

Obergefreiter. Corporal.

Obergruppenführer or **Oberstgruppenführer** (Ob-Gruf). Waffen-SS general commanding an SS Panzerkorps composed of several SS Panzer divisions.

Oberkanonier. Senior gunner.

Oberkommando der Luftwaffe (OKL). High command of the air force headed by Reichsmarschall Hermann Göring. See Luftwaffe and Oberkommando der Wehrmacht.

Oberkommando der Marine (OKM). High command of the navy. See Kriegsmarine and Oberkommando der Wehrmacht.

Oberkommando der Wehrmacht (OKW). Supreme high command of all three German armed forces. The OKW and its three branches (OKH, OKL and OKM) were created in February 1938 following the dissolution of the Reich War Ministry. In theory, the OKW served as the military general staff for the Third Reich, coordinating the efforts of the army, navy, and air force. In practice, it acted as Hitler's personal military staff, translating his ideas into military orders and issuing them to the three services. The motive behind the reorganization reflected Hitler's desire to consolidate his power and authority around his position as führer and reich chancellor (Führer und Reichskanzler), to the detriment of the military leadership of the Wehrmacht (q.v.). The OKW was led by Generalfeldmarschall Wilhelm Keitel (q.v.), who reported directly to Hitler, from whom most operational orders actually originated as Oberster Befehlshaber der Wehrmacht (Supreme Commander of the Armed Forces). At the end of 1941, the OKW's purview was limited to Western Europe, Mediterranean Sea and the Balkans. The front in Russia was then directed by the OKH and Hitler personally.

Oberkommando

Oberkommando des Heeres (OKH). High command of the ground force from 1936 to 1945. The OKH did not plan operations; this task was left to the General Staff. After 1941, the Oberkommando der Wehrmacht (q.v.) de facto directly commanded operations on the western front while the OKH commanded the eastern front.

Oberleitung (OBL). Organisation Todt (q.v.) general director.

Oberleutnant. First lieutenant.

Oberst (Ob). Colonel.

Oberste SA Führer. Title of the supreme commander of the SA. See Sturm Abteilung der NSDAP.

Oberste SA Führung (OSAF). Upper command of the SA. The Oberst SA Führung was a headquarters similar to the Reichswehr (q.v.) because the SA—at least in Röhm's mind—was intended to be the future Nazi Germany's army. Therefore the SA's structure was that of a smaller armed force. It included several Sondereinheiten (special units), such as the Motor Sturm Abteilung (MSA) motorized units; the SA Nachrichten (signal corps); the SA Gebirgsjäger (mountain troops); the SA-Marine (navy); the SA-Flieger (air force); the Streifendienst (a police and patrol service); the Hilfspolizei (a police force in Berlin and Brandeburg province); and the Feldjägerkorps (field or military police). See Sturm Abteilung der NSDAP and Röhm, Ernst.

Oberster Führer SS. Supreme Leader of the SS (q.v.) This function was held by Adolf Hitler himself. Under him came Reichsführer-SS Heinrich Himmler (q.v.).

Obersturmbannführer (Ostubaf). Lieutenant colonel in the SS.

Obersturmführer (Ostuf). SS first lieutenant.

Oder-Warthe-Bend (OWB). See Ostwall.

Odessa. Organization of former SS members. See Organisation der ehemaligen SS-Angehöringen.

Offener Beobachter. Open observatory, a circular observation pit built in the thickness of the wall of a bunker, manned by a single sentry/observer. The observatory did not communicate directly with the inside of the bunker but possessed its own entrance. See Tobruk.

Offizierfeldmütze alterer Art. Officers' field cap, old model. See Schirmmütze.

Offizierlager (Oflag). A permanent camp for officer prisoners of war. Privates and low ranks were detained in Stammlager (Stalag).

Ohlendorf, Otto (1906–1951). A German SS-Gruppenführer and head of the Inland-SD a

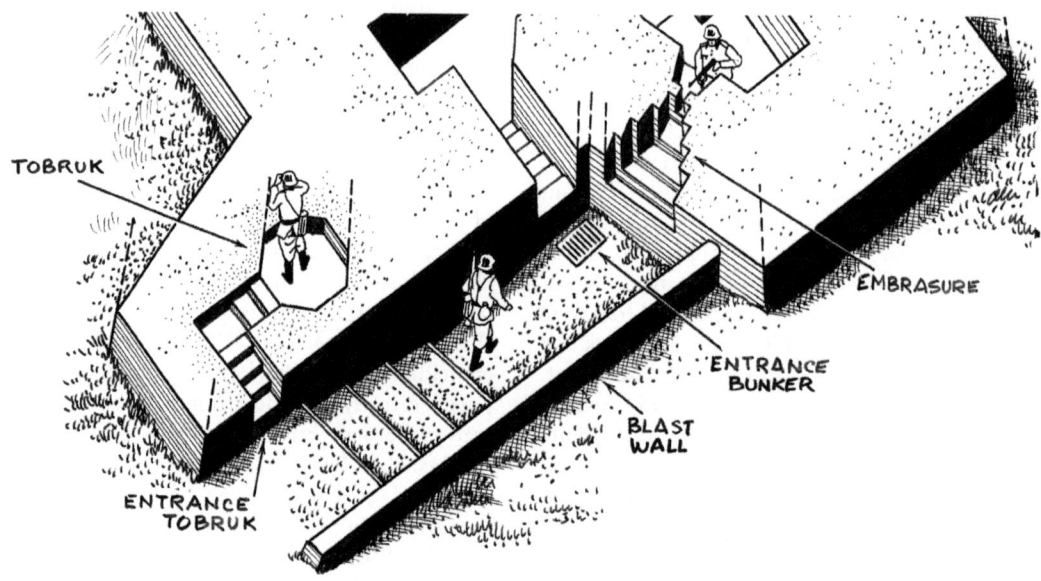

Offener Beobachter.

section of the SD (q.v.) responsible for intelligence and security within Germany. Ohlendorf was the commanding officer of Einsatzgruppe D, which conducted mass murder in Moldova, south Ukraine, the Crimea, and, during 1942, the north Caucasus. As such, Otto Ohlendorf was a Holocaust (q.v.) perpetrator and mass murderer. He was convicted of war crimes and executed after World War II.

Okkupation or **Besetzte Gebiete.** Occupation. At the peak of their strength in the period 1940–1943, the Nazis occupied large parts of Europe. The occupation was not uniform but had four main modes.

(1) unter Reichsverwaltung eingegliederte Gebiete: annexed territories, which had become Gaue, or integral parts of Germany, such as French Alsace-Lorraine, Austria, Sudetenland, Wartheland, Upper Silesia, East Prussia, Memel, Bialystok.

(2) unter Reichsverwaltung angegliederte Gebiete: protectorate, such as Generalgouvernement in Poland, Bohemia and Moravia in Czechoslovakia, Lemberg.

(3) Reichskommissariate in den besetzten Gebieten der UdSSR: Commissariate in Soviet Union occupied territories, including Ostland and Ukraine.

(4) unter Militärverwaltung: territories placed under German military administration, such as France, the British Channel Islands, the Netherlands, Belgium, Denmark, Norway, and a large combat zone in the USSR from Leningrad in the North to Cherson in the South.

OKH. See Oberkommando des Heeres.

OKL. See Oberkommando der Luftwaffe.

OKM. See Oberkommando der Marine.

OKW. See Oberkommando der Wehrmacht.

Old Fighters. See Alte Kämpfer.

Olympic Games, 1936. In spite of controversy and threat of boycott because of the racist nature of the Nazi regime, the Berlin Games of the XI Olympiad was a big success for Hitler, and a great opportunity to present to the world the "smiling" face of Nazism. Hundreds of international journalists acknowledged that Germany had put on the most lavish and biggest Olympics ever. Many thousands of tourists and reporters also left Germany with happy memories of the courtesy extended to them by the Nazis and the German people, and the precise efficiency of the whole event. The world admired the fantastic facilities, including a brand new 100,000-seat track and field stadium, six gymnasiums, swimming pools, many other smaller arenas, and modern innovations such as a closed-circuit television system, a radio network that reached 41 countries, and many other forms of expensive high-tech electronic equipment. Filmmaker Leni Riefenstahl (q.v.) was commissioned for $7 million by the German Olympic Committee to film the events — a record that celebrated the stable, confident community that had staged them. The Nazis had carefully concealed all traces of their ugly regime and had succeeded in getting what they most wanted and expected from hosting the Olympics: international respectability.

One-pot meal. See Eintopf.

Ordensburgen. Castles of the Order; Nazi training schools. These were the finishing schools, the highest residential academies for the training of the future Nazi elite. Those chosen formed a kind of NSDAP university, an institutional core of Nazi brothers united in mysticism. Four Castles of the Order were established in out-of-the-way romantic settings, at Crössinsee, Sonthofen, Vogelsang, and Marienburg. Each castle accommodated about 1,000 students, called Junkers. Supervision was in the hands of 500 instructors and administrative staff. The executive official was Robert Ley (q.v.). He set its standards. Entrants were chosen from among those who had spent six years between the ages of 12 and 18 at the Adolf Hitler Schools, two and one half years in the Reichsarbeitsdienst (q.v.), and another four years in full-time party activity. The candidates were thus in their mid-twenties when chosen. The selection of candidates was controlled by high party and SS functionaries. Graduates entered the highest echelons of the Nazi Party, the SS and the German army. However, the Ordensburgen failed to attract a full complement of students despite the financial inducement and the prestige of attendance. See also Adolf-Hitler-Schule and Nationalpolitischen Erziehungsanstalten.

Ordnertruppen. Gymnastic groups, the first (cover) name of the troop created in the fall of 1920 by Hitler for his own protection. In late 1921 they were renamed Sturm Abteilung der

Ordnungspolizei

NSDAP (q.v.) or SA for short — Storm troopers, NSDAP paramilitary groups.

Ordnungspolizei (Orpo). The regular uniformed police, composed of Schutzpolizei (security police), Gemeinde Polizei (urban police) and Gendarmerie (rural police). The Orpo was charged with assuring interior order, and therefore it was militarily structured and organized with uniforms and ranks similar to those of the Wehrmacht. The Orpo went under control of the SS in 1936 and was headed by SS Oberstgruppenführer Kurt Daluege. Militarized and indoctrinated, the Orpo became far more a military force of the interior than an organization of public servants. Some 100 battalions were raised, each about 550 men who served in the ranks of the Wehrmacht (q.v.) as antipartisan units. Some members of the Orpo were drafted in 1940 to form the 4th Waffen-SS Panzergrenadierdivision "Polizei 1." Some Orpo policemen — particularly those who were under disciplinary punishment — volunteered to constitute Einsatzgruppen (q.v.) in Russia. Other volunteers formed SS-Polizei regiments in 1943. Beginning in 1945, Orpo policemen were drafted into the Volkssturm (q.v.) and to form the 35th Waffen-SS grenadierdivision Polizei 2." The Orpo was considered by the Allies a dangerous service. Right after the German capitulation in May 1945, the police force was purged of its Nazi members, but it was rapidly reactivated to maintain order. In the postwar period it became the Volkspolizei (Vopo) in the communist Eastern Germany (DDR) and — under its original name — Schutzpolizei (Schupo) in Western Germany (BRD).

Ordnungspolizei policeman.

Organisation Consul (OC). A secret ultranationalist group operating in Germany in the early 1920s. It was principally formed of ex-members of the Marinebrigade Hermann Ehrhardt (q.v.), a Freikorps unit which was disbanded after the Kapp Putsch (q.v.) failed to overthrow the German Weimar Republic. The Organisation Consul's aims were cultivation and dissemination of nationalist thinking; warfare against all antinationalists and internationalists; warfare against Jewry, social democracy and leftist-radicalism; and fomentation of internal unrest in order to attain the overthrow of the antinationalist Weimar constitution. At least 354 people were murdered by the organization for political reasons between 1919 and 1922. Some notable victims were the republic's minister of finance, Matthias Erzberger, in August 1921 and Foreign Minister Walter Rathenau in June 1922. Erzberger was murdered because he was the German representative who signed the 1918 armistice. After Rathenau's murder, the OC became the Viking Bund, a league that eventually became related to the Nazi SA (storm troopers). However by 1923, Hermann Göring wrote that the Viking Bund had "declared war against the party and the SA."

Organisation der ehemaligen SS-Angehörigen (Odessa). Organization of former SS members alleged to have been created by Austrian SS after the collapse of Germany in 1945 to help Nazi war criminals and SS men to escape capture and prosecution. Frederick Forsyth's best-selling 1972 thriller *The Odessa File* brought the supposed organization to popular attention. The actual existence of Odessa is contested by many historians, but there were indeed several organizations and authorities that helped, protected and supported Nazi criminals, SS men and pro-Nazi collaborators on the run, notably some Swiss banks, the Vatican, Egypt, Franco's Fascist Spain and some states in South America such as Argentina, Uruguay and Paraguay.

Organisation der Gewerblichen Wirtschaft. Organisation of the Industrial Economy, set up by law in February 1934. An ensemble of bodies and chambers representing the substantial unity of the Nazi dictatorship with big business, finance and industry.

Organisation Todt (OT). The Organisation Todt was a German conglomerate of building and public construction companies created in 1933 by Hitler's architect and engineer Fritz Todt (q.v.). Closely related to the Nazi Party, the OT was entrusted to construct Autobahnen (q.v.) in 1933, and bunkers in the Westwall (q.v.) in 1938. In 1940, the OT became a Werhmachtsgefolge (q.v.). After Fritz Todt's death in February 1942, the OT was headed by Albert Speer (q.v.). Speer became minister of production and armament; he entrusted the OT direction to Franz Xaver Dorsch. The huge OT building conglomerate used private enterprise, improvisation, slave labor, and technical standardization to support the German army. It built and repaired railways, roads, bridges, ports, canals and airfields, it constructed bunkers and fortifications, notably in the Atlantikwall (q.v.), and defensive lines in Italy, such as the Gustav, Hitler, Gengis Khan and Alpine lines. The OT was also charged by the SS with building gigantic underground installations, industrial shelters, concealed armament factories, and concrete launching sites for retaliation V-weapons as well as fortification lines aiming to stop Russian offensives in the East. The Germans utilized all occupied lands' resources to support their war efforts. Slave labor, unlimited looting and methodical plundering became common practice; on a large scale, the OT requisitioned all material, tools, plants, equipment and transportation means. See Arbeitseinzatz and Organisation Todt-Schützkommando.

Organisation Todt-Schutzkommando (OT-SK). Paramilitary protection squad of the Organisation Todt. The OT squads were formed in 1942 to guard OT building sites against theft and sabotage. In addition, the OT-SK supervised the workers, the slave laborers, teams of Jewish slave workers and Soviet POWs. To fill its ranks, the OT-SK had to rely on the recruitment of foreign volunteers because most physically able German

Organisation Todt cipher.

Organisation Todt worker.

OT-SK member.

men were already serving in the armed forces. Many Dutchmen, Flemings, Walloons and Frenchmen volunteered for the OT squads. By the end of World War II, the OT-SK men were employed to guard POWs, criminals and concentration camp inmates. The OT-Schützkommandos were also involved in antipartisan campaigns on the eastern front. In March 1945, all SK companies were disbanded and a great majority of the troops were transferred to the Waffen-SS and other German military formations.

Orpo. See Ordnungpolizei.

Ortsgruppen. NSDAP subdivisions, groups of villages or towns, headed by an Ortsgruppenleiter who often doubled as a town mayor. A various number of Ortsgruppen constituted a "circle," which was a district called Kreis (headed by a Kreisleiter). See Nationalsozialistiches Deutsche Arbeiterpartei.

Ossewabrandwag. Oxwagon Sentinels, an organization officially launched in South Africa in 1939 to preserve the culture and traditions of the Afrikaners (white South Africans of Dutch origin). The organization progressively developed into an anti–British and pro–Nazi paramilitary force which at its peak had 400,000 members and posed a considerable threat to the South African government. Some of its members became Stormjaers (storm troops) and during the war committed various acts of sabotage and subversion with the hope of starting a rebellion. The Ossewabrandwag helped German internees to escape and send information and intelligence to the Germans.

Ost. The East. For the Nazis it meant the Union of Socialist Soviet Republics (USSR), including the Baltic states. The acronym USSR was seldom used by the Nazis, who referred to it as Rußland (Russia) or Ost.

Ostindustrie GmbH. Eastern Industry Ltd., a company set up in March 1943 by Odilo Globocnik (q.v.) for the purpose of utilizing (Jewish) slave labor in the Lublin area in Poland.

Ostmark. The East March, or eastern border. Original Nazi term for Austria, Hitler's birth land. The name "Austria" was no longer permitted in official use and was outlawed owing to increased "anti–Prussianism" among Austrians.

Ostmedaille. Eastern Medal, awarded to soldiers having served on the Russian front in winter 1941–42. It was sarcastically called Gefrierfleischorden (Order of Frozen Meat) by the troops, referring to the cold conditions on that front.

Ostpreußen. East Prussia, a province in Prussia. The capital was Königsberg (today Kaliningrad). The province was divided in 1945 between the Soviet Union and Poland, and all German-speaking people were expelled.

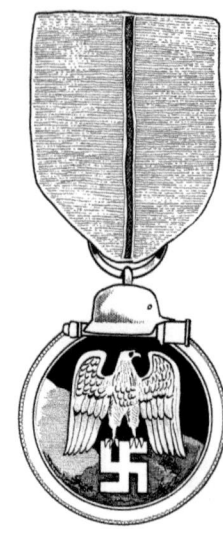

Ostmedaille.

Ostradschlepper. Tractor East. A heavy 4 × 4 tractor with oversized metal wheels designed in 1942 by Ferdinand Porsche and built by the Skoda Company specially intended for the Russian front.

Skoda Ostradschlepper.

Ost-Truppen. Eastern troops composed of men coming from the Soviet Union. Ost-Truppen were volunteers from Armenia, Georgia, Turkestan, Azerbaijan or other Soviet republics. Some men believed that the Third Reich would give them independence once Stalin's regime was crushed (actually a propaganda lie). Other eastern troopers were just young men attracted by an adventurous life or fleeing misery. Others were Russian POWs who enlisted in the German army to escape bad treatment and certain death in prison camps. Because of ill motivation, language and cultural barriers, Ost-Truppen formed poor military units. According to army regulation, Ost-Truppen were to be posted in the least menaced positions on the front and always to be placed between two reliable German units.

Ost-Truppen soldier.

Ostwall (OW). East Wall, a line of fortification planned and partly built at the border with Poland between 1935 and 1938. The so-called East Wall included defensive positions in the isolated province of East Prussia, the Oder-Warthe-Bend line (OWB), the Pomeranian line, and the Oder Line. The East Wall stretched along both Pomerania and Silesia, from Küstrin (today Koszalin in Poland) on the Baltic Sea running along Neustettin, Landsberg, Glogau and Breslau up to Gleiwitz (today Gliwice in Poland). The northern province of Pomerania was totally lacking in natural defenses. It was the most vulnerable sector exposed to a supposed Polish invasion; therefore the Oder-Warthe-Bend line was given full priority and became the strongest position in the East Wall, including three lines of fortifications. The never-completed East Wall was reactivated in the summer of 1944 to resist Soviet offensive but it was no match for the overwhelming Soviet war machine. The term Ostwall also designated a continental-scale line of fortification planned in the East following the AA Line (q.v.). The project of this Eastern Wall was seriously entertained by Hitler. According to the Nazi concept of Lebensraum (q.v.), the Russians were to be chased headlong across the Volga, over the Ural mountains and deep into Asia — their "barbaric home." Intended as another Great Wall of China, the Eastern Wall would have prevented them from ever returning to Nazi-controlled Europe.

Ostwind. Eastern wind. Name given to the self-propelled antiaircraft Flakpanzer IV. The Ostwind, produced from March 1944 onwards, was a converted Panzerkampfwagen PzKfw IV armed with a 3.7 centimeter flak 43 gun placed in a rotating octagonal armored turret.

Oswiecim. See Auschwitz.

OT. See Organisation Todt.

OT-SK. See Organisation Todt-Schutzkommando.

Otto-Programme. A special Wehrmacht scheme developing rail and road facilities through Central Europe to the Russian border for transporting supplies. "Otto" was code for Ost (East). Developed between October 1940 and May 1941, it was intended to prepare for Operation Barbarossa, the attack on Soviet Union.

Pacelli, Eugenio. See Pius XII.

PaK. See Panzerabwehrkanone.

Pakwagen. Antitank car. This term particularly applies to the SdKfz 234/4 Pakwagen (8-Rad), an eight-wheeled reconnaissance armored car armed with a 7.5 cm antitank Pak 40. See Panzerjäger.

Pangermanismus or **Alldeutsche Bewegung.** Pan-Germanism, a political nationalist movement. Originating in the early 19th century, Pan-Germanism promoted the doctrine that all German-speaking people in Europe should live in one state. The policy was one of Hitler's aims. See Großdeutschland and Volksdeutsche.

Panther. The PzKpfw V Panther tank, issued in May 1943, was intended to match the Russian T-34 tank. The Panther included many of its opponent's features, notably large tracks, the sloped front plate, which increased the effective thickness of armor, and a powerful 7.5-centimeter KwK 42 (L/70) gun. The Panther existed in various improved versions. The model D entered service in 1943. Its length was 7 meters, its width was 3.5 meters. Its maximum armor was 80 millimeters and its weight was 43 tons, the engine had a power of 650 hp, its range was about 100 km, its maximum speed was 45 kilometers per hour. It had a crew of five and its main armament consisted of one 7.5-centimeter gun. The Panther, modified and greatly improved, became a formidable weapon, probably the best all-around tank of the war.

Panzer (Pz). Armor. The term seems to derive from the Old French *pancier*, meaning "armor for the belly." It can refer to a tank (Panzerkampfwagen) or to an armored formation (Panzer Division). The adjective for "armored" (train, car, vehicle and bunker) is gepanzert.

Panzer und Lastkraftwagen (PuLK). Armor and Trucks. A tactical term designating a rapid break-through with tanks and trucks carrying troops. See Blitzkrieg.

Panzerabwehr. Antitank defense.

Panzerabwehrkanone (PaK). Antitank gun.

Panzerbefehlswagen (Pz Bf Wg). The commanding tank of any Panzer detachment. Often specially built for command, this type of tank had no armed turret but featured a casemated upper structure allowing storage of extra radio gear.

Panzerbrigade 150. A German unit raised during the operation Wacht am Rhein (Battle of the Bulge in winter 1944), composed of English-speaking Germans wearing U.S. uniforms and equipped with captured Allied vehicles. Commanded by SS Obergruppenführer Otto Skorzeny (q.v.), the Panzerbrigade 150 achieved limited success in military terms but it did sow widespread panic behind the Allied lines. An air of paranoia rapidly emerged and all sorts of rumors began to spread, such as one about an attempt to kill General Eisenhower. Skorzeny's comman-

Panther tank.

PaK 38 antitank gun 5 cm.

Pz Bf Wg SdKfz 265 K1 command tank.

dos breached the rule of war, and those who were captured were shot as spies.

Panzerbuchse (Pz.B). Light portable antitank gun in the form of a large rifle firing heavy armor-piercing ammunition.

Panzerdivision. Armored division. The German Panzerdivision, developed by general Heinz Guderian, was a mixed motorized combat force in which infantry, artillery and tanks (as well as paratroopers and ground-attack airplanes) were combined with supporting services under one commander. See Blitzkrieg.

Panzerfaust. "Armor fist." A short-range, portable, disposable, one-round recoilless antitank weapon (or "wall buster") that fired a shaped charge projectile and was operated by one soldier. Panzerfaust existed in several variants with various penetrating capabilities and range varying from 30 meters to 250 meters.

Panzergraben. Antitank ditch. The excavation had various breadths (about 4.50 meters) and depths (about 3 meters) so as to be impractible to any armored vehicle. The Panzergrabe was either a simple ditch dug in the ground or a permanent and costly installation made of concrete. It could also be filled with water (called then Wasserpanzergraben); in many cases Wasserpanzergraben were rivers, canals and other wa-

Panzerfaust.

terways incorporated as antitank ditches in a defense network.

Panzergrenadier. Infantry private in a motorized infantry unit, generally carried in armored halftrack, but as halftracks were rather scarce also transported in trucks. See Grenadier.

Panzergrenadierdivision. Motorized infantry division.

Panzerjäger (PzJg). Literally "tank hunter," an antitank gun placed either in a casemate (an en-

Profile of Panzergraben.

closed armored firing chamber) or in an open-topped firing emplacement and mounted on a tracked chassis.

Panzerkampfwagen (PzKfw). Armored fighting vehicle; tank. A weapon system incorporating firepower (guns and/or machine guns placed in a rotating turret), protection (given by thick armor plates) and mobility (an engine driving endless tracks giving speed across country and obstacles). The first German tanks, the Panzerkampffahrzeug I (PzKfz I), and the Panzerkampffahrzeug II (PzKfz II), were light armored vehicles. In 1935 a better design was issued, the 15-ton light Panzerkampfwagen (PzKpfw III). The Panzerkampfwagen IV (PzKfw IV) was stronger, more powerful, more heavily armored and better armed; it was the mainstay of armored forces and the only German battle tank to remain in production throughout the war. The new PzKpfw Tiger (q.v.) was undoubtedly the most famous German tank of World War II, and was regarded by the Allies as the symbol of German technological superiority in armored fighting vehicles. The PzKpfw V Panther (q.v.), issued in May 1943, was intended to match the Russian T-34. In May 1944, a new heavy tank was issued, the PzKpfw Tiger B, better known as Königstiger (King or Royal Tiger).

PzKfz IV SdKfz 161 Ausf. A with short KwK 7.5 centimeter.

Panzerkampfwagen Abzeichen. Tank Assault Badge introduced in December 1939 to reward achievements of Panzer personnel who took part in armored assaults. It was designed by Wilhelm Ernst Peekhaus of Berlin, and was instituted by order of Generaloberst Walther von Brauchitsch. As the war continued it became obvious that the single 1939 Panzer Badge was no longer adequate to recognize the growing number of veterans with years of experience, and in June 1943 four new classes of the award were introduced for 25, 50, 75 and 100 engagements.

Panzerkorps. Unit formed of several armored divisions.

"Panzerlied." One of the best known Wehrmacht songs. It was composed by Oberleutnant Kurt Wiehle in June 1933, when Germany was clandestinely starting to develop an armored force in defiance of the Versailles Treaty.

Panzermauer. Antitank wall. The Panzermauer was a heavy, permanent linear obstacle. It was mostly constructed of reinforced concrete and was thus very expensive, so Panzermauern were only built in strategically important sites. Profiles, height (from 1.5 to 4 meters), thickness, solidity, and length varied and depended on local topography and strategic importance. The antitank wall was often built with a zigzag layout, and if special antitank guns placed in concrete casemates were incorporated, the Panzermauer formed a very efficient barrier.

Panzerschreck. "Tank terror." Also called the 8.8-centimeter Raketenpanzerbuchse 53, this antitank weapon was directly copied from the U.S. bazooka (introduced in 1942). The Panzerschreck, operated by two men (a shooter and a loader), fired a 3-kilogram charge from a smoothbore barrel fitted with a shield protecting the gunner; its projectile could penetrate 10 centimeters of armor at a range of about 200 meters.

Panzerspähwagen. Armored reconnaissance vehicles (generally on wheels although halftracks and tanks were also used in that role). The Germans designed a wide range of Panzerspähwagen, four-wheel, six-wheel and eight-wheel, furnished with radio and light arms. The standard eight-wheel heavy reconnaissance car was the schwerer Panzerspähwagen SdKfz 231 (8-Rad eight wheel).

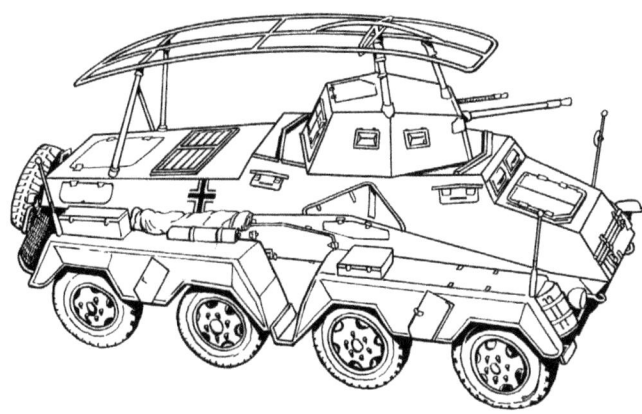

Heavy Panzerspähwagen SdKfz 232 with radio (8-Rad Fu).

Panzerstützpunkt (PzStP). Fortified point, a stronghold including Panzerwerke (q.v.).

Panzertruppen. Armored troops including armored reconnaissance cars' crews. See also Nationalsozialistischen Kraftfahrkorps.

Panzerturm. Armored turret. Generally armed with one or more guns or machine guns, Panzertürme were rotative and placed on top of tanks, warships and even bunkers.

Panzervernichtungabzeichen. Decoration for tank destruction, in the form of a small, rectangular cloth badge displaying a tank. Worn on the upper right arm.

Panzerwaffe. The armored arm, the German tank force.

Panzerwagen (PzW). Armored car, light tank.

Panzerwerk. Concrete bunker including weapons (machine gun, mortar or gun) placed in an armored metal cupola or turret.

Panzerwurfmine (PWM). Shaped charge, hand-thrown antitank grenade. It included a warhead and a tube with attached stabilizing canvas fins. It could penetrate 150-millimeter armored plate, but in combat use the Panzerwurfmine often did not live up to expectations, due to its relatively short range.

Panzerzug or **Eisenbahn Panzerzug** (Eis. Pz-Zug). (See illustration on page 136.) Armored train. Armored trains have been used by most combatants in one form or another since the coming of railways. In the period 1939–40, the Germans had several Panzer trains, including improvised armored convoys and foreign matériel pressed into German service. The equipment and crews of these trains varied a lot, from boxcars armored in a makeshift way with sandbags and light weapons to thick armor with considerable firepower. In January 1942, a construction program was launched involving the Linke-Hoffmann-Werke Company to build armored wagons, the Krupp Company for locomotive armor, the Rheinmetall-Borsig Company for artillery turrets and the Gothär-Wagon-Fabrik to convert civilian rail material. In October 1942, the Germans had ten armored trains in Western Europe, twelve on the Russian front, and two in the Balkans.

Papen, Franz von (1879–1969). A general officer in World War I and later a diplomat and leader of the Catholic Centre Party, the conservative von Papen was among those who believed that

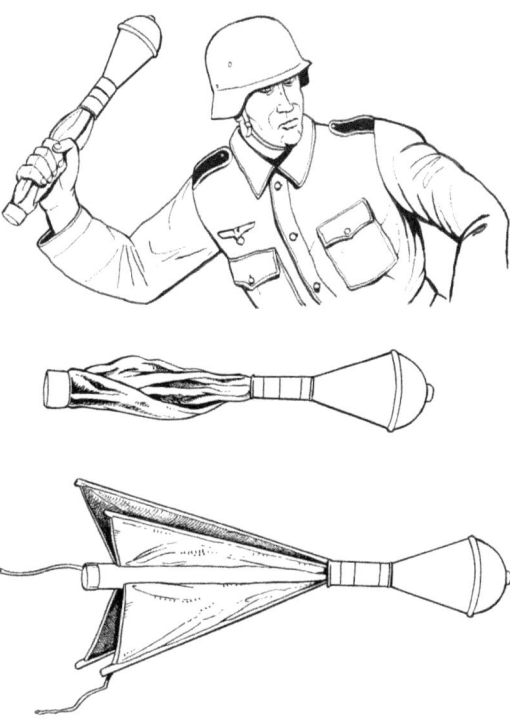

Panzerwurfmine. Top: Throwing the device. Middle: PWM with attached fins. Bottom: PWM with stabilizing canvas fins deployed when thrown.

Papierkrieg

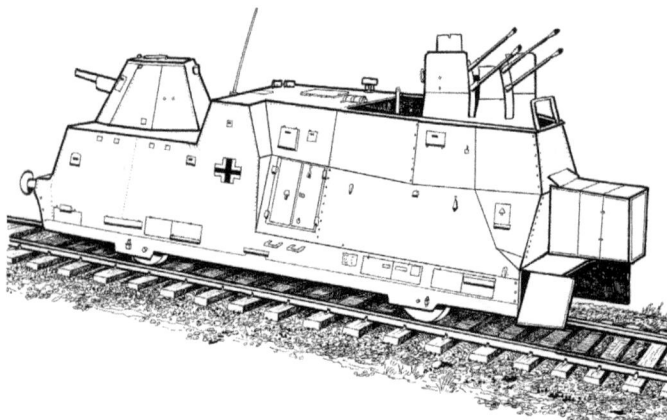

Armored train car in a Panzerzug.

they could control Hitler. He played an important role in the rise to power of Adolf Hitler, who made him vice chancellor in January 1933. Von Papen was special minister, then ambassador to Austria between 1934 and 1938. During World War II he served as ambassador to Turkey. He was tried in 1946 as a war criminal but was acquitted because of insufficient evidence. In February 1947 a German court sentenced him to eight years in prison, but in 1949 he was released because of his age and ill health.

Papierkrieg. Paper war, a German military slang word referring to the struggle to keep up with bureaucratic paperwork.

Parachute troops. See Fallschirmjäger.

Parteigenosse (Pg). Fellow member of the Nazi Party. See Kamerad.

Parteigerichte. Party Courts, established to maintain the NSDAP principles of the Führerprinzip (q.v.). Headed by Walter Buch, the courts imposed discipline in the often complicated, confused and ramshackle NSDAP hierarchy. See also Nationalsozialiste Deutsche Arbeiterpartei and Untersuchungs-und Schlichtungs-Ausschuß.

Parteitagen. Days of the Party, an annual Nazi rally held in Nuremberg in September before World War II. The Nuremberg rally lasted three days and attracted crowds of participants and spectators from all over Germany. The rally featured spectacular demonstrations of Nazi liturgy and power, including marches, speeches, parades, flags and music, all staged to arouse dramatic emotions in order to give frenetic support to the Nazi regime. See also Feiertagen.

Patrone. Cartridge.

Patronengürtel. Cartridge belt for machine gun.

Patronentaschen. Rifle ammunition pouches, generally six attached to the service belt.

Peenemünde. The Heeresversuchsanstalt Peenemünde, or HVP (Peenemünde Military Test Site), located on the westmost extremity of a long sand-spit in the northwestern part of Usedom (Mecklenburg-Vorpommern) on the Baltic Sea coast of Germany, was one of the most modern technological facilities in the world in the years between 1937 and 1945. There, rocket technicians developed, built and tested numerous flight objects equipped with revolutionary technology. From the start this research was directed toward one goal only: achieving military superiority through advanced technology. Slave laborers, concentration camp inmates and prisoners of war provided the work that enabled the construction of the test sites and the later serial production of the rockets, which the Nazi propaganda referred to as Vergeltungswaffen (q.v.).

Pelzmütze. Fur-covered cap. The Pelsmütze was introduced during the winter of 1942–43 to German troops serving at the eastern front. Based on the Russian-style fur hats, it had side flaps that could be tied down under the wearer's chin.

Pelzmütze (fur cap).

Pfarrer Notbund. Emergency league of pastors formed by Martin Niemöller (q.v.) in September 1933 to defend the Lutheran Church against the Nazi Gleichschaltung (q.v.). See Religion in the Third Reich.

Pfeffer von Salomon, Franz Felix (1888–1968). A veteran of the Freikorps (q.v.) and the NSDAP Gauleiter (q.v.) in Thuringia and Westphalia, Pfeffer von Salomon was appointed Leader of the Sturm Abteilung der NSDAP (q.v.) from 1926 to 1930. After the Stennes mutiny (q.v.) of 1930, and a dispute with Hitler, he was dismissed, and Hitler personally took command of the SA until the return of Ernst Röhm (q.v.) from Bolivia.

Pfeifenkopf. Code name for a 1944 German artillery experiment. It was a simple rocket designed to be fired against tanks, but with a rather sophisticated head, which carried a scanning device; this signaled back a dim picture of the target to allow the operator to guide the rocket to the enemy tank. Another version, code-named Steinbocke, used infrared detectors that allowed the missile to home in automatically on the tank without the assistance of an operator. Both experimental weapons were far from being serviceable when World War II ended.

Pg. Short for Parteigenosse (q.v.).

Phony War. See Sitzkrieg.

Pimpf. Literally "little chap," a boy age 10 to 14 belonging to the Deutsches Jungvolk in der HJ (q.v.). See Hitler Jugend.

Pistole. Pistol, a light hand-held weapon which fires small ammunitions automatically or semi-automatically. The Germans did not produce revolvers, preferring the pistol. The main German service pistols were the Luger (q.v.) M 08, the Walther P 38, the 9 mm Mauser (q.v.) C96 and the small Walther PPK. For signaling the Leuchtpistole 42 (flare pistol) was used.

Pius XI, Ambrogio Damiano Achille Ratti (1857–1939). Pope from 1922 to 1939, Pius XI made a number of efforts to bring the Catholic Church into greater harmony with the modern world. Pius XI, however, regarded communism as a much more serious threat to the Catholic Church than Nazism, and thus sought to appease Hitler in the effort to protect the rights of Catholics in Germany. As a result he signed a concordat with Hitler in 1933. It was not until 1937, when he issued the encyclical *Mit brennender Sorge* (q.v.), that he condemned some aspects of Nazism. See Reichskonkordat and Religion in the Third Reich.

Deutsches Jungvolk Pimpf.

Pius XII, Eugenio Pacelli (1876–1958). Eugenio Pacelli was papal nuncio in Munich in 1917 and in Berlin from 1920 until he became a cardinal in 1929. He was Vatican secretary of state, and on Pius XI's death was elected pope in March 1939. Pope Pius XII's actions during World War II and the Holocaust remain controversial. For much of the war, he maintained a public front of indifference and remained silent while German atrocities were committed. Even though he was well acquainted with Germany and was kept informed, he refused pleas for help on the grounds of neutrality, while making statements condemning injustices in general. Privately, he sheltered a small number of Jews and spoke to a few select officials, encouraging them to help the Jews. Many members of the Catholic Church undoubtedly felt betrayed by Pius XII's silence on the issue of genocide. Historians offer many reasons why Pope Pius XII was not a stronger and better public advocate for the Jews: a fear of Nazi reprisals; a feeling that public speech would have no effect and might harm the Jews; the idea that private intervention could accomplish more; the anxiety that acting against the German government could provoke a schism among German Catholics; the church's traditional role of being politically neutral; and the fear of the growth of communism should the Nazis be defeated. Whatever his motivation, it is hard to escape the conclusion that Pope Pius XII, like so many others in positions of power and influence, could have done more to save the Jews. See Religion in the Third Reich.

Plakat. Poster. The poster was an important medium in the Third Reich, notably during elections before 1933, but also after the seizure of power as propaganda. German posters of the period reflected the heroic realistic style imposed by the Nazis, with short and powerful slogans and bold, dynamic layout. Even the typography mirrored the Nazis' official ideology. The use of Fraktur (q.v.) was common until 1941, when Martin Bormann denounced it as "Jewish" and decreed that only Roman type should be used. Modern sans-serif typefaces were condemned as cultural bolshevism, although Futura continued to be used owing to its practicality. See Kunst and Reichskulturkammer.

Pohl, Oswald (1892–1951). Head of the Allgemeine SS (q.v.) administration from 1934, and subsequently head of the Wirtschafts-und Verwaltungshauptamt (q.v.), or WVHA, Main Office for Economy and Administration. Pohl formed companies, obtained monopolies and recruited to the SS businessmen, clerks and administrators, many of whom were more concerned with profits than with Nazism. The WVHA's economic activities, largely deriving from "Aryanized" Jewish businesses, the ruthless exploitation of forced slave labor from concentration camps and booty from extermination camps, brought substantial riches to the SS. Oswald Pohl was sentenced to death in 1947 and hanged in 1951.

Polish Amnesty Decree. A decree made in late 1939 by Hitler giving full amnesty to SS men and units held by the army for atrocities committed in Poland. See Einsatzgruppen.

Polizei. Police. The failure of the Munich Putsch in 1923, which was crushed by the police and not by the army, brought home to Hitler the fact that unrestricted control of the police would be an essential element in the successful establishment of a long-term National Socialist state. Consequently the years after power take-over were marked by the Führer's effort to have his most trusted men, the SS, nominated to senior police positions. In June 1936, Himmler increased his apparatus of repression and terror. He managed to maneuver himself into a position allowing him to become chief of the Ordnungspolizei (q.v.), head of Gestapo (q.v.), Kriminalpolizei (q.v.) and Sicherheitsdienst des Reichsführer SS (q.v.). In 1939, these services were united in one large centralized police department called the Reichssicherheidshauptamt (q.v.), or RSHA—Central Security Department. Although the Nazi police services were basically divided into two main branches with different purposes—Sicherheit (security) and Ordnung (order)—the subject of the German police during the period of the Third Reich is extremely complex, as there were a wide range of sub-branches connected with the state, the party, the SS and the armed forces. The fusion of police and SS led to a fundamental change in the German daily life, the lawless, malicious and faceless bureaucratic SS police being not any longer a public service but an instrument of the Führer's personal will. See Reichsführer-SS und Chef der Deutschen Polizei.

Polnische Wirtschaft. Polish business, a Nazi metaphoric term referring to the fact that the Poles were Slavic subhumans and that Poland stood directly in the way of German expansion in the East.

Pölzl, Klara (1860–1907) Wife (and second cousin) of Alois Hitler (q.v.) and mother of Adolf Hitler. Her father was Johann Baptist Pölzl and her mother was Johanna Hiedler. Her children were: Gustav Hitler (1885–1887); Ida Hitler (1886–1888); Otto Hitler (1887); Adolf Hitler (1889–1945); Edmund Hitler (1894–1900); Paula Hitler (1896–1960).

Stepchildren were: Alois Hitler, Jr. (1882–1956) and Angela Hitler (1883–1949).

See also Raubal, Geli, and Schicklgruber, Maria Anna.

Porsche (P). Automobile company from Stuttgart called Dr. Ing. F. Porsche GmbH. It was founded in 1931 by Ferdinand Porsche (q.v.).

Porsche, Ferdinand (September 1875–January 1951). An Austrian automotive engineer, he is best known for creating the first hybrid vehicle (gasoline-electric), the Volkswagen (q.v.), and the Mercedes-Benz SS/SSK, as well as many automobiles named after himself. Porsche also made a number of contributions to advance World War II German tank designs, including the Tiger I, Tiger II, and the Elefant, as well as the super-heavy Panzer VIII Maus tank, which was never put into production. In 1945, Ferdinand Porsche was arrested for war crimes. He was not tried, but stayed in prison for 20 months. Released in 1947, he started anew a brilliant career in top-quality automobile design and production.

Positives Christentum. Positive Christianity. A movement within Nazi Germany that blended ideas of racial purity with Christian doctrine. It was adopted as part of the official party doctrine at the NSDAP congress in 1920 to express a worldview that was Christian, nonconfessional, and vigorously opposed to the spirit of "Jewish Materialism." Adherents of Positive Christianity regarded Christ not as a Jewish pacifist but as an active preacher, organizer and fighter who opposed the institutionalized Judaism of his day. They rejected Jewish-written parts of the Bible (including the entire Old Testament), they claimed "Aryanhood" and non–Jewishness for Christ, and their political objective of national unity advocated overcoming confessional differences, eliminating Catholicism, and uniting Protestantism into a single unitary Christian national socialist church. Hitler, who was strongly opposed to Christian ethics, was careful not to take a public stand in defence of Positive Christianity, but he was sympathetic to it.

Pour le Sémit. For the Semite. Cynical punning of "Pour le Mérite" (highest German military medal awarded for merit). Pour le Sémit was used to describe the yellow star or Judenstern (q.v.).

Presse. Press. After Hitler took power in 1933, the press fell under Gleichschaltung (q.v.) and soon "Aryanization." The Propaganda Ministry, through its Reich Press Chamber, assumed control over the Reich Association of the German Press, the guild that regulated entry into the profession. Under the new Editors Law of October 4, 1933, the association kept registries of "racially pure" editors and journalists, and excluded Jews and those married to Jews from the profession. Propaganda Ministry officials aimed to control the content of news and editorial pages through directives distributed in daily conferences in Berlin and transmitted via the party propaganda offices to regional or local papers. Detailed guidelines stated what stories could or could not be reported and how to report the news. Journalists or editors who failed to follow these instructions could be fired or, if believed to be acting with intent to harm Germany, sent to a concentration camp.

Prinz Albrechtstraße. Prince Albert Street. The street in Berlin where the headquarters of the Gestapo (q.v.) was located. The name became synonymous with fear and dread.

Prinz Eugen. *Admiral Hipper*–class heavy cruiser, the third member of the class of five vessels. She was laid down in April 1936 and launched in August 1938. *Prinz Eugen* entered service in August 1940. The ship was named after Prince Eugene of Savoy, an 18th-century Austrian general. She took part in several operations and after World War II was taken by the United States, used for testing nuclear weapons and capsized at Kwajalein Atoll in December 1946.

Process of Nuremberg. See Nürnberger Prozeß.

Propagandakompanie (PK). Propaganda company. Front-line reporters, photographers and filmers formed units also called Sondereinheiten der Wehrmacht (special Army squads). Their works were published in the numerous and strictly controlled press magazines and newspapers (*Signal*, for example) and shown in the Deutsche Wochenschau (q.v.). Articles, photographs and both fiction and nonfiction films were of course severely censored and carefully selected in order to glorify the war effort, the achievements of the Nazi regime, and to boost the morale of the population.

Propagandaministerium. Ministry of Propaganda, headed by Joseph Paul Goebbels (1897–1945). The official name was Reichsministerium für Volksaufklärung und Propaganda (RMVP, Reich Ministry for Public Enlightenment and

Propaganda). Propaganda is the organized use of publicity material to spread information, doctrine or practice. It is an instrument of psychological warfare as old as history. In modern parlance it deals with true or invented information and embraces every possible civil and military activity; its effectiveness depends upon the means of dissemination, the literacy and the insight of the people addressed, and upon the skills and talent of the propagandists. After World War I, beside the existing pamphlets, newspapers and posters, new media appeared: the wireless radio broadcast, which brought the voice of propaganda inside many homes, and the motion picture, which brought it into every urban neighborhood. The German Propaganda Ministry directed by Goebbels won enormous success and played a central role in the Nazification of Germany before and after the seizure of power by the Nazis. Goebbels' basic principle was that "an oft-repeated lie eventually would be believed." This became standard practice in the Third Reich. Nazi propaganda was based on the principle that truth was variable and adjustable. It was not intended to try to pass judgment on conflicting rights, giving each its due, but exclusively to emphasize the racist and bellicose values the Nazis were asserting. Propaganda did not investigate the truth objectively, but presented only that aspect of the truth which was favorable to the ideology, and the objective truth was violated, twisted, and reshaped whenever it suited the regime.

Protektorat Böhmen und Mähren. See Böhmen und Mähren.

Protokolle der Weisen von Zion. *Protocols of the Elders of Zion.* A forgery of 19th-century origin used by various European organizations to provoke hatred against the Jews. The fraudulent anti–Semitic document purported to be the minutes of a secret Zionist congress, describing a Jewish plot for achieving global domination by controlling the press and the world's economies, the planning of terrorism, and the undermining and destruction of the Aryan people. In the anti–Semitic context of the time, these exaggerations were widely believed. The protocols were first published in Russia in 1903. They were translated into many languages and disseminated internationally in the early part of the 20th century. Henry Ford funded printing of 500,000 copies, which were distributed throughout the United States in the 1920s. Hitler was a major proponent. The *Protokolle* were studied, as if factual, in German classrooms after the Nazis came to power in 1933, despite having been exposed as fraudulent by the *Times of London* in 1921 and by a Swiss court of law in 1935. The forged document has often been regarded as Hitler's primary justification for initiating the Holocaust (q.v.).

Prussia, August-Wilhelm, Prince of (1887–1949). Nicknamed Auwi, he was the fourth son of Kaiser Wilhelm II (1859–1941) who ruled Germany from 1888 to 1918. A fervent admirer of Adolf Hitler, the prince joined the NSDAP in 1930, and was deliberately used by the National Socialists to obtain respectability and gain votes in elections. However, after the establishment of the dictatorship, the Nazis no longer needed the "little brown-shirted Prince," who himself had secretly hoped that Hitler would one day hoist him or his son Alexander up to the vacant throne of the kaiser. Auwi (described by Goebbels as a "good-natured but slightly gormless boy") was appointed to high honorary ranks in the NSDAP, SA and SS, but was soon completely sidelined and also banned from making public speeches. After the war Auwi was sentenced to two and a half years' hard labor. Due to his confinement since 1945 in an internment camp, in 1948 he was considered to have served his sentence and released.

Puma Sdkfz 234/2 (8-Rad). An eight-wheel armored reconnaissance car, type Sdkfz 234, transformed in 1944 into a self-propelled artillery vehicle, armed with one MG 42, six smoke shell launchers and one 5-centimeter KwK 39/1 antitank gun placed in a rotating oval turret.

Pz. Short for Panzer (q.v.).

PzKfw. See Panzerkampfwagen.

Quisling. A pejorative meaning "traitor," during World War II commonly used as an insult directed at a citizen who collaborated with the Germans in one of the conquered nations. The term was taken from the pro–Nazi illegitimate Norwegian leader Vidkun A.L. Jonsson Quisling (1887–1945), the founder of the Norwegian Fascist Party. Quisling was tried and executed in 1945. See Fünfte Kolonne.

RAD. See Reichsarbeitsdienst.

Räder, Erich (1876–1943). Commander of the German navy from 1935 to 1943, replaced with Karl Dönitz (q.v.) from 1943 to 1945. At the Nuremberg trials, he was found guilty of having planned war, and he was sentenced to life imprisonment. However, he was released in 1955.

Radfahr; Radfahrer. Bicycle; bicyclist. It was a lucky German soldier who even got a ride in a troop-carrier, particularly after 1943, when the number of motor vehicles was decreased, heavy equipment and artillery were horse-drawn and infantrymen just had to walk or make use of cheap means of transportation: the ordinary bicycle.

Radio in the Third Reich. After the seizure of power in January 1933, broadcasting houses were cleansed and coordinated by Gleichschaltung (q.v.). Undesirable employees were sacked or sent to concentration camps for political or racial reasons. Joseph Paul Goebbels (q.v.) was in charge, and henceforth the Nazis alone decided what people were allowed to listen to. Recognizing the importance of radio in disseminating their message, Goebbels approved a scheme whereby millions of cheap radio sets—the Volksempfänger (q.v.)—were subsidized by the government. To make political broadcast more attractive, non-propaganda elements like music, advice, reports, commentaries, serials and other entertainment were introduced. Radio broadcasts, notably Hitler's speeches, were also played over loudspeakers in public places, factories and workshops. Along with domestic broadcasts, the Nazi regime used radio to deliver its message to both occupied territories and enemy states. Nazi propaganda was delivered to Great Britain through William Joyce (q.v.), Norman Baillie-Stewart, Pearl Vardon, Leonard Banning, Susan Hilton, Barry Payne Jones, and Alexander Fraser Grant. Broadcasts were also made to the United States, notably through Robert Henry Best and "Axis Sally," Mildred Gillars (q.v.).

France received broadcasts from Radio-Stuttgart through the anti–Semitic journalist Paul Ferdonnet. Following the occupation of France, Radio Paris and Radio Vichy became the main organs of Nazi propaganda, featuring leading far-right figures such as Philippe Henriot, Jean Hérold-Paquis and Gerald Hewitt. Regularly speaking in support of the Nazis in Belgium was Ward Hermans. Pro–Nazi broadcasts were heard regularly in the Italian Social Republic through Giovanni Preziosi and Luisa Rita Zucca (q.v.), and even in North Africa, where Mohammad Amin al–Husayni helped to ensure the spread of Nazi propaganda in the Arabic language.

Rad-Zugmachine mit Hilfskettenantrieb (MSZ 201). A four-wheeled armored vehicle with additional tracks, designed by certified engineer Diplom-Ingenieur. Heinrich-Ernst Kniepkamp, produced by the J.A. Maffei AG Company in 1931. The MSZ 201 could carry eight soldiers or a 1,000-kilogram load, it could tow a small gun or a trailer, it weighed 5.4 tons and had a maximum speed of 50 kilometers per hour when driving on wheels on good road.

Ranks. See Dienstgrad.

Rasputitsa. Thick mud resulting from the heavy autumn rain on the Russian front in which many German vehicles and tanks got bogged.

Rasse- und Siedlungshauptamt (RuSHA). Central Office for Race and Settlement, run by the SS (q.v.) One of the five key branches of the SS, the Rasse-und Siedlungsamt was headed by the Nazi "philosopher" Richard Walther Darré (q.v.) before the war, and later successively by Otto Hofmann, Richard Hildebrandt and Gottlob Berger. The RuSHA was intended to examine the SS recruits' lineage in order to control the purity of the SS according to Darré's racial principles. The recruits' wives were investigated as well. It was also charged with organizing the Eindeutschung, the colonization of conquered Eastern territories by German settlers following Darré's theory of Blut und Bodem (q.v.)—blood and soil. The conquest of Lebensraum (q.v.), or vital space, was one of Hitler' most important aims. After the 1939–41 victories, a part of this program was set up, not by means of the RuSHA but by the Hauptamt Volksdeutsche Mittelstelle. During World War II, the RuSHA lost a great deal of its significance and took over the management of salaries, pensions and social care for SS members. See Hauptamt Volksdeutsche Mittelstelle and Sippenbuch.

Rassenforschung. Race research, encouraged by the Nazis for teaching Rassenkunde (q.v.).

Rassenkunde or **Rassenlehr.** Racial knowledge. Rassenkunde was one of the pillars of Nazi ideology. It was based on the racist belief that human races were unequal, the superior race being the Aryans. The Nazi ideology was the application and officialization at the state level of the basic biologic principle of "struggle for life," the belief that only the strongest may survive and the weakest have no right to live. It represented a complete break with the traditional European values of Christian forgiveness, charity and love of fellow beings. This criminal ideology was carried out, mainly after 1942, by industrial extermination in the death camps ruled by the SS. See Arisch, *Essai sur l'inégalité des races humaines*, Herrenvolk, Ubermensch and Untermensch.

Rassenschande. Racial shame. Law passed in September 1935 — paragraph 5 of the Nuremberg Blutschutzgesetze (q.v.) — which forbade sexual intercourse between German Aryans and Jews. This "ignominy" was punishable by imprisonment in a concentration camp.

Ratsch-Bumm. Nickname given by the Germans to the Russian 7.62-centimeter M1939 field gun for its distinctive sound when firing.

Raubal, Geli (1908–1931). Hitler's niece. In 1928, Hitler had rented the Haus Wachenfeld on the Obersalzberg near Berchtesgaden, and invited his sister Angela Raubal to move in as his housekeeper. Angela brought along her two daughters, Friedl and Angela, or Geli, as she was known. On the evidence of many Nazi colleagues, Hitler was deeply in love with his niece Geli, and she became his constant companion. They were rumored lovers, but what exactly happened between niece and uncle is still unknown. The relationship degenerated as the hyperjealous Hitler became more and more demanding. Geli Raubal shot herself — or perhaps she was shot by Emil Maurice (q.v.) — on September 17, 1931, and Hitler was devastated. Geli Raubal's life and mysterious death remain great mysteries in Hitler's private life. See Braun, Eva.

Räumboot (R-Boot). Minesweeping boat. Ships equipped with mechanical sweeps to detect and detonate sea mines in advance of other naval operations.

Ravensbrück. The major Nazi Frauenlager (q.v.) was Ravensbrück, located near Furstenberg in North Germany. Established in autumn 1938, and originally intended for the detention and "reeducation" of deviant German women, the camp had to be enlarged four times during World War II as its population grew to include women, babies and young children from 20 different European countries. By the end of 1939 there were 2,290 inmates. By the end of 1941, there were 12,000 prisoners. By the end of 1942, the population was 15,000, and it reached 42,000 by the end of 1943. At that point the concentration camp included some 31 subcamps and work camps and external kommandos where women and children were forced to do hard and heavy work. As in other concentration camps, Ravensbrück had a crematory, and in November 1944, the SS decided to build a gas chamber where those too weak to work were murdered. Ravensbrück was liberated by the Russian army in April 1945. The estimated number of victims is 92,000. See Kommando.

Räumboot T1 Class TB 13–32.

Rednerschule der NSDAP. Nazi Party school for orators. This political institute was created in 1928 by Fritz Reinhardt (1895–1969), and speakers and senior leaders of the NSDAP were trained in oratory, the art of speaking in public.

Regelbau (R). Regular construction. A standardized bunker type specially conceived for functional efficiency and low cost. Every Regelbau bunker had a type number corresponding to a function, indicating dimensions, material quantities, construction delays and issuing date. Beside this indication, each bunker carried a unit number and a letter corresponding to the arm it belonged to.

Reich. Empire. See Drittes Reich.

Das Reich. The [German] Empire, Nazi magazine founded by Rudolf Sparing, Rolf Rienhardt and Max Amann (q.v.) with the agreement of propaganda minister Joseph Goebbels. First published in May 1940, it contained news reports, essays on various subjects, book reviews, and an editorial written by Goebbels. Some of the content was written by foreign pro–Nazi authors, but with the exception of Goebbels' editorial, Das Reich did not share the tone of other Nazi publications. (Das Reich was also the name of the 2nd Waffen-SS Division.).

Reich Central Security Office. See Reichssicherheitshauptamt.

Reichenberg. See V1, V4 and KG 200.

Reichsarbeitsdienst (RAD). National labor service, whose motto was "Arbeit Adelt" (Work Ennobles). It was established on June 26, 1935. Service for six months in the RAD was compulsory for Hitler Jugend (q.v.) members and all males between the ages 18 and 25 before entering military service. The RAD was part of the Deutsche Arbeitsfront (q.v.), DAF, or German Labor Front (q.v.) directed by Robert Ley (q.v.). The Reichsarbeitsdienst Manner, or RAD/M, was set up for men, and later the RAD also included a separate sections for females called the

Left: The depicted Haupttruppführer (Sergeant) wears the brown M1935 RAD uniform with spade-shaped badge indicating battalion and company numbers and red armband with black swastika in a white disc. *Top left insignia:* RAD insignia; *bottom left insignia:* Insignia of the RADwJ (Female Labor Service). *Right:* Young woman in the Reichsarbeitsdienst der weibliche Jugend (RAD/wJ).

Reichsarbeitsdienst der weibliche Jugend, or RAD/wJ. Before World War II, the RAD took part in labor projects such as the reclamation of marshland for cultivation, the construction of dikes, drainage improvement work, vast tree removal operations, the reclamation of fallow or wasted land, and the construction of roads. During World War II the RAD continued to serve its originally established duty of training young men prior to their service in the Wehrmacht by providing construction and agricultural work for the nation, but increasingly it took part in more militarized support roles on all fronts. Soon RAD units were involved in front-line combat, trained and used as antiaircraft units under the control of the Luftwaffe (q.v.). The Reichsarbeitsdienst was disbanded with the collapse of the Third Reich on May 8th, 1945. See Flakhelfer.

Reichsautobahnen. Motorways constructed by the Nazi regime. See Autobahnen and Organisation Todt.

Reichsbahn. German Railway Company.

Reichsbund der Deutschen Beamten (RDB). German Civil Servants' league. The League, headed by Hermann Neef—who was also head of the administrative department of the NSDAP—was intended to control all administrative personnel. It had fourteen administrative groups. In May 1937 the RDB was reorganized, but its activities were suspended in March 1943 for the duration of the war.

Emblem of the RDB.

Reichsbund Deutsche Jagershaft. German National Hunting Association. This association was in existence before the Third Reich. Its main function was to conserve, regulate, control and organize hunting throughout Germany's extensive forests and land. Hermann Göring (q.v.) was eventually appointed as its head and given the title of National Hunt Master. This suited him very well as hunting was one of his favorite pastimes. See Reichsforstdienst.

Reichsburger. Citizen of pure German blood, as opposed to Staatsangehörige ("impure" subject of the state).

Reichsbürgergesetz. Ensemble of laws passed in Nuremberg on September 15, 1935, aiming at reducing the Jews' civil rights. See Nurnberger Gesetze.

Reichsforstdienst. The National Forestry Service. This was in existence well before the Third Reich came into being. It was organized to control and preserve the natural resources of Germany's abundant national forests. The primary objective of the forestry service was the administration of all matters concerning timber and wildlife conservation. Hermann Göring was the head of both the National Forestry Service and the National Hunting Association. The forestry service was charged with prescribing game laws and hunting regulations. The actual policing of the forests was delegated to regional or district Forstmeisters (foresters), who were trained full-time government representatives. Large private landowners were required to hire forestry officials at their own expense in order to safeguard their estates from poachers.

Reichsführer-SS. Leader of the SS, Himmler's title until 1936.

Reichsführer-SS und Chef der Deutschen Polizei. Leader of the SS and Chief of the German Police, Himmler's title after June 1936, when he became chief of the German Orpo (ordinary uniformed police), head of secret state police (the notorious Gestapo, established in April 1933), criminal police (Kripo) and security service (Sicherheitsdienst, or SD). The amalgamation of police and SS made Germany a police state with oppression, repression and terror as only means of ruling. See Himmler, Heinrich; Polizei; and Schutz-Staffeln.

Reichsführung-SS (RfSS). Supreme command of the SS. See Hauptamt Persönliche Stab des Reichsführer-SS.

Reichsgau. Each of the eleven regions formed of annexed territories after 1939. See Gau.

Reichsjugendamt. Reich Youth Office. The service responsible for the administration and training of the Hitler Jugend (q.v.).

Reichsjugendführer. Leader of the Reich Youth. The reserved title for the chief of the Hitler Jugend (q.v.). They were Baldur von Schirach (1907–1974) between 1933 and 1940, and Arthur Axmann (1913–1996) between 1940 and 1945.

Reichskokarde. See Kokarde.

Reichskommissar (RK). Reich commissioner serving as governor in occupied territories.

Reichskommissariat für das Ostland. German administration of conquered Soviet territories, headed by Alfred Rosenberg (q.v.).

Reichskommissariat für die Festigung des Deutschen Volkstums (RKFDV). Reich Office

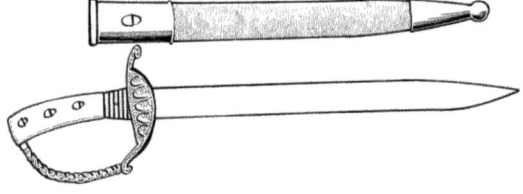

Reichsforstdienst dagger. The dagger had a length of 19 inches.

for the Consolidation of German Nationhood. It was an important SS agency that coordinated two other SS departments: the Rassen-und Siedlungshauptamt (q.v.) and the Hauptamt Volksdeutsche Mittelstelle (q.v.). Created in 1939, the RKFDV was responsible for the program of resettlement of Volksdeutsche (q.v.), the expropriation and displacement of Slavs in the eastern occupied territories, and the consignment of "racially undesirable" people to forced labor, concentration and extermination camps.

Reichskonkordat. Hitler's concordat signed in July 1933 with Pope Pius XI (q.v.). The agreement assured German Roman Catholics freedom to profess and practice religion, the right of the Church to administer itself, and guaranteed of its legal status, its property and its role in education. In return the Catholic Church agreed that priests should take no part in politics.

Reichskriegerbund. National Veterans Organisation.

Reichskriegsflag. War flag officially issued to the German Army on November 7, 1935. The flag, combining tradition and Nazism, was composed of a red background; a superimposed white cross at the junction of which was a small circle containing a black swastika; and in the upper left corner of the flag was a small black iron cross. The term Reichskriegsflag also designated a voluntary paramilitary organization led by Ernst Röhm (q.v.), which formed the nucleus of the SA.

Reichskulturkammer (RKK). National Culture Chamber. It was established in September 1933 by Joseph Paul Goebbels (q.v.) in order to control all cultural activities in Germany. The chamber was a public corporation, a government body, and became a corporate member of the DAF in February 1934. It was divided into seven subchambers controlling music, film, press and broadcast, literature, theater, architecture and sculpture, and visual arts. Membership was compulsory for anyone willing to work as an artist, and limited to culturally valuable "racially pure Aryans" who agreed to be supportive and compliant with the Nazi regime. Persons denied membership were in effect excluded from their professions. See Architecture in the Third Reich, Film Industry in the Third Reich, Kunst, Literature in the Third Reich, Music in the Third Reich, and Radio in the Third Reich.

Emblem of the Reichskulturkammer.

Reichslehrerbund (RLB). Reich Teachers' League, an organization of teachers devoted to the ideals of Nazism, carefully watched by high Nazi officials. See Education in the Third Reich.

Reichsleiter. Reich Leader, official term for Hitler's position as leader of the Third Reich. The term was also used to describe members of the Executive Committee and departmental heads of the NSDAP. See Führer.

Reichsleitung der NSDAP. Reich leadership, term applied collectively to several bureaucrats at the top level of the NSDAP.

Reichsluftfahrtministerium (RLM). Reich Air Ministry or Ministry of Aviation in charge of development and production of airplanes. It was created in April 1933 and personally led by Reichsmarshall Hermann Göring (q.v.).

Reichsluftschutzbund (RLB). Reich Air Defense League. This organization, created in 1934, was composed of volunteers whose task was to coordinate the passive air defense. With the beginning of Allied mass bombing in 1942, the RLB became a large organization for the protection of German citizens from air raids and attacks. See Deutsches Rotes Kreuz and Luftschutzraum.

Reichsmarschall. Marshal of the empire, title of Hermann Göring (q.v.).

Reichsministerium des Innern (RMdI). Ministry of interior, headed by Wilhelm Frick (q.v.) until 1943, then by Heinrich Himmler (q.v.) until 1945.

Reichsministerium für die besetze Ostgebiete (RMO). Reich ministry for occupied eastern territories, headed by Alfred Rosenberg (q.v.) in 1941.

Reichsministerium für Volksaufklärung und Propaganda (RMVP). Reich Ministry for Public Enlightment and Propaganda. Official name of the propaganda service headed by Joseph Paul Goebbels (q.v.). See Propagandaministerium.

Reichsnährstand (RNS). Reich Food Estate. A government body set up in September 1933 in order to regulate food production. Headed by the Nazi ideologist and Reichsbauernführer (National Farmers Leader) Richard Walther Darré (q.v.), the RNS had legal authority over everyone involved in agricultural importation, production and distribution. It attempted to interfere in the market for agricultural goods, using a complex system of orders, rationing, price controls, and prohibitions, through regional marketing associations. Although the RNS had some involvement with the Deutsche Arbeitsfront and the SS, it was and stayed a separate self-sustaining organization. While food shortages never reached a critical level, distribution of foodstuffs was badly disrupted after 1943 as a result of Allied bombing. The Reichsnährstand's argument that Germany "needed" an additional 7–8 million hectares of farmland, and that consolidation of existing farms would displace many existing farmers who would need to work new land, reinforced Hitler's decision to invade the Soviet Union. See Blut und Bodem and Lebensraum.

Reichsparteitag. Yearly national Nazi Party meeting held at Nuremberg, suspended for the duration of the war. See Parteitagen.

Reichssicherheitsdienst (RSH). A special security service for guarding Hitler and the leading members of the Nazi Party. The highly selected members of the RSH were generally recruited from policemen of the criminal police (Kripo) who had proved loyal Nazis.

Reichssicherheitshauptamt (RSHA). Central Reich Security Office, founded in September 1939 and headed by Reinhard Heydrich (q.v.) until 1942, when Ernst Kaltenbrunner (q.v.) took over. The SS Reichssicherheitshauptamt, located in Berlin, was divided into the following subdepartments. Amt I was Personal, Ausbildung und Organisation (administration and personnel) headed by Bruno Streckenbach; Amt II was Haushalt und Wirtschaft (equipment and finance) headed by Werner Best, later by Hans Nockemann; Amt III was the dreaded security service Sicherheitsdienst SD des Reichsführer SS (q.v.), headed by Otto Ohlendorf; Amt IV was the Gestapo (q.v.), the secret state police headed after 1943 by Heinrich Müller (q.v.); Amt V was the Kripo, the Criminal Police, headed by Arthur Nebe; Amt VI was the Foreign Intelligence Service, headed by Heinz Jost, later by Walter Schellenberg; Amt VII was Ideological Research and Evaluation and was headed by Alfred Franz Six. After February 1944, new services were added: Militär Amt was the former Abwehr (q.v.), the military intelligence service of the Wehrmacht, absorbed by the SS; Amt N. Nachrichtenwesen was for telex and radio communication; and Amt S. Sanitätwesen was for medical service. In a regime supposed to be completely centralized, the Nazi German police organization was extremely complicated. This complexity was explained by the nature of the SS, which became a state within the state, and by the fact that, in their regions and districts, the NSDAP servants (Gauleiter, Reichsstatthalter or Oberprezidenten) were powerful men who defended their prerogatives. See Höherer SS-und Polizeiführer and Polizei.

Emblem of the Reichsnährstand.

Reichssportbund or **Nationalsozialistische Reichsbund für Leibesübungen** (NSRL). Reich Sport League or National Socialist Reich League for Physical Exercise. An organization established in July 1934 promoting sports among Nazi Party members, and until 1938 the umbrella organization for sports in the Third Reich. After the Enabling Act, which legally gave Hitler dictatorial control of Germany in March 1933, all sports organizations connected to the Social Democratic Party, the Communist Party, and even to the Churches, were banned. This ban also affected sports clubs of industrial workers. See Gleichschaltung; Olympic Games, 1936; and Sports in the Third Reich.

Reichsstatthalter. Reich lieutenant, senior ranking Nazi deputy given the task of overseeing the fulfillment of Hitler's political guidelines in the state.

Reichstag. Parliament, legislative assembly of the Weimar Republic (q.v.). The Reichstag became largely a figurehead body after its legislative powers were taken away and granted to the Reich government by way of Hitler's Enabling Act of March 24, 1933.

Reichstagsbrand. Burning of the building of the Reichstag on February 27, 1933. The burning of the Reichstag building provided Hitler with an excellent excuse for the rapid persecution of the communist and social democrat opposition. This led to new elections and the passing of the Enabling Act in March 1933. See Ermächtigungsgesetz; Kroll Opera House; and van der Lubbe, Marius.

Reichstrunkenbold. National Drunkard in Chief, nickname given by the German people to two profiteering Nazi officials known for habitual alcoholism: Robert Ley (q.v.) and Heinrich Hoffmann (q.v.).

Reichsverband Deutscher Fleisch-beschauer und Trichinenschauer (RDFuTr). A small organization of meat and intestine inspectors controlling meat quality for human consumption. The emblem of the RDFuTr was a microscope, two crossed butcher knives and a swastika, illustrating how far Gleichschaltung (q.v.) went and how omnipresent Nazi control was in almost every occupation and labor activity. Indeed there was also a German Commercial Employees' Association, a Hair Dressers' Guild, a Berlin Industrial Mechanics Association, a German Stenographers' League, a Painters' Association and many others.

Emblem of RDFuTr.

Reichswehr. Name of the German army in the period 1918–1935. The treaty of Versailles (June 1919) imposed on Germany severe military limitations; the German general staff was disbanded, the navy was limited to 16,500 seamen, submarines were forbidden and ships over 10,000 tons were outlawed, conscription was forbidden, and the ground forces were reduced to 100,000 men with no tanks, airplanes, chemical weapons, heavy guns, automatic weapons or fortifications. Until 1927, the Reichswehr was controlled by an Allied commission, but between this date and 1933 the treaty was secretly breached. In May 1935, the army's name was changed to Wehrmacht (q.v.) when the Versailles treaty was renounced.

Reichswerke Hermann Göring. Hermann Göring National Works. A large corporation created and capitalized by the Nazi regime as a means of keeping big industry in line. See Vierjahresplan.

Reichszeugmeisterei (RZM). Central ordnance office of the NSDAP. The Reichszeugmeisterei, established in July 1934, was a branch of the Treasury Department of the NSDAP, and had exclusive legal authority to design, manufacture, and sell wearing apparel, consisting of shirts, trousers, tunics, overcoats, caps, and other acces-

Examples of RZM control label on SS items.

sories, such as waist belts, belt buckles, belt straps, flags, crash helmets, daggers, knives, standards, buttons, insignia, badges, armbands, car pennants, neckties, drum eagles and all other Nazi regalia. The RZM was charged with making sure that the production of all that they procured was carried out in "Aryan" manufacturing plants, with materials of German origin whenever possible. Producers authorized by the RZM were not allowed to employ "non–Aryan" workers, and had to give preference to Nazi Party members when promoting workers. The RZM system applied to Nazi Party equipment and insignia for the Gliederungen der NSDAP (q.v.), and Angeschlossende Verbände (q.v.) only, the control did not extend to nonparty organizations, like the army, navy and Luftwaffe. The RGBl I-844 law from June 26, 1935, punished by imprisonment any person who insulted or mocked Nazi regalia, uniforms and flags.

Reitsch, Hanna (1912–1979). Germany's leading woman test pilot. Hanna Reitsch held many records for duration, distance and altitude with gliders in the 1930s. She also tested wartime planes, notably the autogyro Fa 61 and the piloted V-1 rocket. Personally devoted to Hitler, she was captured by the Americans in 1945. After being released in 1946, she resumed her career as an international research pilot. See V1 and V4.

Religion in the Third Reich. Hitler and his followers in general rejected Christianity because it was a religion that defended the meek and it was Jewish in origin. Moreover, concepts like forgiveness, mercy and love were anathema to them. Alfred Rosenberg placed Positive Christianity (q.v.) on the NSDAP program, and Heinrich Himmler declared that the church was "for a large part an erotic association of perverted men that has terrorized humanity for one thousand eight hundred years." Hitler, rather bored by religion and religious issues, prudently held ambivalent views on the subject, and did not bind himself to any creed. In fact it suited him that Nazism was regarded by many Germans as a rampart against godless Soviet bolshevism/communism, but there were no doubts that in the long term he would not tolerate religion within Nazi society. In July 1933 he concluded a koncordat that guaranteed the neutrality and the integrity of the Catholic Church, but coming to an understanding with the Protestant Church was more difficult. The Bekenntniskirche (q.v.) — the Confessional Church — worked to maintain the purity of the Evangelical faith, so the Protestants were brought along Nazi lines by force. Two religious groups were singled out for total repression, the Jews and the Jehovah's Witnesses (q.v.). Hitler's struggle with the churches ended with the outbreak of World War II. Then he eased up on the antichurch campaigns, which might have impaired the morale of his soldiers. Hitler was too shrewd a politician to come out openly against Christianity, but should Germany have won the war, both Catholic and Protestant faiths would have been annihilated.

Remagen Brücke. Remagen Bridge, a railway bridge located on the Rhine River halfway between Coblenz and Cologne. It was built during the World War I at the urging of the German generals, so that more troops and war materials could be brought to the western front. Designed by architect Karl Wiener, it is 325 meters long and has a clearance of 14.80 meters above the normal water level of the Rhine. On March 7, 1945, the bridge finally collapsed after many attempts by the German High Command to destroy it. It was never rebuilt and all that remains are defensive towers and foundations.

Reserve. Army reserve composed of Landwehr (men between 35 and 45) and Landsturm, secondary reserve (men over 45).

Rettungsmedaille. Life-saving medal instituted in 1833 in Prussia. It was reinstated in June 1933 with the addition of a swastika on the Prussian imperial eagle. The medal was awarded to any person having rescued someone from great peril or death at the risk of one's own life. The medal was worn on the breast and the ribbon only could be worn in the second buttonhole of the tunic.

Rettungsmedaille.

RF-SS. See Reichsführer-SS.

Ribbentrop, Joachim von (1893–1946). Educated in Switzerland, France and England, and having worked in Canada and the United States, Ribbentrop joined the National Socialist German Workers Party in May 1932. The glamorous pseudo-aristocrat with many connections was a very useful and effective functionary. He quickly moved up the Nazi hierarchy, and in 1933 became Hitler's foreign affairs adviser. The following year he established the Ribbentrop Bureau, a duplicate Nazi organization that worked alongside the official diplomatic authority. Hitler appointed Ribbentrop as the ambassador to London in August 1936, and in February 1938, Ribbentrop replaced Constantin von Neurath as Germany's foreign minister. He worked closely with Hitler in his 1938 negotiations with the British and French governments, and in August 1939 he arranged the signing of the Nazi-Soviet Pact. Ribbentrop became a background figure during World War II but was arrested and charged with war crimes in June 1945 at the Nuremberg trials. Found guilty, he was executed by hanging in October 1946.

Riefenstahl, Leni (1902–2003). A German film director, actress and dancer widely noted for her aesthetics and innovations as a filmmaker. Her most famous films were *Triumph des Willens* (*Triumph of the Will*), made at the 1934 Nuremberg congress of the Nazi Party, and *Olympia*, a record of the 1936 Olympic games (q.v.). Riefenstahl's prominence in the making of the Third Reich's propaganda films, along with her personal friendship with Adolf Hitler, thwarted her film career following Germany's defeat in World War II, after which she was arrested and briefly imprisoned. She was released without any charges.

Ringkragen. Gorget. The Ringkragen was a metal plate worn on the breast and held by a chain. This specific item was worn by selected members of uniformed organizations to denote special service or duty. Two distinct styles of gorget existed: the heart-shaped and crescent-shaped. Both descended from similar regalia used by the Imperial German army. The obverse of each shield bore an appropriate badge and/or inscription, while the reverse was covered in cloth or stiff card and featured a protruding central prong. This prong was hooked through a convenient buttonhole in the tunic during wear, thereby holding the gorget plate firmly in position. The first official Nazi gorgets were produced in the late 1920s for SA standard-bearers. The neck chain was made from tight-fitting nickel-plated wire links, and the backing cloth was dark-colored wool. The gorget was used only when the wearer was actually engaged in the specific function or carrying his regimental flag. Individually designed Ringkragen were subsequently created and manufactured for standard-bearers of the SS, NSKK, NSFK, RAD, HJ, Political Leadership, RLB, TeNo, Polizei, Reichs-

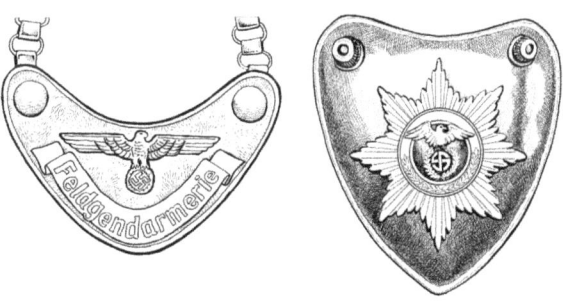

Left: Ringkragen. *Right:* SA standard-bearer's heart-shaped gorget.

Ringstand

bahn, DRK, Army, Luftwaffe and ex-servicemen's associations. Each bore insignia relevant to its own organization. The gorget worn by the Feldgendarmerie des Heeres (q.v.) was treated with luminous paint on the buttons, eagle and lettering so that it was easily visible in the dark.

Military Policeman with Ringkragen.

Ringstand. Small bunker, open observation post or armed pit. See Tobruk.

Ritterkreuz. See Ritterkreuz des Eisernen Kreuzes.

Ritterkreuz des Eisernen Kreuzes. Knight Cross of the Iron Cross. Award for valorous service for those who had already received the Iron Cross. The Knight Cross was the highest award class for bravery under fire or military leadership. Previous recipients of the Ritterkreuz would be awarded a higher degree of the same award, and then successively higher ones. The higher degrees were, in ascending order: Ritterkreuz mit Eichenlaub — knight's cross with oak leaves (890 recipients during the war); Ritterkreuz mit Eichenlaub und Schwerten — knight's cross with oak leaves and swords (159 recipients in total, plus one honorary recipient, the Japanese admiral Isoroku Yamamoto); Ritterkreuz mit Eichenlaub, Schwerten und Brillanten — knight's cross with oak leaves, swords, and diamonds (27 recipients); Ritterkreuz mit Goldenem Eichenlaub, Schwertern und Brillanten — knight's cross with golden oak leaves, swords, and diamonds (only one recipient, Hermann Göring). See Eisernes Kreuz.

Rock. Military jacket or tunic for field use and parades.

Röhm, Ernst (1887–1934). A nonconformist, homosexual World War I front-line professional soldier, a veteran and organizer of the post–1918 Freikorps (q.v.), and an organizer of special political intelligence and secret dumps of weapons and ammunition, Ernst Röhm recruited the then

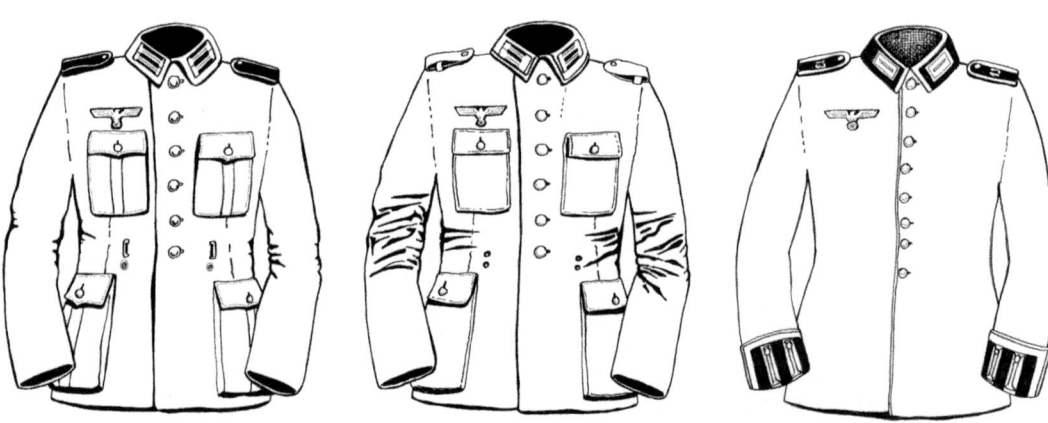

Rock. *Left:* Tunic pattern, 1936. *Middle:* Pattern of 1943. *Right:* Waffenrock for parade.

totally unknown Hitler to infiltrate Drexler's DAP. The two men became close friends and accomplices, and when Hitler imposed himself as leader of the NSDAP, Röhm became the key figure in developing the Sturm Abteilung der NSDAP (q.v.), which he involved in the failed Beer Hall Putsch. When Hitler decided to act legally in order to gain power, Röhm disagreed, resigned and went abroad to Bolivia to work as a military instructor. In January 1931, Hitler recalled him to lead the SA again. Röhm and his SA played an important role in the period 1931–1933, but after the seizure of power they became cumbersome henchmen. Indeed, Röhm had political ambitions and saw the SA as the core of the Nazi revolution. His radical views alienated the landowning Junkers and the industrialists who supported Hitler. In early 1934, the impatient and ruthless SA, as well as Röhm's growing power (and bohemian conduct, drinking, homosexuality and loose aggressive talk) outraged many people, both in and outside the Nazi Party. The "good old pal" had become a threat to Hitler's power, and his troops were a financial burden for the NSDAP, a challenge to the German army, and an embarrassing force that no longer had any purpose. According to Nazi realities this danger had to be eliminated. After some hesitations, Hitler acted with chilling decisiveness. In the last weekend of June 1934, Ernst Röhm, most of the SA leadership and several other annoying and deviating personalities were murdered in the massacre known as the Night of Long Knives. See Nacht der langen Messer.

Röhm Racher (RR). Röhm's Avengers. A secret group of SA men who had remained faithful to their former leader, Ernst Röhm (q.v.), and who dedicated themselves to striking back against the execution of their chief. At least 150 SS men were murdered in retaliation by the unknown avengers. The Gestapo made a serious enquiry but was never able to identify the mysterious Röhm's Avengers. See Nacht der lange Messer and Sturm Abteilung der NSDAP.

Röhm-Purge. See Nacht der langen Messer.

Röhm-Putsch. See Nacht der langen Messer.

Rollbock or **Cointet-Gitter**. Also called Belgian gate, the Rollbock was a captured mobile

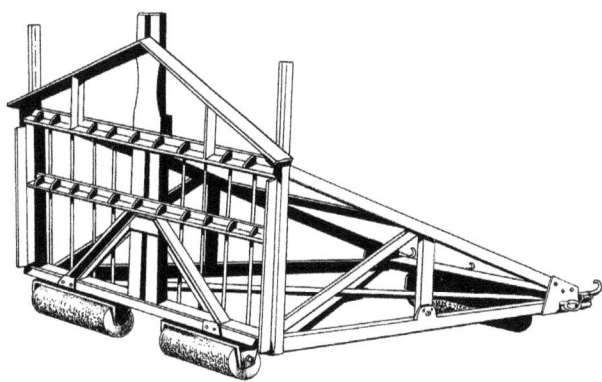

Rollbock.

Belgian/French antitank obstacle composed of a 3-meters-wide and 2.5-meters-high metal gate firmly fixed on a 3.30-meters-long carriage moved by three rollers. In German service it was used as roadblock or beach obstacle.

Rommel, Erwin (1891–1944). Rommel was a German field marshal in World War II. He won the respect of both his own troops and the enemies he fought. He was a highly decorated officer in World War I, and further distinguished himself in World War II as the commander of the 7th Panzer Division during the 1940 invasion of France. However, it was his leadership of German and Italian forces in the North African campaign that established the legend of the Wüstenfuchs (Desert Fox). He is considered to have been one of the most skilled commanders of mobile armored warfare in the conflict. In spring 1944 he spurred the construction of the Atlantikwall (q.v.) and commanded Army Group B during the invasion in Normandy. On July 17, 1944, he was severely wounded during an air attack near the front in France. Although his role in the July 20, 1944, conspiracy to kill Adolf Hitler remains unclear, the Nazis decided to eliminate him. Because the highly regarded and much respected Rommel was widely renowned and popular, Hitler chose to kill him quietly. In trade for assurances that his family would be spared, Rommel agreed to commit suicide, and officially the cause of his death was the injuries suffered on July 17. Rommel was buried with full military honors, and the truth about the circumstances of his real death did not come out until 1946. See Deutsches Afrika Korps and Zwanzig Juli 1944.

Rommelkiste

Rommelkiste. Junk box, an outer locker fitted behind the turret of a tank or added to armored vehicles for stowage of various cumbersome supplies and equipment which could not fit inside a tank, such as tools, food, spare clothes, sleeping accommodations, tent, sleeping bags and so on.

Rommelspargel or **Holzpfahl.** "Rommel's asparagus," or wooden pole. A German Luftlandesperre (q.v.) probably created by Generalfeldmarschall Erwin Rommel, whence its name. It was a simple 2.50-long tree trunk on top of which a mine was fixed. Rommelspargeln were planted in fields and meadows in the hinterland of the Atlantikwall (q.v.). They were placed at 25 or 30 meters from each other. All were connected with barbed wires or cables to detonate the mines.

Rommelspargel.

Rosenberg, Alfred (1893–1946). The Estonian-born Rosenberg went to Germany in 1918, wrote anti–Semitic articles, met Hitler, joined the Nazi Party, and became the editor of its newspaper *Völkischer Beobachter*. In 1930, Rosenberg wrote his principal opus, the cloudy, obscure and rather incomprehensible *Der Mythus des 20 Jahrhunderts* (q.v.) (*Myth of the Twentieth Century*). In 1933, after Hitler came to power, he formed the party's foreign policy office, and in 1934 he was made responsible, in his own words, for the party's "intellectual and ideological education and training." His foreign policy office was soon eclipsed by Joachim von Ribbentrop (q.v.). In July 1941 he was appointed Reich Minister of Eastern Occupied Territories (Ukraine and Ostland). Rosenberg abjured genocide and expulsion, preferring to co-opt the territories to fight Stalin, but he proved quite unequal to the machinations of such power-hungry rivals as Joseph Paul Göbbles (q.v.), Heinrich Himmler (q.v.), and Hermann Göring (q.v.) In October 1944 he intimated in a letter to Hitler, which was never answered, that he wanted to resign. Alfred Rosenberg was sentenced to death at the Nuremberg trials and executed.

Rossbach, Gerhard (1893–1967). A notorious Freikorps (q.v.) leader, Rossbach joined the Nazi Party in 1922 and took command of the Munich SA. He took part to the Beer Hall Putsch and escaped to Austria. Rossbach introduced the light brown SA uniform owing to a stock of unused World War I East African campaign clothes. Although a leading figures of the SA, he survived the June 1934 Nacht der langen Messer (q.v.) massacre, ceased all political activity and lived on in Frankfurt as a businessman.

Rotfront Kämpferbund (RFKb). Combat League of the Red Front, founded in 1924. The paramilitary groups of the German Communist Party (KPD) numbered some 150,000 members at their height. Their worst enemy was, of course, the NSDAP's Sturm Abteilung der NSDAP (q.v.), although, before 1933, Nazis and communists sometimes cooperated in breaking up social democrat meetings. The RFKb

Members of the RFKb (Red Front Combat League) often wore a soft peaked cap and a green pullover tunic. Like their SA enemies they were armed with truncheons and light weapons.

had a youth organization called Rote Jungfront (Young Red Front) for adolescents and young men age 16–21.

Rotte. Squad of nine or ten men in the SA, SS or Waffen-SS, headed by a Rottenführer (corporal).

RSHA. See Reichssicherheitshauptamt.

Rudeltaktik. Tactics of the "wolf pack" used by German submarines for attacking Allied convoys.

Rundfunk. Radio. See Radio in the Third Reich.

Runen. Runes. Alphabet used by the ancient German and Scandinavian tribes. Fascinated by the German ancient culture, Heinrich Himmler adopted some of the German pagan symbolism for his selected SS corps. See also Hakenkreuz.

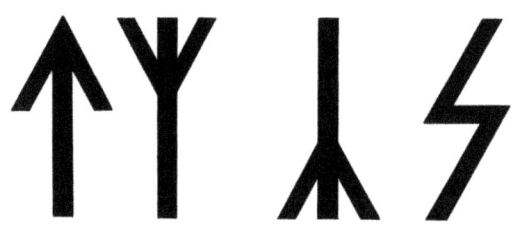

Runen used by the Nazis. Left to right: Teiwaz, or Tyr rune, symbol of energy and of pagan god of war Tyr; Algiz, or Leben rune, symbol of protection, birth and life; Algiz upside down, the symbol of death; Sowelu or Sieg rune (letter S), the strength of life and energy of the sun, symbol of victory, was used as emblem for the Hitler Youth and by the SS.

RuSHA. See Rasse- und Siedlungshauptamt.

Rust, Bernhard (1883–1945). A schoolteacher who joined the NSDAP in 1922, a friend of Hitler's since the early twenties, an SA Obergruppenführer, and Gauleiter of Hannover-South in 1925. Although a follower of the Strasserites (q.v.), Bernard Ruse was appointed minister of education for the Reich in April 1934. He committed suicide in May 1945. See Education in the Third Reich and Erziehung.

RZM. See Reichszeugmeisterei.

SA. See Sturm Abteilung der NSDAP.

SA Wehrmannschaften. SA defense teams. After the purge of 1934 and until the end of the war in 1945, the SA continued to exist as Nazi propagandists, as a sportive organization and as premilitary training units for the SA Reserve and for the boys of the Hitler Youth. For this training purpose, SA Wehrmannschaften were created in January 1939. The SA Wehrmannschaften were also assigned to auxiliary defense police units and some of them, in 1942, were organized as antipartisan fighting units in Yugoslavia. By the end of the war, in October 1944, some formations were incorporated into the Volkssturm (q.v.). See Hitler Jugend and Sturm Abteilung der NSDAP.

Saalschlachten. Hall battles. Political violence in meeting halls, cafés, assembly rooms or beer cellars throughout the Kampfzeit (q.v.) all over Germany.

Sachsen-Coburg und Gotha, Carl-Eduard von (1884–1954). The Nazi-minded duke of Sachsen-Coburg was the president of the German Red Cross from 1933 to 1945. A male-line grandson of the British Queen Victoria and Prince Albert, Carl-Eduard was one of Hitler's favorite royals, but also a considerable embarrassment to the British royal family. See Deutsches Rotes Kreuz.

Sachsenhausen. A concentration and labor camp located near Berlin. Established in July 1934, it was originally intended for the detention and "reeducation" of Gypsies, the "work-shy," vagrants, and political opponents and suspects. In 1941, the camp grew in size with the arrival of thousands of Russian prisoners of war. The camp included workshops and factories, as well as a training center for SS Death's Head guards; an interrogation center; a high-security cellblock where the Gestapo kept special prisoners; and closely guarded offices where skilled prisoners were put to work making forged documents and even counterfeit banknotes for the SS. In April 1945 the camp was vacated, and all surviving prisoners were marched out to the North, thousands dying on the road. See Neuengamme.

Salon Kitty. A high-class brothel used by Reinhard Heydrich's SD security service situated at 11 Giesebrechtstrasse in Berlin. Managed and owned by Madame Kitty Schmidt, the brothel was intended for foreign diplomats, top industrialists, high-ranking civil servants and senior Nazi Party members. The prostitutes were selected and trained by the SD, and the nine bedrooms were fitted with hidden microphones and cameras in order to provide incriminating or embarrassing evidence for blackmail or political pressure. Practically nothing of value to the Nazis ever emerged from Salon Kitty's rooms. The building was destroyed by a bomb in 1942 during an air raid and by then the project was discontinued.

SA-Mann Brand. A Nazi film glorifying the Sturm Abteilung der NSDAP (q.v.). The movie was a box-office disaster. See Film Industry in the Third Reich.

Sanitätsdienst Gefreiter (SDG). Health Service Corporal; a euphemism for executioner in extermination camps. Indeed, the SDG's function had nothing to do with health. He was actually an SS man who brought canisters of poison, and who, wearing a gas mask, poured the granulated contents into an opening on the roof of a gas chamber. See Gaskammer.

Sanitätskraftfahrzeug (Sanka). German field ambulance.

Sauckel, Fritz (1894–1946). A World War I seaman, and a prisoner of war in France, Sauckel was one of the earliest Nazis, joining in 1921. Appointed Gauleiter of Thuringia in 1925, he became the Reich's Plenipotentiary for the Mobilization of Labor in March 1942, following Hitler's decree to mobilize both German and foreign workers to meet the demands of Albert Speer's armaments and ammunitions production. With ruthless efficiency Sauckel moved some five million people from occupied Europe to work as slaves in Germany. In 1945 he was arrested and put on trial at Nuremberg as a major war criminal. He was hanged in October 1946. See Arbeitseinsatz and Speer, Albert.

Saukopf. Pig's head, term used to refer to the shape of a gun mantlet or mount.

Schacht, Hjalmar (1877–1970). Currency commissioner and president of the Reichsbank under the Weimar Republic, and president of the Reichsbank under the Nazi regime between 1933 and 1939. Schacht recruited bankers and industrialists for financial support to Hitler. He was one of the primary drivers of Germany's policy of redevelopment, reindustrialization and rearmament, and was a fierce critic of his country's post–World War I reparation obligations. Released from effective service to the Nazi government in 1939, and replaced by Dr. Walther Funk (q.v.), Schacht was jailed in 1944 after the July 20th bomb plot and narrowly eluded the hangman. He was tried and acquitted at Nuremberg for his role in Germany's war economy. Schacht became adviser to Colonel Nasser of Egypt in the 1950s and died in Munich, Germany, in June 1970. He is often regarded as one of the fathers of the post–World War II capitalist banking system.

Schanzzeug. Entrenching tool. Each German soldier was issued a field entrenching tool for quick digging of a foxhole in case of bombardment. This was a short-handled shovel with steel blade mounted and riveted to a hardwood handle with a pronounced ball end. A later design for a folding tool was similar to the American folding shovel but it was not as sturdily constructed. The tool was kept in a leather cover hanging from the waist belt.

Schanzzeug.

Schar. (1) An SA formation, approximately corresponding to a squad, including 8 to 16 Sturmmannen (privates) commanded by a Scharführer (approximately corresponding to the rank of corporal). Three or four Scharen formed a Trupp (platoon).

(2) In the Waffen-SS the Schar was a platoon generally formed of three of four Rotten (squads). The Waffen-SS Schar was commanded by noncommissioned officers: Unterscharführer (Uscha, sergeant), Scharführer (Scha, staff sergeant), Oberscharführer (Oscha, technical sergeant), Hauptscharführer (Hscha, master sergeant), Stabsscharführer (first sergeant) and Sturmscharführer (Stuscha, sergeant major).

Scharfschütze. Sharpshooter, sniper, or marksman.

Scharnhorst. German battleship named after Gerhard von Scharnhorst (1755–1813). She was the lead ship of her class, which included another ship called *Gneisenau* (q.v.) *Scharnhorst* was launched in October 1936 and commissioned in January 1939. *Scharnhorst* and *Gneisenau* operated together for much of the early period of World War II, including sorties into the Atlantic to raid British merchant shipping. *Scharnhorst* was sunk by the Royal Navy battleship HMS *Duke of York* and her escorts at the battle of North Cape in December 1943.

Scharten. Crenel, embrasure, loophole, porthole (term used in fortification).

Schartenbauprogramm. End of 1943 program dictating that all Atlantikwall (q.v.) artillery emplacements be sheltered under concrete roofed casemates.

Schartenstand. Concrete casemate fitted with a porthole. See Kampfstand.

Schartenturm. Armored turret fitted with portholes.

Scheinminenfeld. Fictitious minefield. Mine danger warnings could be placed in nonmined zones or phony minefields to deceive enemies who would waste valuable time searching for nonexistent mines. See Mine.

Scheinwerfer (Schw). Searchlight, a detection device composed of a powerful but fragile lamp set on a mobile carriage. Searchlights had a range of several hundred meters depending on illuminating strength of the beam and weather conditions. Searchlights were mainly employed to help antiaircraft guns and warships. A less usual use was to shine on low clouds in order to give light to advancing troops (such as during the Ardennes offensive in winter 1944). In 1934, during the Nazi Party rally in Nuremberg, Albert Speer (q.v.) had the idea of using one hundred and thirty searchlights; at night the beams formed the pillars of a gigantic cathedral of light.

Schellenberg, Walther (1910–1952). Schellenberg attended the University of Marburg and then in 1929 the University of Bonn. He initially studied medicine and wanted to be a doctor, but switched to law. Schellenberg graduated in 1933 and joined the SS where he met Reinhard Heydrich (q.v.) who employed him in the Counter Intelligence Department—Sicherheitsdienst des Reichsführer SS (q.v.). From 1939 to 1942 he was Himmler's personal aide. Throughout the war Schellenberg played a key role in many counterintelligence activities and clandestine operations, but also urged Himmler to investigate the possibility of negotiation for peace. At the Nuremberg trials he was sentenced to six years' imprisonment, but he was released in 1951 on the grounds of bad heath. Walter Schellenberg died of cancer in Turin, Italy, in March 1952.

Schell-Programm. Named after General Schell, this program, launched in 1938, was intended to reorganize German military vehicle production.

Schicklgruber, Maria Anna (1795–1847). Hitler's paternal grandmother. In 1837 the unmarried Maria gave birth to a boy whom she named Alois (this was Adolf Hitler's father). Alois's biological father remains unknown. It was later officially accepted that it was Johann Georg Hiedler, whom Maria married in 1842. Other possible candidates were Johann Nepomuk Hiedler (Georg's young brother and Adolf Hitler's step-uncle), and a certain Leopold Frankenberger. This came into question when Hitler began to rise in power and when pure "Aryans" had to have a documented ancestry certificate called Ahnenpass (q.v.). Johann Georg Hielder was officially declared the paternal grandfather of Adolf Hitler, and the Führer of the Third Reich was considered a pure "Aryan." At age 39, Alois assumed the surname "Hitler" instead of Schicklgruber. The name was also spelled "Hiedler," "Hüttler," or "Huettler"; the name was probably regularized to its final spelling by a priest. The meaning of the name is either "one who lives in a hut" (Standard German Hütte), or "shepherd" (Standard German hüten, "to guard," English "heed").

Schienenwolf. "Rail wolf." Sometimes also designated as Schwellenpflug (sleeper plow), or "rail ripper," it was a rail vehicle designed to destroy rail lines through the use of a strongly built, hook-shaped armored plow. In operational use, a locomotive hauled the attached railcar and the hook was lowered into the middle of the track, resulting in breaking the sleepers, tearing up the middle of the track and pulling the rails out of alignment. Used in Hitler's scorched-earth policy of total destruction, especially during the collapse of the Third Reich by the end of World War II, the Schienenwolf was intended to deny the Allies the use of railways into Germany. See Nero Befehl.

Schiffskanone (SK). Navy gun. Heavy naval gun used as a coastal piece, placed in a rotating Panzerturm (armored turret), inside a casemate, or in an open emplacement.

Schirach, Baldur von (1907–1974). A Nazi Party member starting in 1925, Schirach met Hitler, who took a liking to him. Three years later Hitler appointed Schirach head of the National Socialist Students' League. Satisfied with his work, Hitler promoted him to the post of Reich Youth Leader of the Nazi Party, and in 1933 he took over the leadership of the Hitler Jugend (q.v.), or HJ. In 1940, Schirach joined the German army, won the Iron Cross in France, and was replaced as leader of the HJ by Arthur Axmann (q.v.). Later that year Hitler appointed Schirach Gauleiter and Reichsstatthalter (Reich governor) of Vienna. In the latter position, Schirach's responsibilities included deporting Jews from Vienna to ghettos and camps in Poland. At the Nuremberg trials, Schirach was found guilty of crimes against humanity and sentenced to 20 years' imprisonment. He was released in 1966 and died in 1974.

Schirmmütze. Uniform peaked cap, usually worn by senior noncommissioned officers, officers and generals. Made of wool or canvas (stiff or soft), the Schirmmütze had a field-gray top, a dark blue-green cap band and a shiny black patent leather peak. Its front included a chinstrap carrying Waffenfarbe (arm of service) pipings, and the Reichkokarde hemmed with oak leaves around the coat of arms crowned by the eagle/swastika emblem. There was also the widely worn Offizierfeldmütze alterer Art (officers' cap old model), which was a peaked cap rather similar to the Schirmmütze but smaller in outline and unstiffened. Generals wore the same Schirmmütze but with the chinstrap cords in gold-braided material secured with gilt buttons. See Kokarde.

Schlageter, Albert Leo (1894–1923). A World War I veteran and conservative Catholic who signed up with the right-wing Freikorps (q.v.), Schlageter joined the fledgling Nazi Party when it absorbed his Freikorps unit in 1922. The next year, when France occupied the Ruhr to secure war reparations payments, Schlageter conducted antioccupation sabotage in resistance. In May 1923, he was caught, tried, condemned to death and executed by the French. He became a Nazi martyr practically overnight. The place of his execution became a mecca marked with a 90-foot cross and used for party rallies. His name christened a military training vessel, a Luftwaffe fighter wing, two SA units, and several Nazi badges and decorations. There were also statues, plays, poems, and songs about him.

Schlawiener. Viennese Slavs. A sarcastic term used by the Nazis to describe the Austrians. The Anschluß Osterreichs (q.v.) had not stopped the use of derisive names for those who lived outside Germany.

Schleicher, Kurt von (1882–1934). A career army officer, von Schleicher rose to major general by 1929 and became a key figure in the Weimar Republic. His political intrigues helped secure for him the posts of defense minister (1932) and chancellor (1932–33). Seeking to keep the Nazis under the army's control, he offered to participate in a government with Hitler, who refused him and thereafter regarded Schleicher as his chief enemy. Dismissed by Paul von Hindenburg in favor of Hitler, Schleicher was murdered during the purge known as the Nacht der langen Messer (q.v.).

Schmidt, Paul (1889–1970). Hitler's interpreter who was present at all important meetings with foreign VIPs. His memoirs are a

Left: Schirmmütze alterer Art. *Right:* Schirmmütze (stiff).

useful background for Nazi diplomatic history.

Schnalle. Metal belt buckle often decorated with a swastika/eagle emblem or a motto.

Schneeanzug. Snow suit, a generic term for winter dress including quilted anorak, thick trousers, hoods and warm footgear like boots.

Schneeanzug.

Schnellboot (S-Boot). Speedboat generally armed with torpedoes. The concept of light attack boat was based on speed rather than on heavy armor. These small ships were used against submarines and surface vessels, for convoy escort, for patrol or for quick raids. The German S-Boot type S38, used during World War II, was a fine example of this genre. She was built in 1942. Each of her three Daimler-Benz diesel engines produced a remarkable 4,800 hp (horsepower), giving her a top speed of 42 knots. The boat was equipped with two enclosed torpedo tubes forward, and was armed with one 2-centimeter cannon forward and one 4-centimeter gun aft. Eight sea-mines could be carried at the stern.

Schnellboot-Kriegsabzeichen. E-Boat war badge introduced in May 1941. The decoration was awarded after 12 successful operations at sea.

Schnellboot-Kriegsabzeichen.

Schnellfeuerkanone (Sk). An automatic quick-fire gun often used as an antiaircraft weapon. The main automatic-firing light caliber flak guns used by the Germans in World War II were the 2-centimeter 36/38; the 3.7-centimeter 36/43; and the Flak Vierling, composed of four 2-cen-

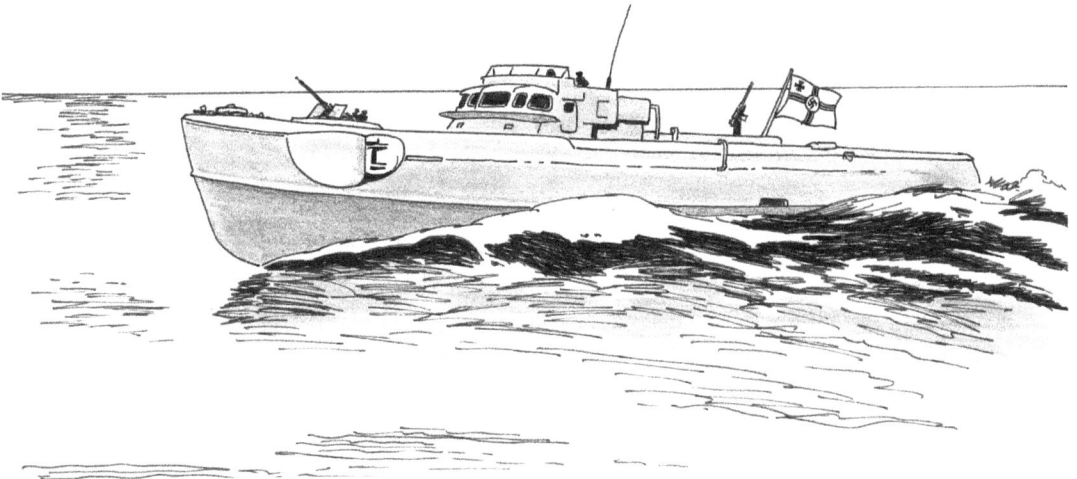

S-Boot type S-38.

Schnurstiefel

timeter 38s. The principal automatic guns (called Maschinenkanone, or MK) mounted on aircraft included the MK 108/30, the MK 103, and the MK 112/55.

Schnurstiefel. Laced top boots.

Scholl, Hans and Sophie. See Weisse Rose.

Scholtz-Klink, Gertrud (1902–1999). A fervent National Socialist, she became leader of the women's section in Baden in 1929. After the seizure of power in January 1933, she was appointed reich women's leader and head of the NSF (Nazi Women's League). Gertrud Scholtz-Klink's main task was to promote male superiority and the importance of childbearing. Giving a good example, she married a factory worker at the age of eighteen and had six children. In July 1934 she was appointed head of the Women's Bureau in the DAF (German Labor Front). In this function Scholtz-Klink had responsibility for persuading women to work for the good of the Nazi regime. After World War II, Scholtz-Klink went into hiding and was not arrested until 1948. Later that year, she was sentenced by a French military court to eighteen months in prison. See Deutsche Arbeitsfront and Nationalsozialistische Frauenschaft.

Der Schöne Adolf. The Handsome Adolf, descriptive term applied to Hitler by German women who regarded the Führer as a sex symbol.

Schönheit der Arbeit (SdA). Beauty of Labor. This was one of the subdivisions of the Deutsche Arbeitsfront (q.v.), responsible for working conditions and regulations. The SdA made attempts to improve working conditions as in the areas of ventilation, security, noise, and worked at increasing cooperation and solidarity in workplaces. See Kraft durch Freude.

Schräge Musik. "Slanted music." Code name for a weapon system consisting of obliquely upward/forward-firing guns placed on the back of a German night fighter.

Schulterklappe or **Schulterstücke.** Shoulder strap, or epaulettes. The Schulterklappen showed the rank and the branch of service (see Waffenfarbe), which was indicated by colored piping. This color was repeated in the form of more piping around the collar, around the cap and around the cuff patches. For security, economy and labor cost, slip-on shoulder straps were introduced. They were detachable for cleaning, fixing on an overcoat or when a soldier was transferred to another unit. Epaulettes often wore the regimental number, though this practice was discarded for obvious security reasons after 1940. See Schwalbennester.

Schupo. See Schutzpolizei.

Schürzen. Outer metal sheets or skirts held by bars placed on both sides of armored fighting vehicles and self-propelled guns. The skirts were intended to protect the tank tracks and to explode enemy AT shells before they could penetrate the tank's vitals.

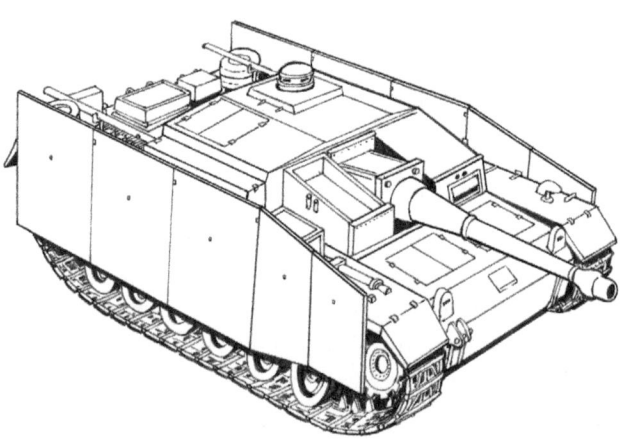

Schürzen fixed on the sides of a Stug III.

Schußsicher. Bulletproof, or a defense protecting against small projectiles and shell splinters. This term was employed to designate any defensive screen, such as a trench parapet made of sandbags, a masonry or concrete wall or an earth entrenchment, anything offering protection against small projectiles and shell splinters. See Laufgrabe.

Schütze. Literally "defender"; private, infantryman, rifleman.

Schützenabzeichen. See Lanyard.

Schützengraben. Foxhole, dugout, temporary field fortification.

Schützenpanzerwagen (SPW). Armored troop carrier, generally a halftrack, which had been converted to a personnel carrier. The vehicle was provided with armor slopes on all sides to deflect hits. Armored infantry carriers greatly improved the quality of armored divisions. Alongside the tanks they carried soldiers in relative safety through enemy fire to the point at which dismounted action began. There was only one problem with SPWs: there were never enough of them. See Halbkettenfahrzeug and Hannoversche Maschinenbau AG.

Schutzhaft. Protective custody. An arbitrary measure in virtue of which the SS police could bypass the regular justice court system, arrest and detain people in prisons and concentration camps for indeterminate periods. The Schutzhaft was introduced in 1933 right after the Nazi seizure of power.

Schutzhaftlager. Camp for preventive custody; another word for concentration camp.

Schützkommando (SK). Generic term for protection squad, armed militia, auxiliary police force.

Schützmannschaft (Schuma). Armed, militarily organized, uniformed formations raised from pro–Nazi local militias and home guard units (mainly Balts, Cossacks and Ukrainians). These auxiliary police forces were completely separated from the Wehrmacht, took their orders from Himmler and Hitler through the Höhere SS- und Polizeiführer (q.v.), and worked closely with the SS in the suppression of resistance groups in Russia, Eastern Europe, the Balkans and, after Italy's surrender in September 1943, in Northern Italy.

Schutzmantel. Protective overcoat. Often issued to motorcyclists, the Schutzmantel (also called Klepper) was practical, thick, double-breasted, waterproof and rubberized. It could be buttoned around the man's legs to permit movement and motorbike riding. See Mantel.

Schutzmütze. Special crash helmet or beret worn by tank crews. It consisted of a soft padded circular beret, which served to protect the heads of the Panzer crew from injuries possible when the vehicle was motoring over rough terrain.

Left: **Schutzmütze worn by armored force personnel.** *Right:* **Schutzmütze worn by Motor SA and NSKK.**

Schutzpolizei (Schupo). Security police. The Schupo was created right after World War I by the Ministry of Interior of the Weimar Republic with a double intention: to fight against interior subversive armed groups (left or right wing); and to constitute an additional military force to help the reduced national Reichswehr (q.v.) oppose any aggression or invasion from abroad. Therefore the Schupo policemen were uniformed, lived in barracks, received professional military training, and were equipped with heavy material including machine guns, armored cars and transport trucks. When the Nazis established the Third Reich in 1933, the Schupo was placed under Hermann Göring's supervision. The personnel was purged, loyal Nazis were appointed to key positions, and SS Gruppenführer Kurt Daluege became head of the organization. When Himmler took control of all German police services in June 1936, the Schutzpolizei was transferred to the Ordnungpolizei (q.v.), or Orpo, and to the Sicherheitspolizei (q.v.), or Sipo. After the German capitulation in May 1945, the Ordnungpolizei was abolished. The German police were purged of Nazi members. However, the Orpo was rapidly reactivated to maintain order. In the postwar period, the Schutzpolizei was reestablished in West Germany as the national security police force and urban constabulary composed of ordinary policemen on foot patrol. See Reichssicherheitshauptamt.

Schutz-Staffeln (SS). Hitler's protection squads. The SS, like no other institution in the Third Reich, represented the arrogance of Nazi ideology and the criminal nature of Hitler's regime. The origin of the SS was a small squad created

Schutz-Staffeln

in 1923 as a personal bodyguard to Hitler called Stoßtrupp Adolf Hitler. In early 1925, the unit was reshaped and took the name Schutzkommando, then Sturmstaffeln, and finally in November 1925 the title Schutz-Staffeln, or SS, meaning protection squads. Under this name it would become notorious. By 1929 the SS numbered only 280 loyal selected guards under command of Erhart Heiden. Hitler had certainly no reason and no intention to let the squad grow in number. On January 6, 1929, the detachment was given a new leader, the ambitious Heinrich Himmler (q.v.), and the growth of the SS began. During the weekend of June 30–31, 1934, the SS participated to the elimination of the cumbersome and rival SA. After this bloody purge, known as the Nacht der langen Messer (q.v.) — the Night of the Long Knives — the SS was charged with the security of the Reich. The formation became independent, and SS Reichsführer Himmler, from then onwards, added enormously to the range of functions that the SS performed and to the responsibilities it carried. From 1934 on, Hitler's former bodyguard group developed into the most important pillar of Nazism, the brutal executor of the regime's most delicate and gruesome tasks. In June 1936, Himmler increased his apparatus of repression and terror, and became chief of the Ordnungpolizei (q.v.) and head of the Gestapo (q.v.), Kripo and Sicherheitsdienst des Reichsführer SS (q.v.). Although the SS police services were basically divided into two main branches with different purposes — Sicherheit (security) and Ordnung (order) — the range of SS activities went far beyond mere police terror. The SS claimed to be a pioneer of the Nazi movement, a model for the youth and the educator of the German people by promoting ideological indoctrination. The SS soon included several major branches, such as the Allgemeine SS (q.v.), the SS-Totenkopfverbände (q.v.), and the Verfügungstruppen (q.v.), later known as Waffen-SS. The war brought massive expansion for Himmler's empire and gave the SS an opportunity to increase its influence in every area of life, both in Germany and in the occupied states of Europe. With the extension of German rule over large parts of Europe, the SS had a unique opportunity for realizing most of its administrative, racial, economical and settlement ambitions. The number of concentration camps for political and racial prisoners expanded enormously, enabling Himmler to utilize a huge reserve of cheap manpower. Slave labor was leased out to German industry, systematically, mercilessly and efficiently exploited in companies created by the SS. Himmler's empire thus gained much control of activities in the economy, industry, agriculture, construction, armaments projects and war production programs. By the end of World War II, the SS had control over more than forty different businesses, comprising about 500 plants and factories. It was involved in quarrying, in the production of food and drink, in agriculture, farming, fishing, stock breeding, forestry, timber and iron processing, leather, textiles and publishing,

SS-Obersturmbannführer (lieutenant colonel).

SS Insignia. *Top left:* Eagle/swastika worn on headgear and on upper left sleeve; *bottom left:* Totenkopf (death's head) worn on headgear; *right:* SS rune insignia worn on right collar patch.

and more. The Nazi program had included since its foundation an anti–Semitic hatred that resulted in the physical elimination of the European Jewish community. The SS was the blindly obedient corps that translated the criminal and hysterical Nazi ideology into action and practice. The Endlösung der Judenfrage (q.v.)—the "final solution" of the Jewish question—was the genocide of the Jews by Einsatzgruppen (q.v.)—intervention groups of the SS. After January 1942 this was conducted on an industrial scale in Vernichtungslager (q.v.)—extermination camps—through inhumane living and working conditions, starvation, monstrous "medical experiments," and mental and physical torture. Gas chambers and crematoria were established for mass murder and burning the bodies of the victims. In the last year of the war, when the Nazi regime was at the brink of ruin, the power of the SS reached its zenith. Himmler was then at the head of a huge and complex organization forming a state within the Nazi state. Controlling almost everything, the SS became the driving force of the regime, dealing out a summary justice, repressing defeatism, with its death camps working at full speed, moving its crowds of wretched slave laborers from project to project. Meanwhile, its private army, the Waffen-SS (q.v.), was fighting with a hopeless and fatalistic savagery at all collapsing fronts.

Schutzwall Ehrenzeichen. Fortification medal, awarded to zealous workers and instituted by Hitler on August 2, 1939. The reverse bore the mention "Für Arbeit zum Schutze Deutschlands" (For work for the protection of Germany).

Schutzwall Ehrenzeichen.

Schwalbennester. "Swallows' nest." Special parade shoulder straps worn by musicians. They were fixed on the field tunic epaulettes by means of metal hooks.

Schwarz, Franz Xaver (1875–1947). One of the earliest members of the NSDAP Schwarz participated in the failed Beer Hall Putsch of November 1923. In March 1925 he became full-time treasurer of the Nazi Party, a function he held until 1945. Schwarz was arrested by the Americans in 1945 and died in an Allied internment camp near Regensburg in December 1947. In September 1948, he was posthumously classified by the Munich denazification court as a "major offender." Schwarz remains an enigmatic member within Hitler's inner circle, due to the fact of his having died without being properly interrogated. Also, he burned his diaries and a lot of NSDAP financial documents in April 1945. Because of this there are considerable gaps in the historical record specifically, by whom the early Nazi Party was financed, how funds were used, and where the money went after the war.

Schwalbennester worn by an SA drummer.

Schwarze Front. Black Front, also called the Kampfgemeinschaft Revolutionärer National-

Emblem of Strasser's Schwarze Front (Black Front) about 1930, composed of a black flag with red crossed hammer and sword.

Schwarze

sozialisten (Combat League of Revolutionary National Socialists, or KGRNS). This dissident, left-oriented anti-capitalist branch of the NSDAP was formed in May 1930 by Otto Strasser (q.v.) and Walther Stennes. Both had been expelled from the Nazi Party, and set up their headquarters in Prague, Czechoslovakia, to lead anti–Hitler activities. The Strasserite Black Front was never able to oppose Hitler effectively.

Schwarze Korps. The Black Corps, another name designating the SS. See *Das Schwarze Korps, Zeitung der Schutz-Staffeln der NSDAP*, and Schutz-Staffeln.

Das Schwarze Korps, Zeitung der Schutz-Staffeln der NSDAP. The Black Corps, Newspaper of the SS of the Nazi Party, published weekly between 1935 and 1945. The newspaper was founded and headed by reporter/chief editor/SS Standartenführer Gunther d'Alquen. The publisher was Max Amann (q.v.) of the Franz-Eher-Verlag publishing company. The first copy of the newspaper was issued in March 1935 and by 1945 the number printed was 750,000 per week. The newspaper contained foreign news reports, analyses of threats, and theoretical essays on Nazi policies. It was vehemently hostile to many groups, with frequent articles condemning the Catholic Church, Jews, communism, Freemasonry and others real or supposed enemies of Nazi Germany. The paper was published in close cooperation with the SS Security Service, which of course had total editorial control.

Schweitzer, Hans. See Mjölnir.

Schwer (S. or schw.). Heavy; for artillery, ammunitions, vehicles, tanks.

Schwimmwagen. Literally, "floating car," meaning amphibious vehicle. See Kübelwagen.

SD. Security service. See Sicherheitsdienst des Reichsführer SS.

SdA. See Schönheit der Arbeit.

SdKfz. Special vehicle. See Sonderkraftfahrzeuge.

Sea Lion. See Seelöwe.

Sebottendorf, Rudolf von (1875–1945?). A Freemason, a practitioner of meditation, astrology, numerology and alchemy, and also an important figure in the activities of the Thule Gesellschaft (q.v.) and editor of the *Münchener Beobachter* (q.v.).

Seelöwe. Sea Lion, code name given to the invasion of the British Isles in August and September 1940. The invasion was several times postponed and finally aborted when it became clear that the German Luftwaffe had lost the Battle of Britain. The great majority of military historians believe Operation Sea Lion would not have succeeded. Hitler displayed a remarkable lack of interest in the preparation of Operation Sea Lion, which he probably considered merely as means of bringing military and diplomatic pressure on Britain. The operation was indeed envisaged, but never really seriously planned.

Sehrohr. Periscope; literally, "looking tube." Used in submarines but also in tanks and bunkers.

Seitenwaffe. Sidearm, including pistol, dagger, combat knife or bayonet.

Selbstfahrlafette. Self-propelled gun (SPG), a hybrid vehicle composed of a gun carried on the hull and chassis of a standard, obsolete or captured light or heavy tank. Selbsfahrlafetten allowed artillery to move without the encumbrance of horses. More powerful guns could be placed than those housed in a limited tank turret space. Troops could open fire within a minute of halting and operate in the most difficult broken ground conditions. Finally, they offered good protection for gunners and guns. German

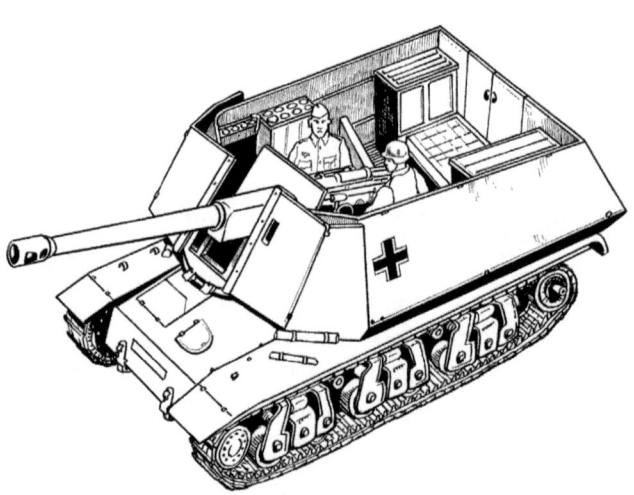

Selbstfahrlafette: Panzerjäger Marder I.

Selbsfahrlafetten were divided into three main categories according to their function and special armament. (1) Sturmgeschutz, Sturmpanzer, Panzerhaubitze and Sturmhaubitze were armed with field guns and howitzers; (2) Panzerjäger and Jagdpanzer were armed with antitank guns firing armor-piercing shells; and (3) Flakpanzer (q.v.) were armed with antiaircraft guns.

Selbschutz. Generic term for self-protection, designating several organizations: (1) Independent militia recruited by the SS from the Volksdeutsche (q.v.) in Poland; (2) A pre–1925 German nationalist self-protection organization; and (3) the self-protection service, part of the Luftschutzdienst (q.v.), made up of air raid wardens.

Selbstgleichschalter. Self-coordinating citizen. A Nazi concept referring to a citizen of the new Reich who accepted Nazi tenets immediately without pressure and without question. Unsaid but implied was that those incapable of this kind of self-discipline were to be removed from Nazi society. See Asoziale, Gleichschaltung, and Volksgenossen.

Seldte, Franz (1882–1947). Cofounder of the militant ex-servicemen's association Stahlhelm (q.v.). The right-wing Seldte and his Stahlhelm took part in agitation against the Weimar Republic (q.v.). The veterans' association was merged with the SA in 1933. Subsequently minister of labor in Hitler's government from 1933 to 1945, Seldte was arrested by the Allies in 1945, but died before being tried.

Septemberling. Johnny-come-lately; sarcastic name given to those who joined the NSDAP after the successful election in September 1930. Other contemptuous names given to those (about one million) who hastened to join the Nazi Party after the seizure of power in January 1933 were Märzgefallene (those who joined in March) or Märzveilchen (March Violets).

Seyss-Inquart, Arthur (1892–1946). A Viennese lawyer, member of the Austrian Nazi Party, later governor of Austria, deputy governor to Hans Frank in the general government of occupied Poland, and Reich commissioner for the German-occupied Netherlands. In the last-named capacity, Seyss-Inquart shared responsibility for the deportation of Dutch Jews and the shooting of hostages. He was found guilty on counts two, three, and four (crimes against peace, war crimes, and crimes against humanity) and sentenced to death. Seyss-Inquart was hanged in October 1946.

Sicherheits und Hilfdienst (SuHd). Security and Assistance Service. The Sicherheits und Hilfdienst was formed in 1935 as a mobile civil defense organization to augment the defensive capacity of the most vulnerable cities and towns in Germany from Allied air raids. It differed from other civil air raid protection services in that it was mobile and was responsible for heavy rescue work. The men of the Sicherheits und Hilfdienst were "kazerniert" (housed in barracks). The service was organized into five main groups consisting of decontamination squads, fire fighting troops, repair work teams, veterinary service groups, and medical units. In June 1942 a brand new organization was established, the Luftschutzpolizei, or Air Defense Police, which came under the full control of the Ordnungpolizei (q.v.)—Orpo, German order police. The existing Sicherheits und Hilfdienst Abteilungen were transferred directly into the Luftwaffe, renamed Luftschutz-Abteilungen (motorized air protection battalions), and continued to operate in fire fighting, rescue work and debris clearing operations.

Sicherheitsdienst des Reichsführer SS (SD). Security branch of the SS. Officially created in June 1934 but formed as early as 1932 by Reinhard Heydrich, the SD was the intelligence organization of the SS and NSDAP. In practice the members of the SD were part of the Gestapo; they wore the SS black or grayish uniform with a black diamond-shaped badge with "SD" on it. After September 1939 the SD became a part of the RSHA. See Geheime Staatspolizei and Reichssicherheitshauptamt (RSHA).

Sicherheitshauptamt (SD Hauptamt). SS central security department. See Reichssicherheitshauptamt.

Sicherheitspolizei (Sipo). Security police. The Sipo was reorganized in 1936 by Heinrich Himmler. Headed by Reinhard Heydrich, it was made up of the Geheime Staatspolizei (q.v.)—Gestapo, secret state police—and Kriminalpolizei (q.v.)—Kripo, the criminal investigation branch. The Sipo was the forerunner of the Reichssicherheitshauptamt (q.v.), into which it was incorporated in 1939.

Sieg Heil! Hail to victory! Popular rallying cry. At the end of a meeting, a gathering, a toast, a ceremony or a speech, the president or the speaker shouted "Sieg!" (victory) and the crowd, the guests or the participants answered "Heil!" It was a kind of hurrah or shout of honor or joy. It was repeated several times to express the German collective triumph and was paired with the Hitler salute. See Deutscher Gruß.

Siegfried lines. Names of two extensive fortification lines built by the Germans, both named after Siegfried, the hero of the anonymous heroic poem the Nibelungen, written in the 13th century. The first Siegfried line, which the Allies called the Hindenburg line, was built during World War I in the period 1916–1917. It was a long field fortification network extending from the south of Belgium to the Swiss border intended to resist French and British offensives. Particularly strong in Champagne and in Somme, the Hindenburg/Siegfried line was a huge fortified network composed of four defensive rows, using all possible natural obstacles (hills, ridges, marshes, rivers, forests), field fortifications (trenches, barbed wires, obstacles) and concrete bunkers (shelters, observatories, MG pillboxes, command posts, artillery emplacements). The second Siegfried line, or Westwall (q.v.), was ordered by Hitler and built in the period 1938–1940 on the west border of the Reich. It extended from Switzerland to the Netherlands.

Siegrunen. The victory rune, letter S of the runic alphabet. A single Sieg rune was used as an emblem for the Hitler Youth, and a double by the SS. It was worn on the right collar patch, on regalia and on flags. See Runen.

Siemens. A company created in 1847 by Werner von Siemens to make telegraph apparatus and insulated cable. The company also produced electric motors and dynamos. In 1866 the firm opened a branch in Britain, and it grew to one of the world's most important manufacturing and electronics concerns. In World War I and World War II, Siemens supplied both Germany and Britain with vital electrical and electronic equipment, notably radar.

Signal. A fortnightly Nazi illustrated news magazine. *Signal* was a special edition of the *Berliner*

SS Siegrunen.

Illustrierte Zeitung published from mid–1940 onwards by the Deutsche Verlage, which was controlled by the Nazi Ministry of Propaganda. *Signal*, based on the layout of the U.S. magazine *LIFE*, reached a maximum circulation of 2,500,000 copies per issue, and was translated into 25 languages and issued throughout occupied Europe. In an effort to rally European occupied nations under the Nazi banner, and to promote and justify German hegemony over Europe, *Signal* glorified German military achievements and Nazism in all its aspects by means of catchy articles and lavish illustrations and photographs.

Sipo. See Sicherheitspolizei.

Sippe. Literally, "tribe" or "clan." In Himmler's mind the SS was not intended to be a "club" exclusively open to men but a Sippengemeinschaft, a large—if selected—community, a kind of tribe of families with wives and children.

Sippenbuch. Clan book. A booklet containing special identification and proofs of ancestry attesting racial purity that was issued to members of the SS. The booklet was introduced in 1932 and its records were kept by the Rassen-und Siedlungshauptamt (q.v.), the Central Office for Race and Resettlement.

Sippenhaft. Kith and kin liability. The crimes of political dissidents were not only their own; instead, mothers, fathers, brothers and sisters were all targets for retribution. Although never enacted into law, collective punishment of one's acquaintances and relatives remained a real threat that defined aspects of the Nazi system of terror-based "justice." Robert Ley (q.v.) once declared, "He who fails or betrays the party and its Führer ... will not thereby merely be deprived of an office, but he personally, together with his family, his wife, and his children, will be destroyed. These are our harsh and implacable laws." With the onset of the war, Sippenhaft gained prominence as a reprisal against resistance on the home front and desertion and treason in the military. The assassination attempt on Adolf Hitler on July 20, 1944 reinvigorated its use and ushered in a harrowing final phase of arrests and threats.

Sitzkrieg. Phony War, a term used to describe the war period of September 1939 to May 1940, during which the western front saw very little action, while most of the German army was engaged in Poland. The very term "Phony War" was possibly coined by U.S. Senator William Borah, who stated in September 1939, "There is something phony about this war." The period was also called at the time the Twilight War by Winston Churchill; der Sitzkrieg in German ("the sitting war"), a play on the word Blitzkrieg; the Bore War (a play on the Boer War); and in French la drôle de guerre ("strange/funny war"). The American news magazine *Time* called the period the Lullablitz.

Skorzeny, Otto (1908–1975). Legendary SS special operations leader of World War II. Born in Vienna, Austria, Skorzeny joined the Austrian Nazi Party in 1930 and was a strong advocate of union with Germany. After the Anschluß he worked under Ernst Kaltenbrunner and was appointed as one of Hitler's personal bodyguards. In February 1940, he joined the German army as an artillery officer, and during the Western Offensive he served with the Waffen-SS (q.v.) and saw action in the Netherlands and France. Promoted to lieutenant, he was sent to Yugoslavia for the Balkan campaign. In September 1943 Skorzeny led an airborne commando raid that rescued the destitute Benito Mussolini (q.v.) imprisoned in the Abruzzi Apennines. In November 1943 Josip Tito was able to establish a government in Bosnia. In February 1944 Adolf Hitler sent Otto Skorzeny to kill Tito. Tito was able to escape, but Skorzeny was more successful in October 1944 when he kidnapped Miklos Horthy, who wanted to surrender Hungary to the advancing Red Army. Skorzeny's next special operation was as leader of 2,000 English-speaking German infiltrators, dressed in American uniforms, who attempted to create havoc behind Allied lines in France during the Battle of the Bulge in the winter of 1944–45. Otto Skorzeny was arrested by American troops in May 1945. He was tried for war crimes but was acquitted in September 1947. He was handed over to the German authorities but managed to escape in July 1948. He went to live in Spain where he received the protection of General Francisco Franco and continued secret pro–Nazi activism.

Sobibor. Extermination camp established in March 1942, in southeast Poland in the province of Lublin (q.v.) near the frontier of the Ukraine Reich Commissariat. It is estimated that 250,000 Jews were murdered by gas at Sobibor. See Aktion Reinhard.

Social Darwinism. See Sozialdarwisnismus.

Soldbuch. German soldier's paybook. The Soldbuch was the pay and ID document for all German soldiers. Issued immediately after entry into active duty, the Soldbuch contained all the soldier's details, including a photo, name, rank, promotions, pay grade, clothing, equipment, next of kin, awards, medical information, and a history of unit assignments. It was to be carried at all times in the left breast pocket of the tunic. See also Erkennungsmarke.

Sonderbehandelung. Special treatment. Nazi bureaucratic term for physical elimination, in fact an euphemism for murder and assassination. See Sprachregelung.

Sondereinheiten der Wehrmacht. Special army units or army propaganda squads. See Propagandakompanie.

Sonderführer. Exceptional leader, or special tasked officer. Sonderführer were persons who were posted in the German army to do an officer's duty not because of their military qualifications but because of their professional ability. It was applied to such persons as administrators, scientists, technicians, lawyers, interpreters, doctors and other specialists. Their ranks were lieutenant, captain and major, but they commanded only in the area of their job. They were not

Sondergericht

armed, though they were issued normal army officer uniforms, badges and insignia. They were distinguished by their own Waffenfarbe (branch of service color), which was grayish blue.

Sondergericht. Tribunal of exception. See Freisler, Roland.

Sonderhänger (Sdh). Two- or four-wheeled trailer, for example designed and used for transportation and action of a gun; usually towed by a halftrack.

Sonderkommando. (1) Special detachment for police and political tasks, subunits of the Einsatzgruppen (q.v.).

(2) Squads of inmates in the concentration camps used by their guards as working parties. In the extermination camps, Sonderkommando were squads of inmates used to remove the bodies from the gas chambers, and sort and repair the victims' clothing, among other things. The Jewish Sonderkommando were killed periodically and replaced by new arrivals, so that they would neither have time to organize a revolt nor survive to tell about what happened in the camp.

Sonderkommando 1005. See Einsatzgruppen.

Sonderkonstruktion (SK). Nonstandardized, exceptional bunker construction. See Regelbau.

Sonderkraftfahrzeuge (SdKfz). Special vehicles. Vehicles standardized and accepted into service in the German forces had an ordinance inventory number, generally three figures, allocated by the Ordinance Department. For example, the PzKpfw VI Ausf E was also known as SdKfz 181. Certain vehicles were given type names as well. The PzKpfw VI Ausf E (SdKfz 181) for example was better known as Tiger. See Panzerkampfwagen, Panzerspähwagen, and Schützenpanzerwagen.

Sonderverband. Special unit, sometimes implying a special operation or elite unit, or simply meaning a unit formed for a special purpose.

Soviet-German Non-aggression Pact. See Hitler-Stalin Pakt.

Sozialdarwisnismus. Social Darwinism. A belief, popular in the late Victorian era in England, America, and Europe, which stated that the strongest or fittest should survive and flourish in society, while the weak and unfit should be suppressed or allowed to die. The theory was chiefly expounded by the British philosopher, biologist and sociologist Herbert Spencer (1820–1903), whose ethical philosophies held an elitist view, and which received a boost from the application of Darwinian ideas such as adaptation and natural selection. Nazi Germany's justification for its aggression was regularly promoted in propaganda films depicting scenes such as beetles fighting in a lab setting to demonstrate the principle of "survival of the fittest," as expressed by the slogan "Alle Leben ist Kampf" (All Life Is Struggle).

Spähtruppen. Scouts, reconnaissance troops. Reconnaissance units of any army had (and still have) perhaps the most dangerous task to do as they formed the point of the advance. They probed forwards until they encountered enemy forces, then they had to remain unseen in order to observe and obtain tactical intelligence; if they were located and attacked they quickly withdrew. Organized in Aufklärung Abteilungen (Panzerdivision's reconnaissance battalions), German Spähtruppen were equipped with motorcycles and wheeled or halftrack armored reconnaissance vehicles. See Panzerspähwagen and Sonderkraftfahrzeuge.

Spanischer Reiter. "Frizzy horse," a mobile obstacle composed a beam resting on crossbars, often reinforced with barbed wires. Often used as a roadblock.

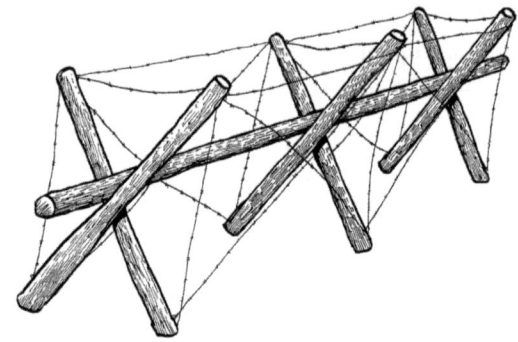

Spanischer Reiter.

Spartakusbund. Spartacus League. A left-wing Marxist revolutionary movement organized in Germany during World War I. The league was named after Spartacus, leader of the largest slave rebellion of the Roman Republic in 73 B.C. The league was founded in 1915 by Karl Liebknecht,

Rosa Luxemburg, Clara Zetkin, and other communists. The league's period of greatest activity was during the German Revolution of 1918, when it sought to incite a Soviet revolution. The ill-prepared Spartakus revolt was brutally crushed in January 1919 by the newly formed paramilitary units called Freikorps (q.v.). The league subsequently renamed itself the Kommunistische Partei Deutschlands (q.v.). It joined the Comintern in 1919.

Spaten. Spade. Emblem of the Reichsarbeitdienst (q.v.).

Speer, Albert (1905–1981). Albert Speer studied at the technical schools in Karlsruhe, Munich, and Berlin, and acquired an architectural license in 1927. After hearing Hitler speak at a Berlin rally in late 1930, he joined the Nazi Party in January 1931. He impressed the Führer so much with his efficiency and talent that, soon after Hitler became chancellor, Speer became his personal architect. He was rewarded with many important commissions, including the design of the spectacular Nuremberg party congress of 1934, filmed by Leni Riefenstahl (q.v.) in *Triumph of the Will*. A highly efficient organizer, Speer in 1942 became minister for armaments, succeeding engineer Fritz Todt (q.v.). In 1943 he also took over part of Hermann Göring's responsibilities as planner of the German war economy. From Todt, Speer also inherited the Organisation Todt (q.v.). Under Speer's direction, economic production reached its peak in 1944, despite Allied bombardment. In the last months of the war, Speer did much to thwart Hitler's scorched-earth policy, which would have devastated Germany. However, Speer is said to have prolonged the war for at least a year, with the consequent death of hundreds of thousands and widespread ruin. Speer's efforts also gave the Nazis more time to pursue their mass murder of Jews, Russians, Gypsies and others deemed not fit to live. On the stand at Nuremberg, Speer stood out amid other prominent accused Nazis, as he was the only one who admitted his guilt and expressed regret for his acts. This probably saved his head. Speer was condemned to 20 years imprisonment. After his release he wrote his memoirs, and until his death in 1981 he worked hard at being a penitent, presenting himself as someone who should have known what was being done but did not want to know. In some ways, Albert Speer offered himself as the scapegoat for Germany's collective guilt.

Sperrballone. Barrage balloon used to hinder the flight of enemy aircraft above a particular target.

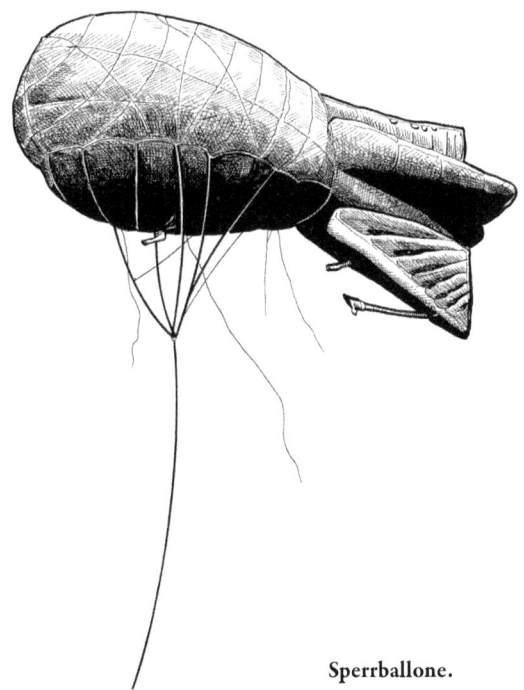

Sperrballone.

Spielmann. Bandsman, musician.

Spielmannzug. A military marching band directed by a Musikführer (bandmaster) that played martial tunes with fife, drum and trumpet. A military band was composed of a various number of musicians wearing a traditional form of detachable shoulder ornamentation known as Schwalbennester (q.v.). All branches of the German army had orchestras and bands but also had (often male) choirs that sang songs with bellicose lyrics.

Spiesser. Philistine. Term sometimes employed by the Nazis, particularly the moralizing Joseph Paul Goebbels (q.v.), to designate the uncultured, unenlightened, prosaic and selfish bourgeoisie.

Sportanzug. Sports uniform issued to German recruits and privates. The Sportanzug consisted of a white cotton vest, black cotton pocketless shorts with elastic waistband, and low brown

Sportpalast

leather lace-up shoes, generally worn without socks. In addition to this, each German recruit was issued a track suit and a pair of swimming trunks for water sports.

Sportpalast. A large indoor sports arena located in the center of Berlin. With a capacity of 15,000, it was often hired by the Nazis in the 1930s for political rallies and meetings.

Sports in the Third Reich. As soon as the Nazis won political power, all sports associations were subjected to Gleichschaltung (q.v.). The idea of a Germanic "master race" was propagated along with the promotion of physical exercises to look after one's own body and to prepare oneself to be a warrior for the German volk (people). The Nazis' vision was that physical exercise would improve the morale and productivity of German workers as well as making sports a source of national pride for the Germans. The aims of the promotion of sports in the Third Reich included hardening the spirit of every German as well as making German citizens feel that they were part of a wider national purpose. Another goal was the demonstration of Aryan physical superiority. The promotion targeted the German youth, and sports skills were made a criterion for school graduation as well as a necessary qualification for certain jobs and admission to universities. Teachers of physical training were now regarded as the most important members of the staff. It should be noted that the Nazi top leadership and Hitler first of all were averse to any kind of physical exercise. See Boxing; Hitler Jugend; Kraft durch Freude;

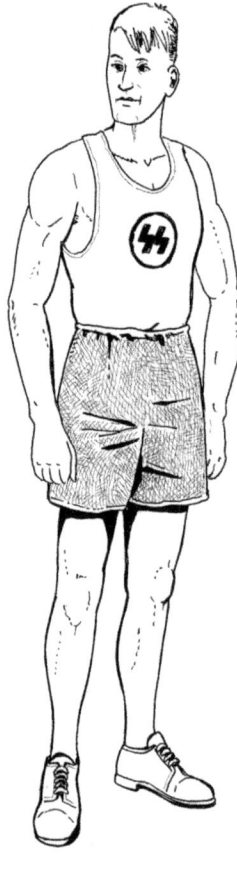

Sportanzug (here worn by an SS man).

Olympic Games, 1936; Reichssportbund; and Ubermensch.

Sprachregelung. Regulation of the language, a special terminology that masked the Nazi policy of extermination. It took the words "extermination," "killing," and "liquidation," and replaced them with euphemisms like "final solution," "evacuation," "special treatment," and "resettlement," or "labor in the East." It was developed to hide the crimes and dehumanize and deceive victims, and to help SS officials avoid facing reality.

SS. Hitler's protection squads. See Schutz-Staffeln.

SS Ehrenführer. Honorary SS member. Some persons of high position or wealth, whose influence could be useful to the SS organization, were made honorary SS officers. These were generally diplomats, scientists, university professors or high-ranking civil or NSDAP servants. Others were bankers, industrialists and holders of significant capital who exchanged substantial financial support to the SS for protection and freedom from the other Nazi organizations. Honorary SS members enjoyed all the privileges of the SS order but were not submitted to its burdens. Ehrenführer had usually the rank of SS-Standartenführer (colonel).

SS-Flakabteilung B. SS antiaircraft battalion "B," posted in Berchesgaden. It was intended to defend the air space above Hitler's residence in the Berghof (q.v.).

SS-Freiwillingendivision. Division of Waffen-SS (q.v.) volunteers composed of Volksdeutsche (q.v.), "racial" Germans from northern and central European Germanic lands who were considered as people of "similar blood."

SS-Führungs Hauptamt (SSFHa). Waffen-SS general command headed by Hans Jüttner. This department, created in August 1940, was intended to be the Waffen-SS's equivalent to the Oberkommando des Heeres (q.v.), or army headquarters. The SSFHa coordinated training, payment of wages, supply of equipment, arms, ammunitions, and vehicle maintenance and repair. It was also responsible for the transport of the SS and police, mail censorship, geology, war archives and medical services. But its military competencies were rather limited, at least until

July 20, 1944, the day of the failed Army generals coup. After that, Himmler's headquarters took a significant part in the war operations, the Reichsführer Heinrich Himmler becoming Befehlshaber des Ersatzheeres, head of all German reserve ground forces.

SS-Hauptamt (SSHa). SS central office charged with recruitment and maintenance of records on noncommissioned personnel. The SSHa was headed by August Heißmayer until 1940, and later by Gottlob Berger (q.v.).

SS-Junkerschule Bad Tölz. Bad Tölz is a town in Bavaria, Germany, about 30 miles south of Munich, where in 1937 the SS-Junkerschule was established. The SS-Junkerschule (SS Officer Candidate School) was a large training center for Waffen-SS (q.v.) officers. The instruction consisted of lectures on Nazi ideology and a mixture of intensive athletics and military field exercises. The center operated until the end of World War II in 1945. A subcamp of the Dachau concentration camp was located in Bad Tölz. It provided labor for the SS-Junkerschule and the Zentralbauleitung (Central Administration Building). In March 1945, staff and students from the school were used to form the 38th SS Division Nibelungen, a unit that never achieved anything near full division status but did actually see some combat in the Landshut area, before surrendering on May 8, 1945. The buildings and training grounds of the former SS-Junkerschule was the base of the U.S. Army's 1st Battalion, 10th Special Forces Group, until 1991.

SS PanzerKorps. SS armored corps, composed of several SS Panzerdivisionen, commanded by an Obergruppenführer (q.v.) or Oberstgruppenführer — General of the Army. The first SS Panzerkorps was created in 1942, called the 1st Leibstandarte; the 2nd Das Reich; and the 3rd Totenkopf. It was later reorganized as 2nd Panzerkorps with the addition of the SS divisions Hohenstaufen and Frundsberg, and the Hitler Jugend. During World War II there were eighteen SS Panzer corps created, with paratroopers divisions, armored brigades, Waffen-SS divisions, assault battalions, police units and foreign troops.

SS Personalhauptamt. SS personnel office headed first by Walter Schmitt and, after 1942, by Maximilian von Herff. As the name suggests, this Hauptamt was concerned with anything regarding the SS personnel, officers and lower-ranking men. In particular it planned organization, transfers, training, and movement of men to field units. It also dealt with promotions and proposals for decorations, degradation or exclusion of the SS order. This was closely monitored by Himmler himself, who as an inquisitor wanted to know in detail everything about his organization; even the simple promotion of a Scharführer to Oberscharführer, for example, had to get his approval. It is worth noting that the promotion from Gruppenführer to Obergruppenführer had to be submitted for Hitler's approval as well because this rank included high responsibility.

SS-Totenkopfverbände (SS-TV). SS "death's head" units. This body, originating from Wachtverbände (guard detachments) and Wachmannschaften (guard teams), was composed of permanent, professional armed uniformed SS men living in barracks. They had a rudimentary military training and were intended to form Bereitschafttruppen (special political mobile troops) stationed in key points across the Reich to protect the Nazi regime from an internal revolt. But rapidly—as no such threat appeared—the anti-insurrection force was assigned to run prisons and concentration camps set up by Hermann Göring in 1933 to house and "reeducate" all political opponents. The concentration camps and the first regiment of SS-Wachtverbände were organized by Oberführer Theodor Eicke (q.v.). In 1936 the SS-Wachtverbände was renamed SS-Totenkopfverbände (SS-TV), becoming part of the SS Hauptamt, headed by Obergruppenführer August Heißmeyer. In time of war the SS-Totenkopfverbände were intended to form a reserve for the Waffen-SS (q.v.) and the police force. However, more than a military unit, the SS-Totenkopfverbände constituted a strictly regulated repressive machine, men of low quality doing the "necessary dirty work." In early 1940 some Totenkopfverbände were drafted to form a Waffen-SS unit called the 3rd SS Panzerdivision Totenkopf. During World War II, there was lots of movement between the KZ guards and the Waffen-SS fighting at the front. Many Totenkopfverbände were regrouped in rear area security groups, frontline fighting brigades and regiments which were transferred to reinforce, provide staff for, or create new Waffen-SS divi-

SS- und Polizeiführer

sions, notably the 2nd Das Reich, the 3rd SS Totenkopf, the 6th Nord, the 8th Florian Geyer, the 15th Lettland, the 18th Horst Wessel, the 19th Latvia and the 20th Estland. The duties of guards in the concentration camps were then taken over by senior members of the Allgemeine SS (q.v.) who were too old for active service, by disabled Waffen-SS veterans, by convicts and common criminals and by foreign volunteers. During the course of the war, Nazi repression and terror were widely expanded and the number and size of camps grew significantly. The Inspektion der Konzentrationslager was entrusted to SS Brigadeführer Richard Glucks and the management of the KZ was placed in 1942 under the authority of the SS Wirtschafts-und Verwaltunghauptamt (q.v.)—the SS office of administration and economics, headed by SS Brigadeführer Oswald Pohl.

SS- und Polizeiführer (SS-PF). SS and Police Leader, a title for senior Nazi officials who commanded large units of the SS, and of the regular German police prior to and during World War II. There were three levels of subordination.

SS- und Polizeiführer (SS-PF), SS and Police Leader; Höhere SS- und Polizeiführer (HSSuPF) (q.v.), Higher SS and Police Leader; and Höchste SS- und Polizeiführer, (HöSSPF), Supreme SS and Police Leader. Answering only to Heinrich Himmler (q.v.) and Adolf Hitler, SS and Police Leaders had great authority and were involved in coordination of deportation in concentration and extermination camps. See Schutz-Staffeln.

Stab. Staff, headquarters, administration.

Stab in the back. See Dolchstoss.

Stabshauptamt of the Reichskommissar für die Festung deutschen Volkstums (StabHa RKFdV). Reich commission for the consolidation of Germanism. See Hauptamt Volksdeutsche Mittelstelle, and Rassen-und Siedlungshauptamt.

Stabsquartier. Headquarters.

Stabwache. Staffguards, the original NSDAP headquarters guards, formed in 1923 from selected members of the SA and from the Nazi Party, later merged in the Stoßtrupp Adolf Hitler, which was the nucleus of the SS (q.v.). See Schutz-Staffeln.

Stacheldraht. Barbed wire, artificial metal thorns wrapped around twisted galvanized wires and coiled on a reel for handling. Intended to stop or hinder infantry progression, the wires were stretched on 1.10-to-2-meter high poles. Between rows, other wires in roll form were set, making a 5-to-6-meter entangled impassable network. Barbed wire was also used as fence and could be electrified, which made them very dangerous or even lethal.

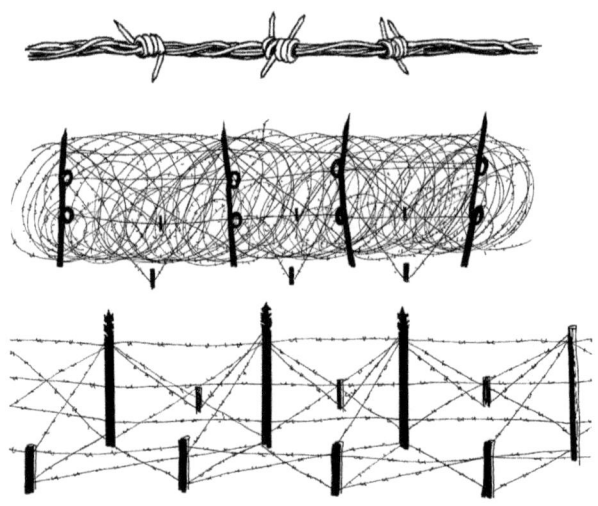

Stacheldraht.

Staffel. Generic term for detachment, or military formation (plural is Staffeln). In the Luftwaffe (q.v.), a Staffel was a wing commanded by a Staffelkapitän and numbering about ten planes of the same type. Several Staffeln formed a Gruppe (q.v.). Three Gruppen formed a Geschwader (squadron). Several Geschwadern formed a Fliegerkorps (air corps) and more Korpsen formed a Luftflotte (air fleet). The Schutz-Staffeln (q.v.), or SS, were originally detachments for protection of the NSDAP.

Stahlhelm. (1) Steel helmet. The steel helmet issued in 1935, the Stahlhelm M35, was the most characteristic item of equipment associated with the World War II German soldier, and was standard issue for all fighting units of the Third Reich (with the exception of the airborne troops, who had a lighter version). Very well designed,

M 35 stahlhelm.

Honor badge of Stahlhelm veterans' league.

offering good protection to face, ears and neck, the German helmet came in five basic sizes to fit all head sizes, and weighed from 0.82 kilograms to 1.20 kilograms.

(2) Stahlhelm was also the name of a monarchist nationalist veteran league. This paramilitary organization for ex-servicemen, formed after World War I by Franz Seldte (q.v.), was absorbed by the SA in 1933.

Stahlpakt. Pact of Steel, a military alliance signed in May 1939 between Italy and Germany.

Stalin, Joseph. See Union der Sozialistischen Sowjetrepubliken.

Stalinorgel. Stalin's Organ. Nickname for the Soviet Katyusha rocket launcher.

Stammlager (Stalag). Main camp; a permanent camp for prisoners of war. Stalags were intended for privates, the officers being detained in Offizierlager (q.v.), or Oflag for short.

Stand. Blockhouse, bunker, concrete shelter or concrete emplacement. The Stand was either passive (when not armed and designed exclusively for sheltering purposes) or active (when intended for combat and then armed with one or more weapons).

Standarte. (1) An SA, SS or Waffen-SS formation, roughly the size of a regiment (comprising between 1,200 and 3,000), headed by a Standartenführer (colonel).

(2) (See illustration on page 32.) A banner for SA and SS regiments copied from the ancient Roman vexillum banner. It had the form of a pole surmounted by an eagle holding a wreathed swastika, below which there was a rectangular frame displaying the letters NSDAP. From the frame was suspended a red flag with a black Hakenkreuz (q.v.) on a white disc. The banner had a red, white and black fringe and carried the motto Deutschland Erwache (q.v.) on one side, and on the reverse Nat. Soz. Deutsche Arbeiterpartei Sturmabteilung.

Ständig Ausbau (St). Permanent construction used for concrete fortification works. It was divided into three subcategories: (1) Baustärke A (StA) was 3.50 meters thick, making A-works capable to resist to 1,000-kilogram bombs. (2) The intermediary 2.50-meter Baustärke A-1 thickness. (3) Baustärke B (StB) was a standardized 2-meter concrete thickness, designed to resist 250-kilogram bombs. Most World War II German bunkers, notably those built in the Atlantikwall (q.v.), were constructed in StB. See Baustärkte StA and StB and Regelbau.

Stauffenberg, Graf Claus Schenk von (1907–1944). Von Stauffenberg entered the German army in 1926 and won distinction as a staff officer with an armored division in the campaigns in Poland and northern France (1939–40). After he was transferred to the front in the Soviet Union, however, he became disillusioned with the German occupation's brutal policies toward Slavs and Jews. At his own request, he was transferred to the North African campaign, where he was a staff officer. In that campaign he was severely wounded, losing his left eye, right hand, and two fingers of his left hand in April 1943. While convalescing from his wounds, Stauffenberg decided that Hitler must be eliminated. In the ever-widening conspiracy of army officers against Hitler, he assumed a leading role and reserved for himself the central task of carrying out the proposed assassination. His chance came in July 1944, after he had been promoted to colonel and reassigned to the post of chief of staff of the Reserve Army Command; this post gave him access to conferences personally attended by Hitler. After two preliminary attempts, Stauffenberg succeeded in placing a bomb in Hitler's headquarters at Rastenburg on July 20, 1944. However, the bomb failed to kill the dictator. A planned simultaneous coup in Berlin likewise miscarried, and Stauffenberg and a few of his co-conspirators were summarily executed on the night of July 20 in Berlin — the first of the several thousands who ultimately died in the bloody purge aftermath of the conspiracy. See Zwanzig Juli 1944.

Stiefel (Marching boots).

Stechschritt or **Stechmarsch** or **Exerziermarsch.** Goose stepping, a ceremonial marching form used in military parade consisting of stepping forward without bending the knees, and bringing the foot down with a loud simultaneous stepping noise and continuing the cycle in unison. Originating in Prussian military drill in the mid–18th century, it was introduced into German military tradition by Leopold I, Prince of Anhalt-Dessau (1676–1747).

Steel Helmet. See Stahlhelm.

Steinbocke. See Pfeifenkopf.

Stellvertreter des Führers. Deputy of the Leader, title for the deputy head of the Nazi Party. The function was held by Rudolf Hess (q.v.) until his flight to the United Kingdom in 1941. After this event, Hitler abolished the function and replaced it with the office of party chancellor, which was given to Martin Bormann (q.v.).

Stennes Mutiny. An SA revolt that occurred in September 1930, named after its leader Walter Stennes, a former member of the Freikorps (q.v.), a follower of Otto Strasser (q.v.) and SA deputy to Franz Felix Pfeffer von Salomon (q.v.). See Röhm, Ernst, Schwarze Front, and Sturm Abteilung der NSDAP.

Stiefel or **Marschstiefel.** Boots or jackboots. These were three-quarter length strong black leather boots with hobnails, toe plates and studded soles; the boots' finish was either pebbled or smooth. Trousers were very frequently tucked into them in order to guard against the cold, mud, brambles and barbed wire. From late 1943, however, material shortages forced a change and the issue of jackboots ceased, as leather had become a precious commodity reserved for industrial use. In place of boots, short black lace-up ankle shoes were issued and these were worn with old-fashioned puttees, canvas or leather leggings, anklets or gaiters fastened by buckles. See Gamasche.

Stoßtruppen. Shock troops or storm troopers. Stoßtruppen were developed within the German army

Stoßtruppen 1918.

at the end of World War I. They were composed of small groups of combatants specially trained for aggressive assault and ambush warfare. The tactics and structure of the shock troops were adopted by the Nazis to form a small bodyguard unit intended to protect Hitler, which would become the SS. See Schutz-Staffeln and Stabwache.

Strasser, Gregor (1892–1934). A World War I veteran and member of the Freikorps, Gregor Strasser joined the NSDAP and became a leading member of the Sturm Abteilung der NSDAP (q.v.). He took part in the Beer Hall Putsch of November 1923, and was imprisoned. In May 1924, he was released due to having been elected to the Reichstag. During Adolf Hitler's imprisonment, he briefly led the party. In 1925, he was appointed NSDAP leader in northern Germany. Together with his brother Otto, Gregor Strasser was a committed socialist and social radical, as was Ernst Röhm (q.v.). Strasser saw a need to redistribute wealth in Germany by nationalization and state control of business and industry. Like Ernst Röhm, Strasser opposed Hitler's policy of catering to the country's major industrialists. His outspoken views -representing the anti-capitalist "left wing" of the Nazi Party caused a deep rift with Hitler and other leaders of the party as their views alienated rich industrialist potential supporters and funders. Hitler was not yet the undisputed leader that he was later to become. In 1932, a meeting of high-ranking Nazi officials was held at which all present repudiated Strasser and declared themselves ready to continue the fight at the sides of Hitler. To maintain unity, Strasser resigned all party positions and found work in a large chemical firm. Gregor Strasser, although having lost all political influence, was murdered on June 30, 1934, during the bloody purge known as the Night of the Long Knives. See Nacht der Langen Messer and Schwarze Front.

Strasser, Otto (1897–1974). German political activist who with his elder brother Gregor occupied a leading position in the Nazi Party during its formative period. His leftist socialist leanings and opposition to Hitler caused his downfall shortly before Hitler's accession to power. When Gregor was murdered on Hitler's orders during the Röhm Purge of June 1934, Otto Strasser managed to escape and go into exile. He finally settled in Canada. Returning to Germany in 1955, he failed in an attempt to reenter politics because of his stained Nazi past.

Strasserite. A "left-wing" Nazi, follower of the Strasser brothers, who took the "socialist" elements in Nazism seriously.

Streicher, Julius (1885–1946). A decorated World War I veteran, Streicher was an early convert to Nazism and became a fanatical and devoted follower of Adolf Hitler. He became the regional Nazi Party leader in Franconia and the editor of the most virulently anti–Semitic Nazi newspaper, *Der Stürmer* (q.v.) This broadsheet was crude and mixed racism with obscenity and pornography. It was in the city of Nuremberg, which was part of Streicher's territory, that a tradition developed of holding huge NSDAP party rallies each fall. Streicher was highly valued and liked by Hitler, but because of his corruption, greed, sexual extravagance and sadism, Hitler was obliged to dismiss Streicher in 1940. Eventually, Streicher continued to edit *Der Stürmer* but held no party or government function. The loud anti–Semite Julius Streicher was tried at Nuremberg, condemned to death and hanged in 1946.

Streifendienst. A patrol service officered by the SS that included old men of the reserve and boys of the Hitler Jugend (q.v.). During the air war above Germany, the Streifendienst was particularly charged of seeing that the blackout was respected, that downed Allied airmen were captured and that the scenes of downed bomber aircraft were guarded and investigated.

Strength through Joy. See Kraft durch Freude.

Stücke. Pieces (in concentration camps). A term for Jews and other undesirables intended to dehumanize them. Victims of the Nazis were no longer humans or persons but things or "pieces." See Sprachregelung.

Studiengruppe für germanisches Altertum. Study Group for Germanic Antiquity. See Thule Gesellschaft.

Stuka. Acronym for Sturzkampfflugzeuge (q.v.), dive bomber airplane. The term is particularly associated with the German Junkers Ju-87, although it actually refers to any dive bomber.

Sturm. SS or SA unit the size of a company. A Sturm was commanded by subaltern officers called Untersturmführer (Ustuf, second lieuten-

Sturm

ant), Obersturmführer (Ostuf, first lieutenant) and Hauptsturmführer (Hstuf, captain). Three or four Stürme constituted a Sturmbann (battalion). The company flag was called a Sturmfahne. It was red with a black Hakenkreuz (q.v.), with piping and the unit numeral.

Sturm Abteilung der NSDAP (SA). Assault battalion of the Nazi Party. As early as August 1920, squads of strong-arms were formed under the camouflage name Gymnastic and Sport Division. They were intended to protect the Nazis' meetings, to provoke disturbance, to break up other parties' meetings, and to beat up political opponents as part of a deliberate campaign of violence and intimidation. In October 1921 the squads were increased in number, notably by an infusion of ex–Freikorps (q.v.), and were officially given the name Sturm Abteilung (SA assault battalion). After 1925 the nickname was Braunhemden (Brownshirts) because of the color of their uniforms. The SA, commanded first by Lieutenant Hans Ulrich Klinze, then by Hermann Göring and finally by World War I veteran and ex–Freikorps leader Ernst Röhm (1887–1934) (q.v.), was a private militia, a Gliederung organized within the Nazi Party. Originally confined to Munich, the SA became a national movement owing to the untiring energy of Ernst Röhm. After the abortive Beer Hall Putsch in Munich, the SA was disbanded and temporarily turned into clandestine units called Frontbann. When Hitler was released from prison, the SA was reactivated, but Röhm's success made Hitler uneasy. Hitler intended the SA to be an instrument of intimidation and propaganda subordinate to the NSDAP. Röhm, on the contrary intended to carry on the political fight, and the disagreement between them became so large that Röhm resigned in 1928 and took service in Bolivia as military adviser. Franz Felix Pfeiffer von Salomon was then appointed as chief of SA staff. During the disastrous financial crisis of 1929, the sinking German middle class flocked to the Nazi Party, including many ruined shopkeepers, unemployed people and students, as well as many opportunists. In 1930, the SA numbered 80,000 active members. Pfeiffer von Salomon having proved unreliable, Hitler asked Röhm to come back to Germany and reestablished him as chief of the SA staff in January 1931. The reorganized Brownshirts became a powerful and massive machine (about 100,000 members), which played a significant role in providing Hitler with the keys to power. After the seizure of power by the Nazis on January 30, 1933, the SA became a sort of auxiliary police force, but they became uncontrollable, mutinous and cumbersome. The brutal and scandalous Ernst Röhm, who had done the dirty work allowing Hitler to seize the power, had political ambitions too, and stood in Hitler's way. In 1934 the SA represented a challenge for the army, a serious threat for Hitler and the Nazi Party, and an unpopular burden to the German people. Tensions culminated and reached an explosive point. During the weekend of June 30, 1934 the Brownshirts organization was decapitated. About three hundred SA men and leaders, including Röhm, were arrested and summarily executed or "committed suicide." After this bloody purge, known as the Nacht der Langen Messer (q.v.), the SA did not disappear, but it never recovered. The Sturm Abteilung der NSDAP were never abolished. The units stayed

SA Scharführer, 1933.

SA emblem.

a Gliederung of the NSDAP but were reduced in size, and completely deprived of political power. Relegated to a backseat role, the SA continued to exist as Nazi propagandists, as street fund collectors, as a sports organization and as pre-military training units for the SA Reserve and the boys of the Hitler Jugend (q.v.). See Gliederungen der NSDAP; Lutze, Victor; and SA Wehrmannschaften.

Sturmbann. SA or SS formation roughly the size of an Abteilung (battalion). It was composed of three or four companies and placed under command of middle-ranking officers called Sturmbannführer (Stubaf, major) and Obersturmbannführer (Ostubaf, lieutenant colonel). Three to five Sturmbanne formed a Standarte (regiment).

Der Stürmer. The Storm-Trooper, a Nazi anti–Semitic newspaper edited by Julius Streicher (q.v.). *Der Stürmer* endlessly harped on anti–Semitism based on misinformation, lies, forged evidence, crude pornography and gossip. The editor claimed that *Der Stürmer* was the only newspaper Hitler read from cover to cover.

Sturmgepäk. Combat pack composed of a waist belt and a leather or canvas frame worn on the back with accouterments, straps and hooks intended to carry a number of items, including canteen, shovel, bayonet, backpack, Zeltbahn (camouflage poncho), bread bag, and ammunition pouches.

Sturmgeschütz (StuG) or **Sturmpanzer.** Self-propelled artillery vehicle armed with a Sturmkanone (StuK or assault gun). Self-propelled guns (SPGs), designed for assault or antitank fire, were cheaper to build than were turreted battle tanks. See Selbstfahrlafette.

Sturmgewehr. Assault rifle, the 7.92-millimeter Machinen Karabiner 43 (MK 43), also called Maschinepistole 43 (MP 43). Designed and manufactured by the Erfurter Maschinefabrik Haenel und Suhl (Erma), the MK 43 was issued in July 1943. It was mostly metal with a wooden butt. It weighed 5.1 kilograms and the detachable magazine contained 30 rounds. In 1944 the MK 43 was slightly improved and renamed Sturmgewehr (StG 44) or MPi 44. It proved an excellent assault weapon. Intended to replace the obsolete Mauser 98K rifles, about 300,000 MK 43/MPi 44 were issued in the last two years of the war. Most of the production was allocated to the elite Waffen-SS. The new rifles came too late to replace other service weapons and they could not make any impact on the outcome of the war. See also Fallschirmjager Gewehr FG 42.

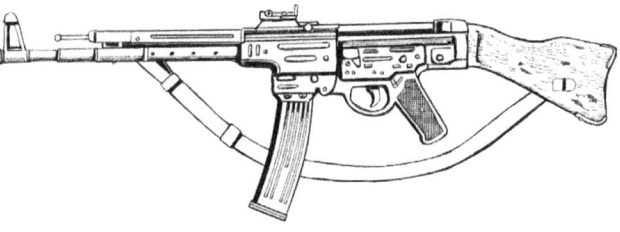

Sturmgewehr MPi 44.

Sturmhaubitze (StuH) or **Panzerhaubitze.** Self-propelled artillery vehicle armed with a howitzer, such as the 10.5-centimeter Wespe SdKfz 124, 10.5-centimeter SdKfz 135, or 15-centimeter Lorraine Schlepper.

Sturmpionier. Military assault engineer.

Sturzkampfflugzeuge (Stuka). (See illustration on page 176.) Dive bomber. A bomber aircraft that dives directly at its targets (between 45 and 90 degrees) in order to provide greater accuracy for the bomb it drops. Diving towards the target reduces the distance the bomb has to fall, which is the primary factor in determining the accuracy of the drop. Additionally, as the bomb's motion is primarily vertical, the complex parabolic trajectory is reduced to one that is much straighter and easy to calculate — even by eye.

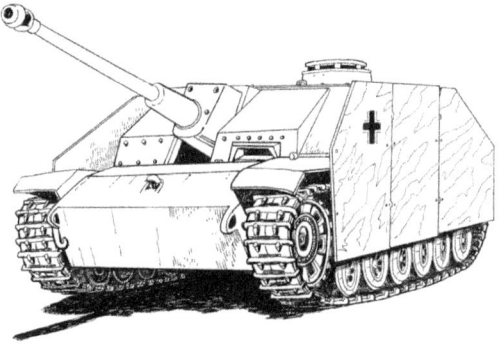

Sturmgeschütz 40 (Stug III Ausf. G).

Stützpunkt

Sturzkampfflugzeuge (Stuka) Junkers Ju 87.

Stützpunkt (StP). Fortified point, stronghold, particularly in the Atlantikwall (q.v.). In theory an StP was the union of two or more Widerstandsnesten (WN) but in practice a small StP could be as strong as a large WN; its surface could vary a lot, from 300 to 500 square meters, some even larger than 1000 square meters. Armament was also variable, including field or permanent fortifications, gun batteries or flak guns depending on the strategic importance of the site. See Widerstandsnest.

Stützpunktgruppe (StPGr). Group of fortified points. In certain particularly important sectors of the Atlantikwall (q.v.), all existing units were regrouped to form a powerful, continuous position on several kilometers along the shore. The StPGr generally constituted a strong block, including army StP and Widerstandsnest (q.v.), navy, army and air force coastal or AA batteries, radar stations, command posts, military hospitals, numerous stores and everything needed to withstand a siege. Stützpunktgruppe status was generally accorded to secondary important harbors.

Sütterlin script. Form of handwriting based on the old German handwriting, designed by the

Sütterlin script. The text, on a sleeve band, reads Feldherrnhalle.

artist Ludwig Sütterlin (1865–1917). Sütterlin was commissioned to create a handwriting script by the Prussian ministry of culture in 1911. The Sütterlin handwriting was taught in all German schools from 1935 to 1941. See also Fraktur.

Swastika. See Hakenkreuz.

Swing. A form of danceable jazz music developed in the United States in the 1930s. Swing jazz was banned by the Nazis, and in both Germany and the European occupied countries it acquired strong resistance connotations.

Swing Jugend. Swing Youth. Urban groups of jazz and swing lovers in Germany in the 1940s, mainly in Hamburg and Berlin. They included 14- to 18-year-old boys and girls in high school, most of them middle- or upper-class students. The Swing Youth formed a kind of spontaneous nonviolent, apolitical sub/counter-culture that sought pleasure, dancing and fun, and defined themselves through British and American swing music. They therefore opposed the National Socialist ideology, especially the Hitler Jugend (q.v.), and rejected any form of militarism and Nazi ultra-nationalism, and Nazi "culture." Jazz music was indeed offensive to Nazi ideology because it was often composed and performed by blacks, and there were a number of Jewish musicians. They called it Negermusik ("Negro Music") or "degenerate music"— a term coined in parallel to entartete Kunst (q.v.)—"degenerate art." Starting in 1941, the violent repression by the Gestapo and the Hitler Jugend shaped the political spirit of the Swing Youth. Also, by police order, people under 21 were forbidden to go to dance halls, bars, and nightclubs, which forced the Swing Youth movement to seek its survival underground. See Edelweiß Piraten and Weisse Rose.

Table Talk. See *Tischgespräche (im Führerhauptquartier)*.

Tapferkeits und Verdienst Auszeichnung für Angehörige des Ostvokan. Decoration for bravery and merit of the eastern people. This medal, instituted in July 1942, was awarded to the thousands of Russians who joined the German auxiliary forces in the hope of freeing themselves and their homeland from the dictatorship of Stalin. Although meant for foreigners, the medal was also awarded to some particularly brave German nationals.

Tarnhelmüberzug. Camouflage helmet cover. See Tarnung.

Tarnjacke. Camouflage smock. As World War II progressed, camouflage tunics became increasingly widespread in the German forces. Tarnjacke combined various colors, such as brown, green, red, pink, yellow, gray and black, printed in various irregular patterns. Camouflage uniforms were rather expensive; a few were issued to the army, but most of them were allocated with priority to elite troops such as paratroopers and Waffen-SS. The special Waffen-SS combat smock had elastic cuffs, was tunic length, collarless and had a lace-up neck. It was worn over the standard tunic and had slits to give access to the tunic pockets. The Tarnjacke was reversible; it had a mottled pattern on one side for autumn wear, and a different pattern featuring mainly green/brown on the other side for spring and summer wear. See Tarnung.

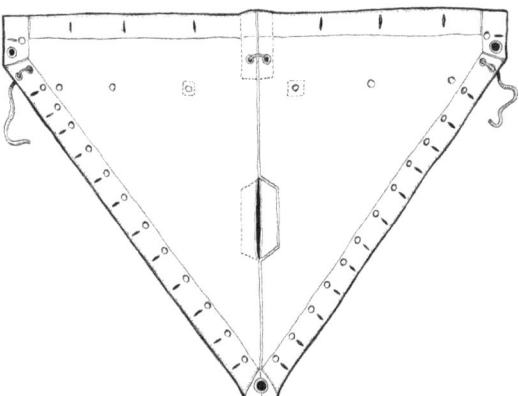

Tarnkappe or Zeltbahn.

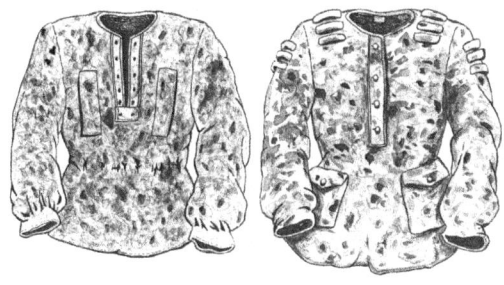

Tarnjacke. *Left:* **Waffen-SS early model.** *Right:* **Waffen-SS late model.**

Tarnkappe or **Zeltbahn.** Camouflage cape or shelter material. Part of a soldier's individual equipment, the Tarnkappe was universally issued throughout the German army. This item was a camouflage triangular cape 203 by 203 by 240 centimeters in size (6 feet, 3 inches, by 8 feet, 3 inches). It was manufactured from tightly woven, water-repellent cotton drill. In its center it had an opening that could be pulled over the wearer's head to use it as a poncho for wind, cold and rain. The edges of the cape were furnished with holes and buttons enabling various combinations, providing both protection and freedom of movement for marching, horse riding and bicycle or motorbike riding. The Zeltbahn was very convenient and multi-purpose, as four or more of these capes attached and held by pins and poles formed a small camouflage pyramidal tent for bivouac. See Tarnung.

Tarnung. Camouflage. Camouflage on a large scale was born during World War I when air reconnaissance was first used. Camouflage has since been very important; fortifications, troops, planes, vehicles and all military installations, and even civilian industrial complexes and factories had to be hidden from sight and thus concealed from enemy fire. They were scattered and placed so as to seemingly "disappear," be totally out of perception from the ground and from the sky. To merge with the surrounding ground they were covered with freshly cut vegetation, painted in appropriate colors showing various patterns, and concealed under camouflage nets that broke up the outline and reduced shadow effects. Camouflage was also art and theatrical bluff. The Germans installed phony bunkers, false airfields, fake supply stores and fake batteries with wooden guns.

Zeltbahn worn as a poncho.

Taschenlampe

Genuine bunkers, installations, supply dumps and even factories and industrial complexes were disguised with tiled roofs, dummy windows, trompe l'oeil, and deceptive patterns, thus appearing to be harmless and peaceful civilian houses or buildings. Camouflage was also introduced into uniforms. German World War II camouflage uniforms included the following: Splittermuster (splinter zigzag pattern introduced in 1932); Platanenmuster (plane-tree pattern mainly used in the period 1937–1942 with spring/summer and autumn/winter variations); Rauchtarnmuster (blurred edge pattern, 1939–1944 with spring/summer and autumn/winter variations); Palmenmuster (palm pattern, ca. 1941 with summer/autumn variations); Beringtes Eichenlaubmuster (ringed oak leaf pattern, 1942–1945); Eichenlaubmuster (oak leaf pattern, 1943–1945 with spring/summer and autumn/winter variations); Erbsenmuster or Flecktarn (pea pattern, 1944–1945 with spring/summer and autumn/winter variations); Leibermuster (Leiber's pattern from 1945); M29 Telo Mimetico (using fabric seized from the Italians in 1943 with medium green, and yellow/ochre in large organic patterns printed over brown basic color); Sumpfmuster (swamp pattern — a camouflage first introduced in 1943, with a variation in 1944).

Taschenlampe. Electrical torch furnished with a spring-loaded hook, commonly worn hanging on the tunic breast pocket. The torch was also a signal device as it could flash and convert white light to blue, red or green.

Tatkreis. Action Circle. One of the many völkisch movements active during the Weimar Republic (q.v.). Tatkreis members were neoconservatives of the radical right who considered themselves to be conservative revolutionaries. They called for a government by an intellectual elite, extolled youth, advocated an end to capitalism and promoted a neomercantilist ideology — a system which encouraged exports, discouraged imports and called for German self-sufficiency. This idea was easily received by the citizens of Germany, who lived through a depression after World War I. The movement had a publication called *die Tat* (*the Action*). After the seizure of power, the Nazis adopted several of Tatkreis's demands but the movement was dissolved.

Tauchfähig. Submersible. This term (from the verb "tauchen," meaning to dive or to submerge) was generally employed for a tank with modified exhaust pipes, snorkel, waterproof chassis and impervious engine that made deep wading and river crossing possible. All light and medium German tanks were able to cross a shallow ford, but a river was always a formidable obstacle. German heavy tanks such as the Tiger and the Königstiger were too heavy for the average road bridge so they were tauchfähig, but for fairly obvious reasons of bulk, no tank was a natural swimmer.

Tausendjährige Reich. Thousand-Year Empire. According to Hitler, the Nazi Third Reich should last for 1,000 years. In fact it lasted for only twelve years.

Technische Nothilfe (TeNo). (See illustrations on page 179.) Technical emergency help. The TeNo troops specialized in rescue and repair. Created in 1919 by the Weimar Republic, the service was continued by the Nazis and became a part of the Ordnungspolizei (q.v.) headed by SS Gruppenführer Schmelcher. Most of the TeNo men had technical skills, and they were equipped with tractors, trucks, mobile cranes, pumps, generators and winches. The primary task of the Technische Nothilfe was to repair breakdowns in vital public services such as gas and electric supplies or telephone communication, for example. These tasks were greatly increased by the Allied bombardments. The TeNo personnel also fought fires, and tunneled under piles of rubble to search for victims and survivors. They would defuse unexploded bombs and demolish houses to create firebreaks; they would also point out looters to the police and guard and search scenes of Allied plane crashes. They worked with and supported the action of the Nationalsozialistische Volkswohlfahrte (q.v). To fill its ranks during World War II, the TeNo had to partly rely upon the recruitment of foreign volunteers because most physically able German males were already serving in the armed forces. Many Dutchmen, Flemings, Walloons and Frenchmen volunteered for the TeNo squads. In late 1944 and early 1945, Germany was exhausted and needed still more combatants. As a result, the youngest and the fittest of TeNo men were transferred into German fighting formations such as the Waffen-SS (q.v.) and the Volkssturm (q.v.).

when confronted with bad news, particularly in the last year of World War II.

Tetraeder. Porcupine, a captured French mobile antitank obstacle formed of three wooden, metal or concrete beams assembled as a pyramid.

TeNo emblem.

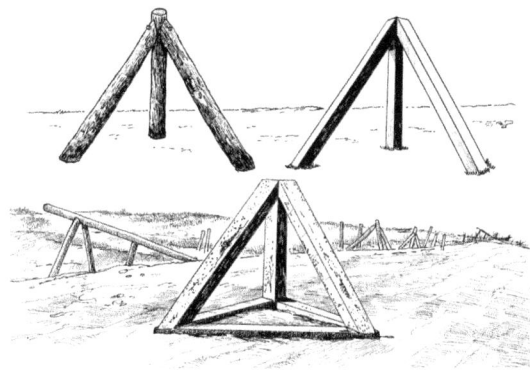

Tetraeder.

TeNo private.

Tellermine (in short T-Mine or T-Mi. 35). German metal-cased antitank mine. The device weighed 9.1 kilograms and contained 5.5 kilograms of TNT, which exploded when submitted to a pressure of 180 kilograms.

Teppichfresser. "Carpet Chewer." Sarcastic term employed to describe Hitler, who, it was said, in moments of rage would drop to the floor and chew the carpet in a fury. There is no evidence for this charge, but Hitler indeed had hysterical moments of anger when contradicted or

Teutonisch deutscher Ritterorden. Teutonic German knight order, created at Jerusalem, Palestine, during the third Crusade (1189–1192). After the fall of Acre in 1291 and the abandonment of the Holy Land, the Teutonic knights were transferred in 1309 to Marienburg, near Danzig (today Gdansk), in Poland. They maintained the spirit of the crusade by evangelizing pagan Slavs populations through force and by conquering vast territories in the Baltic regions. This movement, called Drang nach Osten (q.v.), was to a certain extent the forerunner movement of the Nazi conquest for Lebensraum (q.v.) in Eastern Europe. The Teutonic power reached its apogee in the 14th century, but after the defeat of Tannenberg in 1410, the weakened knights were forced to abandon their territories in Poland. They retreated to Königsberg, where they set up a state which eventually became a dukedom and, later, the kingdom of Prussia. The Teutonic order was suppressed in 1809 by Napoleon, and re-formed in Austria in 1840. Except for the Drang nach Osten and the armed character of both brotherhoods, the SS and the Teutonics had very little in common. Himmler admired and was obsessed with the medieval knights. He tried to create a new order of German knights out of his SS, but he distorted the principles of honor, obedience, bravery and loyalty. And indeed, after the Anschluß Osterreichs (q.v.) in 1938, the Teutonic order was assimilated into Freemasonry, forbidden, many knights imprisoned and their property confiscated. After World War II, the Teutonic order was reestablished in Vienna in 1947, and now the knights assist handicapped people and senior citizens in hospitals and homes. See Freimaurerei.

Theater in the Third Reich. During the era of the Weimar Republic (q.v.), German playwrights, directors and actors achieved a high reputation for excellence. As in all other branches of art, the establishment of the Nazi dictatorship in 1933 caused a total decline. Under the leadership of Dr. Joseph Goebbels, along with all other forms of cultural expression, the German theater was subjected to Gleichschaltung (q.v.). The only established playwright of talent to remain in Germany during the Nazi era was Gerhart Hauptmann. There were good performances of classic plays by Goethe, Schiller and Shakespeare, but on the whole the theatergoing public rejected the boring, heroic and dramatic propaganda productions approved by the Nazi cultural authorities.

Theresienstadt. Terezin (in Czech), located 35 miles north from Prague, was a military fortified town from 1780 to 1882. Under the Nazis it was first a ghetto (q.v.), and later a concentration and transit camp for Jews (notably Czechs from the protectorate of Bohemia-Moravia) bound for Auschwitz (q.v.), Treblinka (q.v.) and Sobibor (q.v.). When initial information about extermination centers began to filter through to the free world, the Nazis decided to show off Theresienstadt to an investigation committee of the International Red Cross as a "humane detention center." The external appearance of the ghetto was changed for this purpose. Serious overcrowding was reduced by additional deportation to Auschwitz. A bank, false shops, a cafe, kindergartens, and schools were set up in the ghetto, and the streets were beautified with flowers. Communal bathing facilities were built as well. Had the committee members tested the water faucets they would have discovered that none of the faucets were attached to plumbing. They were fake. Following the visit of the committee members, the Nazis filmed a propaganda documentary on "the new life of the Jews under the protection of the Third Reich." When filming was finished, most actors, including most of the ghetto children, were deported to Auschwitz-Birkenau and killed in gas chambers.

Thingspielestätten or **Althing.** Open-air medleys, an old Germanic institution revived by the Nazis as a support for their ideology. The Viking Althing was originally a tribal assembly of free men, both a kind of parliament and a court of justice. Under the Nazis the custom was excised from its institutional character and replaced with a mixture of pagan romanticism, militarism and naïve patriotism to build up recruits for Hitler's war machine. The Althing became merely a theatrical show held in rudimentary natural theaters incorporating hilly slopes and ancient ruins. The show included music and songs, commemoration of martyrs, military tattoos and reenactments, pagan oratorios, exhibitions of sports and horsemanship, circus acts and reconstructed battle scenes. These showy and kitschy occasions were no longer held after 1937.

Third Reich. Hitler regarded his regime as a logical extension of the previous German empires. See Drittes Reich.

Thorak, Josef (1889–1952). An Austrian sculptor and medal designer, who, like Arno Breker (q.v.), made powerful and heroic statues representing the Nazi German ideals and the superiority of the "Aryan" race.

Thule Gesellschaft. (See illustration on page 181.) Thule Society, originally named Studiengruppe für Germanisches Altertum (Study Group for Germanic Antiquity) headed by Walter Neuhaus. This German occultist and völkisch (q.v.) group in Munich — named after a mythical northern country from Greek legend — was notable chiefly as the organization that sponsored Anton Drexler's Deutsche Arbeiterpartei (q.v.), which was later transformed by Adolf Hitler into the National Socialist German Workers' Party (Nazi Party). There is no evidence that Hitler ever attended the Thule Society, but there was great enthusiasm among Thule members for Hitler, most notably Rudolf Hess (q.v.) and Dietrich Eckart (q.v.). The occultists believed Hitler to be the redeemer of Germany, and regarded themselves as the first disciples of the new prophet.

Thyssen, Fritz (1873–1951). Multimillionaire industrialist who controlled the United Steel Trust. Thyssen joined the NSDAP in 1923 and

Emblem of Thule Gesellschaft.

helped fund Hitler in the early years. He was one of the industrialists who petitioned Hindenburg to appoint Hitler as chancellor but demanded that Otto Strasser (q.v.), Ernst Röhm (q.v.), and the SA should be repudiated for their continuous attacks on industry and their demands for nationalization. In 1933, he became head of the national employers' association, a powerful industry pressure group that enthusiastically embraced the corporatism of the Nazis. In 1938, however, Fritz Thyssen became disillusioned by the way the Nazis were overturning conventional economics. As a result he fled to Switzerland, and subsequently Göring's Reichswerke took over slices of Thyssen's empire. Thyssen eventually went to France, was turned over to the Nazis by the Vichy government there, and was incarcerated in Dachau concentration camp. After World War II Thyssen was tried for being a supporter of the Nazi Party. He did not deny that he had been a Nazi funder until 1938, and he accepted responsibility for his companies' mistreatment of Jewish employees in the 1930s, although he denied involvement in the employment of slave labor during the war. Thyssen agreed to pay 500,000 deutsch marks as compensation to those who suffered as a result of his actions, and was acquitted of other charges. In January 1950, he and his wife immigrated to Buenos Aires, Argentina, where he died the following year. In 1959, Thyssen's widow and daughter established the Fritz Thyssen Foundation to advance science and the humanities, with a capital of 100 million deutsch marks.

Tiger. The PzKpfw VI (SdKfz 181), better known as Tiger, was undoubtedly the most famous German tank of World War II and was regarded by the Allies as the symbol of German technological superiority in armored fighting vehicles. Although by no means invulnerable, and although a relatively simple, compact, and conventional combat vehicle, the Tiger was at the time of its introduction in 1942 the most powerfully armed and best protected tank in the world. The Tiger, built by the Henschel and Porsche companies, was in production from August 1942 until August 1944. In all, 1,355 were built, surprisingly few considering its tremendous and legendary reputation.

Tiger tank.

Tirpitz. A German battleship named after Grand Admiral Alfred von Tirpitz. She was laid down in November 1936, launched in April 1939 and commissioned in February 1941. *Tirpitz* was sunk by Royal Air Force bombers on November 12, 1944. See *Bismarck*.

Tischgespräche (im Führerhauptquartier). *Table Talk (at Leader's Headquarters).* Records of Hitler's private, impromptu, and informal

Tobruk

conversations published in 1953, 1973 and 2000 with preface and introduction by H.R Trevor-Roper. On Martin Bormann's instructions, Hitler's dinner-table monologues and late-night rambling conversations were all recorded by a team of specially picked shorthand writers from July 1941 to November 1944. In *Table Talk*, Hitler freely spoke about all his familiar obsessions, his numerous enemies, his few friends, his great ambitions, his failures, and his secret dreams, voicing his thoughts to his intimate associates in a didactic and over-confident tone. On the most diverse subjects the Führer had sharp opinions, and could be totally wrong with impunity, outrageous without irony, and boring without limit. Indisputably authentic, *Table Talk* revealed a raw and unretouched look at the inner recesses of Adolf Hitler's crude and narrow mind. The Führer had little education and no humanity. He saw himself as a "Man of Destiny," a political and military genius, when he was only a terrible simplifier, a man who, with no equipment except his own willpower, personality and limited ideas, attempted to bring mankind into a dreadful darkness.

Tobruk or **Tobrukstand** or **Ringstand.** A Tobruk was a small bunker with an open pit generally built in 40-centimeters Vf (reinforced fortification) thickness. It was composed of a small 1.60-meter-high chamber topped with an open pit 80 centimeters in diameter. It was both an observatory and a combat emplacement. It existed in numerous variants, armed with a rotating tank-turret, a machine gun, a mortar, a flame-thrower, a flak gun. This simple bunker, combining full 360 degree firing angle, cheap costs, quick construction, multifunctionality and possibly high firepower, was widely used everywhere, notably in the Atlantikwall (q.v.). When built within a bunker as observation and guard post, the Tobruk was called Offener Beobachter (q.v.).

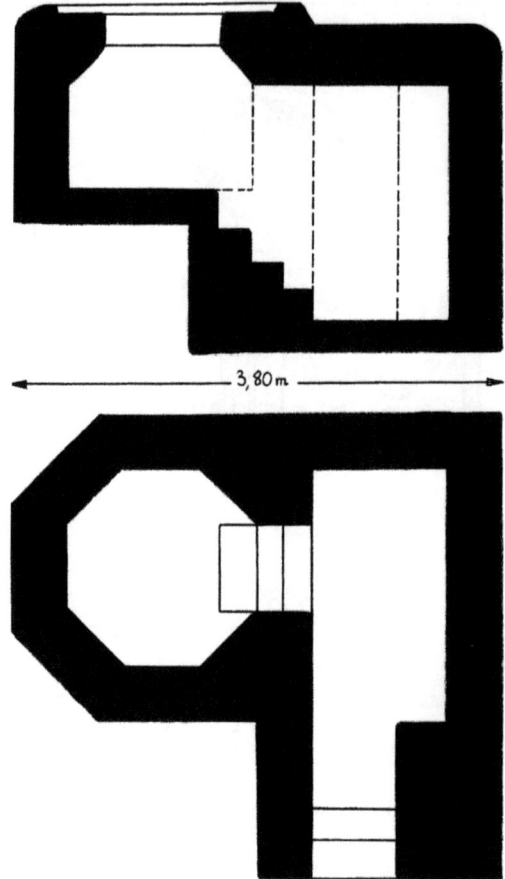

Cross-section and plan of Tobruk.

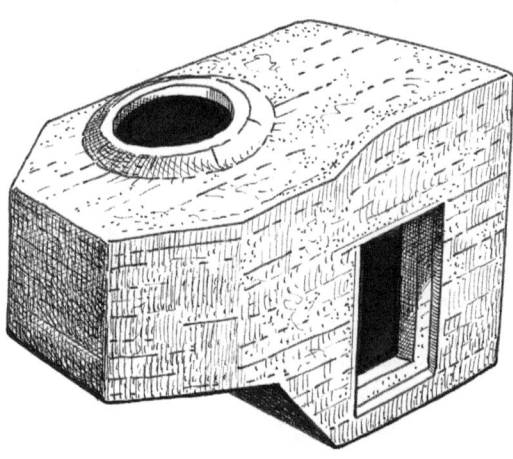

Tobruk.

Todesmärsche. Death march. At the end of World War II when it became obvious that the German army was trapped between the Soviets to the east and the advancing Allied troops from the west, the Nazis, in an attempt to prevent the liberation of concentration camp inmates, forced them to march westward toward Germany proper. Thousands died in these pointless death marches.

Todt, Fritz (1891–1942). After serving in the German army in World War I, Todt studied engineering and worked as a building engineer. He joined the NSDAP in 1922, and, after Hitler's seizure of power in 1933, he was made responsible for the construction of the Autobahnen (q.v.) and given the task of building the Westwall (q.v.) with his conglomerate of companies called Organisation Todt (q.v.). In 1940 Todt was appointed Reich minister for munitions, but by that time he was convinced that the war could not be won. Fritz Todt was killed in February 1942 in a plane crash. Although he was given national funerals, it has never been established whether the cause of his death was an accident or a deliberate assassination. The skilled and competent but defeatist Todt was replaced as minister of munitions by Albert Speer (q.v.). See Atlantikwall and Nationalsozialistischer Bund Deutscher Technik.

Tommy. German slang for a British soldier.

Torgau. City on the Elbe River some 75 miles south of Berlin where on April 25, 1945, Allies and Soviet armies were joined. The Torgau meeting was the occasion of a short celebration by the Allies, marking the defeat of Nazi Germany.

Tornister. Backpack. Based on the World War I model, it was a full marching order fur-covered backpack with rolled blanket, camouflage shelter material, groundsheet, personal gear, mess tin with cooking and eating implements, additional clothing sleeping bags, and all other items needed to maintain the infantryman in combat. In 1937, a new, cheaper, more convenient backpack based on the French alpine pack appeared. Known as the German rucksack type 1937 it was made of canvas, had side pockets, two suspenders and a wooden frame to provide additional support so that a greater load could be carried.

Torpedoboot (T-Boot). Torpedo boat. Larger than a Schnellboot (q.v.), a T-Boot was more like a small destroyer used for coastal defense and escort for heavy fleet units.

Totaler Krieg. Total war. A conference was held in Casablanca from January 14 to 24, 1943, at which the Allies vowed to continue hostilities until a complete, unconditional German surrender. For their part, the Nazis asserted their determination to fight till the bitter end. On February 18, 1943, Joseph Paul Goebbels (q.v.) announced before a carefully selected and fanatical audience in the Sportpalast in Berlin "totaler Krieg," expressing the war radicalization and excluding any diplomatic or political outcome to end the conflict.

Totalitarismus. Totalitarianism. Totalitarianism, as distinct from mere dictatorship, was an outgrowth of a long development in the past. The state was an institution that had continuously acquired new power ever since the Middle Ages. Step by step it had assumed jurisdiction over law courts and men-at-arms, imposed taxes, regulated churches, guided economic policy, operated school systems and devised schemes of public welfare. The 20th century totalitarian states — and more particularly Hitler's Nazi Germany — went even further. National Socialism claimed an absolute domination over every area of daily life and carried the development of state sovereignty and raison d'état to a new extreme. Nazism was not merely anticlerical but explicitly anti–Christian, offering or rather imposing, a total philosophy of life. Churches, both Catholic and Protestant, were "coordinated." The Nazi ideology drew heavily upon a historic nationalism, which it greatly exaggerated. The Nazis held that the nation was a kind of living organism within which the individual person was but a single cell. The individual had no independent existence; he received life itself and all his ideas from the culture of the nation into which he was born and by which he was nurtured. The individual person was meaningless outside the collective body. Hitler claimed to represent the absolute sovereignty of the German people. He was presented as a kind of modern messiah and was the object of a popular worship. Given such a theory, it made no sense to speak of individual's

Left: Model 1937 Alpine tornister. *Right:* Tornister.

freedom. All political parties except the National Socialist were forbidden and destroyed. Valid ideas were those of the Nazis. Even science was "coordinated." There was thus a Nazi science, which was bound to differ in its conclusions from democratic, bourgeois, Western, capitalist, communist and "Jewish" science. All artistic activities — music, painting, poetry, fiction, architecture and others — were good art insofar as they glorified Nazi society. The avowed philosophy of Nazism was basically subjective. Whether an idea was good or true depended on whose idea it was. Truth, beauty and right only corresponded to the inner nature, interest, or point of view of the Nazis. Law itself was defined as the will of the German people operating in the interests of the Nazi state. Propaganda and repression were the principal branches of government. The Nazis demanded total faith in their view of life, they manipulated opinion, they duped the country, they rewrote history and forged "scientific" proofs. The very idea of truth evaporated. Barred from independent sources of information, having no means by which any official allegation could be tested, no one could escape the omnipresent state doctrine, the political expediency, the wishes and self-interests of the men in power. Endlessly repeated, the most extravagant statements came to be accepted — even contradictions, lies and rubbish were believed by the German people. Racism was another further exaggeration or degradation of older ideas of nationalism and national solidarity. It defined Germany in a tribal sense, as a biological entity, as a group of chosen people having the same ancestry, similar physical characteristics, and the "same blood." All through European history, a latent hostility to Jews had always been present in the Christian world, but it arose nowhere so brutally as in Nazi Germany. Jews were considered un–German, and presented as unfair competitors in professions and business. They were also depicted as decaying and parasitical elements putting in danger the "pure" German race and culture. Anti-Semitism was inflamed by Nazi propagandists who wished people to feel their supposed racial purity more keenly and to forget the deeper problems of Germany such as poverty, unemployment and social inequities. The Nazi ideology indeed pretended that differences between rich and poor were of minor importance. It pointed alarmingly to the dark menace of Soviet bolshevism/communism and declared that all social classes stood shoulder to shoulder in slablike solidarity behind the Führer. The Nazis blamed Germany's troubles on forces outside the country. They accused dissatisfied persons of conspiring with foreigners, and opponents were adjudged the tools of Western imperialism, communists and international Jewry. The Nazis transformed the inner conflicts between rich and poor into a struggle between nations and gave the impression that war might be the only solution for social ills. The use, the cult, the acceptance and the glorification of violence were other distinguishing characteristics of the totalitarian state. In Nazi ethics, war was a noble thing and the love of peace a sign of decadence. The Nazi regime indoctrinated the rising generation in schools and universities. It instituted a youth movement, the Hitler Jugend (q.v.). The Nazi ideal was to turn the German people into a race of splendid disciplined animals. Contrariwise, euthanasia was adopted for the insane, and disabled, and was proposed for the aged.

Totenbuch. Death Book. Official ledger used in concentration and extermination camps to register the names of those who were executed. Toward the end of the war, when the Germans were struggling, the record-keeping fell behind the pace of the extermination. Unknown numbers of victims were marched directly from trains to gas chambers in places like Auschwitz without being registered.

Totenburgen. Castles of the Dead. Monumental soldiers' memorials that Hitler planned to construct after the victory of Germany in World War II. Obviously none of these huge commemorative places were ever built. See Kyffhaüserbund.

Totenkopf. Death's head, a skull with two crossed bones. Related to distant Germanic mythology, it was not a Nazi creation; the Totenkopf was a relatively old concept that had always had a strong symbolic meaning. It appeared as a badge on the hats of the Prussian 1st and 2nd Bodyguard Hussars von Rüsch regiments in 1757. It was worn on the headgear of Spanish volunteer units raised in 1808 during the Napoleonic wars, on shakos worn by the 92nd Brunswick infantry regiment in 1809, and also on pirates' flags in the 17th and 18th centuries. In the Nazi period, from 1933 until 1945, the Totenkopf in miniaturized form was worn by the regular army tank troops, by the SS and Waffen-SS.

Totenkopfverbände. See SS-Totenkopfverbände.

Totenvögel. "Birds of Death." Popular name given to NSDAP members charged with informing families of soldiers that their next of kin had been killed in action. They were also charged with organizing subsequent ceremonies to honor the fallen heroes. In this way the NSDAP hoped to take the place of religion in giving solace at a difficult moment.

Tragenriemen. Soldier's equipment composed of waist belt, shoulder belts, suspenders, rings and straps intended to support various individual items such as bread bag, drinking bottle, bayonet, cartridge pouches, gas mask, rolled cape and so on. The straps were Y-shaped, passing from the front of the waist belt on either side of the chest and over the shoulders, converging on a steel ring between the shoulder blades. From this ring a single strap joined to the belt at the center of the back. Straps were fitted with buckles for individual adjustment. The equipment was made of black leather or canvas web.

Treblinka. Nazi extermination camp located on the Bug River 75 miles from Warsaw in Poland. The camp started operations in June 1942, and its sole purpose was extermination of the Jews by gassing. It was the second of the Vernichtungslager (q.v.) after Auschwitz, with an estimated total of 850,000 victims.

Treu Heinrich. The loyal Heinrich, a nickname given by Hitler to his faithful chief of the SS, Heinrich Himmler (q.v.).

Treuhänder der Arbeit. Trustees of Labor. By a law of May 1933, thirteen departmental offices were set up throughout Germany, each headed by a trustee of labor, whose function was the negotiation of work contracts between employers and workers — a clear usurpation of trade union functions. See Deutsche Arbeitsfront.

Triumph des Willens. *Triumph of the Will,* a film directed and produced by Leni Riefenstahl (q.v.) celebrating the Nazi Party congress held at Nuremberg in September 1934.

Troost, Paul Ludwig (1878–1934). Hitler's favorite architect. His style combined a kind of spartan traditionalism with an approach leaning toward classical form. On his death in 1934, he was replaced by Albert Speer (q.v.). See Architecture in the Third Reich.

Trop. Short for Tropisch (tropical). This abbreviation indicated an item, device, piece of uniform or equipment, vehicle or aircraft specially adapted to be operated in tropical or desert conditions. See Deutsches Afrika Korps.

Tropische Anzug. Tropical combat dress issued to the Deutsches Afrika Korps (DAK) during the North Africa campaign between 1941 and 1943. The basic tropical uniform was composed of an olive green four-pocket tunic with open neck, worn over an olive green shirt and tie; olive green straight long trousers bloused at the ankle, slightly flared breeches, or large shorts; and laced ankle boots in either brown leather or olive canvas, or leather or canvas boots reaching to the knee and laced from instep to knee.

Tropische Kopfbedeckung. Tropical helmet; part of the tropical uniform. At the early stage in 1941, a special tropical cork helmet was issued to the soldiers of the German Afrikakorps (DAK) in northern Africa. This helmet, however, covered with khaki cotton or greenish felt, proved cumbersome and of dubious value. The men of the DAK discarded this item of uniform after a few months' experience and reverted to standard 1935 steel helmets or wore the Einheitsmütze, peaked cap.

Trümmerfrau. Rubble Woman. After the fall of the Nazi regime right after the end of the Second

Tropische Kopfbedeckung.

World War, Trümmerfrauen were employed to remove the ruins and clean up the streets. Some 50,000 women were involved in the enterprise, which gained them extra rations. Germany's women were the true force behind the country's reconstruction in the first months of peace after May 1945. As described in Günter Grass's work of fiction *My Century*, "*They had endured too much to give up now.*"

Trümmerfrau.

Trupp. Troop in general, and more particularly the equivalent of a platoon in the SA. Three or four SA-Scharen formed an SA-Trupp commanded by a Truppenführer (staff sergeant). Three or four Truppen formed an SA Sturm (a kind of strong company).

Truppenamt. Troops office. The Truppenamt was formed by General Hans von Seeckt within the remodeled Reichswehr (q.v.) after the German general staff was outlawed by the Versailles Treaty in 1919. The elite unit included technically adept officers who (often in secret) developed new military doctrines and modern weapons such as mechanized, armored, airborne and air forces. The Truppenamt was disbanded in 1935 when Hitler repudiated the Treaty of Versailles and reestablished the general staff and conscription.

Truppenführer. Staff sergeant, a noncommissioned officer in command of an SA Trupp (platoon).

Tschechenigel. "Czech hedgehog." Captured Czech antitank obstacle composed of three steel bars (or three rails) bolted together.

Tscheschish (t). Czech. Designation used for all equipment, tanks and weapons captured from the Czech after the occupation and dislocation of Czechoslovakia in 1939.

Tuchmütze. Cloth cap, the most distinctive form of Reichsarbeitsdienst (q.v.) headgear, designed by Reichsarbeitsführer Konstantin Hierl (q.v.). Introduced in 1934, the soft peaked cap was a cross between an old style peasant's cap and a huntsman's hat. It is commonly referred to as a Robin Hood hat within the collector community.

Turnvereine. German and Austrian callisthenic leagues. They were composed of children, men and women in identical uniforms making perfectly synchronized, rhythmical exercises and move-

Tschechenigel.

ments in performance during Nazi mass meetings, feasts and celebrations displaying group cohesion, discipline and physical fitness.

Übermensch. Literally "upper human," or "over human." Concept appropriated from the work of the philosopher Friedrich Wilhelm Nietzsche (q.v.). Nietzsche proposed the Übermensch as a goal for humanity in his 1883 book *Also Sprach Zarathustra (Thus Spoke Zarathustra)*. The concept was misappropriated and used by the Nazis to describe what they considered the racially superior Germanic "Aryan" people. See Arisch and Untermensch.

U-Boot. See Unterseeboot.

U-Boot-Kriegsabzeichen. Submarine Badge, an award instituted by Oberbefehlshaber der Kriegsmarine und Großadmiral Erich Raeder in October 1939 for all ranks of U-Boat personnel who had served on at least two sorties against the enemy or who had been wounded in action.

U-Boot-Kriegsabzeichen.

Unconditional Surrender (of the Third Reich and Japan). Policy announced by U.S. President Franklin D. Roosevelt and British Prime Minister Winston Churchill at the Casablanca Conference (North Africa) held in January 1943.

Und Ihr habt doch gesiegt. A saying in a speech by Adolf Hitler, which became a slogan meaning "And yet Victory is yours" or "And you were victorious after all." The phrase was inscribed on the Blood Order medal, among other uses. See Blutorden.

Union der Sozialistischen Sowjetrepubliken. Union of Soviet Socialist Republics (USSR). The Soviet Union was a federation of countries created after Vladimir Lenin led the overthrow of the unpopular czarist autocratic government. The largest and most important of the countries in the union was Russia, and the capital city of the Soviet Union was Moscow. The Soviet Union existed from 1922 to 1991. It was the first country to have an official communist government. Ioseb Vissarionovich Jugashvili, alias Josef Stalin (1878–1953) cooperated with Hitler before World War II, and finally in 1939 they made an agreement to invade, conquer and divide Poland. However, in June 1941, Hitler turned against Stalin and attacked the Soviet Union. Then the USSR joined with the Western democratic Allies to defeat Germany.

Unsere Ehre heißt Treue. Our Honor Is Called Loyalty. Slogan of the Schutz-Staffeln (q.v.) inscribed on blades of daggers, among other uses.

Unserer Führer-unser Glaube. Our Leader—Our Faith. Motto of the SA inscribed on belt buckles decorated with eagle and wreathed swastika.

Unterführer. Literally, "subleaders." All-encompassing term for noncommissioned officers.

Untermensch. Subhuman. A term used by the philosopher Friedrich Nietzsche to describe the common man. Likened to sheep, the Untermensch is a social animal spouting pacifist and liberal morality. But according to the racist Nazi ideology, which saw the basic law of nature in the "battle for existence" and was based on a romanticized vision of history, a false interpretation of biology, and racism, the concept of "subhuman" was applied to handicapped people, Slavs, Gypsies and Jews, who were considered mentally and spiritually lower than animals. They were denied membership in the human race, and this justified their physical extermination.

Unterscharführer. Sergeant in SA and SS.

Unterseeboot (U-Boot). Submarine. When Hitler came to power the U-Boot force was developed by Admiral Karl Dönitz (q.v.). During World War II, in the Battle of the Atlantic, German submarines demonstrated their capability against Allied convoys by attacking at night on the surface in dense "wolf packs." The mainstay of German navy was the reliable and maneuverable Unterseeboot type VII. The main subma-

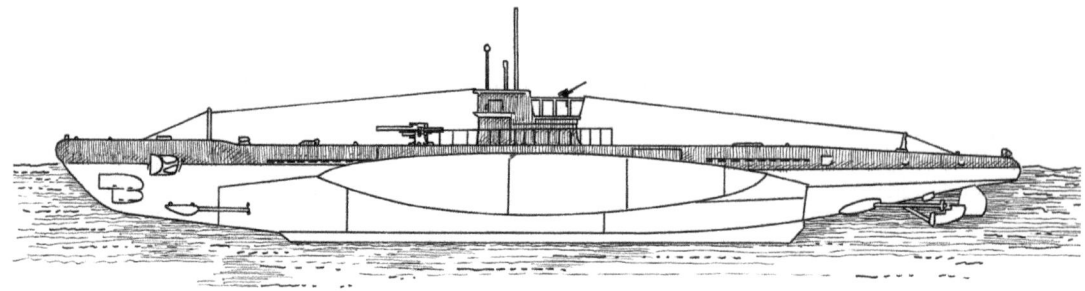

U-Boot type VII C.

rine bases for operations in the Atlantic Ocean were Brest, Lorient, Saint-Nazaire, La Rochelle-La Pallice and Bordeaux in occupied France. See Festung and Kriegsmarine.

Unterstand. Concrete shelter, generally an unarmed bunker.

Untersturmführer. Second lieutenant in SA and SS.

Untersuchungs und Schlichtungs-Ausschuß (Uschla). Committee for Investigation and Settlement. A court of justice headed by former general Heinemann and set up by Hitler in 1926 intended to settle intraparty problems and disputes and channel criticism within the Nazi party. Later, headed by Major Walther Buch, Ulrich Graf and Hans Frank, the committee turned a blind eye to dishonesty, crime and immorality, except insofar as these affected the efficiency and unity of the party. Indeed, the real purpose of the Uschla was preserving party discipline and the authority of Hitler, and settling disputes so as to keep them quiet, rather than to achieve substantive justice between the disputants or to enforce any moral code. In the end the arbitration committee became an effective instrument for Hitler's tight control over the NSDAP.

Unzuverlässige Elemente. According to Nazi ideology, "unreliable societal elements" including Jews, communists, homosexuals, and other undesirable persons. See also Asoziale, Gemeinschaftsfremde, and Untermensch.

Uschla. See Untersuchungs-und Schlichtungs-Ausschuß.

V1. Officially named Fieseler Fi 103 or FZG-76, the flying bomb V1 was a mid-wing monoplane missile driven by a pulsating flow duct motor. Carrying a 1,870-pound explosive warhead, it had a range of 130 miles and a speed of about 200 miles per hour. Guidance was preset before launch and thus the flight was secure against any form of electronic interference or jamming. It was developed in June 1942 and mass production started in March 1944. About 35,000 were produced, of which 9,251 were fired against England and 6,551 against Antwerp in Belgium. See Vergeltungswaffe and Wunderwaffen.

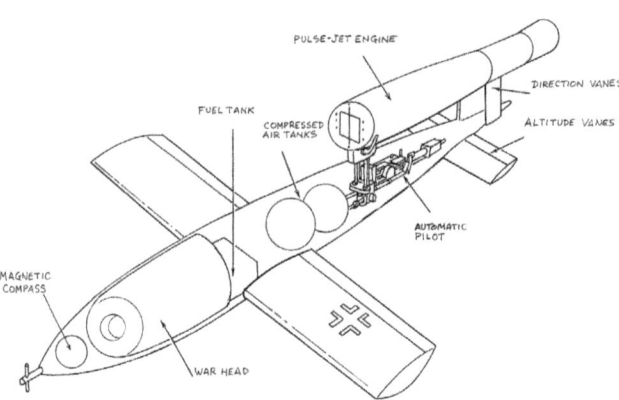

Inside the V-1.

V2. Officially designated Aggregat 4 (A-4 in short), the V-2 was a bullet-shaped rocket propelled by a motor that used liquid oxygen and alcohol, and carrying a one-ton explosive warhead. An immensely portentous invention, the sophisticated V-2 could be fired from practically any clear space of a few square yards. It was transported and erected on a special Meilerwagen (trailer) and rapidly launched. Once the rocket was launched, the site was rapidly evacuated,

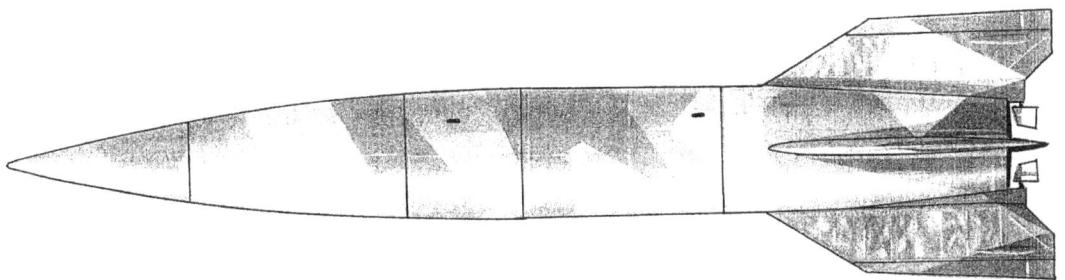

V-2 rocket.

making the detection of a launching unit almost impossible. Besides, the missile flew at supersonic speed, so it was extremely difficult to detect. In all, some 10,000 V-2 rockets were produced and operational use began in September 1944 against England and Antwerp. See Vergeltungswaffe.

V3. Under the cover name of Fleissiges Leichen Wieze, also High Pressure Pump, and nicknamed Busy Lizzie by the Allies, the secret project V3 was installed in the Mimoyecques forest near Landrethun in northern France, 152 kilometers (95 miles) from London. Invented by Dr. Cönders of the Röchling Werk company, the project V3 consisted of a long-range gun battery intended to destroy London. Each gun was a 127-meter-long barrel divided into individual sections fitted with a chamber containing an explosive charge which could be ignited automatically the moment the missile had passed. As the projectile passed successive explosive chambers, each explosion increasing its speed, it left the barrel with extreme velocity with a range of over 160 kilometers. The guns were given an angle of 40 to 50 degrees and aimed in the direction of London. Barrels, facilities and installations were built 67 meters underground in heavy concrete galleries. When the incomplete installation was located, the Allied air forces destroyed it with 6,000-kilogram Tallboy bombs in July 1944. In May 1945, without consulting the French, the British engineering corps completed the total destruction of the dangerous installation. See Vergeltungswaffe.

V4. Also known as Reichenberg, this secret weapon was a piloted variant of the flying bomb V1 (q.v.). The single-seat manned craft was intended to be launched from a mother plane and aimed at its target by the pilot, who would bail out in the final seconds before hitting. The project was never completed. See KG200, V1, and Vergelgungswaffe.

VB. Short for the Nazi newspaper *Völkischer Beobachter* (q.v.).

Vegetarianism. Hitler refused to eat meat and was harshly critical of others whom he described as "eating carcasses." He was a teetotaler who was also vehemently opposed to smoking.

Verband. Formation or unit usually not smaller than a battalion and not larger than a regiment. Plural is Verbände.

Verbandpackchentasche. Field-dressing pack issued to fighting units for emergency medical care.

Verfallskunst. Fallen or degenerate Art. See also Entartete Kunst and Kunst.

Verfügung. Edict, decree, disposition.

Verfügungstruppen (SS-VT). SS troops, after 1939 called Waffen-SS (q.v.).

Vergeltungswaffe (V). Arms of vengeance. Germany was much more advanced than the Allies regarding development of rockets and missiles. As soon as 1937, a special center was created in Peenemünde (q.v.) near Stettin on the Baltic Sea shore. Theoretical research and experimental work were directed by Werner Wernher Frieherr von Braun (q.v.), who carried out many military projects for the Nazis. Several programs were launched concerning secret retaliation weapons. Among these so-called Vergeltungswaffen, the most effective and best known were V1 (q.v.) and V2 (q.v.). In spite of numerous fiascos and serious accidents, Vergeltungswaffen became efficient and formidable weapons that caused many casualties among innocent civilian populations, notably in Britain and Belgium. Hitler had great expectations from these wonder weapons — he hoped they would sow horror, panic, confusion, and paralysis in the Allied camp. He considered that those revolutionary weapons would enable Germany to win the war and he was almost right. Although Hitler far overestimated their effects, the Vergeltungswaffen caused serious casualties, and if the V1 weapons offensive had been launched against England six months earlier or directed against military targets, D-Day might have had to be postponed indefinitely. But, German technologists saw their achievements come to nothing through interservice rivalries and an utter lack of vision at the top. Hitler's secret weapons played an important part in the development of postwar guided and unguided missiles.

Vernichtungslager. Extermination camp or death camp. These camps differed from other detention, work and concentration camps because their sole purpose was genocide, the physical elimination of people, particularly Jews and Gypsies, on a systematic industrial scale by gassing. While there were victims from many groups, Jews were the main targets. This genocide of the Jewish people was the Third Reich's "Final Solution to the Jewish question." Treblinka, Sobibor and Belzec, together with Chelmno and Strutthof, were death camps. Two others, Auschwitz-Birkenau and Maidanek, were combined concentration, work and extermination camps. For political and logistical reasons, Nazi Germany built most death camps in remote places in occupied Poland where most of the intended victims lived (Poland had the greatest European Jewish community), and where the camps could be kept secret from the German civil populace. Prisoners were first rounded up and gathered in prisons, ghettos (q.v.) or Durchgangslager — transit camps (q.v.). Then they were transported for days or even weeks in inhumane conditions, with little or no food and water and packed in rail freight boxcars, in which many died before reaching their destination. Each extermination camp operated differently, yet each was identically designed for quick and efficient industrialized killing by using poison gas to kill the victims and incinerating their bodies in crematoria or on pyres. The Nazi attempts at Jewish genocide are collectively known as the Holocaust (q.v.), or Shoah in Hebrew. The Holocaust killed approximately six million European Jews. The use of camps equipped with gas chambers for the purpose of systematic mass extermination of peoples was a unique, incredible and unprecedented feature in history. Never before had there existed places with the express purpose of murdering people en masse.

Versailler Diktat. Versailles Dictation. The view was widely held in post–World War I Germany that the Treaty of Versailles was an imposed, vindictive and unfair settlement. See Novemberverbrecher and Versailler Vertrag.

Versailler Vertag. The Treaty of Versailles (June 1919) redrew many European and colonial borders. It reduced German territory and imposed severe penalties on Germany, which had to pay enormous compensation sums of money, and had to recognize its war guilt. In military matters, the German general staff was disbanded, the navy was limited to 16,500 seamen, submarines were forbidden and ships over 10,000 tons were outlawed. Conscription was forbidden, and the army was reduced to 100,000 professional soldiers deprived of tanks, airplanes, chemical weapons, heavy guns, automatic weapons and fortifications. The terms of the treaty were harsh for Germany and caused a widespread feeling of injustice. Hitler's first objective was the repudiation of the hated treaty of Versailles, which was achieved in March 1935. See Dolchstoß, Novemberverbrecher, and Reichswehr.

Versorgung (V). Logistics department.

Versorgungskolonne. Motorized supply column.

Verstärkt feldmäßig (Vf). Reinforced field fortification. Verstärkt feldmäßiger Ausbau included masoned and concrete defense works able to resist direct hit by light artillery. Bunkers of category Vf had roofs and walls 30 centimeters thick for subcategory D, 60 centimeters for subcategory C, 1 meter for subcategory B-1 alt and 1.50 meters for subcategory B-2 neu.

Versuchs. Experimental, hence the "V" designation for any German military aircraft or tank prototypes.

Versuchskraftfahrzeug (VsKfz). Experimental vehicle.

Verteidigung. Generic term for defense.

Verteidigungsbereich (VB). Defended zone. After the repulsed attack on Dieppe in August 1942, the German high command was convinced that important European harbors would become priority objectives when the invasion came. Den Helder, IJmuiden, Hoek van Holland and Vlissingen in the Low Countries; Ostende in Belgium; and Boulogne, Le Havre, Cherbourg, Brest, Lorient, Saint-Nazaire, Royan, La Rochelle and Bordeaux in France were then declared Verteidigungsbereiche. These defensive sectors received full priority regarding garrison, weapons and fortifications. See Atlantikwall and Festung.

Vertrauensmann. Intelligence agent, spy or informer.

Verwundeten Abzeichen. Wound badge. The Verwundeten Abzeichen, reinstituted by Hitler in May 1939 for German volunteers wounded in the Spanish Civil War (1936–1939), was awarded during World War II in three classes; gilt for five or more wounds, for total disablement or permanent blindness; silver for three or four wounds, or for the loss of a hand, foot or eye or for deafness; black for one or two light wounds. The wound badge, worn on the left breast without ribbon, was similar to that of World War I but with a swastika added to the steel helmet.

Verwundeten Abzeichen.

Vichy France. French regime set up under Marshal Philippe Pétain (1856–1951) in collaboration with the Germans following the fall of France in June 1940. The Vichy regime maintained some legal authority in the northern zone of France (the occupied zone), which was occupied by the German Wehrmacht, but was most powerful in the unoccupied southern zone libre (so-called free zone), where its administrative center, Vichy was located. In November 1942, following the Allied landing and conquest of North Africa, the southern "free" zone was also occupied and fully subjected to German rule, thus making Vichy entirely a puppet regime.

Vierjahresplan. Four Years' Plan launched under Hermann Göring's direction in August 1936. The plan was intended to develop a blockade-free autarkic economy in which materials vital for war would be produced at home instead of imported. The organization initiated expensive investment programs in basic chemicals, synthetic fuel oil, synthetic rubber, aluminum, and iron-ore extraction, all designed to reduce German dependence on outside sources. The plan introduced a program of improvement in agriculture to ensure that Germany would not be starved into submission in a future war. A program of labor was launched to make sure that the depth of skilled labor needed for a war economy would be in place. Side by side with the economic strategy, the plan aimed to create an economy geared more closely to the conduct of war. Hitler ordered a very great increase in military expenditure designed to bring the armed forces to a state of war readiness by 1940.

Vierling. (See illustration on page 192.) Quadruple, referring to any weapons mount that used four machine guns or autocannon of the same make and model, in a single traversable and elevatible mount.

Viking Bund. See Organisation Consul.

Volk ohne Raum. *People Without Land.* This was the title of a novel published in 1926 by Hans Grimm claiming the need for German territorial expansion. The expression was taken over by the Nazis as a popular slogan. The aim of the Nazis was to lead people out of towns and back onto land, since the "racial hygienists" of the Blut und Boden (q.v.) theory believed they detected a biological degeneration in urban dwellers. Restoration of roots in blood and soil was seen as the means of restoring the nation to health, and therefore the peasant's lifestyle was put forward

Völkisch

20 mm Flak Vierling 38.

Emblem of the Volksbund für das Deutschtum im Ausland in 1935. The emblem displays the profile of a cornflower and the Gothic letters VDA.

as a prerequisite for the renewal and preservation of the German nation. From this were derived the demand for "seizure of land" and colonial settlements in the East, known as Lebensraum (q.v.).

Völkisch. A quite common Nazi concept, rather difficult to translate, meaning generally from/for the people, popular, populist ethnic, with emphasis on the German race, blood and soil.

Völkischer Beobachter. People's Observer, a newspaper purchased by the Nazis in 1920 for sixty thousand marks, raised by Major General Ritter von Epp, by the journalist and playwright Dietrich Eckhart (q.v.) and from army secret funds. It was the official newspaper of the NSDAP, and after 1933 the first national paper, with a popular rather than an elitist style. It remained the leading Nazi Party newspaper until 1945.

Volksbund für das Deutschtum im Ausland (VDA). The League for the Germanity Abroad was a German cultural organization that promoted German culture and language worldwide. Founded in 1881 by the lawyer Julius Scharlach, and originally called Verein für Deutsche Kulturbeziehungen im Ausland (VDA), the league was taken over by the NSDAP in 1933. The league was later denazified and reestablished in 1955. See Hauptamt Volksdeutsche Mittelstelle (VoMi).

Volksdeutsche. German-speaking communities living abroad, notably in Sudetenland, French Alsace-Lorraine, and Luxembourg, but also Germanic people originating from northern Schleswig and southern Tyrol, German minorities from Banat, Bohemia-Moravia, Slovakia, Poland, Hungary, Rumania, Serbia, Croatia, Bulgaria, and from the Volga region. Volksdeutsche, considered as having "similar blood" as the true Germans' were to be joined to the Volksgemeinschaft (q.v.), if need be by conquest. Volksdeutsche were often accused of being fifth columnists, but on the whole their importance in helping the invading German armies was exaggerated.

Volksdeutsche Mittelstelle (VoMi). See Hauptamt Volksdeutsche Mittelstelle.

Volksempfänger. Literally, "popular receiver," a cheap radio sold on the German domestic market purposely designed to receive only the German national and local stations, so as to ensure that only Nazi propaganda broadcasts would be heard at homes all over the country. To this end, most Volksempfänger lacked shortwave bands and did not follow the practice, common at the time among other radio manufacturers, of marking the approximate dial positions of major European stations on its tuning scale. Generally only German (and later Austrian) stations were marked, and cheaper models did not even have a proper scale at all. See Radio in the Third Reich.

Volksgemeinschaft. A concept that means national solidarity; popular ethnic community; classless folk community; national community; ensemble of the Germans and Volksdeutsche (q.v.). Hitler envisaged a biologically homogenous German people led by a new civilian and military elite. The aim was to have selected soldiers and leaders for a greater cohesion for war, by the ruthless exclusion and elimination of all ideological and biological enemies, the so-called asocials. The reorganization of the German people into a community of blood and destiny was supported by a common Weltanschauung (q.v.). The concept of Volksgemeinschaft led to an integrated society without social barriers, even at the price of individual freedom. It satisfied a psychological need for solidarity, idealism and self-sacrifice. It gave the Germans a sense of purpose and national pride that the Weimar Republic had failed to achieve. This egalitarian drive created favorable conditions for social mobility and advancement through merit and achievements. However — never quite certain of the cohesion of the Volksgemeinschaft — the populist and authoritarian Nazi regime relied on a carrot-and-stick approach, combining bribes and threats, savage penalties and calls for decency to keep the German nation in its grip.

Volksgenossen. Fellow countrymen, or national comrades, addressed as such by Hitler or any other Nazi speaker at the beginning of a speech. A "national comrade" was expected to be of "Aryan" race, erbgesund (genetically healthy), leistungsfähig (socially efficient), hardworking, politically reliable, and an active participant in the various organizations of the Nazi regime.

Volksgericht. People's Court. A dreaded court set up in Berlin to render a quick verdict for accused traitors. The court, presided over by judge Roland Freisler (q.v.) was composed of two professional judges and five others selected from among NSDAP officials, the SS (q.v.) and the Wehrmacht (q.v.). The court sat almost continuously from midsummer 1944 to February 3, 1945, when the building was destroyed during an Allied air raid, and pronounced hundreds of death sentences. There was no appeal from the verdicts.

Volksgrenadier Divisions. People's grenadier divisions. These units were raised in September 1944 to replace troops lost in the German-Soviet war and in the Normandy campaign. The term was a morale-building honorific given to low-grade infantry divisions raised or reconstituted in the last months of the war. These were formed of rear echelon units or from remnants of other troops decimated in battle. There were about fifty Volksgrenadier divisions, but each was only about half the strength of a regular division. They had few heavy supporting arms and little mobility, and their training was reduced to six or eight weeks.

Volksschädling. Literally "harmful to the people" or "enemy of the German people." In Nazi Germany this was a term used for persons who voiced criticism of the Nazi regime. The concept was also employed for "misfits" who in the eyes of the Nazis "harmed the public welfare" and "threatened society." Initially a label used mainly for Germans, later it was also employed to characterize Poles. A person so labeled could be sentenced to the most severe punishment, in many cases imprisonment in a concentration camp or even the death penalty. There were basically three types of "enemies of the German people." Firstly, there were ideological enemies who propagated or held beliefs and values regarded as hostile to the Nazis. Secondly, there were the so-called asocials, whose behavior went against the social norms of the Nazi national community. And thirdly, there were the biological outsiders, those regarded as a threat because of their non-Aryan race or because they suffered from a hereditary defect or sickness. See Asoziale, Gemeinschaftsfremde, and Jude.

Volkssturm or **Deutscher Volkssturm.** Home defense units created in September 1944. The idea originated from plans made by General Heusinger

Volkssturm conscript with Panzerfaust.

of the OKH to raise a territorial army. The plan was first put in action in summer 1944 by Gauleiter Koch, who raised all able men to form a small army called Ostpreussen Volksturm, which fought with some success in Goldap and Gumbinen. Pushed by Goebbels, who saw a possible propaganda exploitation, Hitler decided to develop the Volkssturm on national scale. All able-bodied men between 16 and 60 years of age were drafted for the defense of the Heimat (fatherland) in four waves of men born between 1884 and 1928 to make a planned strength of 6 million. Authority over the Volkssturm was mixed. It was equipped and armed by Himmler's SS but it was recruited, organized, politically led and commanded by the Nazi Party (NSDAP) under Martin Bormann's authority; the Volkssturm was actually Bormann's private army and escaped Himmler's control. The members of the Volkssturm were poorly trained and not issued regular uniforms, but they used a great variety of articles available, such as army, party and paramilitary equipment. The only standard identifiable item was an armband indicating "Deutscher Volkssturm Wehrmacht." Weapons, ammunition and equipment, too, consisted of whatever could be found in army stores. It goes without saying that the Volkssturm represented an ill-prepared, poorly armed, heterogeneous body composed of old men, civilians and young boys, none of them bloodthirsty. The Volkssturm showed Hitler's determination to fight to the last man; it was the expression of complete despair, the Götterdämmerung (q.v.), the total collapse of the Third Reich, and the death of the entire German people. Hitler considered that if Germany lost the war, that meant that the nation had not stood the test of strength and in that case Germany deserved to be destroyed and doomed. The Volkssturm was deployed at the front line in 1945. The total number of casualties has never been precisely known. About 175,000 were listed as missing in action after the war.

Volkssturm Gewehr. A cheap submachine gun designed by the Gustloffwerke Suhl Company in late 1944. It fired the 7.92-millimeter short cartridge and was easily put together by nonspecialist factories from nonessential materials. Only a few Volkssturm submachine guns were ever made and none were issued to the front-line troops.

Volkswagen (VW). "People's car," a cheap popular car designed in 1936 by engineer Ferdinand Porsche. It was promised to be part of each German home according to Nazi social propaganda. Because rearmament and war production were industrial priorities, the project came to naught, but there was a military version. Reactivated and denazified after World War II, Volkswagen became a major German car company. It notably designed the popular "Beetle," an immense commercial success in the 1960s and 1970s. See Kraft durch Freude and Kübelwagen.

Volkswagen.

VoMi. See Hauptamt Volksdeutsche Mittelstelle.

Vorpostenboot. Civilian ship transformed into scout or patrol unit.

W2. Code name for a headquarters built for Hitler between Soissons and Laon in northern France. The decision to build the huge underground concrete shelter was ordered by Hitler in spring 1944, as the Führer wanted to be able to personally conduct the expected military operations in case of an Allied landing in France. Headquarters W2—built by the Organisation Todt (q.v.)—cost millions of marks, mobilized hundreds of workers, and consumed large quantities of concrete and hundreds of miles of telephone cable. The expensive installations of W2 were visited only once by Hitler, on June 17, 1944. The bunker was never used. Hitler found the installation unsafe as it was within range of Allied airplanes and allegedly in the heart of a partisan-ridden zone.

Wachdienst. Watch or Surveillance Service, intended for home protection, composed of elderly men. This service should not be confused with the military Volkssturm (q.v.).

Wachenfels. Hitler's house in Berchtesgaden. See Berghof.

Wachmannschaft. Early SS guard units in concentration camps, eventually increased in number and renamed SS-Totenkopfverbände (q.v.).

Wachverbände. SS guards in the concentration camps. See SS-Totenkopfverbände.

Waffenfähig. Capable of bearing arms, able bodied, good for military service.

Waffenfarbe. Colored piping indicating branch of service. Introduced in the German army in September 1915 and continued to be used in the Reichsheer (see Heer), later in the Wehrmacht and Waffen-SS. The main World War II German Waffenfarben were as follows: infantry, white; armored troops, pink; cavalry, golden yellow; reconnaissance units, copper brown; artillery, bright red; general staff officers, carmine red; signal, lemon yellow/light brown; administration, dark green; engineers, black; panzer grenadiers, apple green; mechanized supply troops, light blue; mountain troops, light green; medical corps, cornflower dark blue; recruiting officers, orange; veterinary officers, crimson; propaganda, light gray, and chaplains, violet.

Waffenrock. Uniform tunic.

Waffen-SS. Combat units part of the Schutz-Staffeln (q.v.); the armed branch of the SS, organized in 1935 by Reichsführer SS Heinrich Himmler (q.v.). The military SS, called Verfügungstruppen (SS-VT, reserve or task troops) appeared in the form of a personal Stabswache (bodyguard squad), then a ceremonial regiment for the Führer, the Leibstandarte Adolf Hitler commanded by Josef "Sepp" Dietrich. The Leibstandarte, formed in September 1933, grew to a

Waffen-SS cuff titles. *Top:* First SS-Panzerdivision Leibstandarte Adolf Hitler. *Bottom:* SS-VT Regiment 1 "Deutschland," part of the 2nd SS Panzerdivision Das Reich.

Waffen-SS soldier.

Fez worn by Muslim soldiers of the 13th Waffen-Gebirsdivision der SS "Handschar."

brigade and finally became a motorized division. Himmler was determined that the SS military branch should become the nucleus of a postwar German national police and army service. In 1939, three new SS regiments were created, Deutschland, Germania and Der Führer, in addition to the elite Leibstandarte Adolf Hitler. In July 1940, the Verfügungstruppen were renamed Waffen-SS. Owing to potentialities and the action of the Allgemeine SS, exploiting the law arbitrarily to suit himself, Himmler could swell his army. He recruited Germanic foreigners and found ways and funds to equip his force, notably by ruthlessly confiscating Jewish property. Although the regular Heer watched the SS with dislike and distrust and although the generals tried to obstruct him, Reichsführer SS Himmler managed to assemble a formidable force, which had grown to thirty-eighty divisions by the end of the war. After 1940, the Waffen-SS was opened to Volksdeutsche ("racial" Germans from northern European Germanic lands considered as people of "similar blood"), and in 1942 "non-pure" volunteers from southern and eastern Europe were also welcome. The Waffen-SS was virtually a private army with its own staff. It was organized separately from the regular Heer and had its own badges of rank and emblems. The most noteworthy were the Siegrunen (double SS lightning bolts), the Totenkopf (Death's Head) and the Hoheitabzeichen (national eagle/swastika emblem), which was worn on the left arm instead of on the right breast pocket as in the army. During the war, all individual and collective weapons as well as personal equipment issued to the Waffen-SS were the same as the army's, but Waffen-SS troopers were the first military units to be issued with camouflage clothing as a group. The Waffen-SS built up a reputation as hard fighting soldiers, but they were not ordinary combatants. They were not an ordinary corps or — as has been often suggested — merely a fourth service of the Wehrmacht. They were, on the whole, ultra–Nazis, fanatical SS who committed numerous atrocities and war crimes, both on and off the battlefield. The Waffen-SS was therefore declared a criminal organization at the Nürnberg trials in 1946. See Britisches Freikorps; Eicke, Theodor; Freie Indien; Hilfsgemeinschaft auf Gegenseittigkeit; Höhere SS- und Polizeiführer; Legion, Leibstandarte SS Adolf Hitler; ODESSA; SS-Führungs Hauptamt; Skorzeny, Otto; and Tarnjack.

Waffen-SS Feldgendarmerie. Field military police of the Waffen-SS, recruited among former civil policemen or experienced combat noncommissioned officers with four years' service. Every Waffen-SS division had a military field police unit composed of one Kompanie divided into three Züge (platoons). The military policemen were mobile and equipped with motorcycles with sidecars, trucks, buses and small cars of the Kübelwagen type (a sort of jeep). They controlled traffic, maintained military order, collected and escorted prisoners, checked papers of soldiers on leave, apprehended deserters, and provided street patrols, just to mention a few of their numerous tasks. Their most typical feature was the Ringkragen, a duty gorget similar to that worn by the Feldgendarmerie des Heeres (q.v.).

Wagner, Richard (1813–1883). A German composer, conductor, theater director and polemicist primarily known for his grandiose operas. Wagner was also an anti–Semite who attacked in his writings Jewish contemporaries (and rivals) Felix Mendelssohn and Giacomo Meyerbeer, and accused Jews of being a harmful and alien element in German culture. Adolf Hitler was an admirer of Wagner's music and saw in his operas an embodiment of his own vision of the German nation. There continues to be debate about the extent to which Wagner's views might have influenced Nazi thinking. In fact, the Nazis used those parts of Wagner's thought that were useful for propaganda and ignored or suppressed the rest. Because of the associations of Wagner with anti–Semitism and Nazism, the performance of his music has been a source of controversy, notably in Israel.

Wagner, Winifred (1897–1980) née Williams. The daughter-in-law of Richard Wagner (q.v.), and the widow of the composer's son Siegfried, she was a special friend of Adolf Hitler.

Walther P 38. German pistol. The Walther P 38 was the standard-issue pistol. Modern, cheap and easy to manufacture, the P 38 had eight rounds in a magazine contained in the grip, it weighed 0.96 kilograms and was robust, reliable and accurate. It was an immensely successful design widely issued to officers and troops, and a popular trophy among Allied soldiers.

Wandervögel. Birds of Passage. A youth movement that began in 1896 in a suburb of Berlin consisting of youth-led nature hikes and excursions. Its blend of romantic anti-capitalism and patriotism provided fertile ground in which early Nazi concepts could grow. See Hitler Jugend.

Wannsee-Konferenz. The Wannsee Conference was a meeting of senior officials of the Nazi regime, held in a villa in the Berlin suburb of Wannsee on January 20, 1942. The purpose of the conference was to inform administrative leaders of departments responsible for various policies relating to Jews, that Reinhard Heydrich had been appointed chief executor of the Endlösung der Judenfrage (q.v.), the infamous "Final solution to the Jewish question," which ordered the physical extermination of the European Jewish community. The high-ranking representatives of the SS, the Nationalsozialistische Deutsche Arbeiterpartei and various ministries also discussed their cooperation in the planned genocide. Today the Wannsee House, where the conference was held, is a Holocaust memorial and a historical document center.

Warschauer Getto. Ghetto of Warsaw. Following the German invasion of Poland in September 1939, Nazi German officials ordered all Jewish residents of Warsaw to move into a designated area, which German authorities sealed off from the rest of the city in November 1940. The population of the ghetto, increased by Jews compelled to move in from nearby towns, was estimated to be over 400,000 Jews. German authorities forced ghetto residents to live in overcrowded conditions in an area of 1.3 square miles, with an average of 7.2 persons per room. The population suffered severely from starvation, exposure, and infectious disease. Between 1940 and mid–1942, 83,000 Jews died of starvation and disease. From July 22 until September 12, 1942, German SS and police units, assisted by auxiliaries, carried out mass deportations from the Warsaw ghetto to the Treblinka (q.v.) killing center. In January 1943, SS and police units deported thousands of the remaining approximately 70,000–80,000 Jews in the ghetto to forced-labor camps for Jews in Lublin District of the Government General. This time, however, many of the Jews, understandably believing that the SS and police would deport them to Treblinka, resisted deportation, some of them using small arms smuggled into the ghetto. After seizing approximately 5,000 Jews, the SS and police units halted the operation and withdrew. On April 19, 1943, a new SS and police force appeared outside the ghetto walls, intending to liquidate the ghetto and deport the remaining inhabitants to the forced labor camps in Lublin. The ghetto inhabitants offered organized resistance in the first days of the operation, inflicting casualties on the well-armed and -equipped SS and police units. They continued to resist deportation as individuals or in small groups for four weeks before the Germans suppressed all opposition on May 16. The SS and police deported approximately 42,000 Warsaw ghetto survivors captured during the uprising to the forced-labor camps at Poniatowa and Trawniki and to the Lublin/Maidanek concentration camp. At least 7,000 Jews died fighting or in hiding in the ghetto, while the SS and police sent another 7,000 to Treblinka.

Warthegau. The name of western Poland after annexation by Nazi Germany in 1939.

Wassermann. Aquarius, code name of radar Funkmeßgerät FUMG 402. Wassermann, designed and produced by the Siemens company, was an early warning device ranging about 200 kilometers. It was composed of a strong 40-meters-high mast supporting a flat, vertical, rectangular metal aerial; this framework was 30 to 37 meters high and 13.50 to 21 meters broad. The mast and thus the aerial could fully rotate, giving a complete 360-degree angle of action. Wassermann was placed in special bunkers sheltering equipment and servants.

Wassermann radar FuMG 402.

Wasserpanzergraben. Antitank ditch filled with water. See Panzergraben.

Wasserversorgungstand (WvSt). Water-supply shelter, generally a bunker housing a well or a cistern with various installations such as pump and filter.

Wehrkraftzersetzung. A decree regarding subversion of the war effort. This anti-sedition decree, issued in 1938 in preparation for the coming war, specified the death penalty for persons who attempted to persuade military personnel to refuse to obey orders, or anyone who tried to undermine the war effort. The Wehrkraftzersetzung decree led to the creation of military courts. In 1943 there were some 1,000 military courts with 3,000 military lawyers. For civilians there was the Verordnung gegen Volksschädlinge (Decree against Enemies of the People), issued in

September 1939, that served the same purpose. Statistics reveal that a total of 21,000 persons were tried and executed up to May 1945.

Wehrmacht. Defense forces, regrouping all three German armed forces, composed of Heer (ground army), Kriegsmarine (navy) and Luftwaffe (air force). The "Wehrmacht" replaced the Reichswehr (q.v.), the reduced German post–World War I army. The term Wehrmacht was sometimes wrongly applied only to the ground force (Heer). The Wehrmacht was placed under command of the OKW, Oberkommando der Wehrmacht (q.v.).

Wehrmacht-Einheitskanister. A robust standard fuel container also called Benzinekanne (q.v.), and nicknamed a "Jerry can" by the Allies.

Wehrmachtsgefolge. Armed Forces Auxiliaries. These included several organizations that were not a part of the armed forces but which served such an important support role that they were given protection under the Geneva Convention and/or militarized. The armed forces auxiliaries consisted in part of the Reichsarbeitsdienst (q.v.), Nationalsozialistisches Kraftfahrer-Korps (q.v.), Organisation Todt (q.v.), and Volkssturm (q.v.).

Weimar Republic. The period in German history between 1919 and 1933 when the government was a democratic republic governed by a constitution that was laid out in the German city of Weimar. Technically, the Weimar Constitution lasted until 1945, when the German government was formally dissolved in the wake of World War II, but most people date the end of the Weimar Republic to January 1933, when Adolf Hitler took control and the constitution became effectively meaningless under his dictatorial regime. Under the Weimar Constitution, Germany was divided into 19 states (the largest being Prussia and Bavaria). All citizens (including women) had the right to vote, electing members of the Reichstag (q.v.), or German Parliament, along with the president. The president in turn appointed a chancellor and an assortment of cabinet members. As many historians have noted, on paper, the Weimar Constitution was a brilliant document, and Germany under the Weimar Republic was a true democracy. However, even from the start, the Weimar Republic was deeply troubled. When the constitution was first established, many Germans were highly suspicious of the new government, and extremists on both the left and the right rejected its authority and undermined its effectiveness. While the government was theoretically a coalition comprising numerous political parties, it was beset on all sides, making it difficult to assert its authority. Hitler rejected the Weimar Republic because he associated it with the malign forces of the Jewish-bolshevik conspiracy, and blamed it for having accepted the armistice and the hated Treaty of Versailles. He also attributed to it—quite unfairly—the responsibility for the chaotic, inflation-ridden condition of post–World War I Germany. Hitler rejected equality and democracy in principle, which according to him inevitably led to the rule of the mediocre, weak and inferior. See Führerprinzip.

Weisse Rose. White Rose. Name given to a nonviolent, intellectual resistance group in Nazi Germany consisting of students from the University of Munich (notably Hans and Sophie Scholl and their friend Christoph Probst) and their philosophy professor, Dr. Kurt Huber. The group, motivated by ethical and moral considerations, became known for an anonymous leaflet campaign, lasting from June 1942 until February 1943, that called for renewal of German noble spirit and thus active opposition to Hitler's regime. The six core members of the group were arrested by the Gestapo, hastily tried, and executed by decapitation in February 1943.

Weltanschauung. View of the world, attitude toward life in general, a comprehensive view or personal philosophy of human life and the universe. One of Hitler's favorite terms, which included the belief that Jews should be eliminated, and that European countries were merely pawns for him to use in his game of world dominion.

Weltanschauungskrieg. Ideological war. War was the focus and natural extension of the violent Nazi system. War was not only Hitler's main and ultimate goal, it was also the centerpiece of the reconstruction of German society and the German state on the basis of conquest, subjugation, domination, and annihilation of others. See Krieg.

"Wenn ich 'Kultur' höre, entsichere ich meinen Browning." "When I hear the word 'culture,' I release the safety catch of my Browning." A famous line composed by the writer Hanns Johst in his play *Schlageter* in April 1933. The line, subsequently adopted by so many Nazi Kulturkampfers as "When I hear the word 'culture,' I reach for my gun," was regularly misattributed, sometimes to Hermann Göring (q.v.) sometimes to Heinrich Himmler (q.v.).

"Wer Juden ist, bestimme ich." "I decide who is or is not a Jew." Statement attributed to Hermann Göring (q.v.) who on certain occasion appointed "non–Aryan" officers to Luftwaffe senior posts.

"We're A-gonna hang out the washing on the Siegfried Line." A popular British Sitzkrieg (q.v.) song during the winter of 1939–1940. Composed by Jimmy Kennedy and Michel Carr, the song illustrated the boring days of the Phony War.

Werkfeuerwehren. Auxiliary part-time firefighting groups formed by the management of individual factories and manned by employees of the company.

Werkluftschutz Dienst. Factory Air Protection Service. As the Allies increased their air attacks upon Germany, each important industrial site developed such a service composed of squads of firewatchers, firefighters, decontamination men, and first aid helpers. The squads were drawn from staff and employees, and members were also responsible for providing instructions and precautions and running air raid shelters for the personnel. The Werkluftschutzdienst also included squads of Werkschutzpolizei (Factory Air Protection Police), who were lightly armed men privately employed by industrial concerns to act as factory overseers, guards and watchmen. It must be remembered that the German industry employed not only German workers but also many foreign volunteers and many more foreign forced laborers and prisoners. Members of the Factory Air Protection Police were to see that forced laborers were kept working, disciplined, obedient and subdued.

Werwolf. Werewolf. When Germany was on the verge of defeat in the closing days of World War II, a number of fanatical SS and Hitler Youth members were to enlist in the so-called werewolf scheme. They would form fanatical guerrilla units who would put up last-ditch armed resistance to the Allies in all parts of Germany, notably in the Alps. Their intention was to engage in combat (using sniping, arson, sabotage and assassination) behind the Allied lines. The German propaganda ministry issued crude pamphlets threatening revenge on those who refused to support them. At the time of surrender, the leader of the organization was SS-Obergruppenführer Hans Prützmann. In early 1945, the threat was taken seriously by the Allied forces. However, the Werwolf group, which totaled a maximum of 200 members drawn from the Hitler Jugend (q.v.), never became an effective fighting force, as Hitler's successor, Admiral Karl Dönitz (q.v.), ordered all members of the organization to cease operations and disband. Thus no such resistance ever appeared, and the Werwölfen proved to be merely another creation of Goebbels's propaganda machine. See Alpenfestung.

Wessel, Horst. See "Horst Wessel Lied."

Westwall (WW). West wall, a fortification system established on Germany's western border, called by the Allies the Siegfried Line. The Westwall, lasting from 1937 to 1939, was about 630 kilometers long. It extended from the north near the border with the Netherlands, then followed the borders with Belgium and Luxembourg. It faced the French Maginot Line along Lorraine and Alsace and ended up in the south at the border with Switzerland. Bunkers and military installations were designed by the German army engineer corps directed by General Otto-Wilhelm Förster and the construction was entrusted to the Organisation Todt (q.v.). The Westwall was designed to provide protection to the regular German infantry, to repulse any attack from the west and to serve as a base for a direct counteroffensive. It was composed of bunkers, field fortification (trenches, MG and mortar nests, barbed wire) obstacles, and minefields. After the conquest of Western Europe in mid–1940, the Siegfried line was redundant. In mid–1944, however, the retreating Germans rearmed the Westwall. In winter 1944–45, the line was attacked and outflanked, and could not stop the Allies' progression.

Wewelsburg. Medieval castle situated near Paderborn in Westphalia. Himmler considered the SS as an order and a rebirth of the Teutonic knights' spirit based on honor, obedience, bravery and virility. For his SS "knights," the Reichsführer had restored the fortress of Wewelsburg and several other medieval castles were turned

Wewelsburg

into SS sanctuaries and study centers, such the Teutonic fortress Marienburg near Gdansk in Poland, built between 1309 and 1344. Medieval knighthood, ancestor worship, German Aryan superiority, racism, belief in immortality and the "blood and soil" myth were elements of Himmler's confused Nazi faith glorifying the messiah and savior Adolf Hitler.

Wewelsburg Konferenz. A meeting of senior SS officers held in early 1941 in the Wewelburg castle. During the conference Himmler made preparations for the invasion of the Soviet Union, and gave orders for the murder of 300 million Russian Slavs.

Widerstandsnest (W or WN). Army resistance nest. A small fortified post armed with light infantry weapons placed in field fortifications, excavations reinforced by sandbags, earth entrenchments, temporary troop shelters and facilities which were linked together by trenches. Elements were camouflaged and defended by barbed wires and mines. Sometimes, in the Atlantikwall (q.v.), for example, WNs were given a permanent character: firepower was increased, bunkers, trenches and shelters were made of concrete, and the position was further defended by barbed wire, antitank ditches and minefields. See Stützpunkt.

Wiederwehrhaftmachung. Military preparedness. A Nazi concept according to which war was the goal of a process of social reconstruction with racial purification and domination of the Germans over "inferior races." See Krieg and Weltanschauungskrieg.

Wiesenthal, Simon (1908–2005). Surviving four and a half years in German concentration camps such as Janowska, Plaszow, and Mauthausen during World War II, the Austrian Jewish Simon Wiesenthal dedicated the rest of his life to tracking down and gathering information on fugitive Nazis so that they could be brought to justice for war crimes and crimes against humanity. Simon Wiesenthal is buried in Herzliya, Israel. See also Klarsfeld.

Wilde Lager. Wild Camps. Makeshift prisons and improvised detention centers were hastily set up by the SA right after the seizure of power in January 1933, where untried suspects were illegally detained. The "wild camps" were closed down in late 1933 when the SS, under Theodor Eicke (q.v.), took over the construction, development and administration of the concentration camps for "enemies" of the Nazi regime.

Windjacke. Parka, wind jacket, usually worn by mountain troops. Pullovers were called Windbluse.

Windjacke.

Winkel. Embroidered or stitched chevron worn by noncommissioned officers on the upper left arm indicating rank.

Winterhilfswerk (WHW). Official German winter relief organization. This charity campaign, launched in the winter of 1933–1934, was organized on annual basis by the Nationalsozialistische Volkswohlfahrte (q.v.)—NSV, or Nazi People's Welfare Organization. The Winterhilfswerk was supported by members of the NSDAP, Hitler Jugend and DAF, as well as by prominent artists, functionaries, and sportsmen with the aim of collecting money, food, warm clothing and other items for the poorest Germans. The Jews and asocials were of course excluded from the organization's benefits. The WHW also worked with blackmail. The Nazis made lists of persons who despite financial ability refused to make donations to the organization, and signs called "Boards of Shame" were publicly shown and names were also published in the Nazi press. In 1937 helping the Winterhilfswerk was made compulsory; everybody had to pay a special winter tax (10 to 15 percent of salary) from October to March. During the war, the organization Kriegwinterhilfswerk continued the activities, and collected for Russian front soldiers, widows, and civilian victims and homeless due to the Allied air bombardments.

Winterwaffenrock. Winter suit. The Winterwaffenrock was first issued on the Russian front in winter 1942–43 as a result of the bitter experience of the previous winter. Designed specifically to combat the severe subzero weather conditions encountered on the eastern front, the smock and overtrousers were made of two thick layers of windproof and waterproof cloth with a woolen lining; the double-breasted smock was fitted with a detachable hood. The winter suit was generally worn over the regular field service uniform. Ammunition pouches, holsters and other items were carried on the normal belt under or over it. The suit had patch pockets and the trousers had side pockets. It was reversible, all white on one side and camouflaged on the other. Some fortunate units got white quilted winter parkas or warm sheepskin coats, fur-lined greatcoats with a fur collar, but these luxuries were always in short supply. See Schneeanzug.

"Wir fahren gegen England." "We Are Sailing against England," a popular German marching song. Sometimes called "das Englandlied" ("the England Song"). Also a German Third Reich wartime board game displaying a map of the North Sea with card set, dice, and plastic ships, which players had to sink.

Wirbelwind. Whirlwind. The Panzerflak IV Wirbelwind, introduced in December 1943, was a self-propelled antiaircraft gun similar to the Möbelwagen (chassis of a Panzerkampfwagen PzKfw IV armed with a Vierling 38 four-barreled 2-centimeter gun) but the fighting emplacement was improved by an open-top octagonal revolving turret designed to give better protection to the Vierling 38 and its gunners.

Wirtschaftliche Forschungs-Gesellschaft (WiFo). Economical study society, cover name of a predatory organization created by the Germans to acquire by all means old metal and scraps in occupied Europe.

Wirschaftlich wertvoller Jude (WWJ). Literally "economically useful Jew" thus a Jew, who was tolerated by the Germans as long as he was economically productive. Useful Jews, and sometimes members of their families as well, were immune from deportation for extermination so long as they served the Nazis' purposes and interests. A famous French WWJ was Joseph Joanovici (1905–1965), a Jew of Russian origin. He lived in Paris in the period 1940–1944 and supplied the Germans with various goods and metal scraps on an industrial scale.

Wirtschafts- und Verwaltungshauptamt (WVHA). Main Office for Economy and Administration. This important SS branch was headed by SS-Obergruppenführer Oswald Pohl (q.v.). It was in charge of all SS farming and agricultural undertakings, mining, forestry, construction programs, financial management, and

Winterwaffenrock lined with sheepskin.

industrial businesses into which in March 1942 the concentration and extermination camp system was also integrated. During the war, the Wirtschafts-und Verwaltungshauptamt became a huge and powerful economic, financial and industrial organization with wealth coming from regular businesses, but also from requisitions, confiscation, large-scale looting, black market, blackmail, swindles, thefts and exploitation of Jews and camp prisoners. The activities of the WVHA resulted in the death of all but a handful of the millions of people it controlled and exploited. The huge sums that flew into SS coffers strengthened and maintained the financial autonomy of Himmler's organization.

Wizernes. A deserted stone quarry located near Saint-Omer in northern France. Important works were carried out by the Organisation Todt (q.v.) at Wizernes to create a vast underground factory to assemble, store and launch V2 rockets. The subterranean structures—constructed at the edges of the 30-metre quarry face—were protected by a gigantic concrete one-million-ton dome 5 meters thick and 72 meters in diameter. Additional workshops, barracks, and rocket storage were excavated in the chalk from which two tunnels ran into the quarry. A railway was installed right through the hill to facilitate the handling of components. The impressive Wizernes installation was planned to fire fifty V2 missiles per day, which would have been a terrible threat to southern England, and predictably became one of Hitler's favorite schemes. Fortunately the site was never completed. Rapidly spotted, it was heavily bombarded from March 1944 onwards by the dropping of six-ton earthquake bombs. The site was made unreachable, and in July 1944, destruction was so complete that the Germans had to stop all activities there.

Wochenschau. See Deutsche Wochenschau.

Wohngebiet der Juden. Jewish district. See Ghetto.

Wolfsangel. Rune letter used as insignia by members of Germanic SS in the Netherlands, and by the Werwolf (q.v.).

Wolfsschanze. Wolf's Sconce, always but incorrectly translated as "Wolf's Lair" in English. Code name for Hitler's headquarters near Rastenburg, East Prussia (now Ketrzyn, Poland).

Wolfsangel.

Wunderwaffen. Miracle weapons designed at the end of World War II which were intended to turn the outcome of the war in favor of Germany. See Pfeifenkopf, V1, V2, V3, Vergeltungswaffe, and Wizernes.

Wunschkonzert. Popular music concerts broadcast and introduced by Heinz Goedecke during World War II. The concerts were selected by radio listeners and dedicated to relatives and parents, and also to soldiers at the front with personal messages. These programs that united front and homeland were intended to boost the morale of both civilians and soldiers.

Wurfkörper (WK). Self-propelled bomb. The Würfkorper was an 80-kilogram self-propelled cylindrical bomb electrically launched from a metal framework to a range of about 2 kilometers. There were two main kinds: the 28-centimeter WK (Spr.) was high explosive; and the 32-centimeter WK (Fl.) was incendiary. They were placed in field batteries or fixed on the side of a halftrack vehicle for mobility and organized in Werferbrigade. See also Nebelwerfer.

Würzburg. German radar. Würzburg (officially designated FUMG 39) was a close range precision device detecting up to 40 kilometers. Two types were developed, C and D. Type Würzburg C was mobile, and installed on a four-wheeled trailer. To be put in action, the device was rolled to an open concrete pit, wheels were removed, and the radar was set up on screwjacks. Type C was generally sheltered in a garage-bunker when not in action. Würzburg type D was fixed and mounted on a rotating cabin quite similar to Freya (q.v.) and Würzburg-Riese (q.v.).

Würzburg-Riese. German radar. Würzburg-Riese radar (FUMG 65), designed and produced by the Telefunken company, ranged about 60 kilometers. The device rested on a concrete base fitted with a platform upon which a cabin could fully rotate. The cabin housed aiming, radio and calculating instruments served by a crew. Access to the cabin was by means of a ladder. The cabin was fitted with two strong orientable arms holding a parabolic round aerial with a 7.50-meter diameter. Close range radar Würzburg-Riese was particularly designed to direct fighters and to conduct flak fire. It was used by both the Luftwaffe and the Kriegsmarine, and about 1,500 specimens were built.

Würzburg-Riese radar.

Wüstenfuchs. Desert Fox. Nickname given to Erwin Rommel (q.v.).

Yellow star. See Judenstern.

Y-Gerät. "Y-device" or "Y-equipment"; radio navigation equipment used on German aircraft.

Yule. Winter solstice, December 21, shortest day of the year. This was an old Germanic pagan feast revived by the Nazis. The celebration took place around a big fir tree, symbolizing the life force in winter, promising rebirth. Poems were read, songs were sung, stories were told, candles were lit and dedicated to living or dead persons; the biggest candle was burned in honor of the Führer, Adolf Hitler.

Zählappelle. Roll call in barracks and concentration camps. The Zählappelle was intended to count the soldiers and prisoners, checking for desertion or evasion. In the Nazi concentration camps it was also a form of torture, held two or three times a day, in the camp main square and in work places in all weather. It lasted sometimes for hours, during which the weakened, underfed and poorly dressed inmates had to stand motionless in heat, wind or cold.

Zapfenstreich. Curfew. In Nazi occupied territories, at night, inhabitants had to close their shutters or windows and turn off any light. Without an Ausweiß (q.v.), people were forbidden to go out during the night. During the day, numerous regulations, interdictions, censorship and propaganda made the occupation increasingly unbearable.

Zehnerstaffeln. Groups of ten elite SS men created in 1925 in every district, intended to provide in each German city a small group of Nazis of proven toughness who would act in all circumstances out of total loyalty to Hitler and to protect him during his political campaigning. The volunteering Zehnerstaffeln were the forerunners of the non-permanent Allgemeine SS (q.v.). See Schutz-Staffeln.

Zellen. Cells. Subdivisions of the Nazi Party composed of several Blocken (q.v.). A Zelle (headed by a Zellenleiter) usually comprised a village or a neighborhood in a city.

Zerstörer. (See illustration on page 204.) Literally, "destroyer," name given to a number of ground attack aircraft, notably the twin engine Messerschmitt Bf 110, and also to self-propelled antitank guns.

Zimmerit

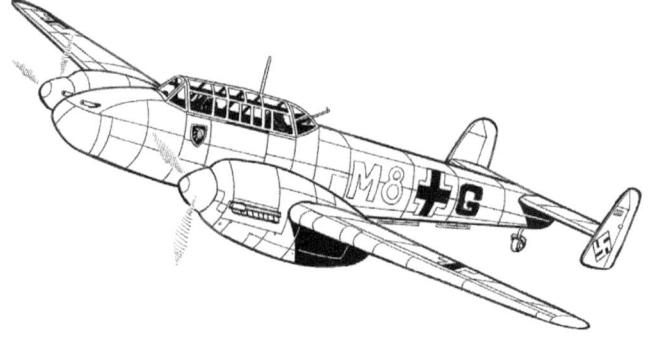

Zerstörer: Messerschmitt Bf 110.

Zimmerit. Zimmer paste. A light gray cement paste designed by the Chemische Werk Zimmer AG Company. It was a coating intended to counteract sticky explosive devices and magnetic mines being fixed to the armor of tanks, armored vehicles and self-propelled guns. Zimmerit possessed no antimagnetic properties of its own; rather it defeated the mines by disallowing contact and providing distance. Zimmerit was applied to vertical and near vertical surfaces but rarely to horizontal or upper surfaces, gun barrels or running gears. It was normally ridged to increase the overall thickness. This spacing reduced magnetic attraction and caused magnetic mines to fall off due to their own weight and the vibration of the vehicle.

Zitadelle. Code name for the attack on the Kursk salient on the eastern front. The Kursk offensive—from July 5 until August 23, 1943—was the greatest tank battle of World War II. It was a gigantic clash of armor vast in scale and terrible in intensity. The German attacks, aiming to regain the strategic initiative in Russia, were utterly shattered. After the defeat in Kursk, the Wehrmacht never recovered.

Zossen. Wehrmacht command headquarters situated near Berlin.

Zucca, Luisa Rita (1912–?) Italian-American radio announcer who broadcasted Axis propaganda to Allied troops in Italy and North Africa. She became known as one of the "Axis Sallys," along with Mildred Gillars (q.v.), who broadcasted out of Berlin, Germany. After the war Rita Zucca was sentenced to four and a half years' imprisonment, but was released after nine months. Barred from returning to the United States, she lived in obscurity in Italy for the rest of her life.

Zug. Army infantry company consisting of three Gruppen (squads) totaling about thirty soldiers.

Zugkraftwagen (ZkW). Tractor, generally intended to tow artillery in the field. See Sonderkraftfahrzeuge.

Zugwache. Train guards; army troops assigned to police military trains and rail centers. The train guards were intended to maintain order and discipline, to escort trains used by High Command staff, and to protect convoys passing through territories which were unsafe because of partisan activities. They wore a duty Ringkragen (q.v.)—a gorget similar to that of the Bahnhofswache (railway guards) with a scroll bearing the legend "Zugwachabteilung." An armband with the same legend could be worn instead of the gorget.

Zur besonderen Verwendung or **zur besonderen Verfügung** (z.b.V.) Literally, "for special employment" or "for special mission." This term was used for retired officers who could be recalled in an emergency. The term was also employed for special units. For example, the Baulehr-Batallion z.b.V. 800 was subordinated to the Abwehr for special sabotage and secret operations.

Zur Verfügung (z.V.) Literally, "at disposal" or "available for duty." This term was used for active reserve officers with no current assignment but who were immediately available for duty. It was also used for certain units. For example, the SS had z.V. troops called SS-Verfügungstruppen. See Waffen-SS.

Zwangsarbeiter. Forced/slave laborer.

Zwanzig Juli 1944. July 20, 1944. On that day a cadre of German military officers launched an assassination plot against Adolf Hitler. The conspirators, led by Graf Claus Schenk von Stauffenberg (q.v.), planned to kill Hitler at his East Prussian headquarters known as Wolf's Lair. The plot, known as the "July Plot," revolved around a plan to assassinate Hitler with a briefcase bomb planted near the Führer. According to various accounts, Stauffenberg either placed the bomb too close to a table support or it was accidentally moved by a member of Hitler's staff.

Von Stauffenberg armed the bomb and then left the room. At 12:42 P.M. the bomb exploded, and Stauffenberg left the compound thinking Hitler had been killed. Though three persons were killed by the bomb, Hitler escaped with only minor injuries. Probably an oak table shielded Hitler, but the dictator believed his survival was a token of good luck and a sign of his infallibility. Less than twelve hours later, von Stauffenberg was executed by firing squad. Three other conspirators faced the same fate. The failed assassination was followed by a ruthless purge, and many conspirators and suspects were arrested and executed.

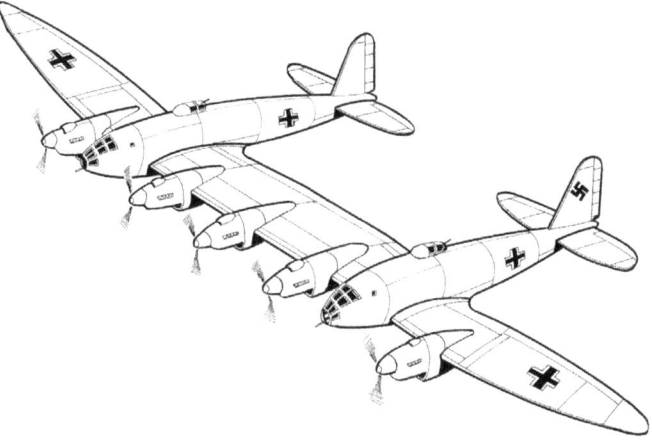

Zwilling: The Heinkel He 111 Z was composed of two He 111s and was intended to tow heavy gliders.

Zweites Buch. See *Mein Kampf*.

Zwilling. Twin. Used for artillery but also for aircraft.

Zwillingslafette. Twin mount, composed of two machine guns or two guns, generally placed on a vehicle or in a fire emplacement, usually for an antiaircraft role.

Zwischenwiderstandsnest (ZWN). Interval fortified position. ZWNs were created at the beginning of 1944 in the Atlantikwall (q.v.), between existing positions to fill gaps in the defense, to increase firepower and improve mutual flanking. See Stützpunkt and Widerstandsnest.

Zyklon-B. Trade name of a hydrogen cyanide–based pesticide (prussic acid, Blausäure in German, hence B) infamous for its use by the Nazis to murder people in gas chambers of extermination camps during the Holocaust (q.v.). Breathing the dust of these crystals made them dissolve in the moisture of the mouth, nose, throat and stomach, which hydrolyzed the cyanide into hydrocyanic acid and resulted in death by paralysis of the respiratory muscles. See Gaskammer and Vernichtungslager.

CHRONOLOGY

1889
April 20: Birth of Adolf Hitler in Braunau am Inn, Austria

1918
November 9: The German emperor Wilhelm II abdicated after revolts and mutinies. Republic proclaimed by social democrat Philip Scheidemann and a new government installed
November 11: Armistice signed between Germany and the Allies, marking the end of World War I

1919
January 5: Founding of the Deutsche Arbeiterpartei (DAP)
January 11–15: Spartakist communist revolution crushed
February 6: Republic of Weimar instituted
May 2: Communist revolt in Munich smashed
June 28: Treaty of Versailles signed
September 10: Austro-Hungarian Empire broken up
September 1919: Hitler joins the German Workers' Party

1920
January 10: The Treaty of Versailles comes into effect
January 10: League of Nations created in Geneva
February 24: First meeting of NSDAP and publication of the Nazi program
March 12–17: Failed Kapp Putsch in Berlin
April 1: Hitler renames the German Workers' Party as the National Socialist German Workers' Party, or Nazi Party
August 7: Official creation of Nazi Party (NSDAP) by Hitler

1921
February 3: First Nazi mass meeting in Munich
July 29: Hitler made first chairman of the NSDAP
November 4: Creation of the SA
November 12–February 1922: Disarmament conference in Washington (U.S., Britain, Japan, France and Italy)

1922
March: Hitler proclaims the first Nazi Party youth group (future Hitler Jugend)
October 31: Fascist march on Rome, after which Mussolini came to power

1923
January 11: Ruhrgebiet occupied by France (until July 1925)
January 28: First Nazi Party day, held in Munich
July: Rampant inflation in Germany (U.S. $1 = 1 million marks)
November 8–9: Marsch auf die Feldherrnhalle Beer Hall Putsch unsuccessfully attempted by the Nazis at Munich
November 11: Hitler arrested

1924
February 24: Nazi Party forbidden, beginning of the trial of Hitler for treason
April 1: Hitler condemned to five years in prison; serves short sentence (from April 1924 to December 1924) during which he writes *Mein Kampf*
December 20: Hitler released from prison, relaunches Nazi Party

1925
February 26: Nazi Party reestablished and reactivated
April 27: Field marshal Paul von Hindenburg elected president of the Weimar Republic
July 18: Publication of Volume 1 of Hitler's book *Mein Kampf*
November 9: Creation of the Schutz-Staffeln (SS)
December 8: Official publication of *Mein Kampf*

Chronology

1926
July 3: Nazi Party day held in Weimar
September 8: Germany becomes member of the League of Nations
December 1: Goebbels appointed Gauleiter of Berlin

1927
March 10: Lifting of public speaking ban on Hitler
August 19–20: Nazi Party day

1929
January 6: Heinrich Himmler appointed head of the SS
April: The Hitler Youth declared the only official youth group of the Nazi Party
August 2: Nazi Party day held in Nuremberg with 150,000 participants
October 24: Collapse of the New York Stock Exchange resulting in American and world economic crisis

1930
June 30: Occupation of Germany by Allied troops ends
February 23: Death of Horst Wessel
September 2: Hitler becomes head of the SA
September 14: Nazi electoral breakthrough
October 30: Baldur von Schirach appointed Hitler Youth (Hitler Jugend) leader
December 31: SS Central Office for Race and Settlement (RuSHA) set up by Walther Darré

1931
July 13: Germany stops payment of World War I reparations
October 11: Conference of rightist political parties (including the NSDAP) against the Weimar Republic
October 16: Large SA demonstration in Brunswick

1932
January 27: Contact between Hitler and Rhineland industrialists in Düsseldorf
February 25: German citizenship granted to Hitler
March 13: Hitler's party receives 13.7 million votes
April 10: Hindenburg reelected president of the Weimar Republic
April 14: The SA, the Nazi Party and the Hitler Youth are temporarily banned by the Weimar government
June 16: Ban on the HJ, SA and SS lifted
July 31: Nazi success in election; win 230 out of 608 seats
December 6: Hermann Göring elected president of Reichstag

1933
January 4: Secret meeting between Hitler and von Papen
January 30: Machtergreifung, Hitler appointed chancellor of Germany
February 2: Nazi program exposed in the *Völkischer Beobachter*
February 27: Burning of the Reichstag
February 28: Nazi laws passed to "protect the German people and the State"
March 1: Official army support to the Nazis
March 9: Himmler made police chief of Munich
March 13: Goebbels made chief of propaganda
March 24: Hitler given full power by Enabling Act granted by the Reichstag
March 17: Creation of the SS Leibstandarte (Hitler's bodyguards unit)
March 21: Special courts established for the prosecution of political enemies
April 1: Nazi boycott of Jewish shops
April 21: Rudolf Hess made deputy Führer of the NSDAP
April 26: Formation of the Gestapo
May 2: Dissolution of the labor unions
May 10: Proscribed books burnt publicly throughout Germany
May 17: Right to strike removed in Germany
June: Baldur von Schirach named youth leader of the German Reich
July 14: Nazi Party declared only political formation allowed in Germany. Creation of the first concentration camps
July 20: Signing of concordat between Hitler and Pope Pius XI
October 14: Germany withdraws from the League of Nations

1934
January 30: Reorganization of the Reich
April 20: Himmler made chief of Prussian Gestapo
June 30: Night of the Long Knives: Ernst Röhm and main SA leaders liquidated
July 20: SS made independent from SA
July 25: Failed Nazi putsch to take power in Austria; chancellor Dollfuss killed
August 2: Death of Marshal Hindenburg; Hitler declares himself Reich Führer of the Third Reich. The Reichswehr (armed forces) required to swear an oath of loyalty to Hitler

1935
January 13: Saarland returned to Germany by plebiscite
March 16: Creation of the SS-Verfügungstruppen (later called Waffen-SS)
March 16: Reestablishment of military service in Germany and beginning of rearmament. Official creation of Luftwaffe
June 18: Naval pact between Britain and Germany
June 26: Creation of the Reichsarbeitsdienst (RAD National Work Service)
September 15: Nuremberg anti–Jewish laws passed in order to "protect the German blood and honor"
October 3: Italy invades Ethiopia

1936
March 7: The demilitarized Rhineland reoccupied by Hitler
March 29: The SS totals 3,500 members
June 17: Himmler appointed head of all German police services
July 18: Beginning of Spanish Civil War (lasts until March 1939), with German and Italian support for Franco. Franco will be dictator until November 20, 1975
August: Olympic Games in Berlin
September 9: Economic four-year-program launched, directed by Göring
October 25: Italo-German Axis Pact signed
October 25: Germany and Japan sign Antikomintern pact

1937
April 27: Guernica, Spain, bombed by German air force
May 28: Neville Chamberlain appointed British prime minister; will pursue a policy of appeasement of Hitler
November 5: Hoßbach conference, outlining Hitler's plans for European domination
November 6: Italy signs Antikomintern pact
December 11: Italy withdraws from the League of Nations

1938
February 2–4: Purge in German army; Generals Blomberg, von Fritsch and several others dismissed, Hitler becomes commander of the OKW (German armed forces supreme headquarters) with General Wilhelm Keitel appointed chief of High Command
February 12: Beginning of Austrian crisis
March 12 and 13: Anschluß—Austria annexed to the German Reich to form Großdeutschland (Great Germany)
April 24: Beginning of Sudetenland crisis
September 15, 22 and 24: British Prime Minister Neville Chamberlain and Hitler meet
September 29–30: Munich Agreement signed by France, Britain, Italy and Germany: Czechoslovakia broken up. Chamberlain declares "Peace for our time"
November 9–10: Kristallnacht (Night of Broken Glass or Crystal Night)—anti–Jewish violence and burning of shops, property and synagogues all through Germany
December 3: Nazi law passed for confiscation of Jewish property

1939
March 15: Bohemia-Moravia (Czecslovakian provinces) annexed by Germany as protectorate
March 23: Region of Memel occupied by German troops
March 25: Compulsory membership/conscription of all German boys aged 10 into the Hitler Youth
April 1: End of Spanish Civil War, Franco enters Madrid
April 7: Albania conquered by Italians
May 22: Italy and Germany sign military "Steel Pact"
August 22: After month of secret negotiations, signing of treaty of nonaggression between Germany and Soviet Union
September 1: Germany invades Poland
September 3: France and Britain declare war on Germany. Beginning of World War II
September 4: Australia, New Zealand, South Africa and Canada declare war on Germany
September 5: USA proclaims neutrality
September 17: Russian invasion of Poland
September 27–28: German occupation of Warsaw. Poland capitulates and is divided between USSR and Germany
October 7: Nazis began forcing Polish farmers off their land
November 8: Failed assassination attempt of Hitler in Munich
November 30: Beginning of the "Winter War" between Finland and Russia
December 17: German battleship *Graf Spee* sunk off Montevideo

1940
March 12: End of war between Finland and Russia
April 9: Operation Weserübung, German invasion of Denmark and Norway

Chronology

May 10: German invasion of the Netherlands. Beginning of the western campaign against Belgium and France. Winston Churchill appointed British prime minister
May 14: Destruction of Rotterdam by Luftwaffe
May 15: Netherlands capitulate
May 17: Brussel captured by Germans
May 28: Capitulation of Belgium
May 26–June 4: Evacuation of 336,427 British troops in Dunkirk (operation Dynamo)
June: War begins in Libya
June 10: Italy declares war on France and attacks Nice and Alps
June 14: Undefended Paris occupied by Germans
June 17: Surrender of France
June 18: General De Gaulle in London called for resistance
June 22: Signing of armistice between Germany and France in Compiègne
June 24: Signing of armistice between Italy and France in Rome
July 11: Marshall Philippe Pétain becomes chief of (Vichy) French State
July 3: French fleet destroyed by Britain at Mers-el-Kebir
August–October: Battle of Britain
September 13: British possession in Egypt attacked by Italians, repulsed in December
September 17: Invasion of Britain (Operation Sea Lion) postponed
September 27: Signing of military Axis pact between Germany, Italy and Japan
October: Italian attack repulsed in Greece
October 24: Meeting between Pétain and Hitler at Montoire

1941

January 22: Fall of Tobruk to the British
February 12: Arrival of General Rommel in North Africa
March 2: German invasion of Bulgaria
March 24: German offensive in North Africa
April 6: Beginning of war in the Balkans; German invasion of Yugoslavia and Greece
April 17: Capitulation of Yugoslavia
April 23: Capitulation of Greece
May 10: Rudolf Hess's flight to England to negotiate peace; Hess imprisoned and replaced as vice president of the NSDAP by Martin Bormann
May 20: German paratroopers attack Crete (Operation Merkur)
May 27: Sinking of the battleship *Bismarck* in the North Atlantic Ocean
June 1: Crete taken by German paratroopers (Fallschirmjäger)
June 22: German invasion of Soviet Union (Operation Barbarossa)
June 27: Finland enters war on German side
June 27: Hungary enters war on German side
July 20–25 August: Battle for Smolensk
August 24: Novgorod seized by Germans
September: SS Einsatzgruppen begin widespread murder
September 8–19: Kiev taken by Germans
October 24: Charkow taken by Germans
November 3: Kursk taken by Germans
November 18: British counteroffensive in northern Africa
December 5: Germans reach the outskirts of Moscow
December 7: Japanese attack on Pearl Harbor; U.S. entered the war
December 7: Germany and Italy declare war on U.S.
December 19: Hitler assumes command of the Wehrmacht

1942

January 20: Secret conference of Wannsee during which Nazis formalized plans for the Endlösing der Judenfrage (Final Solution of the Jewish question)
January 21–31: Rommel's success in North Africa
February 9: Albert Speer appointed minister of war industry to succeed Fritz Todt
February 8–May 1: German troops encircled in Demjansk
February 23: Russian counteroffensive begins in central front
March 21: Gauleiter Sauckel appointed head of the Arbeitseinsatz
April 20: German army allows the formation of foreign volunteer units
May 6–June 30: German troops encircled in Cholm
May 12: First record of mass murder with gas in Auschwitz
May 17–28: Battle for Charkow
May 29: Reinhard Heydrich assassinated
May 30–31: Massive RAF air raid on Cologne
July 22–October 3: Warsaw ghetto uprising repressed
August 19: Canadian landing in Dieppe repulsed
August 21: German troops reach Mount Elbruz (5633 meters) in the Caucasus
October 23: Beginning of Battle of El-Alamein (Operation Lightfoot)

October 25: German offensive to Stalingrad
November 5: Beginning of German/Italian retreat to Tunisia
November 7–8: Allied landing in North Africa (Operation Torch)
November 11: Germans occupy southern Vichy France and Corsica
November 19: Beginning of Russian counteroffensive on southwest front (Stalingrad)
December 28: German withdrawal from Caucasus

1943

January 14: Conference of Casablanca, demanding total unconditional German surrender
January 19: Russians recapture Leningrad
January 30: Ernst Kaltenbrunnen made chief of SD and RSHA
January 31–February 2: Von Paulus's Sixth Army surrenders at Stalingrad
February 18: "Total War" proclaimed by Goebbels
March 13: Failed attempt to kill Hitler by von Tresckow in Smolensk
March 21: Failed attempt to kill Hitler in Berlin
March 25: Around-the-clock air attacks on Germany begin
April 8: Russian offensive in Crimea
April 19–May 16: Second revolt of the Jews in the Warsaw ghetto
May 7–11: Axis forces in northern Africa surrender
June 12: Soviet summer offensive in Orel begins
July 4–August 23: Battles for Kursk (Operation Zitadelle)
July 10–August 17: Allied landing in and battle for Sicily
July 25: Mussolini arrested and made destitute; replaced by General Pietro Badaglio
August 11–23: Battle of Kharkov
August 24: German withdrawal from Smolensk
August 25: Himmler appointed minister of the interior "to combat defeatism"
September 3: Allied landing in southern Italy
September 8: Unconditional surrender of Italy
September 9: Allied landing in Salerno
September 12: Mussolini, imprisoned at Gran Sasso in the Abruz, rescued by German paratrooper commando
September 15: Mussolini creates the Fascist puppet republic of Salo in northern Italy
October 13: Italy joins the Allies against Germany
November 6: Kiev recaptured by the Russians
November 28–December 1: Stalin, Roosevelt and Churchill meet in Tehran
December 22: Hitler orders the presence of Nationalsozialistische Führungsoffiziere in the army
December 24: General Eisenhower made supreme commander of the Allied forces
December 24: Beginning of Soviet winter offensive
December 26: German battleship *Scharnhorst* sunk off North Cape

1944

January 3: Soviet troops reach former Polish border
January 12- May 18: Battles for Monte Cassino
January 19: Twenty-nine-month siege of Leningrad relieved
January 22: Allied landing in Anzio en Nettuno, Italy
February 1: Russian forces reach Narwa
February 4–7: Battle on the Dnieper
March 4: Soviet spring offensives begin
May 9: Sevastopol retaken by Soviets
June 4: Rome liberated by U.S. forces
June 6: Allied landing in Normandy (D-Day, Operation Overlord)
June–August: Battle of Normandy
June 12: First V1 launched onto London
July 13: Beginning of Russian offensive in Ukraine
July 20: Failed attempt to kill Hitler at Rastenburg by Graf Claus Schenk von Stauffenberg. Himmler appointed head of reserve army
July 25: Allied breakthrough in Avranches (Operation Cobra)
July 28: Brest-Litowsk retaken by Russians
August 1–September 16: Warsaw uprising in Poland
August 7–8: trial against the plotters of July 20, 1944
August 15: Allied landing in southern France (Operation Dragoon)
August 16–19: German forces encircled in Falaise
August 25: Paris liberated. Romania declares war on Germany
August 26: German withdrawal from Greece
September 3: Brussels liberated
September 8: First V2 bombs fall on London
September 11: First Allied troops reach the border of the Reich
September 17–27: German forces repulse Allied attack (Operation Market Garden) in Arnhem, Netherlands
September 25: Hitler creates the Volkssturm to defend Germany to the bitter end
October–November: Belgrade and Budapest

taken by Russians; German withdrawal from Greece and Balkans
October 5: German troops encircled in Kurland
October 10: Russian troops reach East Prussia
October 14: Suicide of Rommel
November 21: German withdrawal from Finland
December 3: Allies reach the industrial Ruhr region
December 8: Bulgaria declares war on Germany
December 16: German counteroffensive in the Ardennes (known as "Herbstnebel," Autumn Fog, or Battle of the Bulge)

1945

January 12: Russian offensives in East Prussia
January 14: Beginning of Russian offensives in northern front
January 17: Warsaw taken by Russians
January 18: Krakow and Lodz taken by Russians
February 4–11: Allied conference at Yalta
February 7: Ardennes offensive halted
February 19: Himmler's contact with Count Bernadotte of Sweden
March 7: The western Allies conquer Cologne and cross the Rhine at Remagen
March 11: The western Allies take Coblence
March 19: Hitler orders the Nerobefehl, the total destruction of all military, industrial and economic installations in Germany
April 1: The western Allies reduced the Ruhr pocket
April 11: The western Allies reach the river Elbe; Germany collapses on all fronts
April 16: Beginning of the Battle of Berlin
April 21: Collapse of German resistance in Italy
April 20: Hitler's 56th birthday
April 25: Western Allies and Soviet forces meet in Torgau
April 28: Mussolini, his mistress and several senior Fascists executed by Italian partisans near Lake Como
April 29: Marriage of Hitler and his mistress Eva Braun
April 30: Suicide of Hitler and Goebbels in the Berlin Führer bunker

May 1: Admiral Karl Dönitz appointed head of German state
May 2: Surrender of the last defenders of Berlin to Soviet troops
May 7: Unconditional surrender of German armed forces signed by General Alfred Jodl at Reims. End of World War II in Europe. Germany occupied and divided in four sectors (U.S., Great Britain, France and Soviet Union).
May 8: Amsterdam liberated
May 9: Göring arrested
May 23: Suicide of Himmler
July 16: First atom bomb test at Los Alamos, New Mexico
August 2: Allied conference in Potsdam
August 6: Atom bomb dropped on Hiroshima
August 8: Soviet Russia declares war on Japan
August 9: Atom bomb dropped on Nagasaki
September 2: Capitulation of Japan signed on the U.S. warship *Missouri*. End of World War II
November 20: Opening of the Nuremberg International Military Tribunal

1946

October 1: End of the Nuremberg trials
October 16: Execution of Nazi criminals at Nuremberg

1949

May: Partition of Germany. In the west, the Federal Republic of Germany (BRD) is created with the capital Bonn. It is a sovereign state intended to create a rampart against the eastern communist Democratic Republic of Germany (DDR, with the capital Berlin), a Soviet satellite.

1950–1991

The "Cold War" culminated in the construction of the Berlin Wall in August 1961 and the Cuban missile crisis in October 1962. The reunification of Germany on February 3, 1990, and the collapse of the Soviet Union in December 1991 marked the end of the Cold War and closed the post–World War II period.

Bibliography

Absolon, Rudolf. *Wehrgesetz und Wehrdienst 1935–1945.* Boppart: H. Bolt, 1959.

Achille-Delmas, François. *Adolf Hitler, Essai de Biographie psycho-pathologique.* Paris: Librairie M. Rivière, 1946.

Angolia, J.R., and D. Littlejohn. *Labor Organizations of the Reich.* San Jose, CA: R. James Bender, n.d.

Arendt, Hannah. *The Origins of Totalitarianism.* New York: Harcourt, Brace, 1951.

Ayçoberry, P. *La Société Allemande sous le IIIe Reich.* Paris: Editions du Seuil, 1998.

Bartov, Omer. *L'Armée d'Hitler, la Wehrmacht, les Nazis et la Guerre.* Paris: Hachette Littérature, 1999.

Bessel, Richard. *Life in the Third Reich.* Oxford, UK: Oxford University Press, 1987.

Bishop, C., and A. Warner. *German Weapons of World War II.* London: Grange Books, 2001.

Bleuel, Hans-Peter. *Sex and Society in Nazi Germany.* New York: Bantam, 1972.

Blücher, Wipert von. *Gesander zwischen Diktatur und Demokratie; Erinnerungen aus den Jahren 1935–1944.* Wiesbaden: Limes Verlag, 1951.

Boog, H. *Die deutsche Luftwaffenführung; Führungsprobleme, Spitzenliederung, Generalstabsausbildung.* Stuttgart: Deutsche Verlags-Anstalt, 1982.

Broszat, Martin. *German National Socialism.* Santa Barbara, CA: ABC-Clio, 1966.

Buchheim, Hans. *Gutachten des Instituts für Zeitgeschichte.* Munich: Selbstverlag, 1958.

Burleigh, Michael. *Death and Deliverance: "Euthanasia" in Germany 1900–1945.* New York: Cambridge University Press, 1994.

_____. *The Third Reich: A New History.* Pan, 2001.

Carman, W.Y. *A Dictionary of Military Uniform.* Tiptree: Anchor Press, 1977.

Chant, Christopher. *The Nazi War Machine.* London: Tiger Books International, 1996.

Childers, T. *The Nazi Voter.* Chapel Hill: University of North Carolina Press, 1983.

Cook, C., and J. Stevenson. *Weapons of War.* London: Artus, 1980.

Daniel, J. *Le problème du châtiment des crimes de guerre d'après les enseignements de la deuxième guerre mondiale.* Cairo: R. Schindler, 1946.

Davis, W.J.K. *Wehrmacht Camouflage and Markings 1939–1945.* New Malden, UK: Almark, 1972.

Delagarde J. *German Soldiers of World War Two.* Paris: Histoire & Collections, 2005.

Ehrlich, C. *Uniformen und Soldaten — Ein Bilderricht vom Ehrenkleid unserer Wehrmacht.* Berlin: Verlag Erich Klinkhammer, 1942.

Evans, Richard. *The Coming of the Third Reich.* London: Allen Lane, 2003.

Eyck, Erich. *Geschichte der Weimarer Republik*, 2 vols. Stuttgart: E. Rentsch, 1956.

Faure, Edgar. *La condition humaine sous la domination nazie.* Paris: Office Français d'Edition, 1946.

Fest, Joachim. *The Face of the Third Reich.* London: Penguin, 1979.

_____. *Inside Hitler's Bunker, The Last Days of the Third Reich.* New York: Macmillan, 2004.

_____. *Plotting Hitler's Death: The German Resistance to Hitler, 1933–45.* New York: Weidenfeld & Nicolson, 1996.

Fitzsimons, B. *Tanks and Weapons of World War II.* London: BC, 1973.

Fleischer, W. *Feldbefestigungen des deutschen Heeres 1939–1945.* Wölersheim-Berstadt: Podzun-Pallas Verlag, 1998.

Funcken, L., and F. Funcken. *Uniformes et Armes des Soldats de la Guerre 1939–1945.* Paris: Editions Casterman, 1972.

Gisselbrecht, André. *Le fascisme hitlérien.* Paris: Editions de la Nouvelle Critique, 1972.

Goldhagen, Daniel. *Hitler's Willing Executioners.* London: Little, Brown, 1996.

Grebing, Helga. *Der Nationalsozialismus.* Munich: Isar Verlag, 1959.

Grunberger, Richard. *A Social History of the Third Reich.* London: Weidenfeld, 1971.

Hanfstängl, Ernst. *The Missing Years.* London: Eyre & Spottiswoode, 1957.

Bibliography

Harding, D. *Weapons: An International Encyclopedia from 5000 B.C. to 2000 A.D.* London: Diagram Visual Information, 1980.

Hierl, Konstantin. *Im Dienst für Deutschland*. Heidelberg: Kurt Vowinckel, 1954.

Höhne, Heinz. *The Order of the Death's Head*. London: Secker & Warburg, 1969.

Kammer, Hilde, and Elisabet Bartsche. *Jugendlexikon National-sozialismus*. Hamburg: Rowolt Taschenbuch Verlag GmbH, 1985.

Keegan, J. *Encyclopedia of World War II*. Feltham: Bison Books/Hamlyn Publishing Group, 1977.

Kershaw, Ian. *The Nazi Dictatorship: Problems & Perspectives of Interpretation*. Baltimore, MD: Arnold, 2000.

Kirstein, Lincoln. *Art in the Third Reich*. New York: Magazine of Art, 1945.

Klose, Werner. *Generation im Gleichschritt, Ein Dokumentarbericht*. Hamburg and Oldenburg: Gerhard Stalling Verlag, 1964.

Kogon, Eugen. *Der SS-Staat*. Frankfurt: Europäische Verlaganstalt, 1965.

Landemer, Henri. *Les Waffen-SS*. Paris: Balland Livre de Poche, 1972.

Lang, Karl. *Hitlers unbeachtete Maximen*. Stuttgart: W. Kohlhammer, 1968.

Laqueur, Walter. *Young Germany*. New York: Basic Books, 1962.

Lattimer, John. *Hitler and the Nazi Leaders: A Unique Insight into Evil*. Shepperton, UK: Ian Allan, 1999.

Layton, Geoff. *The Third Reich, 1933–1945*. London: Hodder, 2000.

Lukacs, John. *The Hitler of History*. New York: Knopf, 1997.

Lynch, Michael. *Nazi Germany*. London: Hodder Arnold, 2004.

Mann, Chris, and Matthew Hughes. *Inside Hitler's Germany: Life Under the Third Reich*. Dulles, VA: Brassey, 2000.

Mann, Erika. *Zehn Millionen Kinder, Die Erziehung der Jugend im Dritten Reich*. Munich: Verlag H. Ellermann, 1986.

Manvell, Roger, and Heinz Fraenkel. *A History of German Cinema*. London: Dent, 1971.

McInnes, C., and G.D. Sheffield. *Warfare in the Twentieth Century: Theory and Practice*. London: Unwin Hyman, 1988.

Mollo, A. *German Uniforms of World War II*. London: MacDonald & Jane's, 1976.

Montgomery, B.L. *A Concise History of Warfare*. Ware, UK: Wordsworth Editions, 2000.

Müller, Klaus J. *Das Heer und Hitler. Armee und nationalsozialistisches Regime, 1933–1940*, Stuttgart: Deutsche Verlagsanstalt, 1969.

Newman, Aubrey. *The Holocaust*. London: Caxton Editions, 2002.

Nicolaisen, H-D. *Der Einsatz der Luftwaffe-und Marinehelfe im 2. Weltkrieg*. Berlin: Bernard & Graefe Verlag, 1981.

Noakes, J., and G. Bridham, *Nazism, 1919–1945: A Documentary Reader*. Exeter, UK: Exeter University, 1988.

Overy, R.J. *The Penguin Historical Dictionary of the Third Reich*. London: Penguin, 1996.

Parker, G. *Warfare*. Cambridge: Press Syndicate of the Cambridge University, 1995.

Peukert, D.J.K. *Inside Nazi Germany*. New Haven, CT: Yale University Press, 1987.

Poliakov, Leon. *The Aryan Myth*. New York: Basic Books, 1974.

Ropp, T. *War in the Modern World*. Durham, NC: Duke University Press, 1959.

Rühle, Gerd. *Das Dritte Reich*. Berlin: Hummel-Verlag, 1936.

Schellens, J.J., and Mayer, J. *Histoire Vécue de la Seconde Guerre Mondiale*. Verviers: Editions Gérard & Co. (Marabout Université), 1962.

Shirer, William. *The Rise and Fall of the Third Reich*. London: Secker & Warburg, 1960.

Sklar, Dusty. *The Nazis and the Occult*. New York: Dorset Press, 1977.

Speer, Albert. *Inside the Third Reich*. New York: Avon Books, 1970.

Stern, J.P. *Hitler, the Führer and the People*. New York: Fontana/Collins, 1975.

Stibbe, Matthew. *Women in the Third Reich*. Arnold, 2003.

Stoffel, G. *La Dictature du Fascisme Allemand*. Paris: Editions Internationales, 1936.

Tagg, M. *De Wereld in Oorlog*. Harmelen: Ars Scribendi BV, 1993.

Tippelskirch, Kurt. *Geschichte des zweiten Weltkriegs*. Bonn: Athenäum-Verlag, 1951.

Toland, John. *Adolf Hitler*. New York: Random House, 1976.

Trevor-Roper, H.R. *The Last Days of Hitler*. London: Macmillan, 1962.

U.S. War Department. *Handbook on German Military Forces*. Washington, DC, 1945.

Von Senger und Etterlin, F.M. *Die deutschen Panzer 1926–1945*. Munich: J.F. Lehmanns Verlag, 1968.

Wilmot, Chester. *The Struggle for Europe*, New York: Harper, 1952.

Zentner, Kurt. *Illustrierte Geschichte des Dritten Reiches*. Munich: Südwest Verlag, 1965.

Ziptel, Friedrich. *Gestapo und Sicherheitsdienst*. Berlin: Arani Verlag, 1960.

INDEX

agriculture 28, 62, 75, 77, 160
air force (Luftwaffe) 6, 8, 15, 17, 21, 27, 44, 45, 47, 50, 52, 55, 65, 67, 71–73, 77, 83, 84, 90, 92, 95, 103–106, 108, 111, 117, 118, 125, 127, 143, 148, 150, 156, 162, 163, 199, 209, 210, 213, 214, 227
aircraft carrier 49, 52
airplane 8, 21, 35, 36, 49, 51–53, 67, 74, 83, 90, 93, 104, 110, 133, 147, 173, 190, 194
ancestry 5, 6, 11, 155, 164, 184
antiaircraft 19, 20, 21, 50, 51, 52, 72, 75, 77, 103, 106, 107, 112, 131, 143, 155, 157, 163, 168, 201, 205
antitank 12, 73, 74, 78, 83, 84, 88, 111, 131, 132, 133, 134, 135, 151, 163, 175, 197, 186, 197, 200 203
architecture 10, 16, 17, 78, 145
Armistice (Nov. 1918) 27, 35, 124, 128, 198, 207, 210
armored vehicle 36, 50, 70, 89, 100, 109, 122, 132, 133 134, 141, 152, 155, 159, 166, 181, 204
Atlantic Ocean 12, 48, 95, 96, 155, 187, 188, 210
Atlantic Wall 12, 48, 73, 92, 111, 123, 155, 176, 182, 183, 205
automobile 7, 94, 139
auxiliary 11, 15, 25, 50, 59, 71, 73, 75, 77, 91, 98, 153, 159, 174, 176, 199
Axis 4, 14, 31, 53, 62, 64, 102, 114, 141, 204, 209, 210, 211

Bachem, Erich 14
badge 3, 8, 11, 15, 37, 51, 52, 64, 68, 79, 83, 84, 85, 97, 100, 115, 119, 134, 135, 143, 149, 156, 157, 163, 171, 184, 187, 191

banner 16, 22, 32, 44, 76, 91, 164, 171
Barbarossa (Operation) 3, 16, 210
Beer Hall Putsch 17, 22, 26, 37, 38, 45, 46, 54, 55, 65, 74, 75, 78, 87, 98, 103, 113, 114, 151, 152, 161, 173, 174, 207
Belgium 56, 66, 67, 98, 115, 127, 141, 164, 188, 190, 100, 210
black market 28, 202
Board of Shame 201
Bolshevism 16, 138, 148, 184
boxing 23, 168
Britain 4, 12, 22, 27, 28, 34, 56, 65, 74, 95, 96, 102, 113, 141 162, 164, 190, 207, 209, 210, 212
British Channel Islands 48, 78, 79, 88, 111, 127
Brown Shirts 24, 174

camouflage 7, 50, 51, 61, 94, 1175, 177, 178, 183, 201
casemate 17, 88, 132, 133 134, 155, 156
Catholicism 71, 114, 135, 138, 139, 145, 148, 156, 162, 183
charity 120, 142, 200
coastal defense 12, 72, 100, 102, 107, 155, 176, 183
communism 78, 90, 137, 138, 148, 162, 184
concentration camp 6, 9, 10, 12, 14, 17, 18, 21, 23, 24, 26, 27, 29, 32, 37, 38, 39, 41, 44, 51, 53, 54, 55, 59, 62, 63, 66, 76, 80, 81, 82, 84, 86, 93, 96, 97, 100, 102, 108, 115, 123, 139, 142, 143, 153, 159, 160, 166, 169, 170, 173, 180, 181, 182, 184, 190, 193, 195, 197, 200, 202, 203, 208
concrete thickness 16, 102, 126, 134, 171, 182, 204

conscription 34, 37, 82, 103, 147, 190
conspiracy 3, 26, 44, 54, 56, 88, 109, 151, 172, 198
convoy 12, 96, 103, 135, 157, 187, 204
Czechoslovakia 22, 27, 28, 57, 66, 71, 76, 93, 113, 162, 186

dagger 9, 34, 35, 77, 144, 148, 162, 187
Daluege, Kurt 128
Darwinism 6, 165, 166
decoration 3, 4, 14, 22, 39, 40, 51, 64, 124, 135, 156, 157, 169, 176
decree 17, 28, 35, 83, 92, 115, 125, 138, 154, 189, 197
Demjansk (Battle of) 48
democracy 5, 35, 40, 51, 56, 106, 128, 198
denazification 7, 14, 28, 42
Denmark 20, 26, 115, 127, 209
deportation 15, 16, 29, 32, 39, 59, 85, 163, 170, 180, 197, 201
Desert Fox 151, 203
desertion 44, 165, 203
destroyer 83, 95, 183, 203
Dieppe (attack on) 12, 191, 210
dive-bomber 61, 86, 173, 175
dueling 37, 110
Duke of Orleans 5

education 9, 38, 43, 71, 77, 87, 91, 92, 98, 115, 116, 117, 119, 121, 142, 145, 152, 153, 182
emblem 4, 29, 31, 32, 50, 58, 76, 115, 118, 119, 120, 122, 144, 145, 147, 153, 156, 157, 161, 164, 167, 174, 181, 192, 195, 196
euthanasia 15, 23, 43, 57, 99, 184
extermination (of the Jews) 6, 9, 13, 18, 20, 24, 27, 28, 29, 37, 39, 40, 57, 59, 60, 62, 63, 68,

Index

76, 80, 81, 88, 93, 100, 102, 109, 123, 138, 145, 165, 166, 168, 184, 185, 187, 190, 201, 202

fascism 29, 55, 114, 124, 213, 214
film 4, 11, 30, 49, 50, 64, 70, 127, 139, 145, 149, 154, 166, 167, 180, 185
"Final Solution" 13, 29, 41, 50, 57, 113, 125, 161, 168, 196, 210
flag 10, 16, 22, 24, 39, 44, 45, 68, 69, 76, 77, 84, 91, 136, 145, 145, 174, 184
flak 50, 52, 72, 77, 93, 100, 103, 105, 106, 107, 112, 118, 122, 131, 143, 157, 163, 168, 176, 182, 192, 201, 203
flamethrower 50, 182
Focke, Heinrich 52
Forsyth, Frederick 128
fortifications 1, 12, 17, 66, 71, 75, 129, 131, 147, 155, 158, 161, 164, 171, 176, 177, 191, 199, 200, 227
fortress 7, 27, 48, 83, 90, 107, 108, 199, 200
France 3, 12, 16, 17, 20, 21, 26, 27, 28, 35, 36, 37, 45, 49, 51, 56, 66, 67, 68, 73, 78, 79, 85, 88, 102, 113, 115, 127, 141, 149, 151, 154, 156, 165, 171, 181, 188, 189, 191, 194, 202, 207, 209, 211, 212
freedom 9, 41, 91, 106, 145, 168, 177, 184, 193

Gies, Miep 53
Graf Zeppelin 49, 52
grenade 58, 65, 66, 195, 123, 135
Grim, Hans 191
gypsies 12, 18, 27, 28, 40, 68, 84, 93, 120, 153, 190

Heissmayer, August 115
helmet 46, 48, 61, 86, 122, 148, 159, 170, 171, 172, 177, 185, 191
Hitler, Adolf: doctors 23, 112; nationality 78; testament 78
holidays 80, 94
homosexuality 12, 55, 59, 80, 150, 151, 188
Huber, Kurt 198
human right 57, 91

insignia 1, 3, 13, 15, 20, 31, 48, 65, 68, 76, 143, 148, 150, 160, 166, 202
intelligence 7, 13, 40, 53, 70, 71, 80, 87, 114, 116, 130, 146, 150, 155, 163, 166, 191
Italy 7, 8, 36, 63, 65, 66, 67, 113, 114, 129, 155, 159 171, 204, 207, 209, 210, 211, 212

Japan 4, 8, 11, 36, 150, 187, 207, 209, 210, 212
Jerrycan 18, 198
Joanovici, Joseph 201
Junkers, Hugo 86
justice 54, 61, 71, 86, 115, 116, 120, 125, 137, 159, 161, 165, 180, 188, 190, 200

Kantzow, Karin von 89
komintern 8, 209

law 5, 9, 10, 13, 22, 32, 41, 42, 43, 44 48, 49, 50, 54, 55, 56, 60, 61, 62, 64, 72, 75, 79, 80, 83, 84, 85, 86, 87, 96, 105, 113, 115, 116, 117, 120, 125, 128, 130, 138, 139, 140, 141, 144 147 148, 155, 165, 183, 184, 185, 187, 195, 208, 209
lesbianism 80
Lightning War 21, 122
literature 32, 102, 145
Luger, Georg 105
Lutheran Church 18, 27, 71, 91, 137

machine gun 107, 175
Manhattan Project 12
marriage 22, 29, 38, 62, 71, 85, 91, 212
medal 13, 14, 15, 22, 39, 48, 50, 68, 94, 100, 114, 130, 139, 149, 161, 176, 177, 180, 187
memorial 110, 19, 91, 184, 196
million-dollar wound 72
miracle weapon 202
motherhood 25, 38, 114, 116
motto 9, 16, 32, 94, 109, 243, 1157, 171 187
Moulin, Jean 16
music 12, 17, 25, 32, 50, 70, 87, 102, 113, 114, 136, 141, 145, 158, 161, 167, 176, 180, 184, 196, 202

nationalism 57, 78, 121, 176, 184
nationality 78, 123
navy 4, 12, 20, 35, 51, 56, 65, 68, 71, 72, 75, 95, 106, 107, 125, 126, 141, 147, 148, 155, 176, 187, 190, 198
Netherlands 17, 21, 26, 53, 56, 60, 67, 82, 93, 163, 165, 199, 202 210
newspaper 7, 8, 12, 70, 85, 109, 111, 113, 116, 123, 140, 152, 162, 173, 175, 189, 192
Norway 12, 21, 26, 82, 95, 115, 127, 209
nuclear warfare 12, 139

obstacle 21, 38, 44, 55, 73, 88, 97, 99, 103, 134, 151, 164, 178, 179, 199
overseas organizations 13

paratroop 23, 44, 45, 84, 92, 100, 103, 104, 133, 169, 177, 210
Petacci, Clara 114
Phony War 137, 165, 199
Picasso, Pablo 68
pilgrimage (places of) 19, 24, 89, 122
pistol 20, 46, 51, 101, 105, 137, 162, 196, 199
pope 57, 111, 137, 138, 145, 208
protective custody 86, 96, 159
Protestantism 18, 22, 41, 71, 113, 139, 148, 183

racism 4, 10, 34, 115, 121, 173, 184, 187, 200
radar 50, 51, 54, 56, 80, 105, 106, 164, 176, 197, 202, 203
railway 10, 13, 15, 27, 29, 35, 40, 55, 96, 123, 135, 136, 144, 148, 155, 202, 204
range finder 42, 101, 106
ranks (table of) 33, 34
Red Cross 31, 32, 60, 89, 120, 153, 180,
religion 18, 22, 29, 57, 84, 91, 93, 113, 122, 123, 137, 138, 145, 148, 185
resistance 3, 21, 71, 74, 80, 83, 90, 156, 159, 165, 198, 199, 200
rifle 19, 24, 30, 33, 45, 56, 58, 61, 66, 77, 84, 99, 107, 114, 132, 136, 158, 175
rocket 4, 14, 23, 35, 110, 123, 136, 137, 148, 171, 188, 189, 202
rune 32, 38, 153, 202

Saint-Nazaire 12, 188, 191
Scholtz-Klink, Gertrud 118, 158
Schweitzer, Hans 112
science 38, 43, 61, 62, 117, 124, 181, 184
seachlight 20, 50, 72, 105 106, 155
self-propelled gun 7, 20, 83, 84,

89, 123, 131, 140, 158, 162, 175, 201, 204
Shoah 80, 190
slang 1, 28, 72, 83, 85, 90, 95, 112, 136, 183
slogan 9, 30, 32, 33, 39, 59, 65, 74, 84, 87, 91, 138, 166, 187, 191
smoking 33, 189
song 33, 43, 50, 72, 81, 102, 114, 134, 156, 167, 180, 199, 201, 203
speech 10, 25, 26, 46, 106, 109, 136, 138, 140, 141, 164, 187, 193
Stalingrad (battle of) 65, 211
submachine gun 19, 20, 42, 43, 107, 195
submarine 12, 35, 45, 49, 93, 95, 96, 125, 153, 162, 187, 188, 190

Teutonic knights 36, 100, 109, 179, 180, 199, 200

theater 30, 85, 145, 180, 196
traitor 3, 54, 56, 78, 84, 124, 140, 193
Treaty of Versailles 35, 53, 96, 102, 104, 116, 117, 134, 147, 186, 190, 198, 207
trench 48, 66, 98, 99, 158, 164, 199

uniform 6, 9, 13, 15, 20, 24, 25, 46, 59, 61, 68, 71, 77, 132, 143, 148, 152, 156, 163, 174, 185, 195, 201
United States of America 16, 18, 24, 33, 48, 51, 60, 113, 125, 132, 134, 164, 165, 169, 187, 207, 210, 211, 212, 214
Urvolk 10

Vatican 93, 111, 128, 137
veteran 8, 22, 28, 53, 55, 70, 75, 97, 98, 119, 134, 137, 145, 150, 156, 163, 170, 171, 173, 174

Weimar Republic 1, 35, 38, 51, 54, 88, 110, 128, 147, 154, 156, 159, 178, 180, 193, 198, 207, 208
welfare 8, 31, 59, 71, 75, 98, 119, 120, 183, 193, 200
Wulf, Georg 52
Wüst, Walter 5

yellow star 83, 85, 139, 203

Zander, Elsbeth 118

ALSO BY JEAN-DENIS G.G. LEPAGE
AND FROM McFARLAND

*British Fortifications Through the Reign of Richard III:
An Illustrated History* (2012)

*Vauban and the French Military Under Louis XIV:
An Illustrated History of Fortifications and Strategies* (2010)

French Fortifications, 1715–1815: An Illustrated History (2010)

Hitler Youth, 1922–1945: An Illustrated History (2009)

Aircraft of the Luftwaffe, 1935–1945: An Illustrated Guide (2009)

The French Foreign Legion: An Illustrated History (2008)

*German Military Vehicles of World War II:
An Illustrated Guide to Cars, Trucks, Half-Tracks,
Motorcycles, Amphibious Vehicles and Others* (2007)

The Fortifications of Paris: An Illustrated History
(2006; 2010 paperback)

*Medieval Armies and Weapons in Western Europe:
An Illustrated History* (2005; 2014 paperback)

*Castles and Fortified Cities of Medieval Europe:
An Illustrated History* (2002; paperback 2011)

www.ingramcontent.com/pod-product-compliance
Ingram Content Group UK Ltd.
Pitfield, Milton Keynes, MK11 3LW, UK
UKHW050528150426
5217IPUK00026B/1852